Business, Finance and International Development

Series Editors: **Catherine Dolan**, SOAS, University of London, **Paul Gilbert**, University of Sussex, **Lena Lavinas**, The Federal University of Rio de Janeiro, **Emma Mawdsley**, University of Cambridge, **Dinah Rajak**, University of Sussex, **Farwa Sial**, SOAS, **Jessica Sklair**, University of Cambridge

---

This series is dedicated to interdisciplinary work on business, finance and international development, drawing on cross-cutting conversations in the disciplines of anthropology, critical management studies, development studies, economics, geography and socio-legal studies.

Forthcoming in the series:

Varieties of Impact Investing:
Creating and Translating a Label in Local Contexts
Edited by **Philip Balsiger**, **Daniel Burnier** and **Noé Kabouche**

T0319541

Find out more at

bristoluniversitypress.co.uk/
business-finance-and-international-development

Business, Finance and International Development

Find out more at
bristoluniversitypress.co.uk/
business-finance-and-international-development

FEMINISM IN PUBLIC DEBT

A Human Rights Approach

Edited by
Juan Pablo Bohoslavsky and Mariana Rulli

First published in Great Britain in 2024 by

Bristol University Press
University of Bristol
1-9 Old Park Hill
Bristol
BS2 8BB
UK
t: +44 (0)117 374 6645
e: bup-info@bristol.ac.uk

Details of international sales and distribution partners are available at bristoluniversitypress.co.uk

British Library Cataloguing in Publication Data
A catalogue record for this book is available from the British Library

ISBN 978-1-5292-3727-6 paperback
ISBN 978-1-5292-3728-3 ePub
ISBN 978-1-5292-3729-0 OA PDF

Cover design: Nicky Borowiec
Front cover image: Ana Yael ©
Bristol University Press uses environmentally responsible print partners.
Printed and bound in Great Britain by CPI Group (UK) Ltd, Croydon, CR0 4YY

FSC
www.fsc.org
MIX
Paper | Supporting
responsible forestry
FSC® C013604

Contents

Series Editors' Preface

Time and time again, development organizations and policy makers tout plans to mobilize, catalyse or leverage new flows of private finance as solutions to seemingly intractable development problems. Aid is increasingly dispersed through development finance institutions that look and behave like private investment firms, while philanthropies become tangled up with donors and private contractors alike. Structural adjustment and policy conditionality for heavily indebted countries has returned (if it ever left), although efforts to restructure sovereign debt are often frustrated by the megalithic asset management firms that hold growing shares of Southern debt. Businesses loudly and proudly declare their intention to fight poverty and shape policy norms through 'multistakeholder' forums. Public–private partnerships are once again being promoted as vehicles for the delivery of assorted development goals. Meanwhile, for-profit consultancies (rather than civil society organizations or academics) have the ear of policy makers and development ministries. As private sector actors become increasingly central to the design and delivery of international development, critical, interdisciplinary research on business, finance and development has never been more pressing.

This series is intended as a home for works which examine the multiple forms that new public–private 'state-capital hybrids' take in contemporary international development. This includes: the role that private sector entities play in producing and legitimating knowledge in/of development; the impact of emerging financial architectures and innovations on the Global South;[1] labour and human rights issues in global supply chains; the place of business and finance in resource extraction and conservation; as well as methodological and ethical issues in the study of private sector actors and international development. It is interdisciplinary by design and by necessity. Efforts to engage with some dimension of business, finance and international development have been ongoing for some time in the editors' respective disciplines (anthropology, business & management, development studies, economics, geography, science & technology studies). Drawing together the approaches, methods and normative concerns that have animated this work across disciplines allows contributions to the series to examine issues such as the technicalities of sovereign debt and impact investing, as well as their distributional consequences and entanglements with racialized and gendered power relations and post-colonial geographies.

Our goal is to spark dialogue between scholars situated in the academy, and those who work in civil society or advocacy organizations, or in policy settings. And from the outset, we intend this series to cultivate critical and engaged studies of business, finance and international development that avoids the alarming dominance of Global North-based scholars that has been documented across all of our disciplines. This first book in our series reflects these commitments, incorporating work that has emerged from civil society mobilization around the gendered impacts of debt and austerity in Latin America. With this volume, Bohoslavsky, Rulli and their contributors draw together work on law, human rights of women and LGBTQ+ people, examinations of the gendered consequences of fiscal policy and critical analyses of the androcentrism and machismo of international financial institutions and their policies. At a time when almost 150 countries are in the grip of austerity, and human rights organizations have documented a widespread backlash against women's rights and legal protections for women, girls and LGBTQ+ people, this could not be more timely. We are privileged to be able to initiate this series with *Feminism in Public Debt*, and hope that you find it as compelling as we have.

Paul Robert Gilbert, Catherine Dolan,
Lena Lavinas, Emma Mawdsley,
Dinah Rajak, Farwa Sial and Jessica Sklair

Note

[1] We use this term advisedly, not as a geographical designation, but to draw attention to the varied movements which have mobilized to contest development in former colonial nations, as well as to the efforts of the South Commission (which both critiqued the role of international business and finance in development and advanced the notion of 'South-South' cooperation). The term is intended to denote a structural, neocolonial relation between North and South, rather than merely imply a spatial location.

List of Figures and Tables

Figures

Tables

Notes on Contributors

Leia Achampong is Senior Policy and Advocacy Officer at Eurodad – Climate Finance. She is a climate change and women's rights activist. She has over ten years of experience working on climate change in policy, advocacy and analysis. In April 2020, Achampong joined Eurodad to launch and lead Eurodad's policy and research work on climate finance. Prior to this, Achampong worked at WWF – European Policy Office, and also at Climate Action Network – Europe and the Climate Change Campaign. She holds a Master's degree in Sustainability Science and Policy from Maastricht University and is currently developing a PhD proposal. Hailing from the UK, Achampong is a strong believer in the EU Project. In 2017, Achampong was fortunate enough to participate in the US State Department's International Visitor Leadership Program (IVLP) on climate change and energy.

Juan Pablo Bohoslavsky is Senior Researcher at Argentina's National Scientific and Technical Research Council (CONICET) at the National University of Río Negro (CIEDIS). He holds a Master's degree in Business Law and a PhD in Law. He defended the Argentine Republic in international arbitrations, participated in the nationalization of the national water supply company (AySA) and was its director representing the national state. He worked as Debt Officer at the United Nations Conference on Trade and Development (UNCTAD) and was the Independent Expert on debt and human rights of the United Nations (UN). He has been a consultant for the UN's Economic Commission for Latin America and the Caribbean (ECLAC), the Office of the United Nations High Commissioner for Human Rights (OHCHR), the United Nations Development Programme (UNDP) and human rights organizations. His research focus lies on the interlinks between finance and human rights.

Magalí Brosio is a PhD candidate at the University of Birmingham Law School, and holds a Master's in Labour Economics (University of Turin/Sciences Po) and a BA in Economics (University of Buenos Aires). Her research interests lie at the intersection between gender, economic development and international law. At the professional level, Magalí has worked as a programme coordinator in the area of economic policy in various civil society organizations, including the Center for the Implementation of Public Policies for Equality and Growth (CIPPEC) and the Center for Women's Global Leadership (CWGL), and as an external consultant on economic and gender issues for UN Women and the International Labour Organization (ILO).

Francisco Cantamutto is Senior Researcher at CONICET, based at the Economic and Social Research Institute (UNS-CONICET), and teaching assistant in Argentine Economic Structure and Problems of Recent Argentina, Department of Economics. He holds a BA in Economics (UNS-Argentina), a Master's in Social Sciences (FLACSO-Mexico), and a PhD in Social Science Research, mention in Sociology (FLACSO-Mexico). He specializes in economic development and public debt, with an emphasis on Argentina. He collaborates on articles on political economy in various journalistic media. He is a member of Argentina and Uruguay's Critical Economy Society, being part of the editorial committee of its academic journal, *Cuadernos de Economía Crítica*. He produced the podcast 'Lo Prometido Es Deuda'.

Agostina Costantino is an economist (UNS-Argentina), Master in Social Sciences (FLACSO-Mexico) and PhD in Social Science Research with mention in Political Science (FLACSO-Mexico). She is currently a researcher at Argentina's CONICET and professor at the Economics Department of the National University of the South (Argentina). She also teaches graduate courses at the University of Buenos Aires and the National University of Catamarca. Her research interests focus on the problems of Latin American development with special emphasis on gender inequalities and impacts of the development models and economic policies implemented in the region.

Diane Elson is Emeritus Professor of Sociology at the University of Essex, UK, and a former Chair of the UK Women's Budget Group (2010–16). She has also served as a member of the UN Committee for Development Policy (2013–21), adviser to UN Women (and previously to UNIFEM where in 2000 she initiated the report on 'Progress of the World's Women') and as Vice President of the International Association for Feminist Economics (2004–06). She has published widely on gender equality, human rights and economic justice. She was awarded the 2016 Leontief Prize for Advancing Frontiers of Economic Thought by the Global Development and Environment Institute at Tufts University.

Dorothy Estrada-Tanck is Chair of the UN Working Group on Discrimination against Women and Girls, Professor of Public International

Law at the Law Faculty of the University of Murcia and Co-director of its Legal Clinic. Dorothy holds a PhD in Law from the European University Institute, an MSc in Political Theory from the London School of Economics and Political Science (LSE) and a Law Degree from Escuela Libre de Derecho (Mexico), and enjoys broad academic and professional experience in the UN, State bodies, NGOs and universities in Mexico, Italy, Spain, the US and Canada, focusing on human rights, gender equality, human security, migration and socioeconomic justice. She is author of *Human Security and Human Rights under International Law: The Protections Offered to Persons Confronting Structural Vulnerability* (Hart Publishing, 2016; Best Book Award 2017, Inter-American Bar Association).

Iolanda Fresnillo Sallan is Policy and Advocacy Coordinator at Eurodad – Debt. During the last two decades, Iolanda has been very involved in local, national and international social movements and has participated in campaigns on development finance, debt, human rights, feminism, environment, peace, trade and responsible consumption. She has worked for more than ten years as a researcher, campaigner and communications officer at the Observatory on Debt in Globalization and as a research consultant at Eurodad, Médecins Sans Frontières (MSF) and the Transnational Institute, among others. Iolanda holds a Master's degree in Development and Cooperation and a Bachelor's degree in Sociology, both from the University of Barcelona. Since 2019 she has been working on the interrelations between debt and the climate crisis, with several articles and publications.

Penelope Hawkins is Senior Economist in the Debt and Development Finance Branch of UNCTAD. She focuses primarily on sustainable sovereign debt, financing for development and the nexus between debt and climate finance. Previously, as the founder and Managing Director of Feasibility (Pty) Ltd, Penelope undertook leading research projects in the financial sector in Southern Africa, commissioned by regulators, policy makers and the private sector. She has a PhD. In her thesis she examined the financial constraints of small open economies, and extended the analysis of financial fragility, vulnerability and exclusion to nations as well as businesses. Most recently, she has edited, together with Ioana Negru, a two volume Festschrift in honour of Professor Sheila Dow (2022).

Alicja Paulina Krubnik is a PhD candidate at McMaster University and a political economy and comparative public policy scholar. Her research applies critical and intersectional feminist perspectives to the exploration of how international financial agreements and debt impact the environmental and social policies of low-income and emerging economy countries. Alicja's work also extends to the policy sphere, where she has worked with local community organizations and non-governmental organizations, as well as the Senate of Canada, as a policy researcher in the areas of poverty reduction and social protections. Alicja holds an MSc in Political Economy from the LSE, an MSc in Economics and Governance from Leiden University and a Bachelor's from the University of Toronto.

Christina Laskaridis works on the political economy of sovereign debt, financial crises and international organizations. She is leading a grant on environment-related financial risks and regulatory capital requirements funded by INSPIRE and a project on debt sustainability. Her thesis, 'Debt sustainability: towards a history of theory, policy, and measurement', received the 2022 Joseph Dorfman Best Dissertation prize. Christina has a PhD in Economics from SOAS, University of London, and is a Fellow of St Edmund Hall and Saïd Business School at the University of Oxford, where she teaches a postgraduate course on Financial Crises. Christina uses her expertise to advise on debt and development issues, such as to OHCHR's Independent Expert on foreign debt and human rights, UNCTAD, the Overseas Development Institute (ODI) and several NGOs working on sovereign debt issues.

Lena Lavinas is Professor of Welfare Economics at the Institute of Economics at the Federal University of Rio de Janeiro and Research Associate in the Department of Economics at SOAS, University of London (2022–24). In 2021–22 she was a Leverhulme Visiting Professor at SOAS, and in 2020–21 she was a member of the School of Social Science at the Institute for Advanced Study (IAS) at Princeton. Most of her research examines how welfare regimes adjust to changes in contemporary capitalism, especially under the aegis of financialization, investigating how the restructuring of the social reproduction sphere reshapes social policies and impacts wellbeing. She has published extensively on the financialization of welfare regimes, social policy reforms, gender issues and labour market reforms.

Flavia Marco Navarro is a lawyer, Master in Economic Law and specialist in gender studies. She is a consultant for UN agencies and international cooperation agencies, a researcher at the Center for Participation and Sustainable Human Development (Bolivia) and postgraduate lecturer. She has published books and articles in various countries in Latin America and Europe on social security, care, employment and other issues related to social policies. She is a member of the National Platform for Social and Public Co-responsibility of Care (Bolivia), the Global Carework Network and the Latin American Council of Social Science's (CLACSO) Gender and Care Working Group.

Ulrike Marx is Lecturer in Accounting at Queen Mary University of London. Her research mainly focuses on social studies of accounting, such as the emergence and translation of new (management) accounting phenomena as a response to crisis and political problematizations, for example the emergence of gender budgeting as 'accounting for equality', or more recently the emergence of managing and measuring wellbeing. Interdisciplinary in nature, her research draws upon organization theory, feminist theory, political philosophy and science and technology studies in order to develop insights to inform organizational, social and political action. Her research has been published in international journals such as *Gender, Work and Organization* and she is a member and affiliated researcher in a wide range of national and international research networks and communities.

Patricia Miranda holds a Master's degree in Finance from the Technological and High Studies Institute (ITES) of Monterrey in Mexico under an agreement with EMI in Bolivia, and a postgraduate degree in External Finance from Debt Relief International in England. She was Programme Officer for Latin America at Development Finance International in England, and at the Center for Latin American Monetary Studies in Mexico in a capacity building programme in public finance for highly indebted poor countries. As a Debt Analyst at Fundación Jubileo, she promoted and conducted a debt sustainability analysis with a human development approach. Currently, she is Director of Global Advocacy and Coordinator of the New Financial Architecture Area of the Latin American Network for Economic and Social Justice (LATINDADD).

Florencia Partenio is a sociologist (University of Buenos Aires) and holds a PhD in Social Sciences from the University of Buenos Aires. She is a member of the executive committee of the global south feminist network Women for Alternative Development for a New Era (DAWN). She coordinates the Feminist Digital Justice Project promoted by DAWN and IT for change and co-coordinates the School of Feminist Economics. She has been an expert consultant for the Inter-American Centre for Knowledge Development and Vocational Training (CINTERFOR), ECLAC and ILO. She teaches in undergraduate and graduate programs at public universities in Argentina. She teaches in the Master in Feminist Studies at the IDAES-UNSAM School. She is co-author, jointly with Corina Rodríguez Enríquez, of the book *Sostenibilidad de la vida desde la perspectiva de la economía feminista*, published by Madreselva Editorial.

Laura Pautassi is a principal researcher at Argentina's CONICET and the Institute of Legal and Social Research, A. Gioja, School of Law, University of Buenos Aires and Adjunct Professor at the School of Law (University of

Buenos Aires). She is a lawyer (University of Córdoba) and holds a PhD in Social Right from University of Buenos Aires. She is director of the Interdisciplinary Working Group on Social Rights and Public Policy and a founding member and president of the Latin American Team for Justice and Gender (ELA). She specializes in economic, social and cultural rights, gender approach and public policies.

Marita Perceval is Professor of Philosophy, teacher and Argentine politician. She served as National Senator for the province of Mendoza in the National Congress between 2001 and 2009. She was Argentina's Ambassador to the United Nations between 2012 and 2015 and the UN Children's Fund (UNICEF) Regional Director for Latin America from March 2016 until September 2019. She was Secretary of Equality and Diversity Policies of the National Ministry of Women, Gender and Diversity from 2021 to 2022; and as of 2023 she was appointed, by Presidential decree, as the first Special Representative for Feminist Foreign Policy in the Ministry of Foreign Affairs and Worship of the Argentine Republic.

Diane Perrons is Professor Emerita in Feminist Political Economy at the LSE. She authored *Is Austerity Gendered?* (Polity 2021 – blog at https://www.politybooks.com/blog-detail/is-austerity-gendered); *Globalisation and Social Change* (Routledge, 2004); and co-authored *Gender, Migration and Domestic Work. Masculinities, Male Labour and Fathering in the UK*, with Majella Kilkey and Ania Plomien (MacMillan, 2013). She co-directed the LSE's Gender, Inequality and Power Commission (2016) and is a member of the UK Women's Budget Group Policy Advisory Group.

María Nieves Rico is Argentinian, a feminist and a migrant. She holds a Social Anthropology degree from the National University of Rosario, Argentina, and has a Master's in Sociology of Development and in Urban Development and Local Administration, and a Bachelor's degree in International Relations from Sociedad de Estudios Internacionales de Madrid in Spain. She was a UN official between 1992 and 2020, former Acting Director of the Social Development Division and former Director of the Gender Affairs Division of ECLAC. She was also an advisor to Latin American and Caribbean governments on gender equality policies. She is the author of several books and articles on women's rights and the rights of children and adolescents in fields such as care, poverty, the labour market, education and environmental sustainability. Currently, she is an international consultant on public policies with a gender and human rights approach.

Corina Rodríguez Enríquez is an economist (University of Buenos Aires), a Master in Public Policy (Institute of Social Studies, the Netherlands) and has a PhD in Social Sciences (Latin American School of Social Sciences – FLACSO). She is an independent researcher at Argentina's CONICET, based at the Interdisciplinary Centre for the Study of Public Policy (CIEPP), a member of the Executive Committee of Development Alternatives with Women for a New Era (DAWN), chair of Economics and Gender at the University of Buenos Aires, a postgraduate lecturer at several national universities and a consultant for UN agencies. She works from feminist economics on issues related to fiscal and social policies, organization of care, corporate power and public-private partnerships.

Julieta Rossi is a lawyer who graduated from the Law School of the University of Buenos Aires. She holds a Master's Degree in Law from New York University. She is a PhD candidate in Human Rights from the National University of Lanús. She is a member of the United Nations Committee on Economic, Social and Cultural Rights for the period 2023–26. She is also Director of the Master in Human Rights at the National University of Lanús, research professor at the same university and Professor of the Master's Degree in Human Rights at the Law School of the University of Buenos Aires and of the Master's Degree in Human Rights and Democratization at the National University of San Martín. She is Assistant Attorney General of the Attorney General's Office in the area of proceedings before the Supreme Court of Justice of the Nation (on leave of absence).

Mariana Rulli holds a PhD in Social Sciences from FLACSO. She is a political scientist (University of Buenos Aires), Master in Families and Society (specialization in gender) from the University of Barcelona and Master in Design and Management of Social Policies (FLACSO). She is Professor of Political Science and a researcher at the National University of Río Negro. She has been a consultant on gender and human rights issues for UN Women, UNDP, the United Nations Research Institute for Social Development (UNRISD), the International Institute for Democracy and Electoral Assistance, Inter-American Development Bank, CLACSO and Federal Council of Investments (CFI) in Argentina. She has held scholarships from CONICET, the German Academic Exchange Service (DAAD) and Fulbright. She has done research stays at the Max Planck Institute in Heidelberg and at UNRISD. She has been an advisor to Argentina's Ministry of Women, Gender and Diversity and to the Special Representative for Feminist Foreign Policy of Argentina's Ministry of Foreign Affairs.

Verónica Serafini Geoghegan is a feminist economist. She is a gender advisor for Latindadd, she has a Master's degree in Social Sciences and a PhD in Economics. She is a categorized researcher in the national system of researchers of Paraguay, as level II. She researches topics related to labour markets, poverty and inequality with a gender perspective, fiscal policy and social protection. She teaches at universities in Paraguay and is a guest lecturer in several countries. She cooperates with civil society and international cooperation organizations.

Special Procedures of the United Nations Human Rights Council is a body composed by independent human rights experts with (group and individual) mandates to report and advise on human rights from a thematic or country-specific perspective. The system of Special Procedures is a central element of the United Nations human rights machinery and covers all human rights: civil, cultural, economic, political and social. Special Procedures conduct thematic studies and convene expert consultations, contribute to the development of international human rights standards, undertake country missions, engage in advocacy and provide advice for technical cooperation.

Ariel Wilkis holds a PhD in Sociology (EHESS-UBA), is a CONICET researcher, professor at the University of San Martín and dean of the School of Interdisciplinary Advanced Social Studies (EIDAES) in the same university. He specializes in economic sociology. He is the author of *Las sospechas del dinero* (Paidos, 2013), *The Moral Power of Money* (Stanford UP, 2017) and *¿Por qué importan las deudas?* (Siglo XXI, 2023) and co-author of *Dólar. Historia de una moneda nacional* (Critica, 2019). He edited the books *El laberinto de las finanzas* (Biblos, 2015), *El poder de (e)valuar* (Unsam edita/ Universidad del Rosario, 2018) and *Las formas elementales del endeudamiento* (UNL ediciones, 2020). His books have been translated into English, French and Chinese.

Camila Villard Duran is an international legal expert with an interdisciplinary research background. She works on issues related to international monetary law, central banking, regulation of crypto-assets, climate finance and gender equality. Currently, Camila is an associate law professor at the ESSCA School of Management in France. From 2013 to 2022, she was a professor at the University of São Paulo (USP) in Brazil, where she was awarded her 'Livre docência / Habilitation' in international economics from the Institute of International Relations. Camila is a former Oxford-Princeton Global Leaders Fellow. She holds a joint PhD in international economic law from the USP and the University of Paris 1 Panthéon-Sorbonne.

Marina Zucker-Marques is a postdoctoral researcher at SOAS, University of London (Department of Economics). She is affiliated to the project 'Debt Relief for a Green and Inclusive Recovery', which aims to address developing countries' debt crisis and support their green and sustainable development.

Previously, she worked at UNCTAD in the Debt and Development Finance Branch (Globalization and Development Strategies). Marina holds a PhD from the Freie Universität Berlin, where she defended her thesis on institutional and political-economic drivers of renminbi internationalization. Marina is Brazilian and holds a Bachelor's degree from FACAMP, and a Master's from Zhejiang Gongshang University.

Acknowledgements

We would like to thank the following persons and institutions:

Contributors, for joining this polyphony of voices that are interwoven in the book.

Diane Elson, for having contributed with her foreword, and Jayati Ghosh, Isabel Ortíz and Ilias Bantekas for their reviews on the back cover.

Bretton Woods Project (BWP), Friedrich Ebert Stiftung (Argentina office) and the Open Society Foundations (OSF), for supporting in various ways the production, publication and dissemination of this book.

Valeria Cardozo, Yessica Cernus and Cecilia Picariello, for translating into English the chapters originally written in Spanish.

Finally, Bristol University Press for its enthusiastic support of this editorial project.

Juan Pablo Bohoslavsky and Mariana Rulli (eds)
Viedma, January 2024

Foreword

Diane Elson

This path-breaking book challenges conventional approaches to government indebtedness by proposing that government debt is a feminist issue. It focuses on debt-distressed low- and middle-income countries, especially in Latin America, providing new conceptual and empirical analysis, and suggestions for alternative, more gender-equitable policies relating to sovereign debt. It is particularly original in counterposing the rights of international creditors to the human rights of people living in debt-distressed countries, and arguing that human rights should take precedence.

Of course, lending and borrowing are everyday vital activities for governments, businesses and people. In the right circumstances, they can contribute to enhanced wellbeing, improved livelihoods and accumulation of valuable community assets, especially if organized through systems that have a high degree of mutuality, such as credit unions. However, lending and borrowing are more often marked by very unequal power. In financial markets, relations between creditors and debtors are not symmetrical: the laws that govern these activities are marked by creditor bias, privileging the rights of creditors over those of debtors (Young et al, 2011). An extreme form of creditor bias can be seen in the devastating debt trap in which almost all governments of low- and middle-income countries now find themselves. They are held responsible for State debt whether or not they themselves accumulated this debt. They are facing increasingly unfavourable conditions in the international economy (relating to interest rates, exchange rates and demand for their exports) over which they have no control. It has now become impossible to service this debt, on which interest has to be paid to foreign creditors in foreign currencies. Businesses faced with similar conditions can repudiate their debts through applying for bankruptcy: the rights of creditors are overridden by the imperative to sustain conditions for capitalist entrepreneurs to flourish, enabling them to start up and close down debt-financed businesses and move on (with maybe a short pause) until they find a profitable activity. But no such option is open to governments: there is no regular legal mechanism for unwinding sovereign debt. Governments must apply for debt relief on a case-by-case basis to the International Monetary Fund (IMF), which conducts a so-called debt sustainability analysis and invariably concludes that austerity measures are required to make the debt sustainable. As this thought-provoking book demonstrates, measures that supposedly make government debt sustainable are making life unsustainable, with deepening poverty, worsening health and additional burdens on poor women.

This book illustrates how this biased system of lending and borrowing is a *gendered system*, both in terms of the way that women and men are positioned in the financial system, and the way that the financial system interacts with the process of social reproduction, in which women have most of the responsibility for unpaid care work. Women are disproportionately debtors, men are disproportionately creditors. Men dominate most of the key financial decision-making positions in businesses, banks, regulatory institutions, governments and international financial institutions (Young et al, 2011). Women are disproportionately among those adversely affected by austerity measures. However, as contributors to this book show, promoting more women to leadership positions in the financial system will not solve the problem because the data and models that are used to analyse debt and debt sustainability exclude the unpaid care economy which is vital for social reproduction. There is a 'strategic silence' about the way that the unpaid care economy underpins the financial system (Bakker, 1994) and an implicit assumption that the impact of austerity measures can be absorbed by households without irreparable harm, in effect assuming that women's unpaid work can stretch to compensate for shortfalls in provision of public services and in income from the labour market and the social protection system (Elson, 1991). This book shows in heart-rending detail that this is not the case.

In posing government debt as a feminist issue, this book highlights issues that are obscured in conventional economic analysis, including the way that violence (actual or threatened) and dispossession are utilized to discipline debtors. It illuminates the way that attempts to reduce government debt through austerity measures lead to increases in household debt, especially for the poorest women, arguing that when social rights fail, their debt increases. It argues that non-financial debts should be recognized as well as financial debts: finance capital is indebted to women and to nature for unpaid services that underpin its activities. In the balance sheet of who owes what to whom this should be taken into account. It reverses the morality tale that is often told about debt. Instead of seeing the debtors as uniquely irresponsible, it reveals the irresponsibility of creditors in creating a flawed international financial system that generates booms and busts in liquidity. The risks in this system are not pooled and shared but are downloaded from the dealing rooms of financial markets to the kitchens of poor women (Elson, 2002, 2011).

This book rightly pays a lot of attention to the IMF, as a lynchpin of this system. Although the amount of money that debt-distressed governments owe to the IMF is dwarfed by what they owe to other creditors, both public and private, the IMF plays a key role in disciplining debtor governments, as approval from the IMF is necessary to unlock debt relief and new loans of various kinds. As shown in this book, such approval is conditional on countries implementing austerity programmes that have very adverse impacts on low-income women. It is worth highlighting that the IMF conditions do not in fact lead to debt sustainability because they dampen economic growth. IMF analysis does not reveal this because it uses models that build in over-optimistic growth projections. Even on its own terms, IMF debt sustainability analysis is not fit for purpose. It serves as a rationale for extending new conditional loans to debt-distressed countries but does not lead to effective action to tackle the root causes of debt distress, which lie in the dysfunctional international financial system. As contributors to this book argue, the discovery by the IMF that 'gender equality' is a 'macro-critical' issue, and the elaboration of an 'IMF gender strategy', has done nothing to address the ways in which the operations of the IMF itself adds to gender inequality.

A similar critique is provided in this book of the fashionable initiatives to create 'gender bonds' in which governments issue bonds that specify that the return will not only be financial but also the achievement of particular gender equality goals. The assessment of achievements is outsourced to private companies. If they judge there to be a shortfall in achievements, the government must pay a higher rate of interest to the financial companies that own the bonds. UN Women is promoting gender bonds as a way to mobilize more finance directly linked to gender equality goals. But as contributors to this book point out, this introduces private conditionality and means that fulfilling women's rights is no longer subject to public and democratic debates between States and feminist movements.

Encouraging governments to borrow more is a strange way to address debt distress and the burdens it places on women, especially low-income women. What is needed is a fundamental reform of the international financial system. As this book suggests, the adoption of a human rights approach to the issue of sovereign debt, including conducting human rights impact assessments of debt-related policies, could play an important role in providing a moral justification for debt restructuring and debt cancellation, both within countries and in intergovernmental fora. This moral justification asserts that the rights of creditors should be subordinate to human rights obligations, and would put the fulfilment of women's rights at the centre of the governance of systems of borrowing and lending, both nationally and internationally.

To put this into practice requires changes in law, both nationally and internationally, and in the operation of the international financial system.

Contributors to this book make important proposals for concrete reforms, and also emphasize the importance of cooperation between countries in the Global South to bring about change and the participation of women's organizations that adopt a transformative approach to gender equality to design and monitor reforms to ensure that the benefits are distributed in ways that reduce gender inequality. In this context, contributors call for gender-responsive budgeting efforts to be transformed so that they are given power and resources to move beyond very limited micro-level monitoring to contribute to the development of macroeconomic policies that would lift women's burdens and support gender equality.

The principles of mutuality and reciprocity between creditors and debtors need to be rediscovered and put at the heart of reforms. The proposals put forward by Keynes at the Bretton Woods Conference in 1944, which was convened to set up a new international economic system after the Second World War, did rest on such principles, in the shape of an International Clearing Union organized on cooperative lines. But in the system actually set up, these principles were only very partially accepted, and subsequently further sidelined as the US dollar and private finance came to dominate the system. Provisions for the IMF to provide automatic bridging loans to assist member countries that were in difficulties were not accepted and conditionality became the guiding principle of IMF lending (Elson, 1994).

Human rights scholars can join with progressive economists to urge reforms to end debt distress, and feminists can join with other progressive organizations, such as those campaigning for workers' and farmers' rights, to ensure reforms are designed and implemented in progressive ways. There are signs of new thinking among some governments, such as the 2022 Bridgetown Initiative by the government of Barbados, calling for reform of the global financial architecture, urging that 'We must act now. We cannot be good at rescuing banks but bad at saving countries'.[1] The initiative has been backed by the UN Secretary General and is being widely discussed in the run-up to the UN Climate Change Conference (COP28) in December 2023.

If progress is made, the challenge will still remain of ensuring that freeing governments from debt distress will be translated into improvements in wellbeing and reductions in inequality. Here feminist movements have a vital role to play. This innovative book shows the benefits of a feminist approach to the sovereign debt crisis because it goes well beyond a concern with increasing economic growth to pose as a key test: what will reforms mean for poor women? Will their debt distress be ended? Will their human rights be fulfilled? This book should be widely read and discussed. Everyone should be in no doubt that sovereign debt is a feminist issue.

Note

1 See at https://www.foreign.gov.bb/the-2022-barbados-agenda/

References

Bakker, I. (ed) (1994) *The Strategic Silence,* London: Zed Books.

Elson, D. (1991) 'Male bias in macroeconomics', in D. Elson (ed) *Male Bias in the Development Process*, Manchester: Manchester University Press.

Elson, D. (1994) 'People, development and the international financial institutions: an interpretation of the Bretton Woods system', *Review of African Political Economy*, 21(62): 511–24.

Elson, D. (2002, 2011) 'International financial architecture: a view from the kitchen', *Femina Politica*, 11: 26–37, reprinted in N. Visvanathan, L. Duggan, N. Wiegersma and L. Nisonoff (eds), *The Women and Development Reader* (2nd edn), London: Zed Books.

Young, B., Bakker, I. and Elson, D. (eds) (2011) *Questioning Financial Governance from a Feminist Perspective,* London: Routledge.

Preface

The purpose of convening and bringing together scholars and activists from the South and the North, as well as representatives of national and international institutions, to discuss the phenomenon of sovereign debt from a feminist and human rights perspective, responds to the need to sharpen diagnoses and agree on global strategies on how to resist and transform finances that exaction, mainly, women.

We should not underestimate the political ability of creditors to uphold double standards: they can proudly beat their chests when promoting microcredit programmes for 'women entrepreneurs' while draining from the same countries debt services with interest rates above 20 per cent, even though pandemics, floods, droughts and fires kill those same borrowers; or push green bonds while promoting the fossil industry to strengthen the debt repayment capacity. We have reached the point at which debt can be considered sustainable even if life and the Earth are not.

The book, through its chapters, navigates a number of fundamental questions to which it attempts to contribute: Do human rights have something to offer in terms of dismantling radical inequalities? And to eradicating gender-based inequalities and discrimination? Is public debt with a feminist approach, under the current economic system, an oxymoron? And are we always attentive to the performativity of the 'gender approach', driven by actors who do not really want to transform the patriarchal society?

Juan Pablo Bohoslavsky and Mariana Rulli (eds)
Viedma, January 2024

Introduction: Feminist Sovereign Debt – Utopia or Oxymoron?

Juan Pablo Bohoslavsky and Mariana Rulli

1. Introduction

Recognizing that the matrix of gender relations is a variable that permeates all economic activities (Elson, 1995), the type, the contractual conditions and the volume of public debt, their legal implications (Villard Duran, 2021), as well as the economic policies that are consequently implemented, could never be neutral from a gender-based perspective. Thus, due to the historical and persistent conditions of gender inequalities in the whole world, and particularly in Latin America, sovereign over-indebtedness, the criteria used to assess debt sustainability, and the adjustment policies frequently implemented to ensure the full repayment of debts, affect women's human rights in all their diversity in a differential way.

The gender-based debt narrative that is deployed in this book seeks to dismantle the complex causalities that link debts to women's human rights in all their diversity, and particularly to gender inequalities.[1] Throughout this book, it can be confirmed that economy – and specifically debt – is something too complex to leave only to economists. Besides, debt implications for human rights are too serious for those in charge of making decisions in this field not to adopt a feminist approach.

Debts, even when (or precisely because) they often involve the spoliation of the debtors, are collected. The anthropologist David Graeber in his monumental work titled *Debt: The First 5000 Years* (2011) rebuilds a historical ethnography of violence as an element inherent to debts. In fact, debt has been a domination weapon of colonialist countries (Pénet and Zendejas, 2021).[2]

This book postulates that gender violence, specifically economic violence (as the cause and materialization of the discrimination against women), is also a component of the capitalist system, and consequently of public debt as we know it. From the beginning of the capitalist system, women have been subject to violence (Federici, 2010): the economic, political and social processes of the consolidation and transformation of the system until the current stage of the deepening of financial capitalism have been violent in terms of gender.[3]

That same violence and gender unfairness is not only materialized in the differential effects of the contractual terms of debt and related fiscal policies, but also in the procedural aspects and/or participatory processes. The idea that public indebtedness in democratic systems is a decision that purely and heroically reflects the 'people's will' is an illusion (Eusepi and Wagner, 2017). Public debt is often promoted, imposed and/or justified by domestic power groups over the other groups of the society (Roos, 2019) that will have to work and produce to repay such debt, and even sacrifice the full exercise and enjoyment of their rights to save enough for their creditors. Debt is an instrument of power through which wealth is regressively redistributed under the slogan '"we" all owe this debt' within countries in a covert, deep and lasting way. This is even more evident in countries where constitutional practices do not include a parliamentary, public and ex-ante debate to decide on taking external sovereign debt. Within that general contractualist *illusion*, it can be noted that the groups of population that will be affected in a differential way by indebtedness, such as women in all their diversity, do not have institutional channels of actual participation in debt management.

There is an aspect on which, in theory, orthodoxy and feminist economy could agree: if actually there is a mutual relation between the macroeconomic performance and the levels of inclusion and social equality (Kolovich, 2018; Davoodi et al, 2022), then fiscal policy (expansive or contractionary) and the levels (and types) of sovereign indebtedness would request that decisions in these two fields are consistent and sensitive to those interrelations and eventually to their impact on gender equality. In order to ensure this intermediate point is reached, impact assessments on debt strategies, and economic policies and reforms in terms of gender equality, should be part of the regular landscape in the national institutional practices (of the ministries of economy and finances, central banks, as well as mechanisms of the advancement of women's rights) and of international credit institutions.[4] However, this does not happen because those assessments, implemented and fully considered, would not be simple monetary quantifications, but would imply the creation of the social reality around the origins of inequalities. And, as we know, austerity is a dangerous idea because it is often immune to empirical refutation (Mark Blyth dixit).

A particular, specific and recent example of that contradiction: the moment the government of Argentina approved a retirement moratoria in March 2023, which mainly benefited women who have worked in care tasks without a social security framework to make contributions; the International Monetary Fund (IMF) questioned this measure and requested a larger fiscal restriction to compensate for the cost of this retirement moratoria.

Therefore, the main goal of this book is to extend and strengthen a feminist approach to the challenges posed by sovereign over-indebtedness (typically denominated in foreign currency) of low- and middle-income countries and the frequently resulting economic policies, which involves researching and reflecting about sovereign debt and economic gender violence, development, climate change, legal standards, United Nations (UN) developments (including world and regional UN conferences on women), international financial institutions' (IMF and World Bank) androcentric policies, the right to care and the right to education, women's private indebtedness, budget and debt (and life) sustainability analyses with a gender perspective, social progress indicators and their relation with debt, feminist reforms in the international financial architecture, gender bonds and the institutionalization of a gender approach in the public debt field. Although academic efforts were made to separately analyze these issues, this book offers to address them in a holistic and integrated manner, as well as in an interdisciplinary dialogue.

2. Debt distress and economic orthodoxy: bad news for women

Even before the beginning of the COVID-19 pandemic in 2020, a large number of countries had high levels of sovereign debt, with debt services that took the lion's share and, in consequence, the possibility to ensure a proper expenditure financing to satisfy basic social needs. With the need to mobilize more resources during the pandemic, and the limited fiscal options that low-income and middle-income countries have, the external debt (both public and private) of these countries grew during the health emergency.

As of October 2022, 60 per cent of low-income countries and 30 per cent of emerging economies were experiencing or close to experiencing situations of debt unsustainability, with a global crisis of debt very likely in the next few years (UNCTAD, 2022a). In 2021, low-income and middle-income countries paid US$400 billion of debt service, more than twice the amount they received in official aid for development. Meanwhile, their international reserves were reduced by more than US$600 billion last year, almost three times the amount they received in support for the COVID-19 emergency through the allocation of the IMF special drawing rights. Added to the very limited extension of the initiative to suspend the debt service and the rise of the interest rate, a high number of countries reduced their budgets intended to ensure the full fulfilment of the economic and social rights of the population (Ortiz and Cummings, 2022). In accordance with the very same IMF projections, in 2024, half of low-income and middle-income

Figure 1.1: Percentage of external debt compared to gross national revenues of all low-income and middle-income countries, and the countries of Latin America and the Caribbean (2010-21)

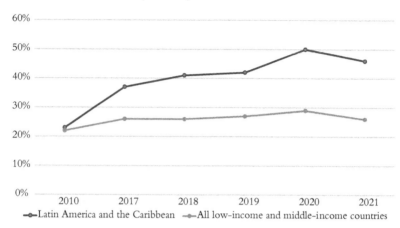

Source: Own creation based on the data from the World Bank (2022)

countries will allocate fewer resources to their health budgets than the ones allocated on average during the 2010–20 decade, and one of the reasons is the significant increase of the amounts allocated to repay the external debt. The relative burden of debt in the countries of Latin America and the Caribbean is considerable, as shown in figure 1.1. The percentage of the external debt compared to gross national revenues of the countries of Latin America has been increasing steadily since 2010, reaching 50 per cent in 2020, and above the same indicator for all low-income and middle-income countries.

Besides, it is worth mentioning that this higher level of indebtedness has not actually benefited women. If we take indebtedness to support growth or finance infrastructure as an example, the growth per se does not ensure a higher or better participation of women in the labour market, and the infrastructure does not usually consider the care economy.

Moreover, as the tax structure of the countries of the region is characterized by being strongly dependent on indirect taxes (consumption tax, which is disproportionally levied on low-income households and especially on those where women are heads of the household) (OECD et al, 2020), the increasing public debt repayment has deepened the already existing inequalities. This is added to fiscal evasion and avoidance, which according to ECLAC (2019) is still one of the main obstacles to move resources for the 2030 Sustainable Development Agenda in the region. The most recent estimates show that fiscal evasion reaches an amount equal to 2.2 per cent of the GDP in the case of the value-added tax (VAT) and 4.1 points of the GDP in the case of the income tax, an amount equal to US$335,000 million (ECLAC, 2019: 7).

While rich countries were able to move trillion-dollar aid and encouragement packages to defuse the recession caused by the pandemic, this fiscal and monetary option was not available for low-income and middle-income countries, including the countries of Latin America and the Caribbean. Capital flight, the collapse of exports and tourism, the price drop of raw materials and demand, as well as the already existing burden of the external debt, created the perfect storm and helps us understand why these countries resorted to a higher indebtedness during the pandemic. International financial institutions (IFIs) provided a series of programmes of financial assistance, while the possibility to accept debt relief both on the principal and the interest was limited to a few countries and for very limited amounts (IMF, 2022).

Debt vulnerability exposes countries to cascade crises (UNRISD, 2022): economic, financial and monetary crises, which result in known and disproportionate impacts on women in all their diversity, whether it is measured in terms of formal participation in the labour market, their presence in politics, educational achievements, or effects on health, among other indicators (Blanton, Blanton and Peksen, 2019). In this aspect, there is a vicious circle: financial and debt crises generate higher inequality, which in turn creates higher levels of debt (Bazillier and Hericourt, 2015).

IFIs, led by the IMF and the World Bank, have been suggesting and requiring, even during the pandemic (Ortiz and Cummins, 2021; Razavi et al, 2021), the need to implement orthodox economic measures (in other words, programmes of structural adjustment) in order to address over-indebtedness.[5] And countries did it: as of September 2022, 143 countries (including 94 low-income and middle-income countries) were already implementing adjustment measures. As of 2023, 85 per cent of the world population is surviving under austerity measures, which will continue at least until 2025, with 75 per cent of the global population (129 countries) under adjustment mandates (Ortiz and Cummings, 2022). The countries of Latin America and the Caribbean have not been exempt from this growing trend to implement austerity programmes: in a context marked by the steady increase of inequality, all the 24 agreements executed by the IMF with 14 countries of the region between April 2020 and May 2022 have contained, to a greater or lesser extent, conditionalities based on adjustment programmes (Oxfam, 2022).

These programmes have a female face as they often disproportionally affect this population group, worsening pre-existent gender inequalities. The first sectors that usually suffer from budget cutbacks are education, health and care (Kentikelenis and Stubbs, 2023), all of which are highly feminized in labour terms. These differential and discriminatory effects occur through a series of causal channels, including the loss of access to public services, fewer opportunities to access (or keep) jobs with decent conditions, a larger burden of unpaid care work, the increase of debt in households, and the weakening of food safety, among others (UN Independent Expert, 2018;

Serafini and Fois, 2021; Saalbrink, 2022); all aspects further analyzed by several chapters of this book.

The large participation of private capital in public services, driven both by the IMF and the World Bank before, during, and after the pandemic, by placing profit as an omnipotent factor, is another policy that disproportionally affects women (Mariotti and Romero, 2022). The negative consequences for women's human rights can be immediately noted, in ways that are more or less obvious (Muchhala and Guillem, 2022), and their effects can last for decades. This is also part of the intergenerational implication of sovereign debt.

In fact, even in the context of the – limited and short-lived – expansive policy of public expenditure that took place during the COVID-19 pandemic, and with the well-known and disproportionate socioeconomic effects on women in all their diversity (ECLAC, 2022), when the fate of these public funds is closely observed, it turns out that men have received twice the resources women have received (Financial Transparency Coalition, 2022: 9).

3. IMF and its (archaic and selective) vision of human rights in debt issues

In an unprecedented way, the IMF, which is an intergovernmental agency and part of the UN system, does not accept that it is bound by international human rights law. Confirming its historical stand, in 2017, in a letter submitted in the context of the elaboration of the Guiding Principles related to the assessments of the effects of economic reforms on human rights, the representative of the IMF stated before the UN: 'The IMF has not accepted the Declaration on Human Rights as the motivating principle of our operations. UN agencies have generally accepted our arguments as establishing the limits of our engagement and obligations on promoting human rights.' (IMF, 2017).

This statement is problematic in at least three aspects. First, because the IMF is the only specialized agency of the UN system self-perceived as being above human rights. The United Nations Charter (Article 1.3) is unambiguous as to the importance of human rights for the activities of the organization. Besides, the IMF Articles of Agreement does not mention 'human rights' in the article (IX) on immunities. Second, stating, as the IMF does in its letter, that UN agencies have accepted such criterion is incorrect. On the contrary, both treaty bodies and the special procedures have repeatedly stated that IFIs (and the IMF is explicitly mentioned) should respect human rights and, therefore, they are internationally liable when they do not comply with such basic obligations. There is no doubt on this since in the 1980s the UN General Assembly ordered the IMF to stop funding the South African Apartheid to prevent it from financing a regime that violated fundamental human rights. Third, considering that several international conventions recognize the right to property as a human right, and in this aspect the IMF does not hesitate when it must pursue its protection, how is this selective criterion justified as to which human rights are binding and relevant for the credit agency and which are not?

In the context of this outlandish legal interpretation that the IMF upholds, the agency launched the self-proclaimed 'gender strategy' in July 2022. As is suggested in a letter that the mandate holders of the UN special procedures submitted to the IMF in 2022, as well as in a number of studies carried out by academics and organizations of civil society, the IMF 'gender strategy' tries to be a justification of orthodox policies.[6] Under this strategy, women's interests are relevant ('macrocritical' pursuant to the IMF jargon) and worthy of being promoted as long as they improve the fiscal situation of the debtor State and promote GDP growth, even at the expense of worsening the rights of women, as is the case when women are incorporated into the labour market with precarious and informal conditions.[7]

In January 2024 the IMF released its 'Interim Guidance Note on Mainstreaming Gender', which offers operational guidance to staff to implementing the gender strategy, discussing 'light touch' versus 'deep dive' approaches to gender analysis. Oddly, the paper does not even mention 'debt' once. The paper states that 'staff would also examine comprehensively how shocks and trends, fiscal, monetary, and financial policies, and structural reforms can have differentiated impacts on men and women and, hence, narrow or exacerbate gender gaps' (IMF, 2024: 9). Yet, this gender impact assessment of the IMF's own conditionalities never takes place.

If anyone still has doubts about the merely instrumental nature of the IMF 'gender strategy', that person needs to know that in 2017 the IMF posted an article on its website, written by (male) economists, where they explained why it was worth investing in the health of women in Rwanda: 'Healthy women will probably work outside their houses, they will have more stamina and energy for physical jobs, and they will work more hours' (Bloom et al, 2017).

This step taken by the IMF to create the 'gender strategy' came to confirm a growing idea in industrialized countries about the importance of gender equality in terms of economic efficiency and good governance, which strengthens the mainstreaming of the gender-based approaches in some institutions. But, at the same time and almost inadvertently, in many cases this has led to the promotion of a more moderate sector of feminism – aligned with neoliberal ideas – that is more willing to instrumentalize and 'rinse' emancipatory demands instead of challenging the neoliberal assumptions that create and support gender inequalities (Budgeon, 2019).

4. Brief genealogy of feminist and debt agendas

The indebtedness problem was included at least four decades ago in the agenda of the feminist movement (including activists and academics) in a broad way and as a priority, highlighting that the debt issue is intrinsically intertwined with other demands and social and political phenomena with a direct effect on women's rights. Yet, the inclusion of these topics in national governmental agendas has been scarce or almost non-existent. Thus, it is key to investigate feminist agendas in a historical and critical manner so as to (re)think the progress of feminism in economic and especially financial issues, as well as the limits and challenges feminist demands have been facing.

In parallel with the beginning of the crisis of the welfare state and of paid work, and jointly with the external debt crisis as far back as the 1970s, as well as the incomplete emergence of the 'New International Economic Order', the third wave of feminism consolidated, wherein the main demands of women focused on power relations that structured family and property, being included in the public scene and transforming the inequalities of the private space.

In the decades that followed, women's labour participation increased and the unfair, invisible and unpaid distribution of domestic and care work started to be questioned. However, when the phenomenon of mass incorporation of women into the labour market started, there was no fair (re)distribution of domestic and care work among the actors of the 'care diamond' (Razavi, 2007), and among men and women; instead, it resulted in the commercialization of much of this work and, consequently, the extension of the double working day for women. Women started to work massively in the labour market and they continued working in their houses. The 'global feminization of work' (Standing, 1989), which involved the increase of women's participation in the workforce – and that included the hiring of women of the Global South with very low salaries for the intensive work in factories for exports (Elson and Pearson, 1981) – was connected to the liberalization of investments and trade (Peterson, 2005).

The 1990s and years well into the 21st century, with an upsurge of neoliberalism and the consolidation of a new model of capital accumulation through the financial capital and indebtedness processes, witnessed the progress of the agendas of feminists and dissidents as to machista violence, participation in politics, the mechanisms of advancement of women's rights, and the recognition of sexual and reproductive rights. Institutional agendas linked to the demands for economic autonomy, participation in the labour market and especially the recognition and the redistribution of the unfair division of unpaid domestic and care work also started to permeate. During these years, progress was also made as to the mainstreaming of the gender-based approach as a principle of public policy (Rodríguez Gustá, 2008; Payo, 2017), and it was included in regulatory, programmatic and budget frameworks.

As far back as the 1980s and the beginning of the 1990s, the feminist movement, mainly from Latin America, suggested that the impact of the macroeconomic policies implemented in the context of the structural adjustment in peripheral countries was not neutral in terms of gender (Birgin,

1992). Indeed, in the Women's Regional Conferences in Guatemala (1988) and Mar del Plata (1994) these problems were raised. In the Beijing Platform of Action (1995), which constituted the basis for the feminist action in the decades that followed, external debt and the orthodox economic policies as actual threats for women's rights were explicitly mentioned. The Beijing Platform went as far as suggesting the need to grant debt relief for highly indebted peripheral countries. This same diagnosis and complaint has been – incipiently and incrementally – present during the decades that followed in world and regional declarations and agreements that address this situation and women's rights.[8] There seems to be an ethical assumption underlying these positionings that understands debt is legitimate providing it fosters human (bodily, cognitive and social) capabilities (Padgett Walsh and Lewiston, 2022).

However, this specific complaint linked to debt, included in official documents and subject to academic research, did not escalate considerably in specific national governmental actions. The feminist and human rights approach in debt issues quickly found its limits. On the one hand, and in a more general way, because in recent decades a neoliberal colonization of human rights has persisted, focusing mainly on civil and political rights, which was not able to touch the economic roots of inequalities, and assumes a perfect compatibility between market economy and human rights (Bohoslavsky and Cantamutto, 2022).

On the other hand, and in a more specific way, due to the recognized tension between the economic redistribution and the sociocultural recognition of the demands of the feminist movement (Fraser, 2000; 2008a; 2008b), which also explains the emergence and consolidation of a sector of moderate feminism, connected to 'progressive neoliberalism', which, while still advocating for the recognition of certain rights and individual liberties, says nothing as to the origins and implications of financial liberalism, and which has softened (or even marginalized) a number of demands of the most radical feminists, as well as institutionalized other more moderate ones, watering down its transformative potential.

For that same reason, the IMF *can afford* to have its own 'gender strategy' that in turn is replicated without fear in a number of national governments, resulting in the institutionalization of a moderate – washed – feminism that, through non-performativity, ends up doing something (institutionalizing) so that nothing changes (Ahmed, 2022); that is, 'non-reformist reforms'. In other words, using this new 'gender strategy', sponsored and supported by the neoliberal agenda, the IMF can appropriate the notion of gender and eliminate any radical and emancipatory ideas of feminist movements to promote public policies whose goal is that women can be useful to capital.

Something similar can be said as to the gender-based approach of the World Bank that is silencing the differential effects of the reform packages, the extractive projects they finance, the private health systems they promote and the unfair systems of microloans they support. Among many other economic and androcentric *delicatessens*, the World Bank obviously focused on 'economically empowering' women (and, in certain cases, on specific civil and political rights – such as the prohibition of discrimination based on gender – with limited fiscal impact), as if gender inequalities do not have a deep structural root, including the unequal distribution of care tasks, which also requires structural solutions (Bruneau, 2023).

In 2018, the World Bank withdrew a loan for education purposes to Tanzania until the government changed its policy of banning pregnant girls from going to school. There was no conditionality aimed at ensuring that a social safety net was in place in the country in order to guarantee that those persons could continue with their studies during the pregnancy and – when this was the case – after the delivery.[9] Also regarding its gender approach, the World Bank announced in May 2023 that it was going to freeze new loans to Uganda because of the country's discriminatory anti-LGBTIQ+ law. Yet, when making this decision, there was no reference to human rights standards but to 'values'; it only focused on discrimination in law but not in practice, there was no comprehensive policy to promote the rights of this group in a vulnerable situation, and the same financial decision was not taken in the case of other client countries with similar discriminatory laws; and it was made, in any case, on an implicit selective use of human rights, as economic and social rights did not deserve any (not even implicit) consideration from the World Bank.

The expansion of the Washington Consensus, the exponential growth of financial neoliberalism, the consolidation of the model of infinite growth leveraged by debt, extractivism and other activities that damage the environment, as well as the higher development of highly masculinized sectors, all had specific consequences for women. The orthodox economic policies to address public over-indebtedness (dismantling public services, weakening networks of social protection, labour flexibilization, higher relative burden of indirect taxes, reduction of standards for environmental protection, and so on) had a different impact on women and caused, for instance, higher private indebtedness for women to satisfy the needs related to social reproduction (Guérin, Kumar and Venkatasubramanian 2023). The result has been the 'financialization of reproduction' that subjects women to be simultaneously exploited as domestic workers and caregivers, as paid workers, as consumers and now also as debtors (Federici, Cavallero and Gago, 2021). The so-called 'gender bonds' that were recently created, subjecting gender equality to the 'forces of the financial market', imply the deepening of this financialization process up to paroxysm.[10] Another irrefutable proof that neoliberalism can cannibalize everything (Nancy Fraser (2023) dixit).

Debt, whether public or private, is key to the systemic and structural discussion of capitalism (Lazzarato, 2015). Just like the core of the capitalist heart has been targeted by the feminist economy denouncing the unfair distribution of domestic and care tasks (Cantilon, Mackett and Stevano, 2023), the limits to indebtedness also affect the logic of modern financial capitalism. Our point here is that feminism from the inside and the outside, as an emancipatory social movement, should not only continue advocating, but also strengthen its demands and improve its strategies in terms of the regulation of the international flow of capital, the international trade of goods and services, the progressiveness of tax regimes, and the actual effects of orthodox economic policies on the human rights of women, as well as the criteria that should guide the granting, sustainability and restructuring of debt that feminism has been defending in the last decades. This is a challenge that goes beyond feminism and overlaps with a number of political struggles, including the workers' struggle connected to production and salary, social protection and the environment. It is evident that the political aspect, as Nancy Fraser suggests, is an essential element to face this challenge and establish the rules and strategies for confrontation, and is the stage for the struggles for redistribution, recognition and representation. It is crucial to continue contributing to the narrative as to how wealth and its concentration is created, the role of debt in them, and their effect on human rights in general, as well as on gender inequalities in particular. That is to say, accepting the sacrifice of human rights on the altar of short-term fiscal discipline – so as to ensure the full repayment of sovereign debt – and admitting that debt can be sustainable even when life is not, implies a major threat for women. The goal of this book is to contribute to the narrative so as to raise awareness and political action.

5. Politics and human rights as transformative feminist tools

The criteria to assess debt sustainability, economic reforms and their results in terms of human rights, including gender equality, are mediated by *politics* (Kendrick, 2020). If the political and social context is androcentric, and the capitalist system is patriarchal, is it realistic to think that economic policies resulting from it will not have that machista bias? Therefore, efforts should not only aim at understanding and reporting the causal connections between economic policies and their effects in terms of gender, they should also focus on how power is created with an androcentric bias, which in turn is the result of a dynamics of interdependent dimensions (Padamsee, 2009); in other words, to re-recognize the supremacy of politics (Karl Polanyi dixit).

Among these dimensions, *positional* factors (how people are placed in material structures or how current institutions and rules are formed) and *interpretative* factors (how we understand and see the world, whether through cultural or psychological means) are found. The feedback dynamics of these dimensions eventually determine the foundations of the social order, and with that the economic reforms and their consequences in terms of gender (Kendrick, 2020).

The conception of family, for instance, has a deep influence on how it is believed domestic care tasks should be distributed and compensated, which in turn impacts on how binding the repayment of debt is considered if this contradicts the obligation to ensure the right to care. Also, what is said and not said has an impact on the representational world that is built from power: a female director of the IMF, who excitedly promotes a 'gender-based approach', takes the attention out of the adjustment persistence (and its effects on the miserly economy of care) and the intrinsic importance of gender equality, presenting equality as 'a means' for the economy to grow more; while the usurious 'surcharges' that debtor States pay to the IMF go untouched, eroding the fiscal space to implement public policies that reduce gender inequalities. The grammar linked to the so-called 'entrepreneurship' of women – that in practice seeks autonomy in the market – erodes arguments connected to the need to address structural inequalities using fiscal policies and other type of public policies. Performing gender-responsive budget assessments (including debt repayments), selecting in an opportunistic way the budgetary lines with positive effects on inequalities, and omitting the consideration of neoliberal elephants, strengthen the meta-idea about the alleged neutrality of debt in terms of gender and thus ends up giving more importance to 'the legitimacy of the political and economic structures of the neoliberal capitalism' (Budgeon, 2019: 1149). And the perception of women, their family responsibilities and their labour ambitions, reflected in the media, contribute to model the level of differential sacrifice of women that is socially accepted as a consequence of the implementation of austerity measures. Building meaning – through semiotic social action – challenges the structures of society, while at the same time being limited by them.

Recognizing the endogenous nature of power relations and their impact on economic policies, and thus on women's rights, forces us to define feminist strategies in the field of debt that cover both aspects: politics and its material and immaterial conditioning factors, and how such dynamics are translated into policies and economic reforms with differential effects based on the sector (to the point that they violate the discrimination prohibition). To tackle both dimensions in a simultaneous and integrated way is not only possible but also necessary. In March 2019, the Human Rights Council of the UN approved the Guiding Principles on Human Rights Impact Assessments of Economic Reforms (United Nations, 2019) that set forth the incorporation to the radar of a wide series of factors that include both the factors that operate the dynamics of power in politics and the relation between economic reforms and the effects on women:

> Principle 8.3 ... The human right impact assessments with a clear gender-based approach and the core participation of women in the assessment process may support the fulfillment of the human rights

of women in practice through a *contextualized analysis*, whose goal is to identify and prevent *direct and indirect discrimination*; address *structural socio-economic and sociocultural obstacles*; correct *current and historical disadvantages*; fight against *stigma, biases, stereotypes*, and *violence*; transform *social and institutional structures*; and facilitate *political participation* and *social inclusion* of women. (United Nations, 2019; emphasis added)

Impact assessments should also consider these before-economic policies factors, even when they generate a lot of discomfort and resistance. As Martha Finnemore and Kathryn Sikkink (1998: 897) explain, 'in order to challenge the existing logics of what is proper, activists will have to be explicitly improper'. If these assessments are carried out, and the factors that in fact determine the economic policies with an androcentric bias are included, they could contribute to a wider struggle to generate and show the truth that compels awareness, claiming in turn its epistemic privilege in politics. Obviously, this implies that assessments contain quantitative and also qualitative aspects,[11] and that they are carried out in a clear, participative and independent way.

We are aware that domestic debt policy manages a series of incentives (elections, lobbying, corruption, conflicts of interest, international geopolitics and so on) which are key to the definition of whether, how much and what type of debt is taken, if it is restructured or defaulted, and to the economic policies that ensure its repayment (Mosley and Rosendorff, 2022). Specifically, performing full impact assessments could release sensitive information into the public domain with the potential to influence the direction of policies; in other words, the 'cognitive moral justification' (Mahlmann, 2023) of economic policies with transformative and emancipatory purposes and effects in the field of human rights would be strengthened.

An approach based on human rights postulates a notion of debt sustainability that considers not only the repayment ability of the country, but also if the agreed level of debt and its service would compromise the minimum fiscal resources of the State to ensure the fulfilment of human rights, including the discrimination prohibition based on gender (Guiding Principles 12.3) and the right to development (UNCTAD, 2022b). Thus, the principle *pacta sunt servanda* ('agreements must be kept') of financial law must be harmonized with the international obligations of human rights and gender equality (Lienau, 2014) which, in turn, may suggest that debt relief is needed (Ghosh, 2022: 9–11).

There exists an essential reason why IFIs do not agree to extend their fiscal and short-term criterion to assess debt sustainability;[12] as long as there are no established global rules regarding debt restructurings which enable the reduction of the agreed amount to all kinds of creditors based on criteria that are objective, agreed and sensitive to human rights and development, creditors will continue stating that a debt is sustainable as long as the short-term fiscal flow shows that the debt is repayable (Laskaridis, 2021), even when debtor countries have to sell their national territory or offer gestational surrogacy to foreign people.

Let's say it openly: the type of sovereign debt aimed for by the emancipatory feminist approach is based on a notion of sustainability that international finances, as they operate nowadays, could not accept. The spread of creditors sacrificed on the altar of the financing of economic and social rights, gender equality and environmental sustainability!? For that reason, the simple idea of suggesting that human rights should be part of the impact assessment of public debt and economic reforms implies assuming a feminist – or radical – stand that does not indulge the bases on which the modern economic system is built. An unmoderated feminism would ask: which source of international law or constitutional provision sets forth that there exists imperative and discretionary public expenditure, and among the former ones the repayment of financial obligation is found, and among the latter ones health, education and care expenses are found? This basic legal question that indicates the transformative potential of human rights in the field of economics (Bohoslavsky and Cantamutto, 2022) is not often reflected in public debates around fiscal policy.

As shown, in the social construction of problems and in their legal understanding, the origin of discriminatory economic policies can be tracked. The point is that '[a]rticulating interests in legal terms redefines the distributive results as preexisting facts or marginal adjustments required by technical considerations. Finally, law permeates our common sense on distributions that are fair, interests that can be heard, and profits that are legitimate' (Kennedy, 2020: 147).

Human rights, as we suggest in this book, challenge one of the legal sacred cows of modern financial law, in other words, that debts shall always be repaid (*pacta sunt servanda*), even when doing so implies extreme material hardship for debtor populations, or redounds to high levels of discrimination and violence. This task is framed in a semantic dispute of a wider scope, where the very definition of human rights and their relation with the market economy and inequalities are subject to an open struggle (Alston, 2021; Whyte, 2019), to which this book also intends to contribute.

6. The chapters

Apart from this introductory chapter, the book has 20 chapters divided into six parts. The first part focuses on 'Debt and feminist agendas' and begins with chapter 2 by Corina Rodríguez Enríquez, where the scope and potential of the notion of economic violence as a result of the operating logic of global financial capitalism is analyzed, in order to explain the material basis of patriarchal violence. The macroeconomic processes and their incidence on material living conditions can be observed through economic violence, recognizing the systemic, and also collective, nature of patriarchal violence that enables the articulation of resistance. With that context, Rodríguez Enríquez offers an analysis on the notions of debt sustainability and life sustainability, as well as reflections linked to the feminist resistance to the indebtedness it generates, which is, according to the author, collective organization, a declaration of the systemic roots of indebtedness and reporting its connection with economic violence.

In chapter 3, Penelope Hawkins and Marina Zucker-Marques describe how the differential impact of sovereign debt on women is not limited to the times when austerity measures are implemented as a solution to a crisis, but they are also connected to the expansive stages of a model of economic development where growth is driven precisely by indebtedness. In the stage of indebtedness-based growth, investment in sensitive areas for gender equality (basic services, care and the labour market) is suppressed, precisely because borrower States need to guarantee a constant flow of debt service, which requires keeping social investment at bay. Finally, they suggest the need to include the long-term sustainable development goals in the analysis of debt sustainability, which requires flexibility to demand repayments in the short term.

In chapter 4, Iolanda Fresnillo Sallan and Leia Achampong offer an analysis on how the twin crises, the debt crisis and the climate change crisis, overburden women in the Global South and threaten the full exercise of their human rights. Through a study that includes how governments implement expenditure cutbacks, higher extractivism and other contractionary or orthodox economic policies, which in fact are deepened to mitigate the current debt crisis, they show how the debt crisis is intrinsically connected to the climate crisis in a cycle that is self-fed and damaging – in a disproportionate way – for women's rights. Moreover, they show the need to advance on reforms of the global financial architecture in order to deal with the twin crises in a comprehensive, systemic and feminist way, for instance, through the cancellation of debt to move resources so as to facilitate the energy transition.

The second part of the book gathers articles on the 'Human rights and debt approach'. In chapter 5, Juan Pablo Bohoslavsky and Julieta Rossi identify and systematize the international and Inter-American legal standards regarding human rights in the field of sovereign debt with a gender perspective. In their analysis, they include the standards applicable to borrower States and public and private creditors, and their implications in terms of specific obligations for both debtors and creditors, for instance, in the field of debt restructurings and the impact assessment of debt, as well as economic reforms for gender equality. The authors argue that the development of this topic is much more prominent in the international field than in the Inter-American one, while they indicate the importance of advancing on feminist reforms in the area of the international financial architecture that enable an equal transformation of societies.

Chapter 6 contains the letter sent in 2022 to the IMF by the holders of special mandates in the UN (Independent Expert on external debt and human rights, Special Rapporteur on the right to development, Special Rapporteur on extreme poverty and human rights, and the Working Group on the issue of Discrimination against Women and Girls) in the context of the consultations this credit agency was making on its announced 'gender strategy'. Although mandate holders recognize the importance of a strategy in this field, they warn that the approach would be focused 'on the macrocritical factors of gender gaps, in line with the IMF mandate', and that, on the contrary, a gender strategy of the IMF implemented with an approach of human rights should recognize and address the differential roles women and girls have in our societies, as well as the obstacles they face because of their sex and gender, and demand the performance of gender-responsive impact assessments of loans and reforms. The letter also shows that a strategy with a human rights approach would imply excluding austerity requirements that the IMF continues to recommend, even in the context of the pandemic crisis. As of April 2023, the IMF has not yet replied to the letter.

In chapter 7, Dorothy Estrada-Tanck presents the mandate of the Working Group of the Human Rights Council of the UN on the discrimination against women and girls (WGDAWG) and presents a selection of excerpts from the thematic report titled 'The gendered inequalities of poverty: feminist and human rights-based approaches' that the Working Group presented in March 2023. The report focused on poverty and socioeconomic inequalities as a result of systemic failures (debt is at the core of them) that violate multiple human rights of women and girls. Furthermore, she enquires into the transversal conditions of gendered socioeconomic inequality, structural discrimination, and drivers within the political, economic, cultural and social system that cause, perpetuate and deepen poverty and inequality experiences of women and girls. In line with the letter of special procedures addressed to the IMF in 2022 (chapter 6), the report shows its criticism to the 'gender strategy' implemented by the IMF, and presents specific proposals and recommendations on the management and restructuring of debt with a gender perspective.

In chapter 8, Marita Perceval and Mariana Rulli systematize and analyze the ways in which sovereign debt and its effects on women have been discussed and agreed upon in the UN World Women's Conferences from 1975 to 1995 and the Regional (Latin American and Caribbean) Women's Conferences from 1977 to 2022. Among the main findings, it is noted that the diagnoses reached and recommendations made at world and regional conferences have been extremely sensitive to the economic, political and social dynamics driven by debt during the periods in which these meetings took place: as early as the regional conferences in Guatemala (1988) and in Mar del Plata (1994), and in the world conference in Beijing (1995), the harmful and differential effects of debt on women's rights were stressed as well as the importance of guaranteeing women's participation in debt and structural adjustment negotiations. The chapter also identifies that in the regional conferences (compared to the world ones) there have been earlier, more robust, continuous and specific denunciations in the field of debt, orthodox economic policies and their differential impact on women, proposing a number of factors that could explain that divergency.

The third part of the book focuses on 'International financial institutions, gender and diversity', and starts with chapter 9, by Camila Villard Duran, who presents a critical perspective on gender mainstreaming in the IMF through an analysis of the historical development of legal and economic narratives of the IMF regarding gender equality based on the scrutiny of official declarations, policies and research documents published in a historical series. This analysis explains the instrumentalization that this agency has made regarding the gender narrative: gender equality as a means to promote macroeconomic stability, not as a value on its own. This instrumentalist approach invisibilizes the adverse effects of the orthodox conditionalities of the IMF on women's rights. Finally, the author suggests the possibility and duty to harmonize international economic law and human rights law, to combine the mandate of macroeconomic stability of the IMF and respect for women's rights.

In chapter 10, Diane Perrons describes how neoliberal economic policies, which are seemingly neutral, produce unequal social effects, especially as to gender. The author removes theoretical and empirical prejudices and fallacies of neoliberal economic thought that have shaped the ideas that in the last decades have dominated national and international policy making (including debt management and the obsession with denying the need of its cancellation), and that have deeply sharpened inequalities, even as a solution to the main current crises. The chapter also explains the existence of alternative economic models, focused on the wellbeing of people.

In chapter 11, Alicja Krubnik analyzes the negative effects in social and gender terms that have been created by the IMF conditionalities (mainly through financialization, privatization, liberalization, deregulation and austerity) in Latin America at the end of the 20th century, and how, despite these results, in the current context of the pandemic, in several cases, the orthodox bias of the IMF has remained and even strengthened in that same direction. Moreover, Krubnik critically analyzes the incomplete and insufficient 'gender turn' the IMF has made and warns with concern that this is a strategy by the IMF to appropriate the gender discourse and shape it to the goals of neoliberal politics.

The fourth part of the book sheds light on 'IMF, women and diversities in Latin America and Argentina', starting with chapter 12 written by María Nieves Rico, which enquires into the interrelation that exists among debt sustainability, life sustainability and care, which happens in a context of already deep structural inequalities. In her analysis, Rico shows how public indebtedness and its consequences have a complex meaning when analyzing their impact on the daily life of people, specifically how the measures adopted (considering the commitments with the IMF) have as one of their greatest consequences – whether directly or indirectly – the reproduction and deepening of gender inequalities. Furthermore, the author analyzes how, considering that socioeconomic situation, women face the costs of family management of care through the implementation of different strategies, such as the reduction of frequent expenses and the need to turn to formal or informal loans and indebtedness so as to satisfy current basic needs. Finally, the author shows the importance of implementing comprehensive care systems in the region to move towards life sustainability.

In chapter 13, Francisco Cantamutto and Agostina Costantino analyze from a gender perspective the impact of public debt and orthodox economic policies on the human right to education in Latin America and the Caribbean. To that purpose, the authors analyze how commercialization and privatizations driven by neoliberal reforms, as well as fiscal austerity (including non-compliance with investment goals in education), have been particularly damaging for the rights of girls, adolescents and women, by excluding them from access and permanence in the education system, blocking training and labour opportunities. The chapter also explains the relation between investment deficits in the education sector and public indebtedness in Latin America and the Caribbean: by increasing the debt service expense in relative terms, investment in education is reduced, with its differential consequences for girls, adolescents and women.

In chapter 14, Florencia Partenio and Ariel Wilkis analyze, in the context of the COVID-19 pandemic and using a qualitative and quantitative study of households of popular classes in Argentina, the relations between the increase of private indebtedness and the deepening of inequalities. In this chapter, the authors suggest that there exists a clear difference of exposition to indebtedness between households with care tasks and households without care tasks, and that private indebtedness was used to finance expenses and consumption to maintain daily care tasks. Then they analyze the dynamics that enhance economic vulnerability when the mechanisms to protect labour rights fail and how economic vulnerability deepens when rights are not recognized paradoxically in an individual way. Besides this, they explain the interface between private and public indebtedness. Finally, they offer reflections as to indebtedness, the care crisis and the lack of access to rights, all of which is reflected in households of popular classes. Thus, the authors show the existing relation between the overload of unpaid care work that is linked to over-indebtedness and the lack of access to social protection for women, lesbians and trans persons.

The fifth part of the book focuses on 'Gender impact analysis: frameworks and experiences'. In chapter 15, Patricia Miranda and Verónica Serafini offer, from the theoretical guidelines of the Feminist Economy, a critical look at the prevailing analysis of debt sustainability. To that end, the authors analyze the theoretical structure of the economic orthodoxy – and the methodology used by the IMF – that gives absolute priority to capital, uses androcentric indicators, excludes tax justice as a key factor, gives an instrumental (non-intrinsic) character to gender equality and invisibilizes the effects of fiscal rules on women. This patriarchal bias of debt sustainability analyses that the IMF uses is a political fact with deep legal implications.

In chapter 16, Ulrike Marx enquires into the connection between feminism and quantification to manage public finances 'using numbers', based on a study of the implementation of gender-responsive budgets in Austria between 2009 and 2012. The quantitative translation of feminists' demands in the transversalization of the gender-based approach, specifically the budgeting practice, risks liquefying feminists' demands by prioritizing efficiency, optimization and competition. While the author recognizes and warns about the political biases in accountability ('numbers are political'), she emphasizes that, even when quantification may depoliticize and democratize feminism, it can also be a powerful political tool to make feminists' demands visible, placing them at the core of the debate and giving them political legitimacy, including on discussion on public debt.

In chapter 17, Flavia Navarro and Laura Pautassi focus on the importance of including the gender-based approach both in the field of State financial obligations and in the field of private debts of women and sexual diversities, and particularly on the development of progress indicators and their implementation. For that purpose, the authors present the main (quantitative and qualitative) indicators of progress that, in accordance with the Inter-American system, are used in current monitoring mechanisms in the region, and consider their potential to measure, with a gender-based approach, the degree of compliance with State obligations connected to debt and their incidence on the level of fulfilment of human rights. Finally, from a critical look at the autonomy approach, the authors highlight the need to promote the recognition of a life free of indebtedness that enables women and sexual diversities to enjoy economic autonomy in all its dimensions.

In the sixth and last part of this book, we focus on 'Work agenda for egalitarian transformations', which starts with chapter 18, where Christina Laskaridis analyzes from a feminist perspective the operation of the international monetary and financial system (IMFS) through their two core institutions: the Group of 20 (G-20) and the IMF. The author argues that these institutions have shown, at a rhetorical level, a growing interest in gender equality, but that concern has not been reflected in efficient policies and actions when reducing gender inequalities, which actually invisibilizes the ways in which the IMFS reinforces gender inequalities and other type of inequalities through the way in which capital flows, sovereign debt and related economic policies, currency hierarchies, liquidity cycles and the operational structures of global economic governance today. The final remarks identify a series of needed reforms from a feminist perspective.

In chapter 19, Juan Pablo Bohoslavsky and Lena Lavinas study what the so-called 'gender bonds' are, how they work, the economic ideas that support them, and which actors promote these gender bonds that have in the last years had an exponential growth, deepening the general phenomenon of financialization. Moreover, the authors critically analyze the limitations, contradictions and problems that these types of bonds pose that – in theory – tend to reduce gender inequalities and promote women's rights through public policies and projects financed by investors that in turn generate profits, but at the end of the day, according to the authors, are 'another brick on the neoliberal wall'.

In chapter 20, the last one, Magalí Brosio and Mariana Rulli warn that, despite the general trend of the last four decades towards a growing institutionalization of gender areas of the State in Latin America and the IFIs, specifically as to gender institutionality in public finances, and particularly as to public debt, progress has been low and, in any case, timid. The authors also provide critical reflections on the proliferation of instrumentalist and performative strategies that have been reflected in gender institutionality at the State (in the case of gender-responsive budgets) and IFIs levels (as in the gender strategy of the IMF), limiting truly transformative approaches. Finally, the authors offer a series of proposals to discuss where and how to deepen gender institutionality in the field of public finances and, more specifically, of sovereign debt.

Acknowledgements

The authors thank Francisco Cantamutto, Laura Pautassi, Emilia Reyes and Verónica Serafini for their critical feedback for this introduction.

Notes

[1] The theatre play called *Con la deuda al cuello* (Up to their neck in debt) of the theatre company 'Las Reinas Chulas', that premiered in Mexico in July 2022, contributes to that end, as by explaining the relations among macroeconomic indicators, material conditions of life, inequalities and gender stereotypes, social indicators, and the increase of public and private debt, it shows how this combination can become a life shredder, mainly for women. In other words, gender violence.

[2] In fact, if we take the period 2009–21 to study the conditionalities imposed by the International Monetary Fund (IMF) to its debtor States, we find that States with the closest diplomatic connections with the US tend to receive a more benevolent treatment by the IMF, while those States closest to China face greater requirements in terms of austerity (Ray, Gallagher and Kring, 2022).

[3] In this regard, see chapter 2 by Rodríguez Enríquez in this book.

[4] See the chapter 20 Brosio and Rulli in this book.

[5] Some of these policies include public service privatizations, health commercialization, public expenditure reduction in highly influential budgetary lines as to the fulfilment of economic and social rights, labour deregulation, weakening of the social protection system, salary and pension reduction, higher tax regressiveness and reduction of standards for environmental protection.

[6] See chapter 6 in this book on the 2022 letter sent by mandate holders of the UN special procedures.

[7] Regarding the 'gender strategy' of the IMF, see chapters 2 by Rodríguez Enríquez, 9 by Villard Duran, 10 by Perrons, 11 by Krubnik and 20 by Brosio and Rulli in this book.

[8] See the chapter 8 by Perceval and Rulli in this book.

[9] And this goes without mentioning that legal and practical barriers to accessing safe abortion implies a violation of human rights.

[10] See the chapter 19 by Bohoslavsky and Lavinas in this book.

[11] See the chapter 16 by Ulrike Marx in this book.

[12] This would lead to a consideration of the immediate effects of debt on human rights and the long-term effects on development perspectives of debtor countries, as well as the level of social resistance to adjustment and other contractionary policies.

References

Ahmed, Sara (2022) *¡Denunciá! El activismo de la queja frente a la violencia institucional*, Buenos Aires: Editorial Caja Negra.

Alston, Philip (2021) 'The past and future of social rights', in S. Jensen and C. Walton (eds), *Social Rights and the Politics of Obligation in History*, Cambridge: Cambridge University Press.

Bazillier, Rémi and Hericourt, Jérôme (2015) 'The circular relationship between inequality, leverage and financial crisis', LEO Working Papers / DR LEO 1968, Laboratoire D'Economie D'Orleans.

Birgin, Haydée (1992) 'La reformulación del orden mundial: el lugar de las mujeres en las estrategias de desarrollo', in Marcela Lagarde et al, Fin de Siglo. Género y Cambio Civilizatorio, Isis Internacional, Ediciones de las Mujeres No 17.

Blanton, Robert; Blanton, Shannon and Peksen, Dursun (2019) 'The gendered consequences of financial crises: A cross-national analysis', *Politics & Gender*, 15(4): 941–70.

Bohoslavsky, Juan Pablo and Cantamutto, Francisco (2022) 'Not even with a pandemic: The IMF and the neoliberal roots of its reluctance to human rights', *Human Rights Quarterly*, 44(4): 759–83.

Bloom, David; Kuhn, Michael and Prettner, Klaus (2017) 'Invest in women and prosper', IMF *Finance and Development*, 4(3): Available from: https://www.imf.org/external/pubs/ft/fandd/2017/09/bloom.htm

Bruneau, Camille (2023) 'The "gender equity" farce: a feminist reading of World Bank policies', CATDM [online] 11 January, Available from: https://www.cadtm.org/The-gender-equity-farce-a-feminist-reading-of-World-Bank-policies#nh2-1

Budgeon, Sally (2019) 'The resonance of moderate feminism and the gendered relations of austerity', *Gender, Work and Organization*, 26(8): 1138–55.

Cantillon, Sara; Mackett, Odile and Stevano, Sara (2023) *Feminist Political Economy: A Global Perspective*, New York: Columbia University Press.

Davoodi, Hamid; Montiel, Peter and Ter-Martirosyan, Anna (2022) 'Macroeconomic stability, adjustment, and debt' in Valerie Cerra, Barry Eichengreen, Asmaa El-Ganainy and Martin Schindler (eds), *How to Achieve Inclusive Growth*, Oxford: Oxford University Press, pp 391–423.

ECLAC (Economic Commission for Latin America and the Caribbean) (2019). 'Panorama Fiscal de América Latina y el Caribe 2019: políticas tributarias para la movilización de recursos en el marco de la Agenda 2030 para el Desarrollo Sostenible' (LC/PUB.2019/8-P), Santiago de Chile.

ECLAC (2022) 'Los impactos sociodemograficos de la pandemia del COVID-19 en América Latina y el Caribe' (LC/CRPD.4/3), Santiago de Chile.

Elson, Diane (1995) 'Gender awareness in modelling structural adjustment', *World Development*, 23(11): 51–68.

Elson, Diane and Pearson, Ruth (1981) "Nimble fingers make cheap workers': An analysis of women's employment in third world export manufacturing', *Feminist Review*, 7(1): 87–107.

Eusepi, Giuseppe and Wagner, Richard (2017) *Public Debt: An Illusion of Democratic Political Economy*, Cheltenham: Elgar Publishing.

Federici, Silvia (2010) *Calibán y la bruja. Mujeres, cuerpo y acumulación originaria*. Madrid: Traficantes de Sueños.

Federici, Silvia; Cavallero, Lucía and Gago, Verónica (2021) *¿Quén le debe a quién?: ensayos trasnacionales de desobediencia financiera*. Buenos Aires: Tinta Limón.

Financial Transparency Coalition (2022) 'Recovery at a Crossroads: How countries spent Covid-19 funds in the Global South', [online], Available from: https://financialtransparency.org/wp-content/uploads/2022/09/FTC-Recovery-at-a-Crossroads-SEPT-2022-V2.pdf

Finnemore, Martha and Sikkink, Kathryn (1998) 'Norm dynamics and political change', *International Organization*, 54(4): 887–917.

Fraser, Nancy (2000) 'Rethinking recognition', *New Left Review*, 3(3): 107–20.

Fraser, Nancy (2008a) 'La justicia social en la era de la política de identidad: redistribución, reconocimiento y participación', *Revista de Trabajo*, 4(6): 83–99.

Fraser, Nancy (2008b) 'From redistribution to recognition? Dilemmas of justice in a 'postsocialist' age', in S. Seidman and J. Alexander (eds), *The New Social Theory* Reader, London: Routledge, pp 188–96.

Fraser, Nancy (2023) *Capitalismo Caníbal. Qué hacer con este sistemaque devora la democracia y el planeta, y hasta pone en peligro su propia existencia*, Buenos Aires: Siglo XXI Editores.

Ghosh, Jayati (2022) '"The writing as on the walls": Debt distress and ways forward in Sri Lanka', *Polity*, 10(2): 7–11.

Graeber, David (2011) *Debt: The First 5000 Years*, New York: Melville House.

Guérin, Isabelle; Kumar, Santosh and Venkatasubramanian, G. (2023) *The Indebted Woman. Kinship, Sexuality, and Capitalism*, Redwood City, CA: Stanford University Press.

IMF (2017) 'IMF and human rights', letter of the IMF Representative of the United Nations to the Independent Expert on Debt and Human Rights, [online] 27 July, Available from: https://www.ohchr.org/sites/default/files/Documents/Issues/IEDebt/impactassessments/IMF.pdf

IMF (2022) 'Covid-19 Financial Assistance and Debt Service Relief', [online], Available from: https://www.imf.org/en/Topics/imf-and-covid19/COVID-Lending-Tracker#WHD

IMF (2024) 'Interim Guidance Note on Mainstreaming Gender at the IMF', [online] 12 January, Available from: https://www.imf.org/en/Publications/Policy-Papers/Issues/2024/01/12/Interim-Guidance-Note-on-Mainstreaming-Gender-at-The-IMF-543779

Independent Expert on Debt and Human Rights (2018), 'Impact of economic reform policies on women's human rights' (UN Doc. A/73/179), UN Human Rights Council, 18 July.

Kendrick, Abby (2020), 'Economic policy and women's human rights: a critical political economy perspective', *International Journal of Human Rights*, 24(9): 1353–69.

Kennedy, David (2020) 'Law in global political economy. Now you see it, now you don't' in Paul Kjaer (ed), *The Law of Political Economy. Transformation in the Function of Law*, Cambridge: Cambridge University Press.

Kentikelenis, Alexandros and Stubbs, Thomas (2023) *A Thousand Cuts. Social Protection in the Age of Austerity*, Oxford: Oxford University Press.

Kolovich, Lisa (ed) (2018) *Fiscal Policies and Gender Equality*, Washington DC: IMF.

Laskaridis, Christina (2021) 'Debt sustainability: towards a history of theory, policy and measurement', PhD thesis, SOAS University of London.

Lazzarato, Maurizio (2015) *Governing by Debt*, Los Angeles: Semiotext(e).

Lienau, Odette (2014) *Rethinking Sovereign Debt: Politics, Reputation, and Legitimacy in Modern Finance*, Boston: Harvard University Press.

Mahlmann, Matthias (2023) *Mind and Rights. The History, Ethics, Law and Psychology of Human Rights*, Cambridge: Cambridge University Press.

Mariotti, Chiara and Romero, María José (2022) 'Demystifying Bretton Woods Institutions' rhetoric on public services', *Development*, 65: 217–27.

Mosley, Layna and Rosendorff, Peter (2022), 'Sovereign debt architecture, suspended', Just Money [online] April, Available from: https://justmo ney.org/layna-mosley-peter-rosendorff-i-will-survive-the-domestic-polit ics-of-debt/

Muchhala, Bhumika and Guillem, Andrea (2022), 'Gendered austerity and embodied debt in Ecuador: Channels through which women absorb and resist the shocks of public budget cuts', Gender & Development, 30(1–2): 283–309.

OECD, Inter-American Center of Tax Administrations, Economic Commission for Latin America and the Caribbean and Inter-American Development Bank (2020), 'Estadísticas tributarias en America Latina y el Caribe 2020', Paris: OECD Publishing, Available from: https://www. oecd-ilibrary.org/fr/taxation/revenue-statistics-in-latin-america-and-the-caribbean_24104736?mlang=es

Ortiz, Isabel and Cummings, Matthew (2021) 'Global austerity alert: Looming budget cuts in 2021–25 and alternative pathways', Working Paper, Initiative for Policy Dialogue, Global Social Justice, International Confederation of Trade Unions, Public Services International, Arab Watch Coalition, The Bretton Woods Project, Third World Network [online], Available from: https://policydialogue.org/files/publications/papers/Glo bal-Austerity-Alert-Ortiz-Cummins-2021-final.pdf

Ortiz, Isabel and Cummings, Matthew (2022) 'End austerity: A global report on budget cuts and harmful social reforms in 2022–25', Initiative for Policy Dialogue, Columbia University [online] 28 September, Available from: https://www.eurodad.org/end_austerity_a_global_report

Oxfam (2022) 'La sombra de la austeridad. ¿Quién paga la cuenta del Covid-19 en América Latina y el Caribe?', [online], Available from: https:// oi-files-cng-prod.s3.amazonaws.com/lac.oxfam.org/s3fs-public/file_atta chments/Diagramación%20Austeridad%20Español.pdf

Padamsee, Tasleem (2009) 'Culture in connection: Re-contextualizing ideational processes in the analysis of policy development', Social Politics, 16(4): 413–15.

Padgett Walsh, Kate and Lewiston, Justin (2022) 'Human capabilities and the ethics of debt', The Journal of Value Inquiry, 56(2): 179–99.

Payo, Mariel (2017) 'Las políticas públicas y las miradas de género. Algunas herramientas para promover su incorporación' in A. Camou and M.L. Pagani (coords), Debates teóricos y metodológicos actuales sobre las políticas públicas, Universidad Nacional de La Plata, Facultad de Humanidades y Ciencias de la Educación.

Pénet, Pierre and Zendejas Juan Flores (eds) (2021) Sovereign Debt Diplomacies: Rethinking Sovereign Debt from Colonial Empires to Hegemony, Oxford: Oxford University Press.

Peterson, Spike (2005) 'How (the meaning of) gender matters in political economy', *New Political Economy*, 10(4): 499–521.

Ray, Rebecca; Gallagher, Kevin and Kring, William (2022) '"Keep the receipts": The political economy of IMF austerity during and after the crisis years of 2009 and 2020', *Journal of Globalization*, 13(1): 31–59.

Razavi, Shahra; Schwarzer, Helmut; Durán-Valverde, Fabio; Ortiz, Isabel and Dutt, Devika (2021) 'Social policy advice to countries from the International Monetary Fund during the COVID-19 crisis: Continuity and change', ILO Working Paper 42 [online], Available from: https://www.ilo.org/global/publications/working-papers/WCMS_831490/lang--en/index.htm

Razavi, Shahra (2007) 'The political and social economy of care in the development context. Conceptual issue, research questions and policy options', Gender and Development, paper N° 3, Geneva: UNRISD.

Rodríguez Gustá, Ana (2008) 'Las políticas sensibles al género: variedades conceptuales y desafíos de intervención', *Temas y debates: revista universitaria de ciencias sociales*, 16: 109–30.

Roos, Jerome (2019) *Why Not Default? The Political Economy of Sovereign Debt*, Princeton: Princeton University Press.

Saalbrink, Roos (2022) 'The care contradiction: The IMF, gender and austerity', ActionAid [online], Available from: https://actionaid.org/publications/2022/care-contradiction-imf-gender-and-austerity

Serafini, Verónica and Fois, Montserrat (2021) 'Women, debt and gender inequalities', Latindaad [online], Available from: https://www.latindadd.org/wp-content/uploads/2021/09/Mujeres-deuda-y-desigualdad-Final_English.pdf

Standing, Guy (1989) 'Global feminization trough flexible labour', *World Development*, 17(7): 1077–95.

UNCTAD (2022a) 'Trade and development report 2022. Development prospects in a fractured world', Geneva [online], Available from: https://unctad.org/tdr2022

UNCTAD (2022b) 'UNCTAD Sustainable Development Finance Assessment (SDFA) Framework: linking debt sustainability to the achievement of the 2030 Agenda', DA COVID-19 Project Paper 16/22, November, Available from: https://mobilizingdevfinance.org/research-material/unctad-sustainable-development-finance-assessment-sdfa-framework-linking-debt

United Nations (2019), 'Guiding Principles on human rights impact assessment of economic reforms', Independent Expert on Debt and Human Rights, UN DOC. (A/HRC/40/57, 19 December 2018); Human Rights Council Res. A/HRC/40/8 (4 May 2019), Available from: https://digitallibrary.un.org/record/1663025?ln=es

UNRISD (2022) *UNRISD Flagship Report 2022. Crisis of inequality: Shifting power for a new eco-social contract*, Geneva: United Nations, Available from: https://www.perlego.com/book/4190879/unrisd-flagship-report-2022-crises-of-inequality-shifting-power-for-a-new-ecosocial-contract-pdf

Villard Duran, Camila (2021) 'The (in)visible woman at the International Monetary Fund: Engendering national economic rule-making', *Journal of International Economic Law*, 24(4): 738–54.

Whyte, J. (2019) *The Morals of the Market: Human Rights and the Rise of Neoliberalism*, London and New York: Verso Books.

World Bank (2022) 'International debt report 2022: Updated international debt statistics', World Bank Group [online], Available from:https://openknowledge.worldbank.org/bitstream/handle/10986/38045/9781464819025.pdf?sequence=8

PART I

Debt and Feminist Agendas

2

Debt, Economic Violence and Feminist Agenda

Corina Rodríguez Enríquez

1. Introduction

The debt phenomenon has increasingly entered into the feminist agenda in Latin America. This happened simultaneously with the expansion of feminisms in several countries of the region, which took place in the last five years, as well as a gradual incorporation of economic topics in academic, activist and advocacy agendas of these feminisms.

Nowadays, this issue has become more important due to the renewed processes of indebtedness that are operating both at a country and household level. In this chapter, this issue will be analyzed from the notion of economic violence, understanding indebtedness as an expression of such economic violence.[1]

The notion of economic violence is powerful because it allows us to notice that patriarchal violence has a material basis, resulting from the functioning logic of global financial capitalism. It enables us to link macroeconomic processes to material living conditions and to the multiple forms of violence (physical, psychological, sexual, labour and financial violence). Thus, the collective nature of violence can also be recognized, going beyond the notion of gender violence and the totalizing figure of the victim (Gago, 2019). Recognizing this systemic and shared nature of violence allows for the coordinating of resistance.[2]

Moreover, thinking of the economic system in terms of violence enables us to recognize that its implications are suffered in the bodies and are lived in a rooted way. It is expressed in the super exploitation of paid and unpaid labour, in the increasingly more precarious living conditions, in bad health conditions that underfinanced public health services cannot properly treat, in the livelihoods that cannot be accessed as a consequence of the agribusiness, the mining exploitations and other misuses of human resources.

The concept of body-territory, coined by women from indigenous communities, acts as a summary of this influence, allowing us to understand how the exploitation of territories-land 'implies to violate the body of each person and the collective body through dispossession' (Gago, 2019: 90).[3] Thus not only are individual bodies connected in a collective body, but also the indivisibility of human bodies with respect to the territories where they live is emphasized.

In their proposal for a feminist reading of debt, Cavallero and Gago (2019) precisely show the need to track the relation between indebtedness and machista violence. Thus they highlight that finances that are presented as something abstract take a specific form in the lives of persons, and particularly in feminized bodies. 'Debt is the one thing that does not allow us to say "no" when we want to ... it ties us to violent relations in the future ... it obliges to keep broken bonds ... it blocks economic autonomy' (p 16). Although debt is also what enables people to move in certain circumstances. For instance, to migrate to seek better situations (even migrate to run away from violence) or to start an independent economic venture. '(W)hether as fixation or as a possibility of movement, debt exploits a future job availability; it restricts to accept any type of job due to the preexisting debt obligation ... in that sense, it is an effective means of exploitation' (p 16).

Debt violence is expressed in multiple ways, all of which are disciplinary. However, any attempt at discipline encounters its resistance. Feminist resistance to debt has been growing and consolidating, and finding new ways of action.

2. The economic logic of patriarchal violence

Capitalism, as an economic and social order, is consolidated through a violent process: the process of primitive accumulation, a concept created by Marx in his analysis of the period prior to the industrial revolution in Europe. As Sen (2014) clearly explains, the appearance of the working class implied the inevitable end of ancient rights to land use and other livelihoods, and even the security provided by feudal relations. The dispossession and the simultaneous creation of private property left large sectors of the population without land and security, and thus obliged to be subject to the hardship of the industrial discipline.

The feminist interpretation of this transaction between feudalism and capitalism made by Federici (2010) explains how in this process the bodies of women, particularly those of 'heretical' women (the heretic, the healer, the disobedient spouse, the woman who dare to live alone; in short, the witches), were objects of specific violence. These types of violence, this 'state of permanent war against women' is repeated, renewed and updated in each new stage of primitive accumulation.[4]

Violent processes have been part of capitalism since then: the accumulation of wealth and privileges in minority groups, systematically replicating inequality; the dispossession of territories and livelihoods; forced migrations for political, religious or economic reasons; armed conflicts; the systematic destruction of the planet.

The neoliberalism imposition by the 1990s gives particular characteristics to capital violence, which imposes its will using repressive (State, parastatal or private) force or debt.

Sovereign indebtedness was the gateway to structural adjustment programmes in the Global South. These programmes carried out wide processes of privatization of public services and state-owned enterprises (with different levels of intensity among countries) that fed the commodification of daily life. People could have access to many goods and services in the past because they were rights, but now they depend on their purchasing power to buy them.

Moreover, in the context of these programmes, flexibilization reforms were advanced in labour relations, worsening the guarantee of rights and making contractual forms, pay levels and social protection more precarious. In this last aspect, the reforms to core social institutions, such as social security systems, eroded the coverage of the systems and the quality of services, making both current and future life more precarious.

In Latin America in the 1990s, the consolidation of the extractivist dimension of neoliberalism also started. The processes of trade and financial opening and liberalization made the entry and exit of transnational capital more flexible, and they created a fertile ground for the foreign ownership of natural resource exploitation. This was when the agribusiness (led by multinational corporations) and extractive industries consolidated. This paradigm will be reinforced in the new century with the appearance of a development strategy based on neo-extractivism, promoted even by the 'progressive' governments of the region, and it will include the growing participation of Chinese investments in the sector (Svampa, 2019).

Debt will also play a key role in this dispossession process. As Sassen (2015) explains, there are two vectors that work in a coordinated way. On the one hand, sovereign indebtedness, which weakens governments and imposes on them the flexibilization of regulations that facilitates the entry and exit of capital, but also limits the possibilities of States to exercise active policies to promote or protect the activities of small agricultural producers or regional economies. This is how the second vector works, as a fertile ground is being prepared in a slow but persistent way for the appropriation (by possession or use) of large tracts of land by transnational companies. 'The gradual destruction of traditional economies in rural areas literally prepared the field for some of the new needs of the advanced capitalism, specifically land for plantation agriculture and to access water, metals, and minerals' (Sassen, 2015: 104).

Indebtedness as a mechanism to discipline and dispossess also works at a micro level. Small rural producers, forgotten by States (that are busy with their own fiscal restrictions), many times are forced to take bank loans to manage funding problems, bad harvests and the consequences of climate events. Then, they cannot fulfil their indebtedness obligations with their income, which is when they are forced to sell or rent their land. The massiveness of these phenomena explains large-scale acquisitions.

The extractive paradigm is not limited to rural areas or the extraction of natural resources. Also in urban and suburban areas a growing extractive process takes place fed by real estate speculation, which results in the displacement of populations with fewer resources, evictions and an increase of the rent value of houses. Moreover, as Gago and Mezzadra (2017) show in their notion of extended extractivism, extractive borders expand to reach virtual territories of data and information extraction, as well as domestic economies that are dispossessed through financial extractivism (Cavallero and Gago, 2019). Debt is thus a violent mechanism of extraction.

3. Debt sustainability or life sustainability?

Prevailing positions insist on the fact that countries and households need to honour their debts. This perspective, which has a moral nature, is based on the assumption that not repaying the debt may lead to chaotic situations that would imply damaging consequences for countries and households. However, this narrative may be challenged for several reasons. First, it hides the origins of indebtedness, which may be as immoral as not repaying the debt, using their logic. Second, the conditions imposed by indebtedness, the cost of repaying the debt, may conflict with the right that all persons have to live a decent life. Or, in other words, what is the social and economic cost of repaying what cannot be repaid? Third, the cost of not repaying the debt is indefinite, and in fact it may not be so high if markets have 'short memory' or if they 'quickly forgive the debt', which often happens if new business opportunities are created.

Unveiling the dimensions of the processes that explain the recurring indebtedness crises of many countries of the Global South may help in this reflection. The prevailing narrative focuses on macroeconomic mismanagement, the bad performance of economies, the failures of governmental management and corruption problems. While recognizing that some of these elements, in different degrees of magnitude, in fact may be part of the conditioning factors that force countries to deepen their sovereign indebtedness, an alternative perspective enables us to recognize the systemic origins of these processes.

In this respect, three elements can be mentioned as the ones that contribute to the dynamics of global financial capitalism and that today explain the key role of debt. First, the process of a growing financialization. The financial logic, boosted by the search for short-term profits, today governs the economic decision-making process. In fact, companies, particularly large transnational ones, increasingly obtain their profits in a greater proportion from financial investments than from investing in the actual economy. Thus there is a permanent need for financial innovation that involves the creation of sophisticated and increasingly more intangible financial assets,[5] and in turn the search for new markets for the financial products.[6] From a feminist perspective, this process has reached a paroxysm with the recent development of the so-called 'gender bonds'.[7] Simultaneously, the deregulation processes of the financial legislation at a country level enable a smoother circulation of money, but also a more obscure one. In this context, corporate power grows.

Second, and in line with this increasing corporate power, States are defunded. The race to the bottom on tax standards as governmental mechanisms to attract direct foreign investment, but mainly the regular practices of tax abuse by companies, reduce the ability of States to collect resources.[8] State defunding has two consequences that jeopardize the possibility to prioritize and guarantee life sustainability (or at least a basic series of human rights). First, States try to seduce private capital by providing fiscal benefits/incentives, and in this way the private sector starts dominating global governance and defining the priorities of the development agenda.[9] Second, governments are increasingly more limited in their ability to finance public policies, and in this way they stop the public provision of goods and services that are key for social reproduction. The third consequence of State defunding is its increasing indebtedness.

Third, and also related to the aforementioned, due to the shrinkage of the State, life is increasingly commercialized (and financialized). Goods and services that are no longer publicly provided must be acquired through the market. As this happens in a context of precarization of work and labour conditions, where salaries are increasingly lower (both in terms of its participation in GDP and in terms of its purchasing power), households need to turn to indebtedness not only to acquire lasting goods or more luxurious consumption, but simply to survive.

For this same reason, low-income households have become an attractive market for formal financial institutions (also for the different mechanisms of informal circulation of money). Even social welfare policies contribute to this phenomenon as they are loan distributors (here numerous experiences of social policies that aim at facilitating so-called financial inclusion can be included) or also serve as collateral for household indebtedness.[10]

No doubt, it is in the restoration of the austerity paradigm where the dispute between debt sustainability and life sustainability is explicitly evidenced. Ortiz and Cummins (2022) make a thorough analysis of the austerity measures implemented or projected in the world between 2022 and 2025. They indicate that, in accordance with the International Monetary Fund (IMF) projections, public expenditure cutbacks are expected in 143 countries, which will affect 85 per cent of the global population. Countries of the Global South will be the most affected ones, with estimated cutbacks in 3.5 per cent of the GDP. More than half of the countries analyzed will make cutbacks that will take their public expenditure to levels lower than before the pandemic.

The type of cutback measures analyzed have direct social impacts and affect significantly women: i) rationalization of social welfare programmes (many of them are feminized); ii) reduction of salaries in public jobs (that have a feminized payroll, particularly in the lowest categories); iii) privatization of companies and public services, as well as promotion of public–private partnerships; iv) labour flexibilization; v) social security reforms (that often limit the access to social security benefits to those who have weaker contributory records, among whom women are overrepresented); and vi) reduction of education and health expenditure (that mainly affect women due to their role in care arrangements, but also because the workforce in these sectors is feminized).

The government in Argentina, which has signed a new agreement with the IMF in 2022 (thus confirming and legitimizing the indebtedness from Macri's government), is also under the pressure of austerity, whose impact can clearly be seen in the last budgets. For instance, in accordance with the reports of the Argentine Budget Office, public investment dropped by 38.3 per cent in real terms in 2022.[11] Meanwhile, the national government gave 33 per cent less in resources in real terms in 2022 to provinces and municipalities, compared to the previous year. This is expected to affect provincial and municipal budgets, and, therefore, the provision of education and health services that are decentralized at these subnational levels. Expenditure on the pension system (the main component of the social public expenditure) went from 8 per cent of GDP in 2021 to 7.7 per cent in 2022, and it is 1.9 per cent lower than in 2017.

As the budget of the national government in Argentina includes a methodology of gender-responsive budgeting (GRB),[12] it can be particularly analyzed how this austerity affects budgetary lines considered to potentially reduce gender inequality gaps. This is what *Asociación Civil por la Igualdad y la Justicia* (Civil Association for Equality and Justice) (ACIJ, 2022) does and indicates for the 2023 budget: i) a reduction of 6.8 per cent in real terms compared to 2022 of social security benefits given through the Plan de Inclusión Previsional (pension inclusion program, that essentially women receive) and 8.8 per cent of non-contributory pensions for mothers of seven or more children; ii) a drop of 11.5 per cent in real terms for the universal child allowance (*Asignación Universal por Hijo*, AUH) and the universal allowance for pregnancy (*Asignación Universal por Embarazo*, AUE), and 32 per cent in *Tarjeta Alimentar* (monetary transfers to buy food); iii) a reduction of 19 per cent in the budgetary line to implement the cash transfer program targeted at the children of victims of gender-based violence; iv) a drop of 45.5 per cent in real terms of the lines that finance the early childhood education programme '*Primeros Años*'; v) a drop of 37.2 per cent of funds for the protection of victims of gender-based violence.

The austerity policy of the Argentine government is also expressed in the reduction of beneficiaries of the main workfare programme, called '*Potenciar Trabajo*'. This reduction also comes with a campaign of symbolic violence (from sectors of the government, the opposition and the hegemonic mass media) against the beneficiaries of this programme (and of welfare programmes of cash transfers in general, who are mainly women), who are accused of corruption (because in some cases the benefit is received without complying with all the requirements), but more extensively are accused of laziness and living at the expense of the State (in a discursive turn that hides huge benefits received by the concentrated capital and high-income sectors of the population through tax laundering, special treatments with respect to the exchange rate policy, tax exemptions and so on).

In order to give perspective to the case of the *Potenciar Trabajo* programme as an example of the economic violence implied by adjustment policies that also affects relatively more women than men, it is worth mentioning that currently the programme has more than 1 million beneficiaries, 63 per cent of whom are women, predominantly young women (83 per cent are between 18 and 45 years old), and most of whom have a low level of education (66 per cent have not completed secondary education). Almost 50 per cent of the beneficiaries comply with the working requirement by working in community kitchens and canteens, in other words, having an essential role for the social reproduction of popular sectors (as was evidenced during the pandemic). Small agricultural activities also predominate to guarantee food safety.

As Giosa Zuazúa (2022) states, despite its role to support the income of the most disadvantaged populations, but also its key role in the social reproduction of these sectors, the programme has been criticized and reduced since 2021. In October 2021, the Minister of Social Development of that time expressed the intention to suspend the subscriptions to the programme and to transform it into a tool to encourage registered paid labour (although he never mentioned how he would do it). In June 2022, the vice-president of Argentina criticized the programme management, especially the role of social organizations as intermediaries between the State and the beneficiaries. In August 2022, the government announced that it would audit the beneficiaries of the programme, a measure that was well received by conservative political and media sectors that defend the controversial narrative of meritocracy. At the beginning of December 2022, 20,000 beneficiaries of the programme were cut off. Ultimately, the context of adjustment and the effective reduction of budgetary lines for this type of programme ends up damaging the material living conditions of the beneficiaries due to transfer loss or payment delays, while a violent narrative is encouraged that accuses them of abuse of the public budget, denying the role that many of these persons play where the State fails (providing food, care and basic social infrastructure in poor neighbourhoods).

The increasing weakness of State mechanisms to provide income and social reproduction force households to increase market exchanges, and as they do not have enough sources of income, they are forced to become indebted.[13] This is how the direct relation between public indebtedness and domestic indebtedness is expressed. Debt as discipline for States, but also for households.

Ultimately, debt sustainability, fulfilling fiscal deficit commitments and how to do it (always through cutbacks of expenditure with questionable priorities, instead of focusing on the sectors that systematically perform tax abuse and defund the State) become a practice of economic violence that puts life sustainability at risk.

4. Feminist resistance to indebtedness

The expansion context of the feminist movement has been favourable to generating resistance to debt from a perspective that aims to challenge both capitalist and patriarchal violence. As Gago (2019: 84) explains, '(i)t is the appearance of a mass feminism that has enabled (and enables) to read the map of the different types of violence as a network'. This stage of feminist activism arose in the mass mobilizations of June 2015, summoned by the motto 'Not even one more dead: We want ourselves alive', precisely as a reaction to one of the more extreme forms of violence against women: femicides.

This claim against the State as being responsible for the violence against women and as an actor that specifically could transform the situation with active policies to eliminate all forms of violence was later connected to the so-called 'green wave', the feminist movement that massively fought for the legalization of abortion (which was achieved at the end of 2020).

It is in the context of this activism that there are actions that show how economic issues, and particularly the debt issue, are pervading the feminist agenda. As told by Cavallero and Gago (2019), on 2 June 2017, an action in front of the Central Bank of the Argentine Republic was organized, where pamphlets were given and a manifesto titled 'We want ourselves alive, free, and debt-free' was read. The manifesto explained this systemic understanding of indebtedness processes, and private, domestic and family indebtedness was made visible and centred in public debate as a feminist issue.

This activist approach to debt problematizes the abstract dynamics of finances in their relation with daily life, the different forms of violence (domestic and institutional) and current mechanisms of labour exploitation (that can also be understood as forms of violence). This approach is summarized in the motto repeated in feminist strikes on each 8 March: 'the debt is owed to us'.

Activism against economic violence and debt is extended to different fields. It is clearly expressed in a part of the feminist trade union activism. It is coordinated with other global social movements in the resistance to and in the G20 and the World Trade Organization (WTO).[14] It challenges the prevailing discourse of financial inclusion as an opportunity.[15] And it is expressed when it criticizes the hypocritical gender strategies of international financial institutions.[16]

At the same time, feminist resistance to debt is transformed into specific practices. They hold themselves in an attitude that proposes to be insubmissive to finances, and that promotes disobedience . For instance, feminist finance is implemented as loans provided by social organizations, they are channelled through experiences of 'ethical finances',[17] they are reconverted to practices of community savings (as in the case of *pasanaku* in the Bolivian community), and they are organized to resist the evictions for real estate debts that cannot be repaid or to propose new regulations in the rent market.[18]

Ultimately, feminist resistance to debt generates collective organization, it reports systemic origins of indebtedness, it makes economic violence visible and it calls for insurrection against what was established as true. Finances can be questioned, challenged and transformed. And this is urgent and imperative.

Notes

[1] The author takes here the notion of economic violence developed by Santillana Ortíz et al (2021).

[2] This movement enables us to 'coin a political word that not only reports the violence against women's body, but it also opens the discussion about other feminized bodies, and even more it moves from a unique definition of violence (that it is always domestic and intimate, and therefore confined) to understand it in relation to an idea of economic, institutional, labour, colonial, etc violence' (Gago, 2019: 62).

[3] To learn more about the genealogy of the concept of body-territory, see Ulloa (2021).

[4] Gago (2019) identifies four scenes of violence that represent the update of this 'war against women': 1) The implosion of violence within homes as a consequence of the de-hierarchization of the figure of the male provider; 2) the appearance of new types of violence in popular neighbourhoods in the context of the proliferation of illegal economies; 3) the pillage of land and common goods by transnational capital; and 4) the coordination of exploitation and extraction of value through the financialization of social life.

[5] An example of this that prevails today in the global agenda of development is the securitization processes that transform the expected returns of investments from the field of development financing into financial assets. This is linked to the processes that seek to leverage the financing of the private sector, and it is very frequent in public-private associations. To learn more about these processes, see Gabor (2019).

[6] This is how the financial sector starts advancing over social sectors that it disregarded in the past, but now considers as new markets. This is clearly the case of loan instruments of low amounts that are spread in popular sectors. To understand this process and its particular feminization characteristic, see Cavallero (2021).

[7] See chapter 19 by Bohoslavsky and Lavinas in this book.

[8] Cobham and Jansky (2020) present a systematization of existing estimates that for developing countries vary from US$77 billion to US$240 billion with respect to the losses of corporate income tax.

[9] To learn more about this idea of corporate capture of States and the development agenda, see Rodríguez Enríquez (2021).

[10] Lavinas (2017) extensively develops this idea in her study of financialization processes of social policies, with special emphasis on the Brazilian case.

[11] Data available online at: https://www.economia.gob.ar/onp/ejecucion/2022#aif

[12] Although the existence of GRB is a step forward, it is also important to mention that this is a first step, which is limited to the identification of budget lines that could have a positive impact on the situation of women and diversities, or on the reduction of gender inequality gaps. In the future, it would be expected that a budget analysis from a feminist perspective be a wider and integrated exercise that analyzes extensively both expenditure and macroeconomic policies (including indebtedness), combining quantitative and qualitative strategies, and that can notice the real impact of public policies on the conditions and quality of life of people.

[13] Partenio (2022) systematizes the findings of a project that particularly researched the relation among debt, work and care in the popular sectors of Argentina, emphasizing the experience of women. There the consequences of the relation between public indebtedness and domestic indebtedness can be seen embodied.

[14] On this matter, see the July 2018 issue of Development Alternatives with Women for a New Era (DAWN) Informa that summarizes the actions and perspectives made in front of the summit of the WTO that took place in Buenos Aires at the end of 2017: https://dawnnet.org/publication/dawn-informa-junio-2018/

[15] On this matter, see the post of Verónica Gago and Luci Cavallero from May 2018 in *Cartografie*: https://studiquestionecriminale.wordpress.com/2021/05/26/los-movimientos-y-las-deudas-veronica-gago-y-luci-cavabello/

[16] On this matter, see Elson and Rodríguez Enríquez (2021), as well as the manifesto signed by more than 100 feminist organizations that rejects the IMF gender strategy: https://www.campaignofcampaigns.com/index.php/en/our-work/actions/354-rejection-of-international-monetary-fund-s-strategy-toward-mainstreaming-gender-2

[17] To learn more about the paradigm of ethical finances, see De la Cruz (2014).

[18] Federici et al (2021) collect a series of experiences of resistance to indebtedness.

References

Asociación Civil por la Igualdad y la Justicia - ACIJ (2022) *Género en el Proyecto 2023*, Buenos Aires: ACIJ.

Cavallero, L. (2021) 'La deuda como dispositivo de violencia financiera en las economías populares feminizadas', PhD thesis, University of Buenos Aires.

Cavallero, L. and Gago, V. (2019) *Una lectura feminista de la deuda*, Buenos Aires: Fundación Rosa Luxemburgo.

Cobham, A. and Jansky, P. (2020) *Estimating Illicit Financial Flows. A Critical Guide to the Data, Methodologies and Findings*, New York: Oxford University Press.

De la Cruz, C. (2014) 'Una lectura feminista sobre el carácter político y el poder emancipador de las finanzas éticas', in Yolanda Jubeto Ruiz, Mertxe Larrañaga, Cristina Carrasco Bengoa, Magdalena Leon Trujillo, Yayo Herrero Lopéz, Cristina de la Cruz Ayuso, et al (eds), *Sostenibilidad de la vida. Aportaciones desde la Economía Solidaria, Feminista y Ecológica*, Bilbao: Red de Economía Solidaria and Alternativa Euskadi, pp 81–96.

Elson, D. and Rodríguez Enríquez, C. (2021) 'Del dicho al hecho: la narrativa de género del FMI y los derechos humanos de las mujeres', *Derechos en Acción*, 6(18): 275–310.

Federici, S. (2010) *Calibán y la bruja. Mujeres, cuerpo y acumulación originaria*, Madrid: Traficantes de Sueños.

Federici, S., Cavallero, L. and Gago, V. (2021) *¿Quén le debe a quién?: ensayos trasnacionales de desobediencia financiera*, Buenos Aires: Tinta Limón.

Gabor, D. (2019) *Securitization for Sustainability. Does it Help Achieve the SDGs?* Washington: Heinrich Boell Stiftung North America.

Gago, V. (2019) *La potencia feminista. O el deseo de cambiarlo todo*, Buenos Aires: Tinta y Limón.

Gago, V. and Mezzadra, S. (2017) 'A critique of the extractive operations of capital: Toward an expanded concept of extractivism', *Rethinking Marxims*, 29(4): 574–91.

Giosa Zuazúa, N. (2022) '¿Victimarias o víctimas? El conflicto con el programa potenciar trabajo', Coyunturas. La política en Disputa [online] December, Available from: https://coyunturas.com.ar/victimarias-o-victimas-el-conflicto-con-el-programa-potenciar-trabajo/?utm_source=newsletter&utm_campaign=68430-Lanzamiento+COYUNTURAS&utm_medium=email

Lavinas, L. (2017) *The Takeover of Social Policy by Financialization. The Brazilian Paradox*, New York: Palgrave Macmillan.

Ortiz, I. and Cummins, M. (2022) *End Austerity. A Global Report on Budget Cuts and Harmful Social Reforms in 2022–2025*, London: Action Aid.

Partenio, F. (2022) *Deudas, cuidados y vulnerabilidad. El caso de las mujeres de hogares de clases populares en la Argentina*, Buenos Aires: CEPAL.

Rodríguez Enríquez, C. (2021) 'Corporate Accountability and Women's Human Rights: an Analytical Approach to Public-Private Partnerships (PPPs)' (DAWN's Discussion Paper #31, February).

Santillana Ortíz, A., Partenio, F. and Rodríguez Enríquez, C. (2021) *Si nuestras vidas no valen, entonces produzcan sin nosotras. Reflexiones feministas sobre la violencia económica*, Buenos Aires: Fundación Rosa Luxemburgo.

Sassen, S. (2015) *Expulsiones. Brutalidad y complejidad en la economía global*, Buenos Aires: Katz Editores.

Sen, G. (2014) 'Reconsiderando la acumulación originaria', in G. Sen and M. Durano (eds), *Refundando los contratos sociales: Feministas en un mundo feroz*, London: Zed Books, pp 139–142.

Svampa, M. (2019) *Las fronteras del neoextractivismo en América Latina. Conflictos socioambientales, giro ecoterritorial y nuevas dependencias*, Wetzlar: Calas.

Ulloa, A. (2021) 'Repolitizar la vida, defender los cuerpos-territorios y colectivizar las acciones desde los feminismos indígenas', *Ecología Política*, 61: 38–48. (the issue number is 61)

3

Debt, Development and Gender

Penelope Hawkins and Marina Zucker-Marques

1. Introduction

Austerity, associated with financial crisis, has long been shown to disproportionally affect women (Elson, 1993; Périvier 2018; Geoghegan and Fois 2021). This chapter makes the point that gender discrimination from sovereign debt relations is not, however, limited to crisis phases, and the seeds of women bearing the brunt of public debt burdens are sown during the expansionary phase of an economic development model dependent on debt-led growth. The chapter goes on to identify some of the pathways that link development policies, debt and gender discrimination throughout the debt-led growth cycle.

Section 2 sets the scene by describing the problem of debt-led growth and gender discrimination. In section 3, the growing indebtedness of developing countries is discussed. In section 4, we consider some of the channels impacting women during the debt-acquisition phases and austerity phases of debt-led growth. Section 5 concludes with some proposals on the sovereign-debt agenda, including a revised conceptual framework for considering debt sustainability that employs a development lens to address gender equality.

2. Debt-led growth and discrimination

There is a widespread acceptance among economists from different traditions that, apart from mobilizing domestic resources, developing countries also need to channel external resources to grow and meet development challenges. To address this, in 1961, a United Nations (UN) General Assembly resolution called on member states 'to pursue policies that lead to an increase in the flow of development resources, public and private, to developing countries'.[1] But six decades on, the mechanisms of international financial debt architecture still fail to generate the necessary quantum of funding and financing at a price that enables such development. Instead, net financial transfers (or net resource flows) continue to flow *from* developing countries to advanced ones, creating a paradox (Kregel, 2004): external resources are deemed necessary to fund development, but this in turn generates return flows of interest payments and profit remittances which may dominate the current account in excess of capital flows (UNCTAD, 2020). Raúl Prebisch, who later became the first Secretary General of the UN Conference on Trade and Development (UNCTAD), pointed out, 'as the stock of foreign capital increases, its financial services also grow, which will demand an increasing proportion of resources from exports, and the more the proportion of these services grows, the less there will be room for importing capital goods with these resources' (Prebisch, 1950: 480, authors' translation).

For this reason, some economists have argued that development hinges on the terms of trade and development aid (Prebisch, 1952).[2] But much-desired aid from developed countries has mostly disappointed and better trade conditions for developing countries have failed to materialize (see section 3). Instead, with foreign direct investment difficult to attract, the default option for growth strategy has become debt-led growth, resulting in a debt treadmill for developing countries: rising indebtedness of developing countries has increased vulnerability and undermined growth prospects, with the impact on women most visible during the austerity phases. In the debt-led growth model, financial markets and mounting financial leverage drive the real economy and, increasingly, the debt sustainability of developing countries is no longer in the hands of the affected sovereigns. In an environment of fragility and spillovers, falling commodity prices and weakening growth, or monetary policy decisions, in developed economies can quickly lead to unsustainable debt burdens in developing countries (UNCTAD, 2019).

Under this debt-led growth strategy, developing countries can be seen to alternate between debt acquisition and austerity phases, and while this may not be entirely binary, it is useful to the later discussion in this chapter to differentiate between them.

In the debt acquisition phase, capital inflows put upward pressure on exchange rates and reserve accumulation takes place. The exchange rate appreciation tends to reduce the competitiveness of the domestic industry (Kregel, 2018), which serves to chill domestic export-led enterprise and export earnings in general. Given that developing countries tend to import capital goods, a long-term reduction in export earnings may undermine the ability of the country to import necessary inputs for investment. More insidiously, as capital flows inward, developing countries have shown a strong predilection to accumulate foreign exchange reserves. Rising reserve accumulation means an opportunity forgone in terms of much-needed investment and social expenditure (Elhiraika and Ndikumana, 2007).

In the austerity, or crisis, phase, the country is obliged to prioritize repayment of creditors, particularly external creditors. Current notions of debt sustainability as the ability of a government to meet its current and future payment obligations without exception arrangements or default thus depends on the willingness and ability of governments to sacrifice domestic objectives to meet foreign claims (7). By doing so, governments put aside human rights commitments, once resources to ensure the realization of economic and social rights are diverted to pay debt claims. While Kregel calls for a new definition of debt sustainability that supports the long-term process of development, which UNCTAD is in the process of fleshing out (see section 5), countries faced by financial crisis have been obliged to reduce fiscal expenditure, in the attempt to generate enough resources to avoid default.

Gender equality is a crucial component of successful development. Financial crisis can force a disproportionate cost on women, increasing their economic vulnerability, and affecting societal outcomes (Floro and Dymski, 2000). Conversely, economic growth that leads to increased female labour force participation without compensatory investments in social care provisioning and better distribution of caregiving responsibilities will ultimately compromise investment and growth (Braunstein, Seguino and Altringer, 2021).[3] Since improving women's status and economic activity has macroeconomic benefits for economic growth and development (Stotsky, 2006), wherever rising debt burdens and debt service payments compete with scarce fiscal resources for health, education and social assistance in normal times – or lead to the cutbacks associated with austerity – progress on gender equality is undermined and development outcomes are unwound.

Building on this, the chapter traces three key dimensions of women's engagement with society and the economy – as employee, as caregiver and as citizen – each of which creates pathways to gender discrimination during the cycle of debt-led growth, not only during crisis. The analysis suggests that the acquisition of sovereign debt itself may inhibit the possibility of necessary compensatory investments in social care provisioning for equality-inducing investment and growth (see section 4). Instead, in developing countries where debt is attracted at interest rates which far exceed those associated with the cost of capital in developed countries, the acquisition of the sovereign debt creates a servicing requirement which imposes a ceiling on investment in public and social services (Persaud, 2022), effectively locking in inequality and ultimately a lower development path.

3. Growing indebtedness of developing countries

During the last 20 years, external debt levels have increased at an unprecedented pace in developing countries, with the total external debt stock for low- and middle-income countries (excluding China) rising from US$1.9 trillion in

Figure 3.1: External debt stocks as share of GDP, by income group (excluding China), 2010–20

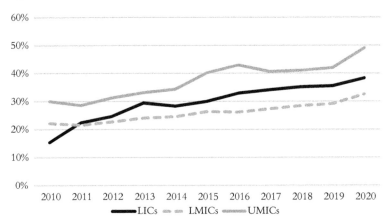

Note: LIC = lower-income country; LMIC = lower-middle-income country; UMIC = upper-middle-income country

Source: Own elaboration based on World Bank (WB) International Debt Statistics and International Monetary Fund (IMF). Classification as per WB (2022)

2000 to US$6.7 trillion in 2020. Given market liquidity preferences during the COVID-19 pandemic, external debt stocks for low- and middle-income countries (excluding China) slightly declined in 2021 (about US$100 billion). But this decline – which highlights the difficulties of developing countries issuing debt when they most need resources – is an exception for the 20 years tendency when external debt stock for middle-income countries more than tripled,[4] while it doubled in low-income countries.[5] As figure 3.1 shows, external debt stocks increased faster than GDP in the ten years up to 2020, hence, for lower-income countries (LICs), debt-to-export ratios increased from 15 per cent in 2010 to 38 per cent in 2020, while for lower-middle-income countries (LMICs) they increased from 22 per cent to 33 per cent and for upper-middle-income countries (UMICs) – excluding China – from 30 per cent to 49 per cent in the same period.

The increase in the debt stock in low- and middle-income countries, in part at least, reflects the insufficiency of alternative sources of external financing: Although Official Development Assistance (ODA) rose to US$167.9 billion in 2021, representing 0.31 per cent of the gross national income (GNI) of donor countries (OECD, 2022), ODA flows have consistently failed to reach the UN target of 0.7 per cent GNI of developed countries.[6] Between 2000 and 2020, the accumulated ODA gap (the difference between the target amount and that actually transferred) accounts for US$3.4 trillion, which represents roughly 70 per cent of the debt stock increase in low- and middle-income countries (excluding China).[7]

The increase in external debt stock over the past two decades featured broadened participation of private lenders in addition to more traditional official lenders (bilateral or multilateral). While official creditors still dominate in LICs, the share of exposure to commercial banks and bondholders tripled to 12 per cent in 2020 from 4 per cent in 2010. Private lenders' largest increase was to LMICs, where this share increased by 20 per cent (from a base of 25 per cent in 2010). For UMICs (excluding China), the exposure increased by only 2 per cent, but private lenders already held 68 per cent of UMICs' debt stock in 2010. The change in composition of the creditor base has worsened borrowing conditions for developing countries (WB, 2022), and the share of debt servicing to private lenders exceeds their holdings by a margin for all country groups. For example, while private creditors make up 12 per cent of the debt exposure of LICS, they receive 22 per cent of LICs' debt servicing. In terms of borrowing costs, loans from private lenders are priced on average 300 basis points more than from official lending. Moreover, official lenders offer longer maturity periods (on average 26 years) than private lenders (average 12 years), with borrowing from private lenders increasing the risks of refinancing at less favourable market conditions.

The growing debt stocks and the deteriorating borrowing costs has meant that debt sustainability indicators have deteriorated for developing countries. For instance, external debt stock as share of exports – a general indicator for external debt solvency – deteriorated for all income groups between 2010 and 2020. For LICs, this ratio increased from 52 per cent in 2010 to 237 per cent in 2020, while for LMICs it increased from 82 per cent to 145 per cent, and for UMICs from 109 per cent to 166 per cent in the same period (see figure 3.2.a). Another relevant debt sustainability indicator is external public and publicly guaranteed (PPG) debt service as share of government revenue, which indicates government capacity used to service external debt. Figure 3.2.b shows how debt service has typically doubled for all country groups, reaching a level of around 10 per cent in 2020.

In the next section, we consider gender discrimination and the debt acquisition and servicing phases, as well as austerity phases of debt-led growth.

4. Pathways of gender discrimination during the debt-led growth cycle

Gender impacts the different roles men and women play in society, and economic and political life. Considering these differences, economic policies and dynamics affect both genders through distinct channels (Périvier, 2018; Ghosh, 2021; de Oliveira and Alloati 2022). In this chapter, we emphasize three – not exhaustive – roles that women perform in the economy and society: as citizens, as caregivers and as employees, to better understand the gendered impacts of the debt-led growth strategy.

Figure 3.2: External debt sustainability indicators, by income group (excluding China), 2010–20

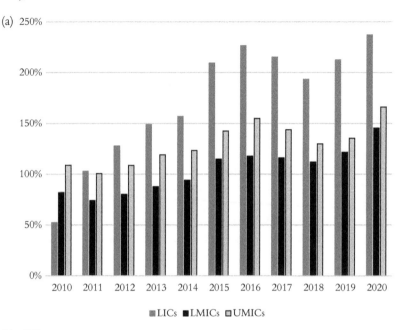

(a)

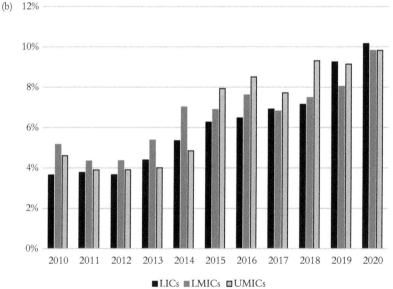

(b)

Note: LIC = lower-income country; LMIC = lower-middle-income country; UMIC = upper-middle-income country

Source: Own elaboration based on WB International Debt Statistics and IMF. Classification as per WB (2022)

By 'women as citizens' is meant the right to access basic and adequate social services and protection, including – but not limited – to healthcare, education and pensions. Regardless of the equal rights men and women may enjoy in any given society, women are made more vulnerable by deficiencies in basic public services for a variety of reasons, including their specific healthcare requirements, gendered expectations around education and work, and the increased likelihood of economic dependency during their working years. As 'caregivers', it is acknowledged that women are still the main providers of social reproduction activities, including household unpaid labour (for example, childcare, elderly care, managing domestic resources and so on). Moreover, 'women as citizens' highlights how these unpaid duties interplay with economic policies and development. Finally, as 'employees', we consider the employment pattern of women in the public sector and the interaction with public spending. Although the three dimensions described here are interrelated, they provide a conceptual device to understand how the debt-led growth cycle affects women not only during austerity, but also during the debt acquisition phase.

Tables 3.1 and 3.2 summarize the discussion, considering the dimensions of the economic and social engagement of women and girls with the

Table 3.1: Phases and dimensions of debt-led growth in expensive debt regimes

Phase of debt cycle/ dimension of gender discrimination	Debt acquisition phase	Austerity phase
Women as citizens	Inadequate basic provision of hospitals and schools – women may forgo treatment or be forced to pay for health services on credit.	Public expenditure cuts result in hospital closures and/or under staffing; access to these services declines.
Women as caregivers	Inadequate social structures and lack of sharing of caregiving responsibilities means general pressure on care-time of women, giving them less time to secure better paid jobs through human capital investment, for example.	Public expenditure cuts mean women are required to provide more care for the elderly, infirm and the young, increasing the disproportionate cost of austerity on women.
Women as employees	Possibility of greater labour market participation of women, but not necessarily at competitive wages. Public sector employment (where most women are employed) may not necessarily increase.	Public expenditure cuts lead to loss of female employment (represent largest share of public sector workers), leading to loss of income and health insurance, increasing vulnerability and making personal debts more difficult to bear.

Source: Own classification

Table 3.2: Life stages and gender discrimination throughout the phases of debt-led growth

Stage of life	Gender discrimination in each stage
Childhood	**Education:** • When education services are scarce and expensive (or rationed during austerity), households may prioritize the enrolment of boys rather than girls. • Girls are more likely to be pulled out of school due to economic necessity. **Food security:** • Girls (and women) more likely to suffer food insecurity relative to men and boys. **Unpaid care and domestic work:** 1. Girls (rather than boys) perform most of the household chores, including child and elderly care. Reduces schooling years for girls during childhood.[a]
Adulthood	**Employment and remuneration:** • Fewer women participate in labour market. • More women are employed in low wage sectors, including informal sector. • Gender-based discrimination affects gender pay gap. • Women are more likely to lose their job because of budget expenditure cuts, or be the subject to a wage freeze. **Health:** • Insufficient health provision for women during reproductive age affects income earnings and longevity. **Unpaid care and domestic work:** • Women perform most of the household chores – this impedes female labour market participation.
Old age	**Retirement:** • Pension systems may pass on lifetime earning inequalities.

[a] https://data.unicef.org/topic/gender/gender-norms-and-unpaid-work/

debt-led growth cycle. The novelty of our contribution has to do with the systematization of gender dimensions and the explicit examination of the acquisition phase of debt, as well as the austerity phase when debt is no longer sustainable. We focus on the provision of health services as an obvious channel as to how these dimensions come into play.

The impact of gender discrimination emerging from sovereign debt relations is not exclusive to adulthood. Instead, during different stages of a woman's life – childhood, adulthood and old age – debt-led growth affects women and girls in distinct ways, given gender biases and asymmetries in access to resources and opportunities throughout their life. Discrimination towards girls influences later outcomes and access to resources and opportunities (for example, fewer years of schooling affects employment opportunities, lower paid positions during adulthood affects old age retirement). Table 3.2 gives some examples of gender discrimination in different life stages.

Achieving gender equality is a Sustainable Development Goal (SDG 5), and to achieve this goal, it is crucial to support other SDGs through public expenditure, in particular SDGs 1–4 (no poverty, zero hunger, good health and wellbeing, quality education). While investing in SDGs 1–4 support both men and women, investment in care, health and education services is seen as female-oriented social investment (for example, Cozzi and De Henau, 2015).

Women as citizens

It is noticeable that during austerity phases, which may include the imposition of a structural adjustment programme, the opportunity cost of privileging debt-servicing and debt-reduction over other fiscal demands means that health facilities in a country may be closed down, not built or be understaffed (Pandolfelli, Shandra and Tyagi, 2014). This has disproportionate impacts on women, as childbearers: for example, sub-Saharan African countries subject to structural adjustment programmes have higher rates of maternal death relative to countries without such a programme (Pandolfelli, Shandra and Tyagi, 2014).

During the debt acquisition phase, women may also have their right to adequate healthcare circumscribed or denied as increasing debt burdens limit social progress since debt service payments compete with scarce fiscal expenditure (WB, 2022, xi). As Figure 3.2 shows, in the last ten years, there has been a tendency for PPG debt servicing to increase faster than health expenditure for all developing country groups.

The situation is most dire for the poorest and most economically vulnerable countries, where the lack of healthcare is often fatal for women. For example, the 46 low- and middle-income countries classified as Least Developed Countries (LDCs) by the UN[8] show that while the external PPG debt service of LDCs already consumed an equivalent share of government revenues as the healthcare budget in 2011, by 2019 (the latest year for which there is data), PPG debt service in LDCs was, on average, 2.5 times larger than health expenditure. Data from the World Health Organization (WHO, 2017) show that the maternal mortality ratio (MMR) in LDCs is 415 per 100,000 live births (where it is 11 per 100,000 live births in high-income countries). While the MMR for LDCs has decreased considerably since 2000 (when the MMR was 763), it is far above the SDG target of 70 deaths per 100,000 live births by 2030. While globally over 80 per cent of births were attended by a professional in 2018, this ratio was 60 per cent for LDCs (WHO, 2021). LDCs currently deploy around 4 per cent

Figure 3.3: Public and publicly guaranteed debt service as share of health expenditure budget, by country groups, 2000–19

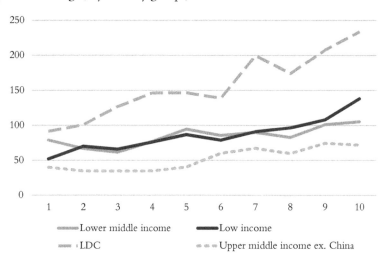

Source: Own elaboration based on WB International Debt Statistics and IMF. Classification as per WB (2022)

of GDP on health expenditure, less than half the global average of 9.8 per cent (WHO, 2021).

Other developing countries also face similar debt-servicing challenges, as can be seen in Figure 3.3. Ninety-four per cent of all maternal deaths occur in low- and middle-income countries (WHO, 2023), where debt-service outweighs expenditure on health – except for upper-middle-income countries (excluding China). During the pandemic, in 2020, some 62 countries spent a larger share of their budget on servicing debt than healthcare expenditure, and for 36 countries, debt servicing was larger than education expenditure (Munevar, 2021).

The lack of an adequate public healthcare system may impose a personal financial burden on women. Lower public expenditure on health is likely to deprive outlying areas of hospitals, clinics and medical personnel, and forgoing treatment may be a poor woman's only option (Smith, 1999). Moreover, given the accumulated backlog in healthcare provision, and the emphasis on generating sufficient public revenues to service the debt, governments are more inclined to acquiesce to pressure to privatize public services, and adopt a user-pays system, while at the same time shifting budget from social services to ensure adequate debt servicing (see for example, the case of Ecuador in Muchhala and Guillem, 2022).

User-pays systems are regressive and the most vulnerable are simply excluded from what should be universal, publicly provided services (Elson, 1993). Both costs and geographical proximity are correlated with women's

Figure 3.4: Share of respondents that 'borrowed any money' versus 'borrowed for health purposes', by income group, 2021

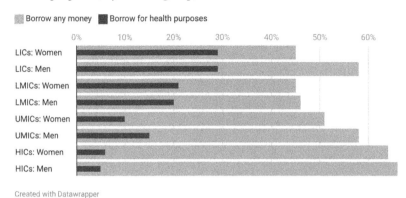

Created with Datawrapper

Note: LIC = lower-income country; LMIC = lower-middle-income country; HIC = high-income country

Source: Own elaboration based on WB Findex Database 2021

use of healthcare services, with women from poorer households seeking less or delaying treatment as it becomes more expensive or less accessible. (Dupas and Jain, 2021). Such behaviour can be detrimental to women's health, particularly to pregnant women, and ultimately results in a higher mortality rate (Taneja and Jadhav, 2022).

For those who are obliged to incur debt burdens to pay for healthcare, this can lead to impoverishment. According to the WHO (2020), in 2015 alone, out-of-pocket health expenditure pushed 89.7 million people into extreme poverty (below US$1.90 per person per day). The same report indicates that, as of 2015, there were at least 927 million people that incurred catastrophic health spending, meaning they spent over 10 per cent of their income on a health crisis or chronic condition. For 200 million people, it corresponded to over 25 per cent of their income, leading in many cases to unmanageable debt.

The use of debt to pay for health expenditure (see Figure 3.4) shows that women tend to borrow as much or more than men (the exception being in upper-middle-income countries), although men are typically more financially included and a larger proportion of them incur debt than women. The tendency for women in poorer nations to borrow more for health services highlights the importance of having a well-resourced, publicly funded healthcare system.

Women as caregivers

Around the world, women spend more time performing unpaid household work (cooking, cleaning, fetching water and firewood, taking care of children and so on), and in some countries, their unpaid workload is ten times longer

Figure 3.5: Labour participation gap between men and women, by income country group, 1990, 2000, 2010 and 2021

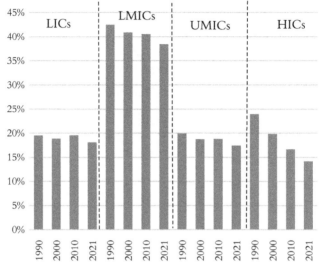

Note: LIC = lower-income country; LMIC = lower-middle-income country; UMIC = upper-middle-income country; HIC = high-income country

Source: Own elaboration based on WB Gender Data Portal

than that of men (Ferrant et al, 2014). Consequently, women are constantly time-poor which often limits or even impedes their participation in paid remuneration (Périvier, 2018). This problem is reflected in the gap between the labour participation rates of men and women.

As Figure 3.5 shows, for all income groups, female labour participation is considerably and consistently lower than for men, and in 2021, the difference between female and male labour participation remained stubbornly high at 38 per cent in lower-middle-income countries. Although the labour market participation gap is decreasing, a decline in the gap of 10 per cent between 1990 and 2021 was achieved only in high-income country groups.

Public expenditure is key to lowering the burden of caregiving on women and freeing them to increase their (renumerated) labour market participation rates. Publicly funded social services, including childcare, have been shown to be of paramount importance, with provision of day care for children increasing maternal employment (Thévenon, 2013; Nishitateno and Shikata, 2017; Andresen and Havnes, 2019). In general, country comparisons show that a decrease in women's unpaid care work by two hours a day may increase women's labour force participation rate by up to 10 per cent (for a given level of GDP per capita, fertility rate, female unemployment rate, female education, urbanization rate and maternity leave) (Ferrant et al, 2014).

Public-sector spending in infrastructure (including electricity, roads, water and sanitation) can ease the barriers for women entering the labour market (Dinkelman, 2011; Lei, Desai and Vanneman, 2019; Fabrizio et al, 2020). Electrification brings general benefits, but women's relative household responsibilities means access to electricity can improve efficiency in time-intensive activities like laundry, food preparation, storage and cleaning, freeing up women to pursue paid work. Despite historical improvements in access to energy, in 2019, for over 940 million people (or about 13 per cent of the world's population) living without electricity was still a reality (Ritchie et al, 2022).

Women as employees

The public sector is the largest employer of women, and globally women represent 46 per cent of the public sector workforce compared with 33 per cent in the private sector (Mukhtarova et al, 2021). Data from the International Labour Organization (ILO) show that in 2019, in 78 of an available sample of 96 advanced and developing economies, the share of women working in the public sector is higher than in the private sector.

This pattern may be explained by the size of public budgets in healthcare and the gendered division of labour. Globally, women make up to over 70 per cent of workers in the health sector, predominantly as nurses and midwives. As figure 3.6 demonstrates, women can be considered over-represented in healthcare and education sectors while the same cannot be

Figure 3.6: Female participation in construction and civil engineering, education and human health sectors, by income group, 2019

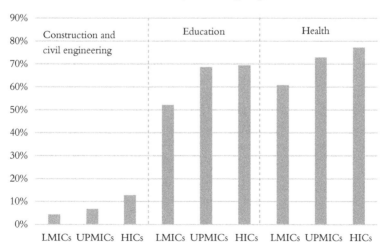

Note: LMIC = lower-middle-income country; UMIC = upper-middle-income country; HIC = high-income country. Given lack of data, low-income countries are not included

Source: Own elaboration based on International Labour Organization. Classification as per WB (2022)

said for construction and manufacturing sectors. The latter sector can be considered better renumerated and less subject to fiscal budgetary cuts. Both of these factors – the gendered division of labour and the lower rate of pay in women-dominated sectors – serve to disadvantage women.

Given the fact that the public sector is a key employer of women, austerity measures as well as constraints of public budgets are detrimental to female employment. While employment losses caused by public expenditure cuts in areas dominated by women – like healthcare – are an obvious concern, the lack of public investment in the healthcare system curbs job opportunity-creation, which therefore affects mostly female workers. Supporting the public health system brings double benefits for women: as citizens, they would have better healthcare conditions, and as employees, higher employment opportunities. This, in turn, is associated with gains in development (Bargawi and Cozzi, 2017).

5. A feminist debt agenda is a development agenda

To build a feminist agenda on debt, it is crucial to rethink the prevailing growth model reliant on external debt, especially from private creditors who offer worse borrowing conditions for developing countries when compared to multilateral and official lenders. A debt-led growth model makes developing countries fragile to external shocks, which in turn worsens gender inequalities. During the debt acquisition phase, increasing debt burdens limit social progress as debt service payments compete with scarce fiscal expenditure for health, education, social assistance and infrastructure investment – areas where public expenditure is essential to improve the socioeconomic condition of women. During the austerity phase, hard-earned improvements in social expenditure tend to be undone, directly and indirectly increasing gender inequality through women's vulnerability to reduced social provision, social protection and employment opportunities. This in turn undermines development.

Supporting developing countries to get out of debt-led growth and expand fiscal space for gender equality-boosting development requires an alternative approach to debt sustainability that can account for social and economic goals, putting human rights at the forefront of this discussion. The UN Human Rights Council has advanced towards this goal by setting up 'Guiding principles on human rights impact assessments of economic reforms', as presented by the UN Independent Expert on debt and human rights in 2018 (Independent Expert, 2018), and with following an adopted resolution (Human Rights Council, 2019) which emphasizes the need to consider debt issues to respect human rights. Part of this shift also requires a new approach to debt sustainability assessments that better bridge creditor and debtor needs and commitments, from an evaluation of short-term flexibility in meeting domestic and foreign claims of creditors to one where more flexibility into servicing debts is introduced, without sacrificing long-term development objectives (Kregel, 2007). In an effort to contribute to this shift, UNCTAD has developed the Sustainable Development Finance Assessment (SDFA) framework for policy makers of developing countries with explicit focus on the achievement of basic development goals and structural development. The UNCTAD SDFA aims at assessing a country's development finance needs to achieve structural transformation through the first four SDGs (mentioned earlier) while at the same time ensuring the sustainability of the external and public sector financial positions (Hawkins and Prates, 2021). This framework incorporates sustainable development finance as a whole, considering all sources of external financing, that is, foreign direct investment (FDI), foreign portfolio investment, remittances and external debt (both public and private). Its objective is to underline that there are a range of policy options to maintain external financial and public sector sustainability while also achieving the SDGs, with the SDFA framework allowing the assessment of these options (UNCTAD, 2022).

A sea-change in debt sustainability analysis that allows for, rather than sacrifices, development is needed. Debt sustainability is linked to the perceived fragility of developing countries and their ability to withstand external shocks. Strategies to scale up development finance need to minimize the exposure to external shocks, cross-border capital flows and external debt service burdens (UNCTAD, 2019). This in turn requires the rekindling of multilateralism to boost official development assistance, the staunching of illicit financial flows and a redesigned international financial architecture where developing countries have access to affordable debt and timely and orderly debt workouts.

Such an approach to debt sustainability upholds gender equality as part of a development agenda which ensures public finances deliver necessary public services. Without this, a feminist development agenda will remain elusive.

Acknowledgements
We are grateful for the helpful comments provided by Gary Dymski and Katie Gallogly-Swan on earlier drafts of this chapter. The views expressed here are our own and do not necessarily reflect the views of UNCTAD.

Notes
[1] General Assembly resolution 1710 (XVI), "United Nations Decade – A programme for international economic co-operation", A/RES/1710(XVI) paragraph 2 (19 December 1961), available from undocs.org/en/A/RES/1710(XVI).
[2] For more about this debate, see Fajardo (2022).

[3] Braunstein et al do not explicitly consider the role of debt in their analysis of growth.

[4] From 2000 and 2020, the increase was from US$644 to US$2,399 billion for lower-middle-income countries, and from US$1,180 to US$4,127 billion for upper-middle-income countries.

[5] Increased from US$79 billion to US$166 billion between 2000 and 2020.

[6] UNCTAD II (1968) adopted resolution 27(II), entitled "Growth, Development Finance and Aid", considered a supplementary target for net ODA of 0.75 per cent of the gross national product (GNP) of developed countries in addition to an overall target of financial resource transfers "of a minimum net amount of 1 per cent of the GNP". UNCTAD II was instrumental in putting development finance and ODA on the international agenda. In 1970, UN General Assembly (UNGA) resolution 2626 (XXV, § 43) adopted a 0.7 per cent of GNP target for ODA, changed to a 0.7 per cent of GNI target in 1993.

[7] Authors' own calculation based on WB International Debt Statistics and Organisation for Economic Cooperation and Development (OECD) Development Assistance Committee (DAC) Creditor Reporting System (CRS).

[8] A full listing is available here: https://unctad.org/topic/least-developed-countries/list

References

Andresen, M.E. and Havnes, T. (2019) 'Childcare, parental labor supply and tax revenue', *Labour Economics,* 61: 101762.

Bargawi, H. and Cozzi, G. (2017) 'Engendering economic recovery: modelling alternatives to austerity in Europe', *Feminist Economics*, 23(4): 225–49.

Braunstein, E.; Seguino, S. and Altringer, L. (2021) 'Estimating the role of social reproduction in economic growth', *International Journal of Political Economy*, 50(2): 143–64.

Cozzi, G. and De Henau, J. (2015) 'The Junker plan must not be a missed opportunity for gender equality', *Euractive*, 12 March.

de Oliveira, A.L.M. and Alloatti, M.N. (2022) 'Gendering the crisis: austerity and the Covid-19 pandemic in Brazil', *Economia Politica*, 39(1): 203–24.

Dinkelman, T. (2011) 'The effects of rural electrification on employment: New evidence from South Africa', *American Economic Review*, 101(7): 3078–108.

Dupas, Pascaline and Jain, Radhika (2021) 'Women Left Behind: Gender Disparities in Utilization of Government Health Insurance in India' (w28972), National Bureau of Economic Research.

Elson, D. (1993) 'Gender relations and economic issues' in Barbara Evers (ed), *Women and Economic Policy*, Oxfam: Oxford.

Elhiraika, A. and Ndikumana, L. (2007) 'Reserves accumulation in African countries: Sources, motivations and effects' (Economics Department Working Paper Series No 24), University of Massachusetts Amherst.

Fabrizio, S.; Fruttero, A.; Gurara, D.; Kolovich, L.L.; Malta, V.; Tavares, M.M. and Mühleisen, M. (2020) 'Women in the Labor Force: The Role of Fiscal Policies. Staff Discussion Notes', IMF [online] 16 February, Available from: https://www.imf.org/en/Publications/Staff-Discussion-Notes/Issues/2020/02/11/Women-in-the-Labor-Force-The-Role-of-Fiscal-Policies-46237

Fajardo, M. (2022) *The World That Latin America Created*, London: Cambridge University Press.

Ferrant, G.; Pesando, L.M. and Nowacka, K. (2014) 'Unpaid care work: The missing link in the analysis of gender gaps in labour outcomes', OECD Development Centre [online] December, Available from: https://www.oecd.org/dev/development-gender/Unpaid_care_work.pdf

Floro, M. and Dymski, D. (2000) 'Financial crisis, gender and power: An analytical framework', *World Development*, 28(7): 1269–83.

Geoghegan, V.S. and Fois, M. (2021) 'Women, debt and gender inequalities', Latindadd [online], Available from: https://www.latindadd.org/wp-content/uploads/2021/09/Mujeres-deuda-y-desigualdad-Final_English.pdf

Ghosh, J. (2021) 'Gender concerns in debt relief', London: International Institute for Environment and Development, Available from: https://www.iied.org/20691iied

Hawkins, P. and Prates, D. (2021) 'Global Financial Safety Nets, SDRs and Sustainable Development Finance: Can the options on the table deliver needed fiscal space?', UNCTAD DA COVID-19 project [online] 14 April, Available from: https://mobilizingdevfinance.org/research-material/global-financial-safety-nets-sdrs-and-sustainable-development-finance-can-options

Human Rights Council (2019) 'The effects of foreign debt and other related international financial obligations of States on the full enjoyment of all human rights, particularly economic, social and cultural rights' (Resolution A/HRC/RES/40/8, 5 April).

Independent Expert (2018) 'Guiding principles for assessing the human rights impact of economic reform policies' (UN Doc. A/HRC/40/57), UN Human Rights Council, 19 December.

Kregel, J.A. (2004) 'External financing for development and international financial instability', G-24 Discussion Paper Series (No 32), Geneva: UN.

Kregel, J.A. (2007) 'Rethinking debt sustainability in the context of the Millennium Development Goals', *BNL Quarterly Review*, 60(242): 225–48.

Kregel, J. (2018) 'The clearing union principle as the basis for regional financial arrangements in developing countries' in *Debt Vulnerabilities in Developing Countries: A New Debt Trap?*, Policy Options and Tools (UNCTAD/GDS/MDP/2017/4), ii, Geneva: United Nations, pp 57–92.

Lei, L.; Desai, S. and Vanneman, R. (2019) 'The impact of transportation infrastructure on women's employment in India', *Feminist Economics*, 25(4): 94–125.

Muchhala, B. and Guillem, A. (2022) 'Gendered austerity and embodied debt in Ecuador: channels through which women absorb and resist the shocks of public budget cuts', *Gender and Development*, 30(2): 283–309.

Mukhtarova T.; Baig F.A. and Hasnain Z (2021) 'Five facts on gender equity in the public sector', 27th September, Available from: https://blogs.worldb ank.org/governance/five-facts-gender-equity-public-sector

Munevar, D. (2021) 'A debt pandemic: dynamics and implications of the debt crisis of 2020', Eurodad [online] 23 March, Available from: https://www.eurodad.org/2020_debt_crisis

Nishitateno, S. and Shikata, M. (2017) 'Has improved daycare accessibility increased Japan's maternal employment rate? Municipal evidence from 2000–2010', *Journal of the Japanese and International Economies*, 44: 67–77.

OECD (2022) 'Official development assistance: ODA data and trends 2021', [online], Available from: https://www.oecd.org/dac/financing-sustaina ble-development/development-finance-standards/official-development-assistance.htm

Pandolfelli, L.E., Shandra, J. and Tyagi, J. (2014) 'The international monetary fund, structural adjustment, and women's health: a cross-national analysis of maternal mortality in Sub-Saharan Africa', *The Sociological Quarterly*, 55(1): 119–42.

Périvier, H. (2018) 'Recession, austerity and gender: A comparison of eight European labour markets', *International Labour Review*, 157(1): 1–37.

Persaud, A. (2022) 'Breaking the deadlock on climate: The Bridgetown Initiative', Group d'etudes geopolitiques: Issue 3, Available from: https://geopolitique.eu/en/articles/breaking-the-deadlock-on-climate-the-bri dgetown-initiative/

Prebisch, R. (1950) 'The economic development of Latin America and its principal problems, New York: ECLA, UN Department of Economic Affairs.

Prebisch, R. (1952) 'Theoretical and practical problems of economic growth' (E/CN.12/221), ECLAC (repr 1973, Santiago: ECLAC), Available from: https://repositorio.cepal.org/bitstream/handle/11362/43904/S150 1407_en.pdf?sequence=1

Ritchie, H.; Roser, M. and Rosado, P. (2022) 'Energy', Our World in Data [online], Available from: https://ourworldindata.org/energy

Smith, M.K. (1999) 'Hospitals in developing countries: A weak link in a weak chain', *The Lancet*, 354: SIV26

Stotsky, J.G. (2006) 'Gender and its relevance to macroeconomic policy: A survey', IMF [online] 1 October, Available from: https://www.imf.org/en/Publications/WP/Issues/2016/12/31/Gender-and-its-Relevance-to-Macroeconomic-Policy-A-Survey-19890

Taneja, A. and Jadhav, N. (2022). 'Experiences of women while availing services in the private healthcare system of India', Oxfam [online] 26 May, Available from: https://www.oxfamindia.org/genderprivatisationhealth

Thévenon, O. (2013) 'Drivers of female labour force participation in the OECD', OECD [online] 23 May, Available from: https://www.oecd-ilibr ary.org/social-issues-migration-health/drivers-of-female-labour-force-participation-in-the-oecd_5k46cvrgnms6-en

UNCTAD (2019) 'Current challenges to developing country debt sustainability', Available from: https://unctad.org/system/files/official-document/gds2018d2_en.pdf.

UNCTAD (2020) 'Topsy turvy world: Net transfer of resources from poor to rich countries' (Policy Brief No 78, May). Available from: https://unc tad.org/publication/topsy-turvy-world-net-transfer-resources-poor-rich-countries

UNCTAD (2022) 'Sustainable Development Finance Assessment (SDFA) Framework: linking debt sustainability to the achievement of the 2030 Agenda', UNCTAD DA COVID-19 Project Paper 16/22 [online] 29 November, Available from: https://mobilizingdevfinance.org/research-material/unctad-sustainable-development-finance-assessment-sdfa-framew ork-linking-debt

WHO (2017) 'Least developed countries health and WHO: Country presence profile', [online], Available from: https://apps.who.int/iris/han dle/10665/255802

WHO (2020) 'Global monitoring report on financial protection in health 2019', [online] 13 April, Available from: https://www.who.int/publicati ons/i/item/9789240003958

WHO (2021) 'WHO country presence in least developed countries (LDCs)', Available from: https://apps.who.int/iris/bitstream/handle/10665/344 255/9789240033412-eng.pdf?sequence=1&isAllowed=y

WHO (2023) 'Maternal mortality fact sheet', [online] 19 September, Available from: https://www.who.int/news-room/fact-sheets/detail/maternal-mortality

World Bank (2022) 'International debt report 2022: Updated international debt statistics', Washington DC: World Bank Group [online], Available from: https://openknowledge.worldbank.org/handle/10986/38045

4

Debt and Climate Change: Twin Crises Burdening Women in the Global South

Iolanda Fresnillo Sallan and Leia Achampong

1. Introduction: debt and climate threats to women's rights

As a new debt crisis is hitting the Global South, governments and economies will face growing difficulties and challenges to deal with the recovery from the pandemic and with climate emergencies. Governments all over are responding to the fiscal constraints and debt increases with spending cuts, a strategy that, far from being gender neutral, will exacerbate existing inequalities. Additionally, the climate emergency also has specific negative impacts on women's rights and gender justice. The intersection of the debt and climate crises is increasingly getting attention from Civil Society Organisations (CSOs), academia, multilateral institutions and governments.

However, the analysis of how these twin rising emergencies are affecting women's rights and exacerbating gender inequalities remains broadly unexplored. This chapter will address precisely how the combination of the debt and climate crises, together with the austerity strategy to face debt distress, is leading to increasing gender inequalities and threatening women's rights, exploring how the existing international financial architecture is unfit to offer gender just solutions and presenting proposals for feminist and systemic responses.

Section 2 of the chapter addresses how governments are responding to the increasing debt crisis with spending cuts and renewed austerity policies, endangering the capacity of public services to advance human rights, including women's rights and gender justice. Section 3 presents how the debt and climate crises are linked in a self-feeding cycle, and section 4 explores how the combination of both crises generate compounding impacts on gender inequalities and women's rights. Section 5 exposes how the global financial architecture falls short in offering gender just and comprehensive solutions to the debt and climate crises. The relation between debt crises, natural resources exploitation and women's rights is addressed in section 6. Finally, section 7 offers proposals on how to deal with the debt and climate crises in a comprehensive, systemic and feminist way.

2. A new debt crisis: renewed threats to women's rights

The world has never been so indebted. Corporations, families and also governments all over the globe have seen a steep increase in their debts, particularly in the last decade, an increase that was exacerbated by the outbreak of the COVID-19 pandemic. The trend is particularly worrying if we look at the public sector in Global South countries, where sovereign debt had already been increasing rapidly since the global financial crisis in 2008. The impact of the COVID-19 shock exacerbated the high debt levels, but debt vulnerabilities kept worsening after 2020 given different factors, including: the food and energy supply challenges and price spikes driven by the spillovers of the war in Ukraine but also by highly speculative markets; interest rates increases driven by monetary policies in advanced economies to tackle the global inflation; currency depreciation and increasing bond yields; and insufficient and inadequate responses from the international community to the multiple crises. Up to 54 countries in the Global South are facing severe debt problems. 'They represent little more than 3 percent of the global economy, 18 percent of the population, but account for more than 50 percent of people living in extreme poverty – including 28 of the world's top-50 most climate vulnerable countries' (Jensen, 2022: 4).

The debt crisis is not only intensifying, but it is also having an undeniable impact on people's lives. Indeed, countries with the highest debt payments are already seeing drops in public spending if we compare the situation to 2019, pre-COVID-19. The most heavily indebted nations are expected to reduce public expenditure by 3 per cent on average between 2019 and 2023 despite the need to counter the impact of spiralling food and energy prices (Woolfenden, 2022a). This tendency is at risk of being exacerbated in the upcoming years, as 94 Global South countries are expected to continue implementing austerity measures between 2023 and 2025, undermining the capacity of governments to provide access to quality public services, including education, healthcare and social protection, among others (Ortiz and Cummings, 2022: 9). This is for instance the case for climate vulnerable countries, such as Small Island Developing States (SIDS), where, while debt vulnerabilities grow, government expenditure as a percentage of GDP is predicted to decrease in 31 out of 37 SIDS between 2022 and 2025 (Fresnillo and Crotti, 2022: 9).

This fiscal consolidation trend, far from being gender neutral, exacerbates the existing gender inequalities in society and the economy, blending patriarchy and neoliberal ideology (Abed and Kelleher, 2022). In effect, the impact of budget cuts on essential public services, and other austerity measures, falls more heavily on women, girls and gender minorities, particularly those who experience intersecting inequalities based on class, 'race', ethnicity, caste and age (Bohoslavsky, 2019). Women, who are typically concentrated more heavily than men in lower-income sectors of society, are more affected by cuts in social protection programmes, maternity and childcare and food or energy subsidies. The gendered impact of austerity also reduces women's ability to access essential public services, which are particularly relevant for impoverished women. It is also women, girls and gender minorities who are deeply affected by the reduction or removal of vital services for survivors of gender violence.

Moreover, it is mainly women who will carry the extra unpaid burden of the care tasks when public services coverage and quality decrease or even stop (Fresnillo, 2020). As Woodroffe and Meeks argue, 'the availability of women's unpaid care as a "shock absorber" is a premise on which cuts to public services are based' (Woodroffe and Meeks, 2019). Austerity does not only rely on the gendered division of labour and the unpaid domestic work, but also on the underpaid work of women, particularly in the care economy (Ghosh, 2021). Public workers' wage caps, typically included in austerity packages, directly impact women's income and economic security, as the public sector tends to be a major source of employment for women (Fresnillo, 2020). For instance, a recent report by Women in Global Health estimated that up to six million women working in the health sector worldwide were either underpaid or not paid (Keeling, 2022). As evidenced, austerity policies affect women's rights, and further entrench economic inequalities and gender justice through different channels and in different ways, but we also need to consider their cumulative impact on communities and families, which can be particularly devastating (Saalbrink, 2022).

3. The vicious circle of debt and climate emergencies

In a recent report, the International Monetary Fund (IMF) acknowledged the harmful self-feeding cycle between debt and climate, recognizing that not only are climate and debt problems closely linked, as climate vulnerabilities and fiscal risks are correlated, but also that 'there is likely causation in both directions' (Chamon et al, 2022). On the one hand, countries with unsustainable sovereign debt tend to have reduced fiscal space, not only to implement development strategies and fight gender inequalities, but also to invest in climate resilience or measures to help face the impacts of climate events.

On the other hand, in a context of increasing sovereign debts, the climate emergency is an additional key element that further exacerbates debt accumulation. The increasing impacts of the climate emergency in the Global South is leading to more external borrowing in order to be able to invest in climate measures. Countries dealing with the emergency of a climate event, including the reconstruction and recovery after the event, have little option but to borrow. As Barbados Prime Minister Mia Mottley described it: 'Tackling natural disasters and protecting the environment are the single most significant causes for increases in our debt' (DRGR, 2020). In fact, climate-extreme events are critical to sovereign debt risks, as they have had a prominent role in some default episodes, such as in Antigua and Barbuda in 2004 and 2009, in Grenada in 2004, in the Dominican Republic in 1998 or in Suriname in 1992 (Fresnillo and Crotti, 2022). Additionally, borrowing usually comes at higher costs for climate vulnerable countries in the Global South, as they have to pay higher interest rates to private creditors than other countries less vulnerable to climate change (Volz et al, 2020). Coupled with this, over 70 per cent of public climate finance delivered in 2020 was in the form of loans (OECD, 2022).

It is deeply unjust that Global South countries have to access loans from bilateral, multilateral or even private sources, in some cases at non-concessional terms, to pay for the impacts of climate change that these countries have historically contributed the least towards (Callahan and Mankin, 2022). As the African Sovereign Debt Justice Network (ASDJN) argues, 'climate change should not impose additional debt burdens on African countries and other least developed and developing countries' (Tamale and Majekolagbe, 2022).

4. Debt and climate crises, a double burden on women

Women, girls and gender minorities are not only more exposed to the impacts of debt crises and the implementation of fiscal consolidation and austerity measures, they also bear a heavier burden from the impacts of climate change and environmental destruction. For UN Women, the climate crisis is not 'gender neutral', as 'women and girls experience the greatest impacts of climate change, which amplifies existing gender inequalities and poses unique threats to their livelihoods, health, and safety' (UN Women, 2022). As a consequence, climate change becomes a threat multiplier for women, girls and gender minorities, impacting and exacerbating 'new and existing forms of gendered inequities' (OHCHR, 2022).

Women tend to be more dependent on natural resources for their livelihoods, particularly in the most impoverished communities. Globally, a quarter of employed women work in agriculture, forestry and fishing (UN, 2022a), but dependency on agriculture as a source of employment is even higher in low- and lower-middle-income countries. According to the International Labour Organization (ILO), 'in Southern Asia and sub-Saharan Africa, over 60 per cent of all working women remain in agriculture, often concentrated in time and labour-intensive activities, which are unpaid or poorly remunerated' (ILO, 2016). However, women have less access to agricultural resources, as ecosystems are increasingly commodified and priced, and less than 13 per cent of agricultural landholders are women (UN, 2022a). The need for increasing resources to repay external debt often leads to an increase in natural resource exploitation to increase export revenue, which can include land-grabbing and, therefore, less access to land for the poor, especially women (Woolfenden, 2022b).

Furthermore, climate change is already impacting ecosystems and food production systems in the agriculture, fisheries and coastal aquaculture sectors, through degraded water quality, soil erosion and lower crop yields (IPCC, 2022). Being more dependent on agriculture and having less access to secured resources means climate impacts on ecosystems and agriculture have a particular burden on women.

As noted, debt crises have the potential of worsening this situation. As debt payments increase and public resources become scarcer, governments, following IMF recommendations or conditions for accessing financial resources, are already cutting subsidies or increasing consumption taxes (Oxfam, 2022). Ortiz and Cummins' latest research shows how in 80 countries the IMF programmes and reports between 2020 and 2022 included advice to reduce food, agricultural, fuel, electricity, gas and other subsidies. Given the disproportionate responsibility for securing food, water and fuel that women bear, such measures increase the time and effort women need to do to provide for their homes. While in the case of energy subsidies, the argument is often the need to curb the global reliance on fossil fuels, we need to consider how to minimize the impact of fossil fuel subsidy reform(s) on communities, and particularly on women. For instance, removal of fuel subsidies will likely lead to increased transport costs, thereby reducing mobility needed for work or education and health services.

In 2022, food and energy price inflation spiked, accelerated by the war in Ukraine, highly speculative commodity markets and the impacts of increasing droughts in different regions of the world, resulting in a major food crisis in many Global South countries. Already in 2021, starvation affected an estimated 828 million people globally, 59 per cent being women (Care, 2022). Hunger and malnutrition, and the gender gap in food insecurity, were already on the rise before the war in Ukraine. In a context of unabated climate change and rising debt crises, the impact of food scarcity and insecurity on women and girls will only get worse (UN, 2022b).

The cumulative impacts of climate change, a debt crisis, austerity measures and food insecurity forces women to adjust, often without public support (or diminishing public support due to spending cuts) and to search for additional financial support. This results in an increased reliance on 'extractive consumer loans', generating or increasing personal debts particularly for households headed by women (Muchhala and Guillem, 2022). The combination of cuts in public services, increased cost of living (exacerbated by climate change impacts) and differentiated consumption patterns leads to an increase in women's indebtedness in order to be able to access basic rights such as health, education and housing. In addition, the increase of precarity and flexibilization of labour rules, often following IMF advice for reforms leading to fiscal consolidation, also leads to indebtedness by women in order to engage in informal work ventures (Serafini and Fois, 2021).

We also need to consider that the impact of climate extreme events and environmental hazards increase the burden of unpaid domestic work for women as they need to invest more hours in securing water, food and energy for cooking and heating the homes (UN Women, 2022). Women and girls are, for instance, responsible for collecting water in almost two thirds of households in developing countries . When a climate hazard occurs, such as a hurricane or flood, routes become impassable and basic services, including water provision, can simply become inaccessible, or women, especially those in rural areas, will have to walk longer distances to access resources. When these impacts occur amidst a debt crisis, the lack of access is exacerbated due to closed or underfunded public services such as health centres, schools and water provision facilities due to austerity packages. According to UN Women, 'this puts added pressure on girls, who often have to leave school to help their mothers manage the increased burden' (UN Women, 2022). Additionally, when struggling with unsustainable debts, governments might find it impossible or will take much longer to reconstruct damaged routes and infrastructure unless they obtain external financial support. Support that, if available, will usually come in the form of new loans that will add to existing debts.

The case of Puerto Rico illustrates this situation. Four months after declaring bankruptcy following a profound debt crisis, Hurricane Maria hit the country in 2017 causing major devastation and losses of US$68 billion, or around 69 per cent of the territory's GDP. An estimated 2,975 people perished from hurricane-related causes. Water and sanitation facilities were also heavily damaged, increasing the burden on women to obtain water (Oxfam, 2018). In some rural areas, water and energy came back only after several months because of the government's limited capacity to finance reconstruction due to its debt crisis and austerity policies put in place.

Damage to infrastructure caused by climate change can also mean that women are at higher risk of living in unsafe and overcrowded shelters, given their lack of owned land or property. In this context, 'women and girls face increased vulnerabilities to all forms of gender-based violence, including conflict-related sexual violence, human trafficking, child marriage, and other forms of violence' (UN Women, 2022). Evidence also suggests that climate displacement disproportionately affects women and girls in the Global South (Care, 2020). Not only are girls more likely to be taken out of school to support household duties, if the situation deteriorates, some families might 'feel they have no choice but to give their daughters away for early marriage, often resulting in early pregnancy' (Action Aid, 2022). In fact, about 12 million more young girls are thought to have been married off after environmental hazards and weather-related catastrophes have been shown to increase sex trafficking by 20 to 30 per cent (Harvey, 2020). Environmental degradation and natural resources scarcity linked to climate breakdown amplify gender inequalities and violence against women and girls (Castañeda Camey et al, 2020). Gender-based violence is increasingly being inflicted on female climate refugees who face extortion, exploitation, rape, sexual harassment, survival sex, forced marriage and human trafficking in transit and/or in destination countries (Harvey, 2020). In the context of over-indebted countries, the lack of fiscal resources makes governments less capable of providing adequate support and shelter for women after a climate event, to secure services for gender violence survivors, or to put policies in place to protect girls from early marriages and trafficking, among other policies to reduce gender violence (Bohoslavsky, 2019).

Finally, climate change and its impacts, and environmental degradation, also have differential gender health effects. These can exacerbate women's and girls' undernutrition and exposure to diseases such as malaria or anaemia, and negatively impact in accessing health care services, aggravating existing gender gaps and damaging sexual and reproductive health and rights (UN, 2022a). This adds to the impacts of debt distress on public health systems and, consequently, on women's health and reproductive rights. According to UNICEF, 'even before the current crisis, one fifth of LMICs spent more on debt service than on education, health and social protection combined', and increasing debt burdens threaten 'to crowd out social spending still further' (UNICEF, 2021). All while at least half of the world's population still do not have access to essential health services and only half of women in developing countries receive the recommended amount of maternal and reproductive health care (UN, 2020).

In conclusion, climate change, as well as debt crises, act as multipliers of existing intersectional gender-based inequalities. According to the Intergovernmental Panel on Climate Change (IPCC) report on impacts, adaptation and vulnerability, 'climate change impacts can be gendered as a result of customary roles in society, such as triple workloads for women (that is, economic labour, household and family labour, and duties of community participation)' (IPCC, 2022). By carrying out climate adaptation measures and diverting their time away from other priorities, women increase their non-paid domestic and care workload. This increased burden also acts as a barrier to them engaging in community participation and political decision making on measures that directly affect them. Various United Nations (UN) agencies have highlighted that women and men can have different solutions to addressing the same climate impact and these responses can impose higher costs and negative consequences for specific groups, shifting exposure and vulnerability (IPCC, 2022). However, when engaging women in defining solutions, it results in better outcomes for all parts of a community (Achampong, 2022b). Which is why it is crucial that women are involved in decision making, project development and policy implementation processes. Yet, multiple barriers exist for women, including female exclusion norms in society on including women within decision and policy making. This forced removal of their political agency means women's knowledge and experiences are missing from decision making, which is exacerbated in the context of increasing climate impacts.

5. Debt and climate finance architecture: unfit for purpose

The debt architecture and climate finance architecture are not fit for purpose to address the compounded impacts of the twin debt and climate crises on women. The continued absence of a multilateral debt resolution framework that ensures a systematic, rules-based and timely approach to orderly, fair, transparent and durable sovereign debt crisis resolution is a persisting gap in the international financial architecture (Perera, 2019). Against this backdrop, in 2020 the G20 approved two initiatives to address the debt problems arising from the COVID-19 shock. The Debt Service Suspension Initiative (DSSI), providing temporary debt payment moratoria to a limited number of countries, and the Common Framework (CF), aspiring to deliver on timely and comprehensive debt treatment for countries with unsustainable debt levels. However, they have proved to be insufficient and inadequate, particularly for climate vulnerable countries and from a development and people's rights approach. Both initiatives are limited to a list of 73 countries, leaving out quite a number of middle-income countries, both in critical debt situations and very vulnerable to climate impacts. Furthermore, the participation of private creditors in both initiatives is voluntary, and the DSSI experience casts doubts on the capacity of the IMF or the G20 to enforce private sector participation in any debt restructuring or cancellation. Within today's debt architecture, the only way to ensure participation of private creditors in debt resolution is to stop paying them. However, countries that default on their debt payments risk legal action from private creditors, particularly for debt issued under New York or London law. Thus it is crucial to ensure there is adequate finance and legislation to protect defaulting countries against uncollaborative creditors.

The uncertainties and lack of clarity regarding the implementation of the CF remains high. Furthermore, participation in the CF is conditional on having an IMF programme. As outlined earlier, such programmes can become a Trojan horse to impose further gendered austerity measures, threatening women's rights and increasing gender inequalities. This is also because debt restructurings are based on the IMF and World Bank debt sustainability analysis, which determines how much debt is sustainable for a country. However, the preeminent approach to debt sustainability is fairly limited to that of capacity of payment, regardless of the resources available to invest in social protection, public services, gender equality or climate resilience. A new approach to debt sustainability should consider the impact of a country's debt burden on its ability to meet its Sustainable Development Goals (SDGs) to fight climate change and to create the conditions for the realization of all universal human rights, including women's rights, overcoming the gender blindness of the existing debt sustainability analysis. In conclusion, the current international financial architecture does not offer an optimal framework or guarantees for a fair, lasting, comprehensive and timely resolution to the debt challenges. Nor does it offer an appropriate approach to debt restructurings considering the climate and gender equality challenges.

In parallel, the current climate finance architecture also comes with important challenges to deliver fair and gender just responses. It is a complex and diverse system of different state and non-state stakeholders very much affected by global economic conditions, such as high inflation, price changes and economic shocks caused by global upheavals. This architecture draws on the development finance model to source solutions, to fill the quantity and quality gap on climate finance. Unfortunately, this has led to the proliferation of lending in development finance to be replicated in climate finance, as 70 per cent of public climate finance in 2020 was delivered in the form of loans (OECD, 2022). Furthermore, public climate finance flows amounted in 2020 to US$68.3 billion, falling short of the existing global, annual US$100 billion climate finance goal, which the OECD predicted would not be met until 2023 (OECD, 2022). Moreover, EURODAD calculations based on OECD data show that the inability to meet the yearly US$100 billion goal has left developing countries at a deficit of US$381.6 billion in bilateral public climate finance and multilateral public climate finance attributable to developed countries between 2013 and 2020 (Achampong, 2022a).

In this bleak context of insufficient responses and inadequate debt and climate finance architecture, numerous voices have been pointing at climate for debt swaps as a possible innovative solution. Debt-for-climate swaps (where liberated funds are invested in climate adaptation and mitigation measures) or debt-for-nature swaps (where funds are invested in conservation goals) are seen by some as 'win–win' solutions that could both relieve some of a country's debt burden and free up resources at a national level to address the climate crisis. However, historical experience tells us that debt swaps have not been efficient when it comes to reducing debt significantly, particularly in cases of unsustainable debt levels. While well-designed debt swaps can free up resources for climate resilience investments, there are risks and challenges that should be taken into consideration. For instance, debtor governments can face challenges in mobilizing counterpart resources, particularly if they were unable to repay the original debt in the first place. Traditionally, debt swaps also have high transaction costs and negotiating debt swaps tends to be a lengthy process. When promoting debt swaps, country ownership should always be protected, avoiding any kind of conditionality or tied aid imposed by the donor. People's rights, including indigenous and other communities' ancestral rights over land use or use of resources, should be guaranteed. For instance, as Andre Standing has argued, 'debt swaps can come with a wider set of obligations, including the privatization of fishing rights, advancing blue carbon trading, expanding high end eco-tourism and commercial fish farming. These are policies that small-scale fishing communities have often opposed' (Standing, 2022). To avoid such risks, civil society participation should be a key element in debt swaps, including by women's and gender minority groups, but in many cases this hasn't been the case. Finally, climate-for-debt swaps should be additional to aid and climate finance commitments. In summary, while progress on debt swaps could help to free up resources for investment needs if well defined, with civil society and women's participation and substantially scaled up, it should not be seen as a solution for unsustainable debts nor as a substitute for climate finance commitments.

The need for adequate and accessible climate finance and finance to address loss and damage that does not exacerbate existing debt problems is vital for countries in the Global South. This was further echoed at COP27, where countries expressed 'deep concern regarding the significant financial costs associated with loss and damage for developing countries, resulting in a growing debt burden and impairing the realization of the Sustainable Development Goals' (UNFCCC, 2022b). Also, the possibility of automatic debt payments' standstills in the aftermath of a climate extreme event would ease the hardship of highly indebted countries when being hit by climate change. Barbados, for instance, is already including climate clauses to its debt issuance to enable a debt service suspension (Cleary Gottlieb, 2020). Lenders such as the Inter-American Development Bank and the government of the United Kingdom are also exploring this option (Wailhe, 2019; UK Export Finance, 2022).

Moreover, despite the United Nations Framework Convention on Climate Change (UNFCCC) recommending that climate finance providers 'improve tracking and reporting on gender-related aspects of climate finance, impact measuring and mainstreaming', data gaps remain (UNFCCC, 2018). Climate finance reporting tables used under the Paris Agreement do not include space for gender to be tracked, but countries may on a voluntary basis include such data under 'additional information' (UNFCCC, 2022a). As we have seen, climate change affects members of communities in different ways, so understanding the gender responsiveness of climate finance is essential to knowing if the differing needs and rights of women, girls and non-gendered communities are adequately being accounted for and addressed in climate action (Achampong, 2022a).

6. Exploiting natural resources to repay debts

With high levels of debt, and in a context of increasing energy and commodity prices, countries in the Global South have been exploiting their natural resources – including fossil fuels, mining or forests – in order to increase exports and use the revenue in foreign currency to repay increasing debts. We have recently seen, for instance, how countries like Suriname are being pushed by its private creditors to pursue future oil extraction in order to be able to repay its debts (Maki, 2022). Several Pacific Island states are already expanding their mining activities in the face of increasing debts. And in the case of Chad, the country has been denied debt relief on the account of increasing oil prices, and therefore the assumption that oil exploitation needs to be continued or even increased. Some countries can even find themselves in a debt-fossil fuel production trap. According to Debt Justice, 'countries rely on fossil fuel revenues to repay debt, anticipated revenues from fossil fuels are often overinflated and require huge investments to reach expected returns, leading to further debt alongside the environmental and human harms caused by such projects' (Woolfenden, 2022b).

When countries turn to increased exploitation of natural resources, women tend to be more impacted; given, for example, the predominant role they play in firewood collection and engagement in forestry value chains as a supplement to their household income (FAO, 2014). In the end, intensifying the exploitation of natural resources to repay public debts will eventually increase climate vulnerabilities, by generating desertification, soil degradation and an increase in carbon emissions. It also exacerbates the countries' dependency on commodities, together with the additional debt vulnerabilities that this may bring, as the infrastructures needed are usually debt financed. In many of these cases, the exploitation of natural resources is encouraged by international financial institutions, donors and creditors. According to a report by ActionAid USA and the Bretton Woods Project, in over half of IMF's 105 member countries, IMF policy advice had endorsed, or directly supported, the expansion of fossil fuel infrastructure between when the Paris Agreement was signed in December 2015 and March 2021, despite the urgent need to reduce emissions (Sward et al, 2021). A striking example of this is the IMF push for Argentina to exploit its oil and gas reserves in Vaca Muerta in order to reduce its reliance on expensive energy imports and increase their fiscal capacity to be able to repay its debts. 'Such incentives for fossil fuel expansion contradict the IMF's advertised climate orientation that centres on aiding countries phasing out of fossil fuel usage' (Stubbs and Kentikelenis, 2022).

Overconsumption of fossil fuels, particularly in the Global North, spurs this dynamic. The hegemony of the Global North distorts the domestic economic priorities of Global South countries, and the extraction of resources to fuel industrialization in the Global North has been a recurring tool to maintain hegemony. Studies on spatial inequality and economic justice show that the economic prowess of richer economies influences other countries' macroeconomic policies (McKay and Perge, 2015). Specifically, in some cases the higher consumption rates of richer countries affects what poorer countries choose to produce and export (Felipe et al, 2014), which in turn contributes to creating the poor environmental and social conditions under which production is carried out.

There is a clear colonial mindset of decarbonizing Global North countries by shifting its fossil fuel infrastructure to developing countries and extracting the resources necessary for building renewable energy infrastructure from the Global South. All in order to maintain the status quo of energy and overall consumption levels in the North, enabling intergenerational wealth accumulation in the Global North and intergenerational inequity in the Global South. Such strategies are actively promoted by multilateral development banks such as the World Bank (World Bank, 2020). This externalization of impacts, often argued for by the need to increase revenue to repay existing debts, not only distorts global power dynamics, but it also increases the risk of severe climate impacts in the Global South, which as we have seen are strongly gendered.

7. How to address the debt and climate crises in a comprehensive, systemic and feminist way

The world today faces several game-changing challenges, among which the climate emergency and the rise of new debt crises stand out. As we have seen in previous sections, the intersection of climate change and debt emergencies has resulted in pervasive inequalities, particularly exacerbating gender inequalities. As evidenced, the twin debt and climate crises have a cumulative impact on communities and families, which can be particularly devastating for women that experience intersecting inequalities based on class, 'race', ethnicity, caste and age . The use of austerity measures and fiscal consolidation to contain debt is affecting the range and quality of public services, increasing unpaid work, and exposing women and gender minorities to more physical climate change and financial vulnerabilities than their male counterparts. These dynamics are made worse by an unfit debt and climate finance architecture that is ill-equipped to provide fair and lasting solutions to the current twin debt and climate crises. The interplay of these phenomena is putting at risk the fulfilment and advancement of women's human rights and towards gender justice in the world, particularly in the Global South, and impacting the Global South journey to sustainable development.

The international community has so far failed to provide adequate support for Global South countries to be able to deal with the dual and compounded impacts of the climate and debt crises. The unwillingness of Global North countries to reform the existing international financial architecture and to fulfil their climate finance and development assistance commitments are at the core of this failure. By endorsing the principle of common but differentiated responsibilities (CBDR) on the climate crisis, but not fulfilling the climate finance commitments, countries in the Global North are showing that there is no real acknowledgement of the responsibility they have for climate change. They fail to acknowledge the climate debt that the Global North has with the Global South due to their disproportionate contribution to carbon and other greenhouse gas emissions (Callahan and Mankin, 2022).

However, the core of the problem is the persisting neocolonial and patriarchal economic dynamics and the fossil fuels and growth obsessions of the capitalist system. Maintaining the current dependency and exploitation of fossil fuels, far from resulting in sustainable development, is a recipe for long-term economic catastrophe, social and environmental disaster, and the exacerbation of existing poverty and inequalities. A fundamental shift in the global economy towards a new model that puts care and people's rights at the centre, respecting the material and natural limits of the planet and atmosphere, is imperative to avoid further climate change. Furthermore, sustainable development is under threat from the disastrous implications of the climate emergency, dwindling natural resources, changing ecosystems and environmental hazards.

A fair response to the multiple crises in the Global South should also address the recognition of climate and other ecological, social and historical debts that countries in the Global North have with them. A debt that started with slavery and colonialism, but that continued with neocolonial resource pillage and unfair trade, financial and political relations that have lasted for centuries. In this historical context, responses to the climate and debt crises should start with the recognition and reparations for climate and ecological debt.

Global North countries, which have historically contributed the most to climate change, need to live up to their commitments in relation to climate action, which are not completed unless they also contribute with financial support to help address the climate impacts they have caused in Global South countries. Doing so is a reparation for causing irrevocable climate change. In this sense, climate finance represents a redistribution of resources between countries to address historical unequal responsibilities for current ongoing climate change (Achampong, 2022a). Climate finance commitments and debt cancellation should be part of a wider set of structural and financial reparations that should also include ecological restoration, phasing out fossil fuel subsidies, ending extractivism and shifting to decarbonized modes of production, distribution and consumption.

Beyond the profound change that we need to see in the world and economic system in order to redress the climate emergency and the unsustainable debt accumulation, there is an urgent need to reform the international financial architecture and climate finance architecture. Such reforms should address the need for a fair, transparent and multilateral framework for debt crisis resolution that includes unsustainable and illegitimate debt, under the auspices of the UN and not in lender-dominated arenas. This should include the delivery of unconditional debt cancellation for climate vulnerable countries and other nations in need and a new approach to debt sustainability, but also of equitable, high quality and new and additional climate finance that contributes to sustainable development in developing countries in the Global South. The entire climate finance architecture needs to be reframed to focus not on investments and cost, but on ownership, debt sustainability, economically-just climate finance flows, transparency and accountability. Finance to address loss and damage, and an automatic mechanism to halt debt payments in the wake of climate extreme events, must also be enacted. Unconditional debt cancellation and effective climate finance flows can be an opportunity to move away from development models that have prioritized growth, industrialization, trade and the interests of development finance providers. Particularly if social structures that facilitate equal access to finance, decision making and policy development and implementation are available.

References

Abed, D. and Kelleher, F. (2022) 'The assault of austerity. How prevailing economic policy choices are a form of gender-based violence' Oxfam [online] 21 November, Available from: https://www.oxfam.org/en/resea rch/assault-austerity

Achampong, L. (2022a) '*Efficient, Equitable and Effective High-Quality Climate Finance: Recommendations for the Post-2025 Global Climate Finance Goal*', Eurodad [online] 12 August, Available from: https://www.eurodad.org/ncqg_2022

Achampong, L. (2022b) 'How lessons from development finance can strengthen climate finance', in C. Cash and L. Swatuk (eds), *The Political Economy of Climate Finance: Lessons from International Development*, Cham: Palgrave Macmillan, pp 21–44.

Action Aid (2022) *Climate Change and Gender*, [online] 27 September, Available from: https://www.actionaid.org.uk/our-work/emergencies-disasters-humanitarian-response/climate-change-and-gender

Bohoslavsky, J.P. (2019) 'The impact of economic reforms and austerity measures on women's human rights', Center for Women's Global Leadership – OHCHR, Available from: https://www.ohchr.org/Docume nts/Issues/Development/IEDebt/WomenAusterity/UserFriendlyVersi onReport_EN.pdf

Callahan, C.W. and Mankin, J.S. (2022) 'National attribution of historical climate damages', *Climatic Change*, 172(40): https://link.springer.com/arti cle/10.1007/s10584-022-03387-y

Care (2020) 'Evicted by climate change. Confronting the gendered impacts of climate-induced displacement', [online] 6 July, Available from: https:// careclimatechange.org/evicted-by-climate-change/

Care (2022) 'Food security and gender equality: A synergistic understudied symphony', Care Evaluations [online] 27 July, Available from: https:// www.careevaluations.org/evaluation/food-security-and-gender-equality/

Castañeda Camey, I.; Sabater, L.; Owren, C. and Boyer, A.E. (2020) *Gender-based Violence and Environment Linkages. The Violence of Inequality*, Gland, Switzerland: International Union for Conservation of Nature (IUCN), Available from: https://portals.iucn.org/library/node/48969

Chamon, M.D., Klok, E., Thakoor, V.V. and Zettelmeyer, J. (2022) 'Debt-for-Climate Swaps: Analysis, Design, and Implementation' (No. 2022/162), International Monetary Fund [online] 12 August, Available from:https:// www.imf.org/en/Publications/WP/Issues/2022/08/11/Debt-for-Clim ate-Swaps-Analysis-Design-and-Implementation-522184

Cleary, G. (2020) 'Government of Barbados in $774 million external debt restructuring', *Cleary Gottlieb News* [online] 21 January, Available from: https://www.clearygottlieb.com/news-and-insights/news-listing/ government-of-barbados-in-774-million-external-debt-restructuring

DRGR (2020) 'PM Mia Mottley's Keynote at the launch of the report "Debt Relief for a Green and Inclusive Recovery"', *Debt Relief for Green and Inclusive Recovery (DRGR)* [online] 18 November, Available from: https://drgr.org/2020/11/18/pm-mia-mottleys-speech-at-the-lau nch-of-the-report/

FAO (2014) 'Women in forestry: Challenges and opportunities' (I3924E/1/ 07.14), Food and Agriculture Organization of the United Nations (FAO), Available from: https://www.fao.org/3/i3924e/i3924e.pdf

Felipe, J.; Kumar, U. and Abdon, A. (2014) 'How rich countries became rich and why poor countries remain poor: It's the economic structure … duh!', *Japan and the World Economy*, 29: 46–58.

Fresnillo, I. (2020) 'Out of service: How public services and human rights are being threatened by the growing debt crisis', Eurodad [online] 17 February, Available from: https://www.eurodad.org/outofservice

Fresnillo, I. and Crotti, I. (2022) 'Riders on the storm—How debt and climate change are threatening the future of small island developing states', Eurodad [online] 11 October, Available from: https://www.eurodad.org/debt_in_sids

Ghosh, J. (2021) *Gender Concerns in Debt Relief*, London: IIED, Available from:https://www.iied.org/sites/default/files/pdfs/2021-12/20691iied.pdf

Harvey, F. (2020) 'Climate breakdown "is increasing violence against women"', *The Guardian* [online] 29 January, Available from:https://www.theguardian.com/environment/2020/jan/29/climate-breakdown-is-increasing-violence-against-women

ILO (2016) 'Women at Work: Trends 2016', International Labour Organization [online] 8 March, Available from:https://www.ilo.org/gender/Informationresources/Publications/WCMS_457317/lang--en/index.htm

IPCC (2022) 'Climate change 2022: Impacts, adaptation and vulnerability'. IPCC Working Group II [online], Available from: https://www.ipcc.ch/report/ar6/wg2/

Jensen, L. (2022) 'Avoiding "Too Little Too Late" on International Debt Relief' (Development Future Series Working Papers), United Nations Development Program (UNDP) [Research-Discussion Papers] 11 October, Available from: https://www.undp.org/publications/dfs-avoiding-too-little-too-late-international-debt-relief

Keeling, A. (2022) 'Subsidizing global health: Women's unpaid work in health systems', Women in Global Health [Policy Report], Available from: https://womeningh.org/our-advocacy/paywomen/

Maki, S. (2022) 'Suriname stranded in default as bondholders ogle oil royalties', Bloomberg [online] 25 July, Available from: https://www.bloomberg.com/news/articles/2022-07-25/oil-dreams-quash-debt-deal-progress-after-suriname-s-default

McKay, A. and Perge, E. (2015) 'Spatial inequality and its implications for growth – poverty reduction relations', in Andrew McKay and Erik Thorbecke (eds), *Economic Growth and Poverty Reduction in Sub-Saharan Africa: Current and Emerging Issues*, Oxford: Oxford Academic, pp 197–226, Available from: https://doi.org/10.1093/acprof:oso/9780198728450.003.0007

Muchhala, B. and Guillem, A. (2022) 'Gendered austerity and embodied debt in Ecuador: Channels through which women absorb and resist the shocks of public budget cuts', *Gender and Development*, 30(1–2): 283–309.

OECD (2022) 'Aggregate Trends of Climate Finance Provided and Mobilised by Developed Countries in 2013–2020', [online] 29 July, Available from: https://www.oecd.org/climate-change/finance-usd-100-billion-goal/

OHCHR (2022) 'Climate change is a threat multiplier for women and girls: UN expert', *Office of the High Commissioner for Human Rights* [online] 5 October, Available from: https://www.ohchr.org/en/press-releases/2022/10/climate-change-threat-multiplier-women-and-girls-un-expert

Ortiz, I. and Cummins, M. (2022) 'End austerity: A global report on budget cuts and harmful social reforms in 2022–25', Initiative for Policy Dialogue (IPD) at Columbia University, the International Confederation of Trade Unions (ITUC), Public Services International (PSI), the European Network on Debt and Development (EURODAD) and the Bretton Woods Project (BWP) [online] 28 September, Available from: https://www.eurodad.org/end_austerity_a_global_report

Oxfam (2018) 'Oxfam America Annual Report', Available from: https://s3.amazonaws.com/oxfam-us/www/static/ media/files/2018_Oxfam_America_Annual_Report.pdf

Oxfam (2022) 'IMF must abandon demands for austerity as cost-of-living crisis drives up hunger and poverty worldwide', [online] 19 April, Available from: https://www.oxfam.org/en/press-releases/imf-must-abandon-demands-austerity-cost-living-crisis-drives-hunger-and-poverty

Perera, M. (2019) 'We can work it out: 10 civil society principles for sovereign debt resolution', Eurodad [online] 17 September, Available from: https://www.eurodad.org/debtworkout

Saalbrink (2022) *The Care Contradiction: The IMF, Gender and Austerity*, Johannesburg: ActionAid International.

Serafini, V. and Fois, M. (2021) 'Women, Debt and Gender Inequalities', Latindadd [online] 14 September, Available from: https://www.latindadd.org/2021/09/14/women-debt-and-gender-inequalities/

Standing, A. (2022) 'Debt-for-nature swaps and the oceans: The Belize Blue Bond', Coalition for Fair Fisheries Arrangements [online] 15 March, Available from: https://www.cffacape.org/publications-blog/debt-for-nature-swaps-and-the-oceans-the-belize-blue-bond

Stubbs, T. and Kentikelenis, A. (2022) 'Mixed messages: IMF loans and the green transition in Argentina and Pakistan', Recourse, Fundeps, PRIED, Alternative Law Collective policy paper [online], Available from: https://www.re-course.org/wp-content/uploads/2022/09/Mixed-messages-IMF-loans-and-the-green-transition-in-Argentina-and-Pakistan-Updatedweb.pdf

Sward, J.; Amerasinghe, N.; Bunker, A. and Walker, J. (2021) 'IMF Surveillance and Climate Change Transition Risks: Reforming IMF policy advice to support a just energy transition', ActionAid, Bretton Woods Project [online], Available from: https://www.actionaidusa.org/wp-content/uploads/2021/08/IMF-x-climate-FINAL-1.pdf

Tamale, N. and Majekolagbe, A. (2022) 'A Brief on Debt and Climate Vulnerable Countries in Africa', African Sovereign Debt Justice Network (AfSDJN) [online] 8 November, Available from: https://www.afronomicslaw.org/category/african-sovereign-debt-justice-network-afsdjn/new-afsdjn-policy-brief-focuses-debt-climate

UK Export Finance (2022) 'UK Export Finance launches new debt solution to help developing countries with climate shocks', UK Government News [online] 8 November, Available from: https://www.gov.uk/government/news/uk-export-finance-launches-new-debt-solution-to-help-developing-countries-with-climate-shocks

UN (2020) 'Good health and well-being: Why it matters', UN Sustainable Development Goals Factsheets, SDG 3 [online], Available from: https://www.un.org/sustainabledevelopment/wp-content/uploads/2017/03/3_Why-It-Matters-2020.pdf

UN (2022a) 'Achieving gender equality and the empowerment of all women and girls in the context of climate change, environmental and disaster risk reduction policies and programmes: Report of the Secretary-General', United Nations Economic and Social Council – Commission on the Status of Women [online] 4 January, Available from: https://digitallibrary.un.org/record/3956348

UN (2022b) 'World Food Day: Another year of global record hunger looms amid food and climate crisis', [online] 13 October, Available from: https://news.un.org/en/story/2022/10/1129522

UNFCCC (2018) 'Biennial Assessment and Overview of Climate Finance Flows', United Nations Framework Convention on Climate Change [online], Available from: https://unfccc.int/BA-2018

UNFCCC (2022a) 'Report of the Conference of the Parties serving as the meeting of the Parties to the Paris Agreement on its third session, held in Glasgow from 31 October to 13 November 2021. Addendum Part two: Action taken by the Conference of the Parties serving as the meeting of the Parties to the Paris Agreement at its third session', United Nations Framework Convention on Climate Change [online] 8 March, Available from: https://unfccc.int/documents/460951

UNFCCC (2022b) 'Sharm el-Sheikh Implementation Plan', United Nations Framework Convention on Climate Change, Conference of the Parties (COP 27), Available from: https://unfccc.int/sites/default/files/resource/cop27_auv_2_cover%20decision.pdf

UNICEF (2021) 'COVID-19 and the looming debt crisis. Protecting and transforming social spending for inclusive recoveries' (Innocenti Research Report, No 01), UNICEF Office of Research – Innocenti, Available from: https://www.unicef-irc.org/publications/1193-covid-19-looming-debt-crisis-protecting-transforming-social-spending-for-inclusive-recoveries.html

UN Women (2022) 'How gender inequality and climate change are interconnected', [online] 28 February, Available from: https://www.unwomen.org/en/news-stories/explainer/2022/02/explainer-how-gender-inequality-and-climate-change-are-interconnected

Volz, U.; Beirne, J.; Preudhomme, N.; Fenton, A.; Mazzacurati, E.; Renzhi, N. and Stampe, J. (2020) *Climate Change and Sovereign Risk*, London, Tokyo, Singapore, Berkeley: SOAS University of London, Asian Development Bank Institute, World Wide Fund for Nature Singapore, Four Twenty Seven, Available from: https://eprints.soas.ac.uk/33524/

Wailhe, K. (2019, July 10). 'Avoiding a debt disaster', *Caribbean Development Trends*. Inter-American Development Bank (IDB). Available from: https://blogs.iadb.org/caribbean-dev-trends/en/avoiding-a-debt-disaster/

Woodroffe, J. and Meeks, P. (2019) 'Push no one behind. How current economic policy exacerbates gender inequality', GADN and FEMNET [online], Available from: https://gadnetwork.org/gadn-resources/push-no-one-behind-how-current-economic-policy-exacerbates-gender-equality

Woolfenden, T. (2022a) 'Countries in debt crisis cut public spending in face of soaring prices', Debt Justice UK [online] 12 June, Available from: https://debtjustice.org.uk/press-release/countries-in-debt-crisis-cut-public-spending-in-face-of-soaring-prices

Woolfenden, T. (2022b) 'Why climate justice must include debt justice', Debt Justice and Climate Action Network International [online] 17 October, Available from: https://debtjustice.org.uk/news/new-briefing-why-climate-justice-must-include-debt-justice

World Bank (Director) (2020) 'Maximizing the Benefits of Oil, Gas and Mining for Developing Countries', [online video] 29 July, Available from: https://www.worldbank.org/en/news/video/2020/07/29/maximizing-the-benefits-of-oil-gas-and-mining-for-developing-countries

PART II

Human Rights and Debt Approach

5

Legal Standards on Debt and Women's Rights

Juan Pablo Bohoslavsky and Julieta Rossi

1. Introduction

In this chapter, current international and Inter-American standards of human rights in the field of sovereign debt from a gender perspective are presented and systematized. These are legal standards that are applied when designing, assessing and implementing economic policies, including public debt management. The standards applicable both to borrower States and public and private creditors, as well as their implications in terms of obligations are presented.

For that purpose, the relevant rules and principles recognized in human rights conventions are identified and articulated, and the vast interpretative development made in this field by special procedures and treaty bodies are presented, such as the Independent Expert on external debt and human rights, the Committee on the Elimination of All Forms of Discrimination against Women (CEDAW Committee) and the Committee on Economic, Social and Cultural Rights (ESCR Committee), as well as the emerging development that is taking place in the Inter-American field (Bohoslavsky and Clérico, 2023). Besides, advances made in World and Regional Conferences on Women are presented. The findings enable us to draw conclusions on the existing legal void and limitations, as well as on the transformative potentiality of human rights in the field of the feminist economy, and to show a roadmap for future development.

The structure of this chapter is as follows. After the introduction, section 2 explains the international and regional standards in the field of sovereign debt with a gender perspective. In this same section, first the general legal framework is described and then the principles related to borrower States and creditors. In section 3, the specific obligations resulting from the earlier-described principles are explained, and in section 4 conclusions are offered.

2. International and regional standards

General legal framework

The development of human rights – mainly economic, social and cultural ones (ESCR) – largely depends on the availability of material resources. Due to the indivisibility and interdependence of all human rights, the availability (or shortage) of resources in turn affects the right to equality and gender-based non-discrimination in its formal and substantive dimensions (Aldao and Clérico, 2022).

Economic policies (including public debt management) may have a deep and long-lasting effect on the effective guarantee of all rights, for instance, through the strengthening or weakening of the fiscal space to deploy efficient social policies so as to reverse situations of vulnerability of certain groups of people, which has an impact on the increase or decrease of poverty and inequality levels, and differential effects based on 'race', ethnicity, social position, age, national origin, gender and sexual orientation, which are aggravated when those factors are combined and/or accumulated. In this respect, it is important to consider that, in the field of the economy and human rights, both States and their creditors have international and regional obligations that will be identified and systematized in the following sections.

It is worth mentioning that the approach presented in this document is not limited to the strict relation between 'debt and human rights', comprising not only the usual financial aspects of loan contracts, but also the broad and growing variety of conditionalities that International Financial Institutions (IFIs), especially the International Monetary Fund (IMF) (see chapters 9, 10 and 11), usually add to loans, including aspects of fiscal, budgeting, monetary, tax, exchange rate, social, labour, gender and environmental policies (Stubbs and Kentikelenis, 2021).

Principles related to borrower States

The Universal Declaration of Human Rights guarantees the right not to be discriminated against (Article 2), which was later broadened and specified in the two International Covenants of the international system. In the Inter-American system, both the American Convention on Human Rights (ACHR) and its Additional Protocol of ESCR expressly prohibit discrimination based on sex (Articles 1 and 3, respectively), to which was later added discrimination based on gender, gender identity, gender expression and sexual orientation (OC-24/17 on gender identity, p 35). This includes equal access to a group of human rights. The Inter-American Convention on the Prevention, Punishment and Eradication of Violence against Women guarantees the full exercise of all rights without violence.

Moreover, the Convention on the Elimination of All Forms of Discrimination against Women (CEDAW) requires States to adopt by all appropriate means and without delay a policy towards eliminating discrimination against women (Articles 2 and 3). The CEDAW Committee, which monitors the compliance of this convention, has addressed on several occasions the danger implied by the economic reforms that adopt policies contrary to gender equality.

A mapping of the situation shows that globalized macroeconomic and political factors, including the privatization of public assets, the unregulated labour markets, the shrinkage of the welfare state, and the austerity measures that are part of policies of structural adjustment and that are required as a condition of loans, often worsen unemployment and poverty, and result in economically unfair situations that disproportionally affect women. These fiscal contraction policies severely erode the capacity of States to execute social policies that can be used as a basis to eliminate structural inequalities, including gender inequality and violations of women's human rights in different areas (CEDAW Committee 2020: paragraph 3). Based on this, when making its Final Observations on Ecuador in 2021, this body noted with concern 'that the austerity measures adopted by the State party in an effort to consolidate public finances have had a disproportionate impact on women in all spheres of life' (paragraph 9).

The Beijing Declaration and Platform of Action of 1995 already proposed an economic agenda of reforms from a feminist perspective. One of its most important strategic goals was to adopt macroeconomic policies and development strategies focused on women and it included a series of specific measures to reduce poverty and economic inequality. Some of those measures targeted multilateral financial and development institutions, including the World Bank, the IMF, and regional development institutions, and others targeted bilateral cooperation (point 59). Furthermore, the recent position document of the XV Regional Conference on Women in Latin America and the Caribbean (2022), the main intergovernmental forum on women's rights and gender equality in Latin America, emphasizes that the high level of indebtedness of countries is part of the trend towards the financialization of economies, which is translated into the growing indebtedness of people and particularly women, which is called 'feminization of debt' (ECLAC, 2022b: 151). It is worth mentioning that in order to achieve sustainable and inclusive development, gender inequality is one of the most important gaps that must be closed, and that the care economy is essential to boost growth dynamics, reduce gender inequalities and facilitate the incorporation of women in the labour market (ECLAC, 2022b: 13).

Based on this integrated regulatory framework, international human rights law has been developing and consolidating legal standards specifically in terms of economic policies, public debt and its potential impact on human rights. The International Covenant on Economic, Social and Cultural Rights (ICESCR) sets forth that States shall allocate up to the maximum of their available resources to ensure the progressive development of ESCR and the continuous improvement of living conditions (Articles 2 and 11). Besides, the obligation of progressiveness results in the prohibition of regressiveness, both in terms of the regulatory scope of rights and the results of the public policies that are implemented for its fulfilment. The ACHR and the Protocol of San Salvador offer similar provisions (Articles 26 and 1, respectively).

Before continuing, it is necessary to clarify two aspects of the principles recently mentioned when they are construed with a gender perspective. On the one hand, the CEDAW does not refer to the progressiveness of rights; therefore, women's rights related to equality and non–discrimination (even when ESCR and the availability of economic resources are at stake) shall be understood as State obligations of immediate compliance (CEDAW, 2010: paragraph 29; CESCR Committee, 2009: paragraph 13); an interpretation reinforced by the *pro personae* interpretative principle (Pinto, 1997).

On the other hand, the standard of continuous improvement of living conditions (Article 11, ICESCR) does not exclusively refer to material aspects, but also to the extra–economic ones, and the conditions for social reproduction is one of them (Goldblatt, 2021); or, its legal translation: the right to care (Pautassi, 2018). This right, which is key to eliminate one of the decisive factors for women's oppression, the unfair gender division of work, has been recognized and developed in different international and regional instances, including the Beijing Platform of Action (1995), the Brasilia Consensus (2010), the Inter-American Convention on Protecting the Human Rights of Older Persons (2015), the Montevideo Strategy (2016) and, more recently, the Buenos Aires Commitment (2022).

In the area of sovereign debt specifically, it is worth mentioning that the principle of debt sustainability exceeds the traditional fiscal criteria such as the ones the IMF and the World Bank use. These agencies focus on achieving a debt rate of change compatible with the expansion of the economy and fiscal resources in order to guarantee the possibility of repayment (whether cancellation takes place or not). However, the debt cannot be considered as sustainable if its repayment requires sacrificing human rights, in particular, the human rights of the most disadvantaged and discriminated social sectors, such as women.

This broad principle of debt sustainability has been reflected in a number of official documents passed by political bodies of the UN system, including: the 'Guiding principles of external debt and human rights' (paragraphs 48 et seq), approved by the Human Rights Council in 2011 (A/HRC/20/23); the 'Basic principles on sovereign debt restructuring processes' (Article 8), approved by the General Assembly in 2015 (A/69/L.84); and the 'Guiding principles on human rights impact assessments of economic reforms' (hereinafter referred to as *Guiding Principles*) (Article 12), approved by the Human Rights Council in 2019 (A/HRC/40/57).

It is also worth mentioning that the maximum allocation of available resources limits the options of economic policy. Measures and reforms in the economic field that have a regressive effect on human rights in general (typically, orthodox economic policies – austerity and fiscal consolidation, privatizations, exchange rate deregulation and labour flexibility, among others) and, especially, those with disproportionate effects on women's rights, even more if there are cumulative and intersectional situations of discrimination and inequality, may be considered, prima facie, as violating the prohibition to discriminate based on gender (Independent Expert on Debt and Human Rights, 2019).

In this regard, several treaty bodies have claimed that policies of fiscal adjustment and austerity measures that are often included in IFI loans have a negative and disproportionate impact on women's rights, both ESCR and civil and political ones. In this context, it can frequently be seen how policies of fiscal adjustment have particularly severe consequences for women in terms of overload of care tasks. In this respect, it is worth mentioning that the reduction of services and social expenditure differentially impacts on women as domestic and care work is mostly done by them. This is a nodal issue because the unfair division of domestic and care work between men and women is at the centre of the discussion, and keeps and reinforces the situation of oppression and structural discrimination. The CEDAW Committee (2020) has expressed that 'reduced social expenditure further shifts the responsibilities for basic social services from the Government to women. Those factors reinforce, and are perpetuated by, discriminatory cultural and social norms that engender the oppression of various groups of women' (paragraph 3).

In this same direction, the CESCR (2016: paragraph 2) stated that:

> reductions in the levels of public services or the introduction of or increase in user fees in areas such as childcare, and preschool education, public utilities and family support services have a disproportionate impact on women, and thus may amount to a step backwards in terms of gender equality. (Articles 3 and 10)

Thus States have the obligation to manage their fiscal policies and to adopt economic policies, ensuring they respect, protect and enforce all human rights, including gender equality from an intersectional and intercultural perspective (Inter-American Commission on Human Rights – IACHR – 2017 and 2018). Resource generation and mobilization must come with coherence and consistency among economic, financial, monetary, social and gender policies (Guiding Principle 11) precisely in line with vast case law of the bodies of the international system, as well as the Inter-American system of human rights, including the Inter-American Court of Human Rights (ICHR) that particularly protects the rights of people in a situation of structural inequality, including women.[1]

However, there are economic situations where resource shortage is a fact and where an emergency may force governments to adopt measures to protect resources and assets that in the long term will be used to protect and enforce human rights, but which in the short term are adversely affected. This is typically the argument used to defend policies of fiscal austerity; sacrificing in the present for a more promising future. However, measures that may cause setbacks in the exercise of those rights are only allowed if States can show that those regressive measures are temporary, legitimate, reasonable, necessary, proportional and non-discriminatory, that they protect the minimum content of social rights, that they are based on transparency and the genuine participation of affected groups, and that they are subject to proceedings of review and accountability (CESCR, 2007, 2012, 2016 and 2018; Guiding Principles, Article 10). This way regressive measures can be compatible with the international framework of human rights only as an exception.

Principles related to creditors

Both public and private creditors have international and regional obligations regarding human rights that include considerations with a gender perspective and particularly involve the field of sovereign debt.

In general, IFIs are self-perceived as being above human rights. However, IFIs are not and could never be above human rights; actually, no State or non-State actor, either national or supranational, could aspire to ignore international human rights law without a negative legal consequence (Bohoslavsky and Cantamutto, 2022).

Even when IFIs, under their own statutes, cannot make political considerations in the course of their duties, it would be problematic to claim that the violation of human rights may be part of 'domestic jurisdiction' (Article 2[7] of the United Nations Charter). In fact, although it is seldom mentioned, the IMF and the World Bank are specialized agencies of the United Nations and, therefore, they must act in accordance with the UN Charter that recognizes human rights as one of its pillars and, in case of conflict, the obligations imposed by the Charter prevail (compare Article 103). In more general terms, as international agencies, IFIs are clearly subject to international law. The CESCR (2016) has highlighted that IFIs and other international organizations are 'bound by any obligations incumbent upon them under general rules of international law, under their constitutions or under international agreements to which they are parties'. This body also specified that those organizations 'are therefore obligated to comply with human rights, as listed in particular in the Universal Declaration of Human Rights, that are part of customary international law or of the general principles of law, both of which are sources of international law' (CESCR, 2016).

Moreover, the ICESCR emphasizes the obligation of the international community to cooperate with the enforcement of ESCR. This way States could not ignore their international obligations by simply creating an international organization that acts on behalf of them. From another perspective, IFIs are formed by States that are obliged to respect human rights and, therefore, they are responsible for the actions taken by the agency (CESCR, 2016).

With regards to the obligations of private creditors, and under Guiding Principle 16, when negotiating transactions with States or other public entities, that kind of creditor shall not erode the capacity of States to respect, protect and comply with their obligations regarding human rights (Guiding Principles on Business and Human Rights, 2011). These creditors shall assess the effects of their own actions and the activities they fund on human rights and gender equality.

3. Specific obligations of debtors and creditors

As results of the principles presented in the two previous subsections, here the specific obligations of creditors and debtors are described, which are not suspended in situations of debt crisis; on the contrary, they take special effect in those critical contexts precisely because the imminent threat on human rights is bigger in those extraordinary contexts.

First of all, debtor States must adopt a comprehensive and gender equality-responsive approach when addressing economic and financial policies; this obligation is also in force in situations of financial vulnerability. The CEDAW Committee (2013) recommended Greece that

> due to the seriousness of the situation and lack of any gender-sensitive approach to the current crisis policy within the State party, the Committee recommends that all important policymakers in Greece, including the European Union institutions and the IMF, cooperate in setting up an observatory to fully evaluate the impact on women of the many measures taken during the economic and financial crisis. (CEDAW Committee, 2013: paragraph 40)

Likewise, as in times of crisis and fiscal restrictions when States often limit social benefits and services, the CEDAW Committee has emphasized the state duty to proceed precisely in the opposite direction, redirecting resources and social investment to avoid damaging and disproportionate effects on women. This body has been consistent in expressing to several countries, including Ecuador (CEDAW, 2021: paragraph 9), Italy (CEDAW, 2017: paragraph 9) and Spain (CEDAW, 2015: paragraph 8), that even in times of fiscal pressure and an economic crisis they must adopt specific initiatives to promote women's rights, keep and extend social investment and protection, and include a gender perspective in policies and programmes, focusing on disadvantaged and marginalized groups of women, and trying to avoid regressive measures.

Likewise, as regards Greece, the CEDAW (2013: paragraph 6) has said that, even in times of fiscal limitations and an economic crisis, special efforts shall be made to respect human rights, keep and extend social investment and protection and use an approach that considers gender, giving priority to women in vulnerable situations.

In this context, it is worth mentioning that the principle of maximum resource allocation has a significant implication in the field of sovereign debt and human rights. First of all, it obliges all States to consider if payments made to repay the principal and interest of public debt, as well as related extra monetary commitments (conditionalities), do not negatively affect the exercise of human rights, including the prohibition to discriminate based on gender (CESCR, 1990 and 2017). How much can be paid of a debt to the detriment of other priorities directly linked to human rights, in particular, when effects are disproportionately damaging and regressive for certain social sectors, such as women?

An essential sub-question in this discussion is how many available resources of the State, in other words, how much of the content of the 'basket of resources', is formed by variables under the domestic control of the State (Kendrick, 2017). It is not the same that the fiscal restriction comes from the unwillingness of other States to comply with the duty of international cooperation through granting debt relief due to debt insolvency if it results from the free implementation of a strategy of debt that affects rights or the implementation of regressive or ineffective tax regimes when it comes to fiscal fraud.

In this respect, internal redistribution of resources shall be ensured for social inclusion and gender equality. In terms of proactive measures to be adopted in situations of economic crises and to face resource shortage, the CEDAW Committee has outlined the duty of States to make reforms that imply an internal redistribution of resources so as to avoid affecting rights and cutbacks of public expenditure in sensible areas for women's rights. Thus it has recommended the State of Ecuador (2021) to enable an internal redistribution of resources that can overcome the consequences of the financial crisis, prioritizing initiatives that foster social inclusion and gender equality. It even recommended adopting measures to correct preexisting gender inequalities that place women and girls in the centre of a recovery strategy in accordance with the 2030 Sustainable Development Agenda, focusing on unemployed women and those living in poverty, women from ethnic minorities, indigenous women, elder women, women with disabilities, migrant women, refugee women and those requesting asylum, lesbians, bisexual women and transgender and intersex persons. Likewise, it held that Suriname shall ensure 'ensure the internal redistribution of its national resources to overcome the consequences of budget cuts and ensure women's access to social benefits and microfinance and microcredit schemes at low interest rates' (CEDAW, 2018: paragraph 41; and 2017b: paragraph 38a). This redistribution obligation implies creating progressive tax regimes, that is to say, relying less on consumption taxes and more on direct taxes, and taxing the largest revenues and fortunes, as well as the effective fight against fiscal fraud.

Consequently, creditors (and in particular IFIs) shall not promote – let alone request – that client States implement economic policies and measures that violate the principles of human rights of their own populations; otherwise, those creditors would incur accountability for complicity in the violation of human rights. Moreover, States shall develop budgets (that include indebtedness and repayment) with a gender perspective. In this regard, in 2018 the CESCR (2018) specified that Argentina must 'adopt and implement the national budget while making every effort to avoid retrogressive measures, and ensure that the budget reflects a human rights and gender-sensitive approach' (paragraph C.6.d).

An additional requirement of strategic importance is to carry out assessments of debt effects and conditionalities on women's rights by governments and IFIs (Guiding Principle 15.1) so as to ensure that the capacity of the borrower State to respect, protect and comply with its obligations regarding human rights is not undermined. One of the main elements of the human rights approach is to assess if, how and to what extent economic policies affect women's rights and the rights of LGBTIQ+ persons. Such assessment shall be carried out assuming the inherent value of gender equality and not with an instrumentalist approach to the services of purely fiscal purposes.[2] Likewise, these analyses shall assume the transformative nature of economic policies, instead of a mere compensatory role considering the worsening that those policies replicate on structural gender inequalities.

A related obligation consists in ensuring effective participation and access to information. Both States and IFIs must pursue the broadest national dialogue possible with the effective, timely and significant participation of all persons and groups, including the groups in a disadvantaged situation and those who are particularly at risk of being affected by the policies to be implemented (Guiding Principle 19.1). Likewise, access to information and transparency must be ensured, as well as the access to justice and accountability (Guiding Principles 20 and 21).

As to creditors specifically, the good faith participation in restructuring processes includes debt relief (such as debt forgiveness or swap, debt rescheduling, debt service reduction and late payment interest) that is necessary and proportional to ensure the provision of public services that guarantee the basic human rights of the population.

4. Concluding reflections

In the last decade, international human rights law has been addressing in a more or less systematic way the impact of public indebtedness and the related conditionalities on the human rights of populations, especially in developing countries with high levels of indebtedness. Specific principles and standards have been developed and systematized, resulting from the current regulatory framework, that try to regulate the actions of States, creditors and IFIs so as to avoid and address adverse consequences in the field of human rights and debt, including from a gender perspective.

Today there is a set of principles and rules of conduct that allocates responsibilities and thus shows a path to be followed, a roadmap to seriously consider human rights with a gender perspective in the field of economy in general and sovereign debt management in particular. Evidently, if the human rights approach is taken seriously, it has the potential to revert and minimize the selective and opportunistic use by financial actors of one of the most important state infrastructures: the legal system (Pistor, 2022).

The international system for the protection of human rights is the most developed one in terms of legal accuracies and responsibility allocation, while the Inter-American system is still significantly underdeveloped in the specific field of debt and human rights. This is an urgent task due to the very high levels of indebtedness after the pandemic that numerous countries of the region have, and the persistent inequalities, including gender inequalities.

There exist specific duties both for debtors and creditors. For instance, regarding impact assessments of debt policy on human rights – including the differential impacts by gender and other relevant factors – and the design of gender-responsive budgeting, and the enforceability of proportional debt forgiveness in order not to excessively erode the fiscal space to the point of affecting the capacity of the State to guarantee the basic rights of the population. A pending aspect is the development of more sophisticated gender indicators in the analyses of debt sustainability that enable the promotion of solutions to debt distress and ensure the resources for an equal transformation (ECLAC, 2022b: paragraph 30).

Besides, States are required to redistribute internal resources through the adoption of progressive tax measures that tax the largest revenues and wealth, and not consumption. In the context of a crisis, adopting regressive measures on rights, including gender equality, will only be valid as an exception. In fact, in those extraordinary contexts, the State duty to strengthen investment in services and social and care benefits reappears, instead of cutting it as is usually the case.

More widely, the mainstreaming of the gender approach in macroeconomic policies in general, including fiscal and public debt ones, is essential to prevent women from being the ones that cushion the effects of multiple crises through the intensification of unpaid domestic and care work (ECLAC, 2022b).

A challenge in this field is to ensure consistency of policies (economic, social, monetary, gender-based, fiscal and so on), including the public debt policy (Guiding Principles 11.e). For that purpose, it is necessary to create and implement an expansion of the institutionalization of feminist demands toward the field of public finances that guarantees a gender perspective in this area.[3] This challenge also includes imposing limits to IFIs, particularly the IMF, which with the so-called 'gender strategy' deepens – instead of relieves – public debt profiles that replicate inequalities against women.[4]

Regarding the deficit of participation of women and LGBTIQ+ persons in the processes of indebtedness and public debt management, this chapter proposes measuring such participation. The CEDAW Committee could develop an indicator to show the extent to which such participation of women and LGBTIQ+ persons is guaranteed (intention) in national legislative branches and what the actual effects (practices) of those rules are, all of which could be perfectly incorporated, and even quantified, in a 'Gender Legislative Index' (Vijeyarasa, 2021).

Lastly, the need to build broader consensus among countries regarding specific institutional rules in the field of debt rescheduling persists; in particular, it is necessary to resume the decision the United Nations General Assembly adopted in 2015 as to the creation of a multilateral legal framework that regulates the processes of sovereign debt and makes them compatible with the obligations and international rules of human rights, including gender equality (Res. A/ RES/68/304, 09/09/2014; see Rossi, 2020). The creation of a widely agreed regime in the field of debt rescheduling constitutes, along with some other structural changes, a part of the necessary feminist reforms in the field of international financial architecture,[5] and the equal transformation of societies depends on its existence.

Acknowledgements

The authors would like to thank Julieta Levín (a lawyer graduated from the University of Buenos Aires and an assistant of the course International

Human Rights Law in the Law School of the University of Buenos Aires) for the invaluable research for this chapter.

Notes

[1] Regarding the right to equality and non-discrimination from a substantive approach, the ICHR has said: 'States shall adopt positive measures to revert or change existing discriminatory situations in their societies with respect to certain groups of people that are in a situation of exclusion or marginalization, including measures in terms of third-party acts and practices' [ICHR (2020), case *Empleados de la Fábrica de Fuegos de San Antonio de Jesus y sus familiares vs Brasil*]. In the same sense, see ICHR (2013); *Comunidades afrodescendientes desplazadas de la cuenca del río Cacarica (Operación Génesis) vs Colombia*, paragraph 352; ICHR (2012) *Masacre de Santo Domingo vs Colombia*, paragraph 273; ICHR (2016), *Trabajadores de la Hacienda Brasil Verde vs. Brasil*, paragraph 336–8.

[2] See chapters 2 and 9 in this book.

[3] See chapter 20 in this book.

[4] See chapter 9 in this book.

[5] See chapter 18 in this book.

References

Bibliography

Aldao, M. and Clérico, L. (2022) 'Transformative constitutionalism and state capture. Challenging business operations through human rights', in A. von Bogdandy, J. Schönsteiner, R. Urueña and C.E. Franz (eds), *Transformative Constitutionalism and International Economic Law in Latin America* (forthcoming).

Bohoslavsky, J.P. and Cantamutto, F. (2022) 'Not even with a pandemic: The IMF, human rights, and rational choices under power relations', *Human Rights Quarterly*, 44(4): 759–83.

Bohoslavsky, J.P. and Clérico, L. (2023) 'El sistema interamericano de derechos humanos y el problema de la deuda' in F. Cantamutto (ed), *Dinámica y reestructuraciones de la deuda argentina, 1998–2019*, Bahia Blanca: Editorial de la Universidad Nacional del Sur, pp 92–108.

Goldblatt, B. (2021) 'The work of living: Social reproduction and the right to the continuous improvement of living conditions' in J. Hohmann and B. Goldblatt (eds), *The Right to the Continuous Improvement of Living Conditions. Responding to Complex Global Challenges*, Oxford: Hart, pp 205–24.

Kendrick, A. (2017) 'Measuring compliance: Social rights and the maximum available resources dilemma', *Human Rights Quarterly*, 9(3): 657–79.

Pautassi, L. (2018) 'El cuidado como derecho. Un camino virtuoso, un desafío inmediato', *Revista de la Facultad de Derecho de México*, LXVIII(272): 717–42.

Pinto, M. (1997) 'El principio pro homine. Criterios de hermenéutica y pautas para la regulación de los derechos humanos' in M. Abregú (ed), *La aplicación de los tratados sobre derechos humanos por los tribunales locales*, Buenos Aires: CELS, pp 163–97.

Pistor, K. (2022) 'The rise of autonomous financial power' in B. Braun and K. Koddenbrock (eds), *Capital Claims: Power and Global Finance*, London: Routledge, chapter 15.

Rossi, J. (2020) 'Los procesos de restructuración de deudas soberanas y los derechos humanos. La necesidad de un marco jurídico internacional', *Jurisprudencia Argentina*, Special Edition, Derecho Internacional de los Derechos Humanos (director: Rolando Gialdino), 2020-II, Fasc. 3, Abeledo Perrot, Buenos Aires, pp 59–86.

Stubbs, T. and Kentikelenis, A. (2021) 'Condicionalidad y deuda soberana: Un panorama general de sus implicancias en los derechos humanos', *Revista Derechos en Acción*, 18(18): 173–215.

Vijeyarasa, R. (2021) 'Quantifying CEDAW: Concrete tools for enhancing accountability for women's rights', *Harvard Human Rights Journal*, 34: 37–80.

Legal documents

CEDAW (2010) 'General recommendation No. 28 on the core obligations of States parties under article 2 of the Convention on the Elimination of All Forms of Discrimination against Women' (CEDAW/C/GC/28).

CEDAW (2013) 'Concluding observations on the seventh periodic report of Grecia' (CEDAW/C/GRC/CO/7).

CEDAW (2015) 'Concluding observations on the seventh and eighth combined periodic report of Spain' (CEDAW/C/ESP/CO/7-8).

CEDAW (2017) 'Concluding observations on the seventh periodic report of Italia' (CEDAW/C/ITA/CO/7).

CEDAW (2018) 'Concluding observations on the fourth to sixth combined periodic reports of Surinam' (CEDAW/C/SUR/CO/4-6).

CEDAW (2020) 'General recommendation No. 38 (2020) on trafficking in women and girls in the context of global migration' (CEDAW/C/GC/38).

CEDAW (2021) 'Concluding observations on the tenth periodic report of Ecuador' (CEDAW/C/ECU/CO/10).

CESCR (1990) 'General Comment 3, The nature of States parties' obligations (article 2, paragraph 1, of the Covenant)' (CESCR, without number).

CESCR (2007) 'General Comment 19, The right to social security (article 9)' (CESCR, E/C.12/GC/19).

CESCR (2009) 'General Comment 20, Non discrimination in economic, social and cultural rights (article 2, paragraph 2, of the Covenant)' (CESCR, E/C.12/GC/20)

CESCR (2012) 'Letter to States Parties from President of the CESCR on the context of economic and financial crisis' (16 May).

CESCR (2015) 'Concluding Observations on the fifth periodic report of Italy' (CESCR, E/C.12/ITA/CO/5).

CESCR (2016) 'Statement on Public Debt, austerity measures and the ICESC' (CESCR, E/C.12/2016/1).

CESCR (2017) 'General comment No. 24 (2017) on State obligations under the International Covenant on Economic, Social and Cultural Rights in the context of business activities' (CESCR, E/C.12/GC/24).

CESCR (2018) 'Concluding observations on the fourth periodic report on Argentina' (CESCR, E/C.12/ARG/CO/4).

ECLAC (2022a) 'The care society: A horizon for sustainable recovery with gender equality' (LC/CRM.15/3), Santiago (document prepared in the context of the XV Regional Conference on Women in Latin America and the Caribbean).

ECLAC (2022b) 'Compromiso Buenos Aires. Decimoquinta Conferencia Regional sobre la Mujer de América Latina y el Caribe'.

Independent Expert on Debt and Human Rights (2019) 'Impact of economic reforms and austerity measures on women's human rights', Human Rights Council, A/73/179

IACHR (2017) 'Report on Poverty and Human Rights in the Americas' (OEA/Ser.L/V/II.164).

IACHR (2018) 'Public policy with a human rights approach' (OAS/Ser.L/V/II00).

ICHR (2012) *Santo Domingo Massacre vs Colombia. Preliminary objections, merits, reparations and costs.*

ICHR (2013) *Afro-descendant Communities Displaced from the Cacarica River Basin (Operación Génesis) vs Colombia. Preliminary objections, merits, reparations and costs.*

ICHR (2016) *Hacienda Brasil Verde Workers vs Brasil. Preliminary objections, merits, reparations and costs.*

ICHR (2017) 'Advisory Opinion OC-24/17, Gender identity, and equality and nondiscrimination of same-sex couples'.

ICHR (2020) *Empleados de la Fábrica de Fuegos en Santo Antônio de Jesus y sus familiares vs Brasil, Preliminary Objections, Merits, Reparations and Costs.*

United Nations Digital Library (2011) *Guiding Principles on Business and Human Rights : Implementing the United Nations "Protect, Respect and Remedy" Framework*, Available from: https://digitallibrary.un.org/record/720245?ln=es

World Conference on Women (4th) (1995) '*Beijing Declaration and Platform for Action*'.

6

Letter from UN Special Procedures to the IMF (2022)

Editors' note

The United Nations Human Rights Council has in place the 'special procedures' system, exercised by independent human rights experts. These Independent Experts and Special Rapporteurs have specific mandates to investigate, report, denounce and make recommendations from thematic or country perspectives. As of 2023, 45 thematic mandates and 14 country mandates are in force.

Mandate holders carry out country visits, contribute to the development of international human rights standards, engage in human rights advocacy and awareness-raising, and provide technical advice, as well as act on concrete and specific situations by submitting communications to States and other actors requesting information in order to formulate recommendations. In March 2022, four mandate holders submitted a letter to Kristalina Georgieva (Managing Director of the International Monetary Fund [IMF]) as part of the IMF's ongoing consultations on its announced 'gender strategy'.

The UN special mandate holders who submitted the letter were: Attiya Waris (Independent Expert on foreign debt and human rights), Saad Alfarargi (Special Rapporteur on the right to development), Olivier De Schutter (Special Rapporteur on extreme poverty and human rights) and Melissa Upreti (in her capacity as Chair of the Working Group on discrimination against women and girls).

With the aim to enrich the discussions on debt and women's rights, the full letter is presented below. One year after it was submitted, as of March 2024, the letter had not yet been responded to by the IMF.

PALAIS DES NATIONS • 1211 GENEVA 10, SWITZERLAND
Mandates of the Independent Expert on the effects of foreign debt and other related international financial obligations of States on the

full enjoyment of all human rights, particularly economic, social and cultural rights; the Special Rapporteur on the right to development; the Special Rapporteur on extreme poverty and human rights and the Working Group on discrimination against women and girls

Ref.: OL OTH 16/2022
(Please use this reference in your reply)

2 March 2022

Dear Ms. Georgieva,

We have the honour to address you in our capacity as Independent Expert on the effects of foreign debt and other related international financial obligations of States on the full enjoyment of all human rights, particularly economic, social and cultural rights; Special Rapporteur on the right to development; Special Rapporteur on extreme poverty and human rights and Working Group on discrimination against women and girls, pursuant to Human Rights Council resolutions 34/3, 42/23, 44/13 and 41/6.

In the context of the current consultations that the International Monetary Fund (IMF) is conducting on its institutional strategy on gender, we would like to seize this opportunity to provide some initial reflections from a human rights perspective before the strategy is presented to the IMF's Board this spring. Our mandates have examined the potentially harmful consequences of gender-blind economic policies and issued recommendations that could inform your strategy and country specific actions, since we also conduct country visits.

We welcome the IMF's initiative to develop a gender strategy that could positively impact women and girls' human rights in the context of its surveillance, lending and capacity development programmes. This step is greatly needed given the current challenges women and girls face in the context of the COVID-19 pandemic and growing backlashes against gender equality, the debt crisis and climate change.

We have noted the inclusion of references to gender-disaggregated data and gender budgeting and expanding the collaboration with other organizations as part of the critical elements of the proposed gender strategy. According to the concept note on the strategy, it will "not consider all aspects of gender issues" and will be "focusing on the macro-criticality of gender gaps, in accordance with the Fund's mandate". While we are fully aware of the IMF's mandate, we would like to stress the interrelatedness and indivisibility of all human rights. As documented by the UN Working Group on discrimination against women and girls, among the many obstacles to gender equality that women and girls face, the most significant challenges remain in the areas of family, culture and sexual and reproductive rights and are those in which there has been a backlash against gains in women's equality. The Working Group regrets that women's economic empowerment and political participation are too often tackled as isolated issues. The interdependence of human rights cannot be overlooked: persistent discrimination in family, cultural and sexual and reproductive rights have a debilitating impact on women's capacity to claim equal standing in all aspects of life. This selective approach towards discrimination against women is an unfortunate practice and is a core problem affecting the way gender equality is addressed and a major obstacle to sustainable progress. Without eliminating discrimination in family, cultural and sexual and reproductive rights, there will be no lasting progress in the other fields (see HRC/38/46).

Furthermore, we would like to stress the importance of ensuring that all IMF staff have the necessary skills and capacity to genuinely mainstream gender issues throughout their work and the need for integration of a gender perspective taking an intersectional approach in terms of substance and process. Macroeconomic policy has an androcentric bias that needs to be addressed on a substantive and definitional level. Women are typically excluded from these processes which leads to their concerns and perspectives being ignored.

We acknowledge the efforts made by the IMF since 2015 to incorporate gender in its work. In that regard, the systematization of experiences issued in the 2018 IMF's paper, "How to operationalize gender issues in-country work", recognizes that macroeconomic policy advice provided by the IMF can deepen gender inequalities and that micro-funded analysis has allowed country teams in the field to measure the specific consequences that fiscal and tax policy recommendations can have on women and girls.

Nonetheless, we regret that the IMF's prescription of austerity measures has affected public investment in areas of particular concern for women and girls. A gender strategy that benefits women and girls in the fulfilment of their human rights could only be achieved if: a) the procedure for the development of the strategy respects a human rights-based approach and; b) the substantive contents reflect gender roles and women and girls different needs (A/73/179). Women and girls are half the world's population, therefore, each and every policy, strategy and operations of the IMF should be gender responsive. Adding a gender strategy to a host of other strategies and an operating system which are gender-blind will not help address the needs of women and girls and end the systemic drivers of their disadvantage and exploitation.

We would like to underscore the importance of the IMF prioritizing the adoption of a fully gender-responsive strategy which would require integrating goals and methods of work that take into account not only systemic biases and the disadvantages that they produce but also the ideologically motivated backlash against gender equality at the heart of which lies an attempt to enforce gendered roles, which are unfortunately often reinforced by gender blind economic policies.

In this regard, the COVID 19 pandemic has increased the effects already observed by the Independent Expert on the effects of foreign debt in the reports to the Human Rights Council and General Assembly as restriction over protection policies against gender-based violence, daily care policies, and the public health sector during the COVID pandemic response and aftermath affected women and girls directly. For example, cuts to contraceptive supplies in the public sector could increase unintended pregnancy and trigger unsafe abortion. Likewise, austerity measures that affect social housing, and shortcuts in programmes that provide shelter to escape domestic violence, exacerbate the constraints women face for autonomy. (see A/73/179).

An IMF gender strategy that includes a human rights approach should recognize and address the differentiated roles of women and girls in our societies and the constraints they face because of their sex and gender. Women's role as unpaid caretakers is reflected in the kind and quality of employment they access. Women are generally segregated to the lower-paid jobs and the informal economy. Also, jobs that are dominated by women, like domestic workers, are largely overrepresented in the informal sector. As a result, when social insurance schemes are tied to work-related criteria, women often do not qualify as beneficiaries; contributory pension schemes, for example, have a differentiated impact on women. In addition, consumption taxes, especially VAT, have a regressive impact on low-income households, which often include female-headed households. This information should be considered when recommending tax measures, such as increases in VAT and other sales taxes, that could further shrink women's available income and reduce their purchasing power (see A/HRC/34/57).

Therefore, as stressed by the Independent Expert in these reports, austerity measures and other restrictive policies on public expenditure affect women and girls disproportionally because of a wide range of socio-economic reasons that could not be explained and analyzed only in terms of macroeconomic results or disparity in opportunities.

Vulnerability and economic disadvantage for women are exacerbated by macroeconomic policies that increase inequalities and reduce social protection floors. This is clearly visible in periods of economic crisis, particularly when governments adopt austerity measures. Although the specific effects of crisis differ by context, the overall picture is one of disparate impact on women, with deepening economic insecurity, an increase in precarious employment and a heavier burden of unpaid care work. Nonetheless, economic crisis merely accentuates existing structural economic disadvantages for women. Therefore, addressing the crisis provides an opportunity to tackle patterns of gender inequality and discrimination entrenched in the economic status quo and shape new gender equality responses. Alternatives to austerity have been applied successfully in some countries. Grounding development priorities in women's human rights is not only a legal and moral imperative but can also enhance effectiveness and accountability (A/HRC/26/39).

For these reasons, as stated by the Independent Expert on Foreign Debt, the IMF should ensure that loan programmes are agreed upon only after human rights with a precise gender dimension have been conducted and that any potential deficiencies are remedied; and that risks of negative impacts on women's human rights resulting from conditionalities, are monitored, and an alternative policy mix are proposed if adverse gendered implications are identified (see A/HRC/40/57).

In the same line, the Special Rapporteur on the right to development has recently stressed that tax policy advice and conditions issued by multilateral development banks and development finance institutions to States, and in particular to developing countries, should be reviewed to take into account their impact on women's income and work, including unpaid labour and unpaid care work, and property and assets ownership (A/75/167, para 60) and that in the framework of COVID recovery measures, the public–private partnerships promoted through loans, projects and other financing arrangements involving multilateral development finance institutions should be subject to independent reviews of their development outcomes, including a thorough examination of their human rights and environmental impacts (A/75/167, para 62). The Guidelines and Recommendations on the practical implementation of the right to development stress that international financial institutions should conduct systematic human rights impact assessments and monitor and evaluate their policies. In particular, human rights impact assessments should be conducted on austerity measures, structural adjustments, securities and trade and investment agreements; (A/HRC/42/38 para 131).

Furthermore, the International Covenant on Economic, Social and Cultural Rights establishes that States should ensure the progressive realization of economic, social and cultural rights by using the maximum of their available resources. Likewise, the Committee on the

Elimination of Discrimination against Women has clarified that those measures should aim to accelerate the achievement of gender equality and address "the structural, social and cultural changes necessary to correct past and current forms and effects of discrimination against women, as well as to provide them with compensation".

We would like to reiterate that the IMF gender strategy should support the full enjoyment of all women and girls' human rights. In the current context of persistent gender inequality and rollbacks which are being exacerbated by rising fundamentalisms of all kinds, coupled with political populism, unchecked authoritarian rule, disproportionate focus on corporate profits over human rights and most recently the devastating impact of the COVID-19 pandemic, the IMF gender strategy should ensure that it does not contribute to further retrogressions in progress made by women and girls in the last decades. We think that our various reports briefly referenced in this letter could support your gender mainstreaming efforts. In this regard, we remain available to continue engaging with the IMF and to engage into a constructive dialogue which could support the genuine and comprehensive inclusion of women and girls' rights in the strategy and throughout your work.

In terms of the current consultation process undertaken, the IMF should ensure public access to information and ample consultation in developing the strategy. In this regard, we welcome the online consultation opened by the IMF on 10 February, but we think that the timeframe proposed might be too tight for various concerned stakeholders to provide substantive contributions, in particular if the strategy is supposed to be presented to the IMF board this spring. In addition, to guarantee transparency, accountability and meaningful and informed consultations, a draft of the gender strategy document should be made available to allow for civil society, women organizations, and other actors to participate in the process. The IMF could also establish an accountability mechanism to inform and promote the participation of women, girls and stakeholders during the development and implementation of the gender strategy.

In conclusion, and without prejudging the current process that the IMF is undertaking to develop its gender strategy, according to the responsibilities of our mandates, and on the basis of the reports mentioned above, we would be grateful for your observations on the following matters:

1. Please clarify how the gender strategy will ensure that all IMF programmes will benefit from a human rights impact assessment with a precise gender dimension and that any potential deficiencies are remedied.

2. Please clarify how the gender strategy will address the risks of negative impacts on women's and girls' human rights resulting from conditionalities, monitoring the effect of subsequent reforms and proposing an alternative policy mix if adverse gendered implications from the proposed conditionalities are identified.

3. Please clarify how the gender strategy will ensure that public investment, including in social and physical infrastructure, is guaranteed so that it supports the realization of women's and girls' human rights.

4. Please clarify how the gender strategy will address taxation and ensure that measures and mechanisms lead to more effective redistribution of resources between women and men.

5. Please clarify how the gender strategy establishes a transparent accountability mechanism to guarantee that the strategy is consulted, monitored, and evaluated with all interested parties' participation.

We would like to inform you that this communication will be made public via the communications reporting website after 48 hours, as well as any response received from your institution. They will also subsequently be made available in the usual report to be presented to the Human Rights Council.

Please accept, Ms. Georgieva, the assurances of our highest consideration.

Attiya Waris
Independent Expert on the effects of foreign debt and other related international financial obligations of States on the full enjoyment of all human rights, particularly economic, social and cultural rights
Saad Alfarargi
Special Rapporteur on the right to development
Olivier De Schutter
Special Rapporteur on extreme poverty and human rights
Melissa Upreti
Chair-Rapporteur of the Working Group on discrimination against women and girls

7

Impact of Debt on Women's and Girls' Human Rights – Introduction to the 2023 Report of the UN Working Group on Discrimination Against Women and Girls, 'Gendered Inequalities of Poverty: Feminist and Human Rights-Based Approaches'

Dorothy Estrada-Tanck

Introduction to the UN Working Group's work. The report in context

In order to put the relevance of an official report addressing debt and women's human rights into perspective, this short note will present what the Working Group does and its role in the international human rights protection system, a holistic understanding of poverty and inequality through a gender lens and the deep gender implications of debt.

The baseline is that women and girls everywhere are still subject to significant disadvantage as the result of discriminatory laws and practices. Full equality has not been achieved in any country in the world, and several pledges to eliminate discrimination have not been fulfilled.

In this context, the establishment of the Working Group on discrimination against women and girls (WGDAWG)[1] by the United Nations (UN) Human Rights Council in 2010[2] was a milestone on the long road towards women's equality with men. It is based on the recognition that while there have been many legal and policy reforms to integrate women's human rights fully into domestic law over the years, progress remains insufficient. Discrimination against women and girls persists in both public and private spheres – in times of conflict and in peace. It transcends national, cultural and religious boundaries. It is often fuelled by patriarchal stereotyping and power imbalances which are mirrored in laws, policies and practices.

The WGDAWG is composed of five independent experts of balanced geographical representation, working collectively as a group, and producing work in the name of the mandate.[3] The Working Group, in establishing its conceptual framework and working methods, stresses that the elimination of discrimination against women in law and in practice requires a comprehensive and coherent human rights-based approach. This approach ensures that women are at the centre of efforts to hold States accountable for implementing international standards guaranteeing civil, political, economic, social and cultural rights.[4]

The elimination of discrimination against women and girls in all fields is addressed by the WGDAWG from the perspective of States' obligations to respect, protect and fulfil women's human rights. It emphasizes that national, regional and international human rights mechanisms, as well as grass-roots activists, play critical roles in ensuring the full enjoyment by women and girls of their human rights. For legal guarantees to benefit all women, implementation frameworks and strategies must be responsive to the intersections of gender-based discrimination with other grounds of discrimination. Indeed, the work of the Working Group covers all women, acknowledging that women are not a uniform group. Nevertheless, there are shared aspects of discrimination against women that persist in all cultures, although with differing levels of intensity and differing impacts.

Furthermore, there is a need to constantly reiterate, even within the human rights system, that women are not just another vulnerable group, as they are often treated by some. They are half of the world population and often the majority of each of the vulnerable groups, hence eliminating persistent discrimination and backlashes against women's rights should be addressed both as a stand-alone goal and as a mainstreaming issue.

To this end, the Working Group engages in constructive dialogue with member states, civil society stakeholders, UN entities, human rights mechanisms and different actors relevant to the realization of women's and girls' human rights. It does so by making full use of a common set of tools available to UN special procedures mandates, namely, communications,[5] annual thematic reports[6] and country visits.[7] In recent years, the content of the annual thematic reports has also been displayed in an interactive, summarized and more practical and user/child-friendly version, including graphics, in the Working Group's microsite (in English and Spanish).[8]

The Working Group also holds an interactive dialogue at the Human Rights Council during the June session on its thematic and country visits reports. It reports orally to the General Assembly in October/November and participates in the Commission on the Status of Women in March each year. Additionally, the WGDAWG undertakes other initiatives, including public statements,[9] amicus briefs,[10] position papers,[11] participation in events[12] and contributions to the work of others in the UN human rights machinery or UN entities. During 2023, the WGDAWG is Chair of the EDVAW Platform − the Platform of Independent Expert Mechanisms on the Elimination of Discrimination and Violence against Women. The EDVAW Platform was launched in March 2018. It is composed of seven UN and regional independent expert mechanisms dedicated to addressing discrimination and violence against women and girls, promoting accountability, and advancing their human rights.[13]

The 2023 annual thematic report of the WGDAWG builds on the previous thematic focus developed by the Working Group of advancing equality in rights and opportunities for women and girls in all areas, namely family and cultural life, economic and social life, political and public life, and safety and health, including sexual and reproductive health. It also reiterates the Working Group's calling, made since 2018,[14] for concerted efforts to counter rollbacks and the increasing attacks against the universality of women's human rights, and reasserts women's and girls' fundamental right to substantive equality, including socioeconomic equality. It is also in line with the arguments made and questions posed in the letter submitted in 2022 by the WGDAWG and other special procedures mandate holders to the International Monetary Fund (IMF) regarding its so-called 'gender strategy'.[15]

As such, in its 2023 report to the UN Human Rights Council, 'Gendered inequalities of poverty: feminist and human rights-based approaches',[16] the WGDAWG focuses on poverty and socioeconomic inequality as outcomes of systemic failures (at the core of which is found to be debt) that violate multiple human rights of women and girls. It analyses the crosscutting conditions of gendered socioeconomic inequality and examines the structural discrimination and drivers within political, economic, cultural and social systems that cause, perpetuate and deepen women's and girls' experiences of poverty and inequality. It draws attention to the deficiency of dominant economic models and methods for understanding, measuring and addressing poverty and inequalities to accurately capture their impact on the substantive equality of women and girls, and it highlights promising alternative approaches. The gender implications of debt cancellation are specifically analysed. Recommendations to States, and to international organizations and corporations, insist upon the urgency of reframing poverty and inequality within and between countries as issues of global concern that necessitate integrated responses informed by intersectional feminist and human rights-based approaches.[17]

Derived from this focus, this piece will concentrate on the parts of the 2023 report which primarily address the intersections of women's and girls' human rights with fiscal and debt policies. It will review the cumulative effects between both gender and socioeconomic inequalities and the heightened risks this creates for women and girls.

Based on this examination of the causes of structural discrimination against women and girls, it will illustrate the way in which macroeconomic policies, including debt policies, at the international and national levels generally lack a human rights-based approach and a gendered perspective, for example, ignoring the highly feminized activities of unpaid care work and domestic work, while lacking a methodology for the articulation of such policies that integrates women in decision-making; and it will also highlight the particular and often disproportionate impact on women and girls of orthodox economic policies that too often come with over-indebtedness.

Lastly, the text will include the recommendations of the WGDAWG's report to States and international and regional economic, financial and monetary institutions in relation to their multiple human rights obligations. A number of recommendations address, specifically, both sovereign debtors and their creditors. These concrete obligations must be understood under the 'umbrella' duty of such international and regional institutions, and their member states, to contribute to the creation of an enabling economic and financial environment for the promotion and protection of all human rights for all persons, in the spirit of Article 28 of the Universal Declaration of Human Rights, legally binding on the entire UN international system, and an essential cornerstone for human dignity, social justice and substantive equality for all women and girls.

WGDAWG Report on 'Gendered inequalities of poverty: feminist and human rights-based approaches' (selected paragraphs):

A. Contextual framework

12. The strengthened neoliberal turn of the last forty years, reflected in the policies of international economic institutions and national governments, has demonstrably increased poverty and inequality both between and within nations.[18] These inequalities, underpinned by patriarchy, slavery, racism, colonialism, militarism and environmental destruction, have been exacerbated by orthodox macroeconomic prescriptions, including structural adjustment and austerity measures[19] designed to offset crippling national debts,[20] the liberalisation of global

trade and the financialization of capital markets,[21] investment, monetary and fiscal regimes,[22] the privatization and commodification of public goods and the retreat of the welfare State.[23] While it is beyond the scope of this report to analyse these phenomena, it is important to highlight that rampant global socio-economic inequality, characterised by the concentration of wealth in the hands of a few people (the majority men), corporations in a limited number of countries, and developed States, has diminished the resources available for policies, services, and programs to advance women's rights and gender equality.[24]

... 15. Dominant approaches to security in times of crises, including economic crises, have also been narrow in scope, human rights being set aside, and disproportionately affecting women and girls. Understanding security integrally as grounded in human rights law,[25] would prioritise preventing and addressing aggravated risks of poverty and inequality for women and girls. In this respect, alongside its role in exacerbating existing inequalities, the Covid-19 crisis has also prompted a re-evaluation of mainstream economic ideologies, including recognition of the central role of care in our societies, as called for by feminists for years, as well as revaluing the State's position (vis-à-vis the market) as an actor in defining and resourcing public policies. The current moment, therefore, presents an opportunity to revisit concepts of unlimited economic growth, often based on deeply embedded forms of structural discrimination, transnational economic inequality, failure to fulfil international solidarity obligations of assistance and cooperation, and inexistent or insufficient networks of social protection and public services to guarantee universally recognized human rights such as health, water, housing, food and nutrition, education, a clean and healthy environment and access to justice.

16. Crucially, poverty and inequality are not inevitable. They are the result of structural discrimination that is reflected in the design of laws and policies which have facilitated present and historical injustices.[26] Social movements advocating for transformative change from the perspective of feminist political economy and human rights, particularly economic, social, environmental and cultural rights, have highlighted the feedback loops between global poverty and inequalities and they have drawn attention to the existence of alternatives to unjust economic and social policies and institutions.[27] These rights-based feminist approaches to inequality and poverty provide key insights, tools, accountability measures and remedies that would enable the structural determinants of poverty and inequality to be identified, challenged and overcome.

... 23. Several social movements are championing a feminist and decolonial Global Green New Deal which would entail a redistribution and revalidation of labour, and investments in the care sector as well as reimagining global public commons and goods so that they are used equitably and sustainably.[28] Feminist workers' alliances are also engaged in the development of alternative economic policies that would promote climate friendly jobs, including those in social care; fundamental rights at work that emphasise adequate wages and maximum hours of work; universal social protection with a global social protection solidarity fund; an emphasis on substantive gender, race and socioeconomic equality; and an inclusive agenda for peace and sustainable development.[29]

D. A feminist human rights-based economy: substantive equality, solidarity, socioeconomic and environmental justice

... 48. The right to be free from poverty cannot be realised in isolation from individual and collective rights to substantive equality.[30] The meaningful participation of diverse groups of women and girls in conceptualising, implementing, and monitoring socio-economic policies, norms and strategies is a core part of this process. The challenge is to move from non-discrimination as a vehicle for the protection of individual rights towards the realization of the relational and redistributive obligations that are also an integral but, as yet largely unrealised, part of international human rights law.[31]

49. The right to substantive equality requires resource mobilization and redistribution within and between countries. The obligations incumbent on States under the ICESCR, particularly its Article 2, and other human rights guarantees to realize economic, social and cultural rights 'to the maximum of their available resources' incorporates positive duties to progressively achieve the implementation of human rights and to seek external resources for that purpose.[32] The current moment of overlapping crises provides an opportunity to examine the human rights impacts of prevailing systems of global economic governance. The commitments made by States under Articles 1.1, 1.2, 5.1, 22 and 23 of the ICESCR, the Declaration on the Right to Development and within the framework of SDG 10, require wealthy countries to assist low-income countries in the realization of economic, social and cultural rights for everyone without discrimination and to cooperate to reduce inequalities between and within nations.[33]

Tax justice

50. As noted above, to fulfil their human rights obligations to reduce gender inequality and poverty, States must direct adequate public resources to comprehensive social protection systems and services. A key mechanism for the redistribution of resources is through proportional and progressive taxation. One of the hallmarks of neoliberal economic policies over the last few decades has been a decline in the fiscal contributions being made by large corporations and high-income earners, while indirect taxes with regressive distributional impacts, such as value added tax, have expanded.[34] In addition to lower direct taxes, illicit financial flows (IFFs) by multinational corporations are depriving countries in the Global South of up to 200 billion USD a year in lost fiscal revenues and failures to effectively curb tax evasion, trade misinvoicing, corruption and money laundering mean that there are fewer public resources available for equitable social and climate spending.[35]

51. Both regressive taxation frameworks and IFFs have a particularly pernicious impact on women and girls who account for a greater proportion of those living in poverty as a result of structural discrimination and who are more likely than men to be responsible for caring for other family members, or to be care-receivers, and are therefore in greater need of social protection and public services.[36] Tax justice, both nationally and globally, is a crucial mechanism for realizing human rights and for tackling socio-economic inequalities and poverty as governments require fiscal revenue to sustainably finance investments in public services, social protection and gender responsive infrastructure.[37] Feminist methodologies for fiscal reform emphasise the need for transparent, gender-responsive taxation frameworks that recognise women's indispensable labour in the economy and equitably redistribute resources from the wealthiest corporations and individuals to fund public provisioning.[38]

Debt cancellation

52. Debt cancellation is a prerequisite for just and human rights-based redistributive public policies. In 2021, in low-income countries, debt repayments represented 171% of all spending on healthcare, education and social protection combined and, in 2022, debt servicing amongst low-income countries globally was estimated at $43 billion.[39] If left unchecked, widespread, lasting debt crises in the wake of the Covid-19 pandemic have the potential to set the achievement of global development goals back by at least a decade.[40]

53. There are alternative models to indebtedness that would not result in increased inequalities through the adoption of austerity and fiscal consolidation measures that lead to reduced social expenditure and that have been shown to undermine the human rights of women and girls living in poverty. In recent years, more than 60 countries have successfully re-negotiated debts, and over 20 have defaulted or repudiated public debt, preferring to invest debt service savings in social programs.[41] Since the COVID-19 pandemic, the G20's Debt Service Suspension Initiative (DSSI) and the IMF's Catastrophe Containment and Relief Trust (CCRT) have provided some debt service relief to highly indebted, poor countries. Additionally, in some country settings, it has been possible for data on the negative impact of austerity measures on the sexual and reproductive health and other rights of women and girls to be put forward to maintain programmes and budgets to guarantee these essential human rights.[42] These interventions have opened space for dialogue on the human rights impacts of debt and fiscal consolidation in specific countries and in particular sectors such as education, health and nutrition, but more could be done with respect to cancelling debt and adopting systematic gender-responsive budgeting and financial processes which would allow governments to reclaim space for the development of feminist and human rights-based economic policies.[43]

III. Conclusions and recommendations

A. *Conclusions*

58. Too little attention has been given to the reduction of socioeconomic inequalities as a prerequisite for effective action to combat poverty. The international human rights framework provides tools to measure and understand how the rights of women and girls to live free from poverty and inequality are being systematically violated by particular political, social, cultural and economic norms and institutions. Human rights instruments also contain important redistributive and solidarity obligations that, if fully implemented, would enable States as well as other duty bearers to create sustainable, feminist, and human rights-based economies.

59. A feminist and human rights-based approach to poverty and inequality is based on the assertion that the role of the economy is to support human dignity, wellbeing, and human rights. A feminist human rights framework focusing on women's human rights, especially their economic, social and cultural rights and their right to participate in all spheres of life, allows specific forms of structural

discrimination to be redressed. This entails examining wealth and income distribution, intra-household dynamics, access to and control over assets, including those that are held in common, environmental protection, time allocation, care and wellbeing, and the right to rest and leisure of women and girls, as pivotal elements of gender equality and sustainable development. This approach also draws attention to the responsibilities of States and other actors to take targeted steps to address inequalities in the distribution of power, resources and entitlements and to advance collective and individual human rights, including the right to development. The adoption of human rights-based and feminist perspectives by States and international organisations to enable the creation of progressive, redistributive global financial governance frameworks is essential for addressing both inequalities and poverty in a comprehensive and effective manner.

60. The right to live free from poverty and not to be discriminated against based on one's socio-economic condition should be further developed as key human rights and appropriate systems should be established to collect disaggregated data on the multiple dimensions of inequalities and poverty. Identifying and effectively responding to intersecting and multiple forms of inequality on grounds of poverty, sex and gender, race, ethnicity, age, ability, religion, geographic location, migration status, sexual orientation, gender identity and other conditions, must be a priority for participatory and targeted policies and strategies at the local, national, regional, and international levels.

61. It is imperative to analyse the ways in which overlapping inequalities drive and amplify ecological, social, political and economic crises and to ensure that poverty eradication policies are directed towards the transformation of unequal power relations through the negotiation of a new human rights-based feminist eco-social consensus. Given the rapidly approaching deadline for the achievement of the 2030 Agenda, and noting the slow rate of progress on SDGs 1, 5 and 10, it is essential to reiterate the centrality of women's and girls' human rights and gender equality to processes of poverty eradication and to combating inequalities both within and between nations.

B. Recommendations

62. States should take positive measures for the realisation of the full range of internationally recognised human rights of women and girls, to eliminate poverty and achieve substantive equality, inter alia, by:

(a) Grounding all laws and policies, especially in the economic and social arenas, in core human rights principles: equality and non-discrimination, meaningful participation of women and girls, accountability, and progressive realisation and non-retrogression of economic, social and cultural rights, and in line with applicable human rights norms and standards for each specific right;

... (g) Carrying out gender-responsive resource redistribution through the recognition of the value of the care economy, fair fiscal policies (including proportional and progressive taxation to high-income earners and corporations), equitable trade and investment policies, debt cancellation or debt relief in case of State insolvency, and corporate accountability;

... (i) Identifying the ways in which crises, compounded forms of structural discrimination, and legal and policy frameworks place women and girls at aggravated risk of poverty and inequality and result in further human rights violations, and prevent, mitigate, and address such risks.

... (n) Complying with the immediate obligations to eliminate discrimination, guarantee the minimum core of all economic, social and cultural rights and their progressive realization; dedicate maximum available resources to the realisation, availability, and accessibility of such rights for all women and girls; and create and promote mechanisms for their full legal recognition and justiciability, including by ratifying the Optional Protocol to the ICESCR and CEDAW.

63. International and regional economic, financial and monetary institutions and their Member States should:

(a) Take concerted steps to move away from growth-centred and neoliberal paradigms that foster inequalities by adopting feminist and human rights-based approaches which prioritize the elimination of poverty and gendered socioeconomic inequality;

(b) Design, construct and implement gender-responsive budgets to realize women's and girls' human rights and gender equality, using gender budgeting tools, increasing financing in ordinary budgets, and through measures such as subsidies, aid, development cooperation, and gender-sensitive loans and financing, and create mechanisms for budget accountability;

... (g) Develop and mainstream gender-responsive and human rights-based macroeconomic policy prescriptions on structural adjustment and national debt repayments in light of significant evidence of their inequitable impacts on the human rights of women and girls. Debt sustainability analysis and impact assessments of economic reforms should consider both the human rights obligations of debtor States and their creditors towards the borrowers' populations, including the prohibition of implementing or promoting debt and macroeconomic policies with disproportionate effects on women.

64. Corporations and the States, international and regional organizations exercising jurisdiction and control over them, should:

… (b) Ensure corporate accountability and tax justice, particularly for transnational and high-profit corporations, through compliance with human rights and fiscal commitments and obligations, and implement the gender guidance to the UN Guiding Principles on Business and Human Rights. States should mainstream a feminist and human rights-based approach into their National Action Plans and other national follow-up mechanisms on business and human rights.

Notes

[1] This is the Working Group's current denomination. The mandate was originally created under the name of Working Group on discrimination against women in law and in practice. The mandate was renewed by consensus at the Council's 23rd session, in resolution 23/7, and then renewed for a further three years, again by consensus, during the Council's 32nd session, in June 2016, through resolution 32/4. In June 2019 the mandate was again renewed through resolution 41/6, and the name of the group became Working Group on discrimination against women and girls. The mandate of the WGDAWG was renewed in June 2022 through resolution 50/18.

[2] See Resolution A/HRC/RES/15/23.

[3] At the time of writing, and during the preparation of the report, the composition of the WGDAWG is: Ms Dorothy Estrada-Tanck (Chair); Ms Ivana Radačić (Vice-Chair), Ms Meskerem Geset Techane, Ms Elizabeth Broderick and Ms Melissa Upreti. For more information on the members, see https://www.ohchr.org/en/special-procedures/wg-women-and-girls/members

[4] See A/HRC/20/28.

[5] See https://www.ohchr.org/en/special-procedures-human-rights-council/what-are-com munications; and https://www.ohchr.org/en/special-procedures/wg-women-and-girls/comments-legislation-and-policy

[6] See https://www.ohchr.org/en/special-procedures/wg-women-and-girls/annual-thema tic-reports

[7] See https://www.ohchr.org/en/special-procedures/wg-women-and-girls/country-visits.

[8] See the WGDAWG's microsite at https://unworkinggroupwomenandgirls.org/

[9] See https://www.ohchr.org/en/latest?MID=WG_Women

[10] See https://www.ohchr.org/en/special-procedures/wg-women-and-girls/submissions-courts

[11] See 'ISSUES IN FOCUS' at https://www.ohchr.org/en/special-procedures/wg-women-and-girls/about-mandate: 'Men's accountability for gender equality'; 'Gender equality and gender backlash' (in English and Spanish); 'Women's autonomy, equality and reproductive health'; 'Women's land rights'; 'Criminalization of adultery'; 'Discrimination against women in nationality'; and 'Women human rights defenders and gender discrimination'.

[12] See https://www.ohchr.org/en/special-procedures/wg-women-and-girls/activities

[13] The EDVAW Platform expert mechanisms include: the UN Working Group on discrimination against women and girls (WGDAWG), Chair; the UN Special Rapporteur on violence against women and girls (SR VAWG); the UN Committee on the Elimination

of Discrimination against Women (CEDAW Committee); the Group of Experts on Action against Violence against Women and Domestic Violence (GREVIO); the Committee of Experts of the Follow-up Mechanism to the Belém do Pará Convention (MESECVI, by its acronym in Spanish); the African Commission on Human and Peoples' Rights Special Rapporteur on the Rights of Women in Africa (A SRWHR); and the Inter-American Commission on Human Rights' Rapporteur on the Rights of Women (IA RWHR).

[14] See the Working Group's Report of 2018, A/HRC/38/46, and its position paper of 2020: 'Gender equality and gender backlash' (in English and Spanish), Available from: https://www.ohchr.org/en/special-procedures/wg-women-and-girls/gender-equal ity-and-gender-backlash

[15] The letter can be read in chapter 6 of this book.

[16] A/HRC/53/39. The excerpts included in this chapter are based on the unedited version of the report as of March 2023, and may differ slightly from the final edited report. The report is available in all UN languages at https://www.ohchr.org/en/special-procedures/ wg-women-and-girls.

[17] On human rights-based approaches to the economy, see also, for example, the Office of the UN High Commissioner for Human Rights (OHCHR), The Surge Initiative and Human Rights, at https://www.ohchr.org/en/sdgs/seeding-change-economy-enhan ces-human-rights-surge-initiative; and https://www.ohchr.org/en/stories/2023/04/ building-economies-place-peoples-human-rights-center

[18] J. Hickel (2018) *The Divide: A Brief Guide to Global Inequality and its Solutions*, London: Penguin; CESCR (2001) 'Statement on Poverty and the International Covenant on Economic, Social and Cultural Rights' (E/C12/2001/10).

[19] Oxfam International and Nawi-Afrifem (2022) *The Assault of Austerity. How Prevailing Economic Choices are a Form of Gender-based Violence*.

[20] A/77/169.

[21] Gender and Development Network (2017) 'Briefing: Making trade work for gender equality'; A.E. Yamin (2020) *When Misfortune Becomes Injustice*, Stanford, CA: SUP.

[22] Oxfam International (2023) *Survival of the Richest. How we Must Tax the Super-Rich now to Fight Inequality*, Oxford: Oxfam International.

[23] A/HRC/44/51.

[24] Focus 2030 (2023) 'Overview of data and resources on gender equality across the world'.

[25] For example, common understanding of human security, UNGA (2012), A/Res/66/ 290.

[26] UNRISD (2022), *Crises of Inequality. Shifting Power for a New Eco-Social Contract*.

[27] For example, L.E. White and J. Perelman (eds) (2011) *Stones of Hope: How African Activists Reclaim Human Rights to Challenge Global Poverty*, Standford, CA: Stanford Studies in Human Rights; see also reports by the Center for Economic and Social Rights, the Global Initiative for Economic, Social and Cultural Rights (GI-ESCR), and Red-DESC/ ESCR-Net.

[28] Feminist Economic Justice for People and Planet Action Nexus (2021), 'A Feminist and Decolonial Global Green New Deal'.

[29] J.P. Bohoslavsky and F. Cantamutto (eds) (2021) 'The IMF and Human Rights: Interviews', LSE Human Rights.

[30] M. Kjaerum et al (eds) (2021), *COVID-19 and Human Rights*, New York and Oxon: Routledge.

[31] UNRISD (2022), *Crises of Inequality. Shifting Power for a New Eco-Social Contract*.

[32] M.E. Salomon (2010) 'Why should it matter that others have more? Poverty, inequality and the potential of international human rights law', LSE Legal Studies Working Paper No. 15/2010.

[33] ICESCR, Article 2.1; CESCR General Comment 3, paragraph 13.

34 J.P. Bohoslavsky and F. Cantamutto (eds) (2021) 'The IMF and Human Rights: Interviews', LSE Human Rights.

35 A/77/169.

36 Global Alliance for Tax Justice (2021) 'Framing Feminist Taxation'.

37 A/HRC/29/31 and A/HRC/26/28. See also R. Balakrishnan, J. Heintz and D. Elson (2016) *Rethinking Economic Policy for Social Justice: The Radical Potential of Human Rights*, New York and OxonRoutledge.

38 For example, AMwA (Akina Mama wa Afrika) (2021) *A Feminist Tax Justice Handbook for Women in the Informal Economy*.

39 Debt Justice (2022), 'The growing debt crisis in lower income countries and cuts in public spending'.

40 A/75/164.

41 J.P. Bohoslavsky and F. Cantamutto (eds) (2021) 'The IMF and Human Rights: Interviews', LSE Human Rights.

42 Views expressed during the Working Group's consultations.

43 I. Grabel (2022) 'Global Financial Governance and Progressive Feminist Agendas', *International Journal of Political Economy*, 51(4): 331–45; IMF (2022) 'IMF Strategy toward mainstreaming gender'.

8

Debt and Human Rights in the World and Regional Conferences on Women in Latin America and the Caribbean

Marita Perceval and Mariana Rulli

1. Introduction

Since 1975 at a global level, and since 1977 at a regional level, Conferences on Women organized by the United Nations (UN) have been taking place. In these conferences, States – through the so-called Mechanisms for the Advancement of Women (MAW) – as well as women and civil society organizations, along with specialized agencies of the UN system, negotiate and establish agreements in relation to the gender agenda and recommendations to move forward in the path towards equality, which are embodied in political declarations and action plans. By reading these official documents, the way States have addressed sovereign debt, related economic policies and their differential impacts on the human rights of women can be traced, reconstructed and analyzed from an historical perspective.

The goal of this chapter is to address the agreements embodied in the official documents of world and regional conferences on women that took place in the context of the UN related to sovereign debt and its consequences for gender inequalities. For that purpose, a systematization, a periodization and a qualitative analysis is made of a corpus composed of 20 official documents of the four world conferences[1] and the ones produced during the 15 regional conferences held in Latin America and the Caribbean until 2022.[2] This research aims at contributing to the lack of feminist literature on the systematization and interpretation of the official documents produced by world and regional conferences on women with a focus on debt and human rights.

The structure of this chapter is as follows. After this introduction, section 2 analyzes the official documents produced in world conferences on women, proposing a periodization. The first stage was marked by more general discussions among developed and developing countries, which are framed within the debates around the 'New International Economic Order' (NIEO). The second stage was marked by a more explicit and direct recognition of the threat that debt poses for women's rights simultaneously with the deepening of the Washington Consensus. In section 3, the historical progression of the official documents and commitments made during regional conferences is presented, proposing the following three stages: the first stage covers the first to the third conference, which highlighted that the underdevelopment of the countries of Latin America and the Caribbean was a consequence of the unfair global economic system, and warned about the impact on the inequalities women suffer. The second stage starts with the fourth conference held in Guatemala (1988) and begins to point out that the problems of the economic, financial and external debt crises, in line with adjustment programmes, had a negative impact on the living conditions of women. Finally, the third stage begins with the Montevideo Conference (2016) and ends with the Buenos Aires Conference (2022), which, without reducing the emphasis on the debt problem and its differential impact, included an approach based on human rights to assess the impact of economic measures on women. In section 4, the main findings are summarized and the conclusions of the research are presented.

2. From Mexico to Beijing: debt in world conferences on women

Although the Commission on the Status of Women was created in 1946 as a commission dependent on the Economic and Social Council, shortly after the creation of the UN, as the main global intergovernmental body exclusively devoted to the promotion of gender equality and the empowerment of women, since 1975, four (until now) world conferences on women and one World Conference on Human Rights have taken place, where a number of consensuses among member states have been adopted, which are analyzed in this section.

These four conferences are studied here considering two different historical periods. The first one, which starts with the First World Conference on Women held in Mexico (1975) and also includes the Second World Conference in Copenhagen (1980) and the Third World Conference held in Nairobi (1985), is marked by debates around the so-called NIEO,[3] which brought together the demands that the 'underdeveloped' countries (as they were called at that time) posed to industrialized countries, focusing on the postcolonialist functioning and the structure of the international economy that perpetuated the inequalities and poverty situation in periphery countries. The political ideas linked to the NIEO proposed to refound a new international economic order based on rules that enabled a balanced and fairer order, including alleviating the burden of external debt and facilitating that more developing countries participate in the International Monetary Fund.

Thus, during the first period, in 1975, the First World Conference on Women was held in Mexico, in the context of the International Women's Year, where an Action Plan was adopted and the General Assembly proclaimed the 'United Nations Decade for Women 1975–1985'. Although the conference had a declaratory nature in general (it did not discuss how different rights would be guaranteed or how violations would be addressed), it was very important from the viewpoint of women's human rights as the Convention on the Elimination of All Forms of Discrimination against Women (CEDAW) was approved afterwards in 1979 (Facio, 2011).

Apart from being important for the evolution of women's human rights that were included in the CEDAW, it is worth revisiting some of the discussions and tensions that took place in the context of the first conference between two different blocks: between women from rich countries and women from 'Third World Countries' (mainly from Latin America). A significant aspect was that although the official framework in which the delegations of States negotiated was anchored during the conference in the drafting of the World Action Plan, it was in the so-called framework of the 'Tribune' (a meeting of non-governmental organizations) where the differences among women according to their country block of origin were clearly evident.

On the one hand, there was the position of women of the 'First World', linked to personal topics, the defence of body individuality and freedom: the main demands were related to sexuality, individual freedom, salary equality and equality within family. And, on the other hand, there was the position of women of the 'Third Word' that considered as political problems those linked to the economic disadvantages they experienced in their countries, compared to industrialized countries. The 'Third World' perspective explicitly linked women's problems to the need for a world reordering, making claims in that same direction (Fuentes, 2014).

It is worth highlighting that the document of the Action Plan that arose from the first conference already mentioned the link between inequalities between women and men (and among women), and the political, economic and social structure dimensions and the level of development of each country (paragraph 7). Moreover, the determinant function of social services and the fact that women are unequally affected compared to men in the stages of development and industrialization were already recognized (paragraph 154).

The Second World Conference on Women took place in Copenhagen in 1980, and, unlike the previous one, it had an evaluative nature and States proposed an Action Plan for the second part of the Decade for Women that would end in 1985 (Facio, 2011).[4] Even though the main topics were related to education, work and health, in a special section the States advanced the theory that inequalities were the cause of the lack of access to resources and the political participation of women. The document of the conference included a special section on the origin of women's inequalities relating to the unequal participation of men and women in the development and impact of the international economic context. Thus, paragraph 12 explicitly mentioned that women's inequalities derived from the underdevelopment of countries that in turn was a by-product of imperialism, colonialism, neocolonialism and unfair international economic relations.

The Third World Conference on Women took place in Nairobi in 1985 and, although the progress and obstacles of the Decade for Women were assessed, it had a strategic nature due to the fact that States signed a document containing the strategies for the advancement of women with a vision until the year 2000 (Facio, 2011). Even though this conference put special emphasis on respecting economic, social and cultural rights, it still talked about women's rights and not about the human rights of women.

The second stage of the periodization that is proposed in this chapter starts with the World Conference on Human Rights held in Vienna in 1993 (even though it was not a specific conference on women, it was very important because there women's rights were recognized as human rights) and ends with the Fourth World Conference on Women held in Beijing in 1995, where the Beijing Platform of Action (BPA) was drawn up, which is considered as the most progressive one to promote the rights of women. This stage took place in an economic context marked by the deployment and deepening of the Washington Consensus and the rise of neoliberal ideas, which were embodied in the implementation of structural reforms and greater public indebtedness and orthodox economic conditionalities that came with this higher debt, particularly in the countries of the Global South, which had a deep and negative impact on living conditions and women's human rights.

The substantive and progressive advance of the World Conference on Human Rights of Vienna (UN, 1993) (with its corresponding action plan and declaration) can be seen in three victories of the feminist movement, activists and advocates of women's human rights: first, violence against women was considered as a violation of human rights. Second, it was agreed that women's human rights[5] should be included in all the activities of the UN and a special call was made to strengthen the CEDAW and to create an Optional Protocol that allows for individuals' requests. Third, which in turn is the most important aspect for this research, women human rights activists managed to have social and economic rights recognized as being of the same importance as civil and political rights, recognizing the interdependence and interrelation of all human rights (Facio, 2011).

In 1995, the Fourth World Conference on Women took place in Beijing, where after having determined that there were still obstacles in the way of achieving equality as to opportunities and women's rights, States adopted the BPA. Apart from the advances made in Vienna, the Beijing Conference is considered as a conference with a 'binding' nature because it connected through its platforms the measures that were proposed for the States to adopt with the legal obligations that were already established in the CEDAW (Facio, 2011).

Furthermore, in the BPA, the unequal impact (based on gender) of external debt, the economic difficulties and the human rights of women are explicitly linked, as well as the resulting need to provide financial relief and to allow the convenience to develop techniques of debt swaps to be applied to programmes and projects of social development. It was highlighted that debt burden and policies of structural adjustment have had a harmful effect on social development and had an impact on poverty, and that:

> As a result of the debt burden and other economic difficulties, many developing countries have undertaken structural adjustment policies. Moreover, there are structural adjustment programmes that have been poorly designed and implemented, with resulting detrimental effects on social development. The number of people living in poverty has increased disproportionately in most developing countries, particularly the heavily indebted countries, during the past decade. (Beijing Declaration and Platform for Action, 1995: paragraph 13)

In line with this, paragraphs 18, 37 and 47 explicitly included the disproportionate consequences for women of the then-called 'mundialization' in the countries with external debt burden that have implemented adjustment programmes. The paragraphs of the Platform for Action also point out that the negative consequences of these policies have worsened the feminization of poverty and that:

> There is a greater acceptance that the increasing debt burden faced by most developing countries is unsustainable and constitutes one of the principal obstacles to achieving progress in people-centred sustainable development and poverty eradication. For many developing countries, as well as countries with economies in transition, excessive debt servicing has severely constrained their capacity to promote social development and provide basic services and has affected full implementation of the Platform for Action. (Beijing Declaration and Platform for Action, 1995: paragraph 38)

Moreover, the importance of an equal participation of women in the revision and modification process of macroeconomic policies is mentioned (paragraph 54), as well as the fact that a gender-based perspective must be included in the analysis of 'integrated macroeconomic and social policies and programmes, including those related to structural adjustment and external debt problems, to ensure universal and equitable access to social services, in particular to education and affordable quality health-care services and equal access to and control over economic resources' (paragraph 54). Furthermore, specific recommendations related to the international financial institutions (IFIs) are made: 'Invite the international financial institutions to examine innovative approaches to assisting low-income countries with a high proportion of multilateral debt, with a view to alleviating their debt burden' (paragraph 59.d).

Although the Beijing Conference was the last world conference on women, in the year 2000, the UN General Assembly[6] approved the carrying out of a review and five-year assessments of the BPA implementation, as well as to undertake studies related to new initiatives, while the Commission on the Status of Women was placed in charge of performing those studies. Since that year, assessments have been made every five years. In the assessments carried out in the year 2000, two documents were adopted: a political declaration[7] and a report, where measures and initiatives were agreed for the implementation of the BPA, and the ones achieved in Beijing were kept.[8] In the document Beijing + 5, where new measures and initiatives were included for the implementation of the declaration and the Beijing Platform for Action, the following issues related to debt were included, among others: 'implement macroeconomic and social policies and programmes, inter alia, through an analysis from a gender perspective of those related to structural adjustment and external debt problems, in order to ensure women's equal access to resources and universal access to basic social services' (Beijing Declaration and Platform for Action, 1995: paragraph 74.c).

In 2005, the Commission on the Status of Women made another follow-up assessment of the BPA and indicated that its goals were crucial for achieving the Millennium Development Goals. In 2010, another assessment was performed and a declaration was elaborated, where the advances achieved as to the BPA were indicated and new measures to attain its comprehensive application were adopted. In 2015, the revision of the BPA was marked by an assessment of the advances made and their connection with the development agenda after 2015, where member states agreed to guarantee the financing for sustainable development through the Third International Conference on Financing for Development[9] in Addis Ababa in July of the same year. This conference was very relevant since the need for development financing with a gender perspective was raised. Finally, in 2020, the last revision was made 25 years since the adoption of the platform.

Likewise, it is worth mentioning that the voting pattern of the most relevant resolutions as to sovereign debt and human rights (with several references to women's rights) passed in the last 15 years by the main political bodies of the UN[10] continue to reflect, in general, the geopolitical division as to the global economic governance that has existed since the discussion of the 'New International Economic Order' in the 1970s, with G77+China promoting these initiatives and high-income countries opposing the fact that finances and human rights can be related, and thus can be included in official documents.

3. From Havana to Buenos Aires: debt in regional conferences on women in Latin America and the Caribbean

Since 1977 in Latin America and the Caribbean, a total of 15 regional conferences on women have taken place, which will now be analyzed according to the following proposed periodization. A first period that begins with the first conference held in 1977 and ends with the third conference held in 1983. The official documents of these conferences, and in line with the considerations of the first two world conferences, linked the underdevelopment of the countries of Latin America and the Caribbean to the unfair global economic system, emphasizing its impact on the inequalities women suffer.

Thus, in the First Regional Conference on Women held in Havana in 1977, it was highlighted that the condition of women could not be dissociated from the development process. It explicitly mentioned that 'the question of inequality of the vast majority of the Latin American female population is indeed closely linked to the problem of underdevelopment, which exists not only because of inadequate internal structures, but also as a result of a profoundly unjust world economic system'. Therefore, it suggested that governments should 'make structural, economic, political, and social transformations in Latin America' so as to enforce the NIEO (Regional Plan of Action for the integration of women into Latin American economic and social development: paragraph 2, page 6). The outcome of the regional conference held in Havana was that the States of the region agreed upon a Regional Action Plan for the Integration of Women in the Economic and Social Development of Latin America, as the first roadmap of the region with the aim to advance towards the active incorporation of women in economic, political, social and cultural life, and make the obstacles they face visible so as to improve their situation regarding multiple inequalities.

The Second Regional Conference held in Venezuela (1979) still mentioned the situation the world was going through, particularly in developing countries, warning that the serious economic crisis affected 'mothers and children with greater intensity' (resolution 1, page 27). Likewise, the Third Regional Conference held in Mexico in 1983 still highlighted that the crisis in the region, linked to international economic problems, seriously affected the participation of women in the integration towards development.

The second period starts with the conference held in Guatemala (1988) and ends in 2013, during which it was mentioned that the problems of the economic, financial and external debt crises, including the related adjustment programmes, had a negative impact on the living conditions of women, particularly in the Mar del Plata conference held in 1994 as a preparation event towards Beijing.

In 1988, the Fourth Regional Conference on Women took place in Guatemala, where significant advances were made regarding the impact of external debt on the living conditions of women, as it was mentioned that 'the financial, economic and social crisis in the developing world has caused the situation of broad sectors of the population to deteriorate steadily, the effect on women being proportionally greater than that on men' (Report of the Fourth Regional Conference, 1988: paragraph 2, page 24). In particular, it was mentioned that 'adjustment programmes have become counterproductive in so far as the economies of some countries of the region are concerned, and the policies that flowed from many of the external debt agreements that were negotiated have not yielded the expected positive results' (Report of the Fourth Regional Conference, 1988: paragraph 3, page 25). Moreover, it was pointed out that 'the external debt cannot be paid in the current conditions and without sustained economic development' and that 'a political dialogue between creditors and debtors and for the establishment of a new international economic order can no longer be postponed' (Report of the Fourth Regional Conference, 1988: paragraph 4). It is worth mentioning that paragraphs 3 and 4 were not accepted by the US government 'because they were considered as inaccurate and extraneous to the issue of the incorporation of women into the economy' Report of the Fourth Regional Conference, 1988: foot note page 25). Finally, it was mentioned that the crises and the debt have had a 'particularly dramatic effect on the living conditions of women' and resulted in a significant reduction of the funds used to finance social policies (Report of the Fourth Regional Conference, 1988: paragraph 5).

Along the same lines, in the Fifth Regional Conference held in Curacao in 1991, it was indicated that the deep transformations made in many countries of the region, due to the economic crisis of the 1980s, translated into higher levels of poverty that especially affected women (Report of the Fifth Regional Conference, 1991: paragraph 19). Furthermore, the importance of avoiding a social and economic regression in the status of women was highlighted while it was recommended to 'adopt a gender-based approach which takes into account the strategic and practical needs of women in recognition of the severe social and economic impact of structural adjustment measures on the situation of women.' (Report of the Fifth Regional Conference, 1991: paragraph 3(e), page 42)

With the Washington Consensus at full power in Latin America and the Caribbean, and a strong and sustained public indebtedness in the countries of the region as a background, in the Sixth Regional Conference on Women held in 1994, the Regional Action Programme for the Women of Latin America and the Caribbean was agreed on and a preparatory regional instance was created for the world conference that would take place in 1995 in Beijing. The Action Programme was very explicit as to references to the external debt problems, their connection with neoliberal policies and their impact on the women's human rights – even before the fourth world conference.

Therefore, in the background and in several sections of the Mar del Plata Programme, the persistence of poverty in the region as well as the increase of productive and reproductive work of women were linked to the huge burden of the external debt and the structural adjustment policies that countries faced:

> The persistence of poverty and extreme poverty in Latin America and the Caribbean is linked to the enormous debt burden in many of its countries and territories, which has propelled them into formally or informally adopting structural adjustment policies with stringent conditionalities. This has impacted negatively on the region's capacity to invest adequately in the human development and institutional resources needed to confront the spread of poverty. For women, the combined effect of the debt burden and adjustment measures has also been to increase their productive and reproductive work, with deep implications for their economic, physical and social well-being. (Mar del Plata Programme, preambular paragraphs)

Besides, some of the recommendations for States are 'to review, modify and integrate macroeconomic and social policies, especially in those countries where debt servicing and structural adjustment policies exist, in order to promote growth and social equity, though, among other actions' (Mar del Plata Programme, Strategic Goal III.1). And international cooperation agencies are urged to 'support the conduct of a critical analysis of the structural causes and the effects of poverty among women, with a view to reorienting and channelling resources to help achieve the objectives of the Regional Programme of Action' (Mar del Plata Programme, Strategic action VIII.b).

One of the new issues included in the Mar del Plata Action Programme (1994) was the recognition of the 'insufficient participation of women in the debt and structural adjustment negotiations, which ultimately has a negative effect on their lives, those of their families and their society'. This recognition is especially important because even though the participation of women has increased since the 1990s in the legislative field in all the State levels of the region with the implementation of affirmative measures first and parity later, as well as in the evolution of gender institutionality and its hierarchization through the Mechanisms for the Advancement of Women, the fact is that no progress was made in terms of gender institutionality in the agencies linked to financial and fiscal issues, beyond the – limited – implementation of gender-responsive budgets.[11]

The conferences held after the Mar del Plata conference continued mentioning the external debt issue with increasing strength and specificity. The Santiago Consensus (1997) urged States to analyze the design and the application of macroeconomic and structural adjustment policies, as well as their impact on the quality of life of women. The Lima Consensus (2000) recognized that economic globalization, trade liberalization, structural adjustment programmes and external debt, as well as the resulting migration patterns, among others, may have specific and negative consequences for the life and situation of women. The Mexico Consensus (2004) stated the concern for the negative social effects of structural adjustment policies and, under certain circumstances, trade opening, one of which aspects is the fragmentation of social policies, as well as for the heavy burden of the external debt service.

However, in the subsequent regional conferences, after the global financial crisis of 2008–09, even though they mentioned the importance of performing 'studies on how the economic, financial, food, energy and environmental crisis affect women and, in particular, internal and international migratory flows and the reconfiguration of all spheres' (Brasilia Consensus, 2010), and to 'adopt measures to ensure that gender equity and equality criteria are applied in relation to the implementation of fiscal policies and that affirmative action is taken to prevent fiscal reforms from exacerbating poverty levels among women' (Santo Domingo Consensus, 2013), there were no explicit references to the problems linked to sovereign indebtedness, and related economic policies and their differential impact on women.

Finally, the third period begins with the Montevideo Strategy (2016) and ends with the last conference held in Buenos Aires (2022), where they went even further than the previous regional agreements as they urged States to ensure that the measures of fiscal adjustment or budget cutbacks aimed at addressing economic slowdown situations comply with the principles of human rights, including the prohibition of discrimination, ensuring that those measures exceptionally cover crisis periods and have a temporary nature, especially avoiding the deepening of all levels of poverty of women, the overload of unpaid and care work that women face, and the reduction of financing and budget for equality policies and mechanisms for the advancement of women.

Also, they recommended to undertake gender-based impact studies of fiscal policies before and after their implementation, ensuring they have no negative (explicit or implicit) effects on gender equality or the rights and autonomy of women, for instance, in the overload of unpaid and care work or in the levels of women's poverty. Moreover, they urged to promote the representation of the countries of Latin America and the Caribbean in the institutions of global economic governance that design and implement international rules as to finances, trade and debt, as well as to ensure that these rules are aligned with the human rights of women. Besides this, they suggested exploring options for debt relief of highly indebted and vulnerable countries in the Caribbean, as well as promoting solutions to face debt distress.

The Santiago Commitment (2020) pointed out the need to implement countercyclical policies sensitive to gender inequalities to mitigate the effects of crises and economic recessions on the lives of women, and to promote regulatory and political frameworks that boost the economy in key sectors, including the sector of the care economy, for which their multiplier effects should be recorded. Furthermore, the document elaborated by the UN Economic Commission for Latin America and the Caribbean (ECLAC) for the conference[12] shows the connection that exists between the financialization phenomenon, the volatility in the entrance and exit of capital flows in the region, the pro-cyclical and short-term nature of foreign investments that tend to focus on high-return assets, and the growing process of public and private indebtedness, particularly in households.[13]

Finally, from the perspective related to strengthening multilateralism as a political strategy, the Buenos Aires Commitment (2022) highlighted a number of actions linked to mobilizing resources to achieve gender equality in the region. In relation to debt, it promotes the need to

> … foster cooperation among States and support for the countries of Latin America and the Caribbean, in order to explore debt relief options for highly indebted countries and promote solutions to address debt overhang and secure the necessary resources for the implementation of the Regional Gender Agenda and the 2030 Agenda for Sustainable Development. (Buenos Aires Commitment, 2022: paragraph 30)

Moreover, it mentioned the need to strengthen regional cooperation to fight tax evasion and avoidance, as well as illegal financial flows, and to improve fiscal collection of the groups with the highest levels of income and wealth so as to have more resources for gender equality policies (Buenos Aires Commitment, 2022: paragraph 29).

4. Conclusions

Since the First World Conference on Women in 1975, the impact of the prevailing economic system on gender inequalities has been increasingly considered and denounced, as feminist movements, activists and academics have persistently claimed in the streets and in books. The diagnoses made and the recommendations offered in world and regional conferences have been sensitive to the evolution and incidences of the more general economic, financial, political and social dynamics that have characterized financial neoliberalism through the years: a legacy of economic asymmetries in postcolonialism, geopolitical alignments as to the 'New International Economic Order', then with structural reforms, the increasing public indebtedness, the weakening of the social protection system, the contractionary economic policies and the increase of inequalities.

In the historical progression of the world conferences, two different periods were identified. The first one begins in Mexico (1975) and ends in Nairobi (1985), where even though there were no explicit references to the problem of sovereign indebtedness, it was recognized that the asymmetry in the structure of the international economy perpetuated inequalities and the poverty situation (especially of women) in those countries. Furthermore, these conferences warned about the existing links among economic restrictions, economic policies and the living conditions of women. During this period, the CEDAW approval and the advances for its ratification in several countries of the world were remarkable milestones.

Afterwards, at a global level in 1993, the World Conference on Human Rights took place and recognized women's rights as human rights, beginning the second period since Beijing (1995), where the threat that external debt posed for the living conditions of women was explicitly and directly recognized. It is worth mentioning that this political process of claiming and acknowledging the effects of external debt on the conditions of women took place at the same time as the creation of mandates on structural adjustment programmes[14] and the effects of external debt on the enjoyment of human rights[15] in the system of special procedures in the UN in the years 1997 and 1998. Besides, addressing the debt issue with a gender-based perspective has been and continues to be supported and developed by treaty bodies and the special procedures of the UN.[16]

In parallel, three periods were identified in the progression of the regional conferences. The first one begins in Havana in 1977 and ends with the conference held in Mexico in 1983, which – following the world conferences of those years – pointed out the consequences that the unfair world economic system had on the underdevelopment of the countries of Latin America and the Caribbean, and, therefore, on gender inequalities. With the Washington Consensus fully deployed in the countries of the region, characterized by an increasing public indebtedness, the second period begins with the conference held in Guatemala in 1988 and ends with the one held in Montevideo in 2016, which explicitly mentioned the impact of public debt on gender inequalities and the emergence of IFIs in economic policy making. Since then, a narrative about the adverse and differential effects of sovereign debt and the related conditionalities that are detrimental for women and gender equality has been developed and extended. Finally, the third period begins with the Montevideo Strategy (2016) and ends in Buenos Aires (2022), during which the narrative to include the human right-based approach for the impact analysis of economic policies and reforms, and the claim for the participation of the countries of the region in the institutions of global economic governance was broadened and strengthened. As has been analyzed, this strategy has not only been defensive as specific recommendations have also been made to address the debt issue, first, with a gender-based approach, and then, with a human right-based approach, with debt relief for highly indebted countries being the main claim, which in turn is opposed by high-income countries.

It is also worth mentioning that several claims and recommendations that have been included in the documents of world and regional conferences have made remarkable advances in terms of their effective implementation through national regulations and public policies. For instance, in the fields of violence based on gender, sexual and reproductive rights, the political participation of women (mainly in the legislative field), the institutionalization of gender agencies in all State levels, and, to a lesser extent, regarding the unfair and unequal distribution of domestic and care work. However, in the field of economy and public finances, and more specifically in the field of debt, similar levels of progress have not taken place. Presumably, this phenomenon is due to the fact that debt is the backbone of neoliberalism (Lazzarato, 2015). Without it, the system would crack, as would happen if the unfair distribution of care tasks was reversed. As is explained in the introduction of this book, a 'feminist debt' sounds very much like an oxymoron.

It is not a coincidence that regional conferences have achieved more (in both quantitative and qualitative political terms) than world conferences as to debt and women's human rights. The awareness of 'Third World women' since the 1970s and the emancipatory potential of the feminist movement and women of Latin America and the Caribbean, plus the political and fiscal need of the governments of the region to reduce the excessive debt burden, largely explains the different progressions between world and regional conferences as to the impacts of external debt on the human rights of women.

Acknowledgement

The authors thank Nieves Rico for the feedback received.

Notes

1   The official documents of the four world conferences on women held in Mexico (1975), Copenhagen (1980), Nairobi (1985) and Beijing (1995) are studied. This last one was followed by a series of five-year reviews made by the Commission on the Status of Women (CSW). This was also included in the corpus of documents of the World Conference on Human Rights held in Vienna in 1993.

2   The official documents elaborated in the regional conferences on women in Havana (1977), Venezuela (1979), Mexico (1983), Guatemala (1988) and Curacao (1991), the Regional Programme of Action for the Women of Latin America and the Caribbean 1995–2001 (1994), the Santiago Consensus (1997), the Lima Consensus (2000), the Mexico Consensus (2004), the Quito Consensus (2007), the Brasilia Consensus (2010), the Santo Domingo Consensus (2013), the Montevideo Strategy for Implementation of a Regional Gender Agenda within the Sustainable Development Framework by 2030 (2016), the Santiago Commitment (2020) and the Buenos Aires Commitment (2022).

3   See Resolutions of the United Nations Assembly (1974), UN Docs 3201 (S-VI) and 3202 (S-VI). Available from: https://legal.un.org/avl/pdf/ha/ga_3201/ga_3201_ph_s.pdf

4   One of the main issues of the second conference was that a special ceremony was held where 64 States signed the CEDAW, and Cuba and Guyana presented their ratification instruments.

5   Some of the rights recognized are: the right to life; the right not to be subject to discrimination or violence for being a woman; the right not to be mistreated or murdered for being a woman; the right not to live with constant fear of being sexually abused with impunity; the right not to be discriminated against in jobs or in the access to economic and production resources; the right to freedom and personal safety; the right to decide about their bodies, sexuality and reproduction without coercion or pressure; the right to freely express themselves and claim their rights without the fear of being incarcerated, persecuted or murdered; the right to a political and public life; the right to elect and be elected; the right to equal conditions between women and men in accessing education and to education without stereotypes; the right to choose their sexual orientation or gender identity; the right to freely choose to get married, without early or forced marriages.

6   See the documents available at: https://www.un.org/womenwatch/daw/followup/beijing+5.htm

7   UN, A/RES/S-23/2 (2000): Available online at: https://www.un.org/womenwatch/daw/followup/ress232e.pdf

8   UN, A/RES/S-23/3 (2000): Available online at: https://www.un.org/womenwatch/daw/followup/ress233e.pdf

9   Information available at: https://www.un.org/esa/ffd/ffd3/

10   'Guiding Principles of external debt and human rights', approved by the Human Rights Council in 2011 (UN Doc A/HRC/20/23); 'Basic Principles of restructuration of sovereign debts', approved by the General Assembly in 2015 (UN Doc A/69/L.84); and the 'Guiding principles on human rights impact assessments of economic reforms', approved by the Human Rights Council in 2019 (UN Doc A/HRC/40/57).

11   See chapter 20 in this book.

12   See the ECLAC position paper (2019) 'Women's autonomy in changing economic scenarios' (LC/CRM.14/3), Santiago de Chile, available from: https://repositorio.cepal.org/bitstream/handle/11362/45032/4/S1900723_es.pdf

13   See the ECLAC position paper (2019) 'Women's autonomy in changing economic scenarios' (LC/CRM.14/3), Santiago de Chile: 7. 78. Available from: https://repositorio.cepal.org/bitstream/handle/11362/45032/4/S1900723_es.pdf

14   CmDH, Res 1997/103.

[15] CmDH, Res 1998/24 (which mandate is joined to the one of structural adjustment in the year 2000, CmDH, Res 2000/82, 26 April 2000).
[16] See chapters 5 and 7 in this book.

References

Bibliography

Facio, A. (2011) 'Viena 1993, cuando las mujeres nos hicimos humanas', *Pensamiento Iberoamericano*, 9: 3–20, Available from: https://dialnet.uniri oja.es/servlet/articulo?codigo=3710875

Fuentes, P. (2014) 'Entre reivindicaciones sexuales y reclamos de justicia económica: divisiones políticas e ideológicas durante la Conferencia Mundial del Año Internacional de la Mujer. México, 1975', *Secuencia*, 89(May–August).

Lazzarato, M. (2015) *Governing by Debt*, Semiotext(e)/Intervention Series, Los Angeles, CA: MIT Press.

Documents of the United Nations World Conferences on Women

United Nations (1975) 'World Conference of the International Women's Year', México City, Available from: https://www.un.org/womenwatch/daw/beijing/mexico.html

United Nations (1980) 'World Conference of the United Nations Decade for Women: Equality, Development and Peace', Copenhagen, Available from: https://www.un.org/womenwatch/daw/beijing/copenhagen.html

United Nations (1985) 'World Conference to review and appraise the achievements of the United Nations Decade for Women: Equality, Development and Peace', Nairobi, Available from: https://www.un.org/womenwatch/daw/beijing/nairobi.html

United Nations (1995) 'Beijing Declaration and Platform for Action', Beijing, Available from: https://www.unwomen.org/sites/default/files/Headquarters/Attachments/Sections/CSW/PFA_E_Final_WEB.pdf

World Conference on Human Rights

United Nations (1993) 'Vienna Declaration and Programme of Action', Vienna, Available from: https://www.ohchr.org/en/instruments-mechani sms/instruments/vienna-declaration-and-programme-action

Documents of the United Nations Regional (Latin American and Caribbean) Conferences on Women

United Nations (1977) 'Regional Plan of Action for the integration of women into Latin American economic and social development', First Regional Conference on the Integration of Women into Latin American economic and social development, La Havana, Available from: https://repositorio.cepal.org/bitstream/handle/11362/16799/S7810189_en.pdf?sequence=2&isAllowed=y

United Nations (1979) 'Report of the Second Regional Conference on the Integration of Women into the Economic and Social Development of Latin America and the Caribbean', Macuto, Venezuela, Available from: https://repositorio.cepal.org/bitstream/handle/11362/41516/S8020333_en.pdf?sequence=1&isAllowed=y

United Nations (1983) 'Report on the Third Regional Conference on the Integration of Women into the Economic and Social Development of Latin America and the Caribbean', Mexico City, Available from: https://repositorio.cepal.org/handle/11362/41505

United Nations (1988) 'Report of the Fourth Regional Conference on the Integration of Women into the Economic and Social Development of Latin America and the Caribbean', Guatemala City, Available from: https://repositorio.cepal.org/bitstream/handle/11362/16829/S8800003_en.pdf?sequence=1&isAllowed=y

United Nations (1991) 'Report of the Fifth Regional Conference on the Integration of Women into the Economic and Social Development of Latin America and the Caribbean', Curaçao, Available from: https://repositorio.cepal.org/bitstream/handle/11362/41454/S9191530_en.pdf?sequence=1&isAllowed=y

United Nations (1994) ' "Regional Programme of Action Mar del Plata": Sixth session of the Regional Conference on the Integration of Women into the Economic and Social Development of Latin America and the Caribbean', Mar del Plata, Available from: https://repositorio.cepal.org/bitstream/handle/11362/47951/S2200521_en.pdf?sequence=4&isAllowed=y

United Nations (1997) ' "Santiago Consensus": Seventh session of the Regional Conference on the Integration of Women into the Economic and Social Development of Latin America and the Caribbean', Santiago de Chile, Available from: https://repositorio.cepal.org/bitstream/handle/11362/47951/S2200521_en.pdf?sequence=4&isAllowed=y

United Nations (2000) ' "Lima Consensus": Eighth session of the Regional Conference on Women in Latin America and the Caribbean', Lima, Available from: https://repositorio.cepal.org/bitstream/handle/11362/47951/S2200521_en.pdf?sequence=4&isAllowed=y

United Nations (2004) ' "Mexico City Consensus": Ninth session of the Regional Conference on Women in Latin America and the Caribbean', Mexico City, Available from: https://repositorio.cepal.org/bitstream/handle/11362/47951/S2200521_en.pdf?sequence=4&isAllowed=y

United Nations (2007) ' "Quito Consensus": Tenth session of the Regional Conference on Women in Latin America and the Caribbean', Quito, Available from: https://repositorio.cepal.org/bitstream/handle/11362/47951/S2200521_en.pdf?sequence=4&isAllowed=y

United Nations (2010) ' "Brasilia Consensus": Eleventh session of the Regional Conference on Women in Latin America and the Caribbean', Brasilia, Available from: https://repositorio.cepal.org/bitstream/handle/11362/47951/S2200521_en.pdf?sequence=4&isAllowed=y

United Nations (2013) ' "Santo Domingo Consensus": Twelfth session of the Regional Conference on Women in Latin America and the Caribbean', Santo Domingo, Available from: https://repositorio.cepal.org/bitstream/handle/11362/47951/S2200521_en.pdf?sequence=4&isAllowed=y

United Nations (2016) ' "Montevideo Strategy": Thirteenth session of the Regional Conference on Women in Latin America and the Caribbean', Montevideo, Available from: https://repositorio.cepal.org/bitstream/handle/11362/47951/S2200521_en.pdf?sequence=4&isAllowed=y

United Nations (2020) ' "Santiago Commitment": Fourteenth session of the Regional Conference on Women in Latin America and the Caribbean', Santiago de Chile, Available from: https://repositorio.cepal.org/bitstream/handle/11362/47951/S2200521_en.pdf?sequence=4&isAllowed=y

United Nations (2022) ' "Buenos Aires Commitment": Fifteenth session of the Regional Conference on Women in Latin America and the Caribbean', Buenos Aires, Available from: https://repositorio.cepal.org/bitstream/handle/11362/48738/S2300106_en.pdf?sequence=1&isAllowed=y

PART III

International Financial Institutions, Gender and Diversity

9

Gender Mainstreaming at the International Monetary Fund

Camila Villard Duran

1. Introduction

> '[W]e now have a framework for integrating gender into the core work of the IMF. This includes our economic surveillance and policy advice, the design of IMF-supported programs, and capacity development. …
> In these ways, we can better support our member countries as they harness the economic dividends of reducing gender inequality.'[1]

With this statement in September 2022, during the Korea Gender Equality Forum, Gita Gopinath, the Fund's First Deputy Managing Director, announced that the International Monetary Fund (IMF) Executive Board finally approved the first comprehensive Strategy for Mainstreaming Gender. Gender mainstreaming consists of 'the process of assessing the implications for women and men of any planned action, including legislation, policies or programs, in any area and at all levels' (ECOSOC, 1997/2: 3). In the last three decades, international organizations (IO) have deployed legal instruments to support member states in translating a set of ideas on gender equality into laws and policies. The 1995 United Nations (UN) Beijing Platform supporting gender mainstreaming strategies triggered this international movement. Various UN agencies and IOs supported the 'global diffusion of gender mainstreaming' (True and Parisi, 2013).

Before 2013, IMF policy documents hardly referred to the word 'gender'. This IO was late in recognizing gender inequality as relevant for the accomplishment of its global mandate. Only in July 2022 was a more comprehensive gender strategy approved.

The IMF is, however, a key IO to the rulemaking process of international economic law (IEL) and can decisively contribute to building a macroeconomic environment that fosters gender equality. International economic regulation consists not only of written rules but also ideas, discourses and the practices of bureaucrats[2] and legal practitioners. Law shapes and is shaped by ideas formulated by IOs and their civil servants.

The IMF has the potential to effectively influence the formation of a more gender-responsive IEL by generating change through the integration of gender equality in the meaning-making process of economic regulation.[3] Gender responsiveness applied to economic laws and policies is the process of recognizing and executing interventions in the global and national economies to effectively address gender gaps and overcome historical gender biases.

Legal and economic narratives matter and are essential to a more gender-responsive IEL. The IMF is responsible for engendering different macroeconomic notions and standards for economic laws, particularly in fiscal, tax, monetary and exchange rate policies, public statistics, and regulation of financial and capital markets. It has the legal power and persuasive institutional mechanisms to translate economic ideas into legal rules at global, regional, and local levels.

Hence, how is the IMF shaping the concept of gender equality and influencing the development of a more gender-responsive IEL? Within its institutional framework, how is the IMF contributing to reduce the gender-blindness of IEL?

This chapter aims to answer these questions and is divided into five parts. Besides this introduction, the following section presents the literature review and identifies the gaps in the current analysis of the IMF gender turn. The third section traces the historical development of the IMF's narratives on gender equality based on the scrutiny of official declarations, policies and research documents published by this IO. The fourth section investigates the role of legal ideas in shaping the Fund's official discourse. The fifth and final section concludes and proposes an alternative legal approach combining the Fund's macroeconomic stability mandate and respect for women's rights.[4]

2. Literature review: the gender turn at the IMF

IMF's narratives on the relationship between macroeconomic rules and gender equality are relevant globally and locally. In all, 190 countries are Fund members.[5] This IO is responsible for overseeing the international monetary and financial architecture. According to Article IV, Section 3 of its Articles of Agreement (AoA), it must advise national policy makers. Hence, the IMF plays a crucial role in shaping diverse macroeconomic concepts within economic law, encompassing perspectives on gender equality. With its mandate and influential institutional mechanisms, the

IMF effectively disseminates regulatory concepts. Since 2013, it also has the political willingness to diffuse how gender equality is to be integrated into the regulatory framework of national economies.

Various studies explored the gendered impacts of global financial and monetary regimes, for example, critical reflections on unconventional monetary policies and their gendered effects (Young, 2018), financial regulation through public–private networks and the role of gender (Young, 2013), the international political structure of remittances and women (Kunz, 2011) and the World Bank's discourses and its policy practices on gender equality (Bedford, 2013; Caglar, 2013; Razavi, 2013; Calkin, 2018), among others.

However, the development of gender-responsive ideas within the IMF has still not been systemically explored by the literature. Academic studies addressing this specific issue remain relatively scarce (Berik, 2017; Coburn, 2019). Notably, there is a significant gap in the reflections on the role of *legal* ideas in shaping the IMF's gendered discourses.

At a country level, the way the IMF shapes ideas on gender equality matters. Narratives wield significant influence in shaping the global economy, delineating social issues, elucidating the roles of national and global institutions in crafting solutions, and delineating the constraints imposed by law and policy when addressing specific subjects (Kennedy, 2016). Hence, ideas carry practical effects, enabling and simultaneously restricting policy interventions.

It was only in 2013 that the IMF began recognizing gender inequality as a critical issue in macroeconomic policies. This acknowledgment came late, despite numerous empirical studies accusing this IO of neglecting the IMF-supported structural adjustments' impact on women's rights, particularly in the 1980s and the 1990s (Benería, 1992; Elson, 1992; Sadasivam, 1997; Aslanbeigui and Summerfield, 2000; Elson and Cagatay, 2000; Ali, 2003; Lingam, 2005; Campbell, 2010; Yoo, 2011; Neaga, 2012; Detraz and Peksen, 2016). In 1987, the United Nations Children's Fund (UNICEF) published one of the first investigations pinpointing the negative effects on women and children in Latin America driven by IMF and World Bank structural programmes (Cornia, Jolly, and Stewart, 1987).

In the case of the IMF, in-house bureaucrats and their precise legal interpretation of its mandate constrained, as well structured, the IO change: women's rights, or their wellbeing, could not be considered an objective per se by the Fund. Women's empowerment was contemplated as instrumental to macroeconomic stability. Inequality, in this context, was conceived as a type of social barrier hindering economic growth.

To better apprehend the internal forces shaping the discourse within the Fund, one must dissect the IMF 'gender expertise': what is the Fund's idea of gender equality; what is its conceptual framework; and who plays a role in shaping this expertise? Analytical tools and legal notions define what the Fund's bureaucrats 'see' and recognize as a relevant subject for economic regulation. They also determine the parameters for gendered analysis and policy recommendations.

3. Explaining the IMF gendered ideas and their place

The IMF has evolved from an IO initially tasked with overseeing the global fixed exchange rate regime under the initial version of the Bretton Woods Agreements to a comprehensive institution dedicated to fostering global economic stability. Throughout its history, the IMF has taken on a more proactive role, extending its involvement to the design of national policies beyond mere monetary concerns. Since 1944, member states have only amended the AoA seven times. Notably, the evolution of the IMF's mandate was significantly influenced by bureaucrats and their legal interpretations of the AoA. The Fund's in-house experts wield a crucial level of autonomy, exerting substantial influence over the IO's practices. They control the agenda-setting process. The staff prepares the policy and legal recommendations to be considered by the Executive Board (Chwieroth, 2010: 5), that is, the political representatives.

In the 1980s, the IMF bureaucrats were a crucial player among other critical actors (including, the US Treasury) in redesigning the IO's mandate. Kentikelenis and Babb (2019) contend that this transformative 'repurposing process' ushered in a new institutional order within the IMF that shifted its mandate from 'a modest assistance for currency stabilization to an all-encompassing structural adjustment program that reshaped developing countries' economies' (Kentikelenis and Babb, 2019: 1723).[6]

In 2013, the IMF staff placed gender inequality in its policy and research initiatives. Former IMF Managing Director, Mrs. Christine Lagarde, emphasized that '[e]xcessive inequality is corrosive to growth ... when women do better, economies do better' (Lagarde, 2013). This discourse marked the commencement of a new narrative within the institution: gender equality, specifically equality for 'women', is crucial for macroeconomic stability. In her words, '[e]mpowering women is good economics ... Gender equality is critical for the economic well-being of both men and women, of society as a whole' (Lagarde, 2016).

The IMF's previous concern with poverty, the environment and military expenditures, that is, non-purely 'economic' subjects for political conditionalities and policy advice, seems to have been triggered by the Executive Board (Barnett and Finnemore, 2004: 63). In contrast, the IMF gender turn appears to have been initiated by its first female leader, Mrs Lagarde. This transition was further bolstered by the ideas developed by in-house lawyers and economists, namely, the Fund's bureaucrats.

In 2013, the IMF published a unique policy guide offering analytical insights into job creation and inclusive growth (IMF, 2013). This document explored women's participation in labour markets, illustrating the significance of gender for economic growth (IMF, 2013: 3). This specific paper (IMF, 2013), crafted by the Fund's staff, triggered the gender equality discourse within this IO.

Before the release of this official paper, the IMF had solely published scattered gender-related studies lacking systematic treatment. For example, these studies addressed various aspects, such as gender bias in tax systems (Stotsky, 1996), the gender gap in education in Eritrea (Comenetz et al, 2017), the effects of social spending on women in the Middle East and North Africa (Laframboise and Trumbic, 2003), gender budgeting (Sarraf, 2003) and women's participation in labour markets in Canada (Tsounta, 2006).

Subsequently, the IMF identified gender equality as a 'macro-critical' issue, including gender perspectives into the guidelines for ongoing Article IV reports (IMF, 2015). Up to 2019, the institution provided policy guidance on gender equity to 40 member states as part of its surveillance function (IMF, 2019). Similarly, the IMF initiated the inclusion of gender-related conditions in its financial support programs (for example, the cases of Argentina, Egypt, Jordan and Niger – IMF, 2019). Gender considerations were also integrated into the agenda of technical training for national bureaucracies and as part of the IMF's assistance whenever required by member states (IMF, 2019).

However, despite the advancement of a more gender-responsive agenda, specialists have observed a disparity between economic research papers and the IMF policy guidance on gender equality for member states (Bretton Woods Project, 2017; Donald and Lusiani, 2017; Mariotti et al, 2017). Remarkably, the IMF does not consistently evaluate the distributional impacts on women within its comprehensive catalogue of macroeconomic policies.

In a guideline published in 2018 (IMF, 2018), the Fund directed its bureaucrats to incorporate gender considerations into policy recommendations and conduct detailed gendered analysis in country work only under specific conditions: (1) there was a 'macroeconomic significance' for the gender component; (2) it was aligned with national 'authorities' priorities' (that is, a political concern). The 2022 IMF Strategy Toward Mainstreaming Gender confirmed this guideline and limited the IO's gender scope to macro-critical gender gaps that are 'in accordance with its mandate' (IMF, 2022: 10). The view of the Executive Directors is that gender-related policy advice 'need[s] to be carefully considered vis-à-vis country authorities' implementation capacity and policy priorities' (IMF, 2022: 3). It is noteworthy that gender diversity within the Executive Board remains low. In 2023, the number of women in the Executive Director position has remained at 3 out of 24. Additionally, the number of women in the Alternate Executive Director position has declined from 5 to 3 out of 31 (IMF, 2023).

It appears that gender equality is not yet recognized as an issue that cuts across multiple areas within the Fund. Instead of embracing an integrative approach, this IO is adopting a 'compensatory approach' (Mariotti et al, 2017) to tackle inequalities, neglecting the effective integration of gender considerations into its legal and policy frameworks. As highlighted by the UN members' opinion on the IMF's gender strategy, 'adding a gender strategy to a host of other strategies and an operating system which are gender-blind will not help address the needs of women and girls and end the systemic drivers of their disadvantage and exploitation' (UN, 2022: 2). The Fund's macroeconomic approach is deemed 'selective towards discrimination against women', demonstrating a disregard for the interconnectedness and indivisibility of fundamental human rights (UN, 2022: 2).

4. The role of legal ideas and the invisible aspects of the IMF gender narrative

Institutions are 'constitutive of actors as well as vice versa' (Keohane, 1988: 382). The preferences and motives of the IMF's bureaucrats are not an exogenous factor; instead, they are influenced by institutional structures, prevailing interpretations of the Fund's mandate and the recruitment process, which may favour specific educational and professional backgrounds. The IMF leverages its macroeconomic expertise to establish a new specialized domain within the institution ('gender expertise'), fostering the formation of in-house professionals ('gender experts'). This initiative involves translating 'feminist knowledge' into actionable policy concepts (Kunz et al, 2019).

Yet, this expertise is more than just technical knowledge. Instead, gender expertise encompasses complex political struggles in both its practice and development (Kunz et al, 2019), occurring either within institutions or across diverse epistemic communities' boundaries. To advance the gender equality initiatives within the Fund, economists needed to overcome a legal barrier associated with this IO's 'purely' economic mandate. Simultaneously, their focal point for contemplating gender issues is entrenched in a specific disciplinary field: mainstream macroeconomics. The combination of macroeconomic stability and gender equality discourses can give rise to tensions, inconsistencies and significant areas of invisibility, potentially influencing outcomes.

Historically, the IMF asserted that '[w]hile its mandate and policies have evolved over time, it remains a monetary agency ... not a development agency' (Gianviti, 2002: 42). François Gianviti, a former General Counsel and a distinguished legal scholar in IEL, stated that the IMF 'contributes to providing the economic conditions that are a precondition for the achievement of the rights set out in the Covenant [on Economic, Social and Cultural Rights]' (Gianviti, 2002). If member states believe the Fund should take a more direct approach to human rights, they would propose an amendment to the AoA (Gianviti, 2002).

Therefore, only an AoA amendment could incorporate human rights into the IMF mandate. Legal bureaucrats would understand any other interpretation of the AoA as contra legem. However, UN treaty bodies and legal scholars have contested this argument. Despite the IMF bureaucrats' opinion, the IMF is bound by international human rights law (for example, CESCR, 2016: 3; Bohoslavsky and Cantamutto, 2022).[7] But, even in the aftermath of the 2008 global crisis, the IMF legal opinion remained unchanged: '... all of the enumerated purposes are of an economic nature, ... unlike some other organizations, the IMF is precluded from using its powers for political objectives' (IMF, 2010).

In 2018, the former Deputy General Counsel conveyed to the UN Special Rapporteur on extreme poverty and human rights that, according to international rules, the IMF is not bound by human rights obligations, 'except perhaps in cases of genocide' (UN, 2018: 7). In a document co-authored by one of the IMF's lawyers in 2021 (Giddings and Blair, 2021), it was sustained that: '[s]ince the IMF is an institution concerned primarily with addressing economic issues, it is prohibited from using its authority to directly address gender equality and other human rights' (Giddings and Blair, 2021).

This discourse, crafted by skilful legal bureaucrats, establishes an ideational border separating, on one side, the Fund's 'economic' mandate from, on the other, the pursuit of political or social goals, including human rights. These statements reveal a narrow conception of human development (Bohoslavsky et al, 2022) and demonstrate the bureaucracy's legal understanding of gender issues. Although the IMF 2022 Strategy Towards Mainstreaming Gender was approved by the Executive Board, during the Board's discussions, certain directors even stated that, given the IMF's mandate and core competencies, the role of this IO in tackling gender disparities is 'relatively limited' (IMF, 2022).

Hence, the Fund's strategies on gender equality are embedded within a specific conceptual framework, an assemblage of legal narratives that shape and limit transformative actions. This process also unveils the depoliticization of feminist issues. The integration of feminist ideas into this IO has given rise to a form of feminism more inclined to preserve prevailing norms than to confront them (Kendrick, 2020), which some authors would label as 'moderate liberal feminism' (Budgeon, 2019: 4).

However, diminishing the significance of women's rights in the meaning-making process of IEL has concerning implications. An excerpt from an article circulated by an IMF flagship magazine (Finance & Development), and co-authored by respectable economists from European and American academic institutions, sheds light on the depth of this conceptual framework.

In this context, the economists drew upon evidence from Rwanda to support the assertion that investments in women's health and education foster economic growth: 'healthy women are more likely to work outside the home, have the stamina and energy for physical labour, and work more hours' (Bloom et al, 2017).[8]

This sentence is, to say the least, alarming. It also unveils three invisible aspects of the Fund's legal and economic narratives and their impact on developing a more gender-responsive IEL. Firstly, it underscores the instrumentalization of women. For instance, the Convention on the Elimination of All Forms of Discrimination against Women (CEDAW) is conspicuously absent from the IMF policy documents. The CEDAW emphasizes women as autonomous rights-holders and not as role-players in family and society, the latter rooted in the conceptual exclusion of the private domain. Since 1979, the CEDAW has been the bedrock of the global women's rights discourse. Instead, the IMF prefers to reference the UN 2015 Sustainable Development Goals (SDG), particularly SDG 5 (gender equality), in lieu of human rights treaties.

This political choice also unveils broader trends in the IEL field: (1) the significance of metrics and benchmarks as valuable tools to global economic governance; and (2) the quest for legal flexibility in engaging States and IOs in pursuing shared international goals through less biding mechanisms of compliance.

Secondly, one may observe that the IMF does not directly address the inequalities stemming from the care economy. Across different countries, women predominantly bear the responsibility for social reproduction. The unpaid work provided by them is still invisible in national accounts. There exist technical methodologies to incorporate household work in public statistics' rules on Gross Domestic Product (GDP). This omission is not due to a lack of scientific understanding but rather a deliberate political choice.

GDP quantifies the monetary value of goods and services in a given national economy in a certain period. The UN formulates rules and ideas governing GDP and national public statistics in collaboration with other economic IOs, including the IMF. The System of National Accounts (SNA) serves as the globally accepted standard for compiling measurements of economic activity. The boundaries of the unproductive sector are a matter of 'convention', that is, a political choice made by the IO responsible for designing the SNA and the correspondent legal framework (European Commission et al, 2008). This phenomenon is also intertwined with economic ideas and discourses, that is, the approach to household work is underpinned by 'the utility theory of value: what is valuable is what is exchanged on the market' (Mazzucato, 2018).

Thirdly, the Fund's gendered ideas unveil the oversight of additional dimensions of inequality, that is, how racial and social disparities intersect and reinforce gender inequity. The IMF 2022 gender strategy explicitly states that even though 'intersectionality is an important aspect of defining an individual's identity, it is not considered in this paper. ... This paper focuses squarely on what is possible under the IMF's mandate: mainstreaming gender where gender gaps are macro-critical' (IMF, 2022: 8). This discourse reflects economic notions of gender that compartmentalize women's and men's experiences into different categories, which are not racialized, have no sexual orientation or social-economic status. There are factors that both unite and divide women, necessitating a more gender-responsive IEL that takes them into account.

Legal narratives concerning the historical development and interpretation of the IMF's mandate have constructed conceptual boundaries. Hence, the IEL conceptualized by the Fund's bureaucrats is markedly isolated from other international law areas. Legal scholars labelled this phenomenon as the 'fragmentation of international law' (Koskenniemi, 2004) or referred to it as 'the misery of international law' (Linarelli et al, 2018). Human rights are not yet conceived as constitutive of markets in the same way as property and contract rights.

5. Conclusion: is there an alternative legal approach to a more gender-responsive IEL?

This chapter elucidated how the IMF's bureaucrats contributed to formulating more gender-responsive global economic rules and policies. It identified key legal and economic narratives. The Fund's ideas on gender trace back to the first woman nominated as managing director, Mrs Christine Lagarde, and in-house experts, who mobilized their knowledge to promote gender-sensitive rules. They also shaped the IMF legal narrative, viewing gender equality as a *means* to achieve macroeconomic stability; no intrinsic value is attached to equality. They also overcame institutional constraints rooted in a conceptual barrier: the strictly legal interpretation of the IMF's 'economic' mandate.

Yet, this conceptual framework for gender equality exposes areas of invisibility and, therefore, of ineffectiveness of the IMF's so-called 'gender strategy'. The Fund's actual policy recommendations and conditionalities unveil another facet of the visible woman: the invisibility of women's individual rights and wellbeing, the inherent discriminatory nature of the unpaid economy and the unequal burdens associated to intersectionality.

Is it possible to envisage an alternative legal approach to the IMF's ideas fostering the development of a more gender-responsive IEL? Human rights ought to be conceived as an intrinsic social content of macroeconomic policies and rules. This narrative provides a potential legal avenue for harmonizing two international frameworks: human rights and IEL.

In 2019, Juan Pablo Bohoslavsky, the UN Independent Expert on foreign debt and human rights, released the 'Guiding principles on human rights impact assessment of economic reforms' (A/HRC/40/57). These principles were later endorsed by the Human Rights Council (Res. A/HRC/RES/40/8). Legally, these guidelines mandate the execution of both ex-ante and ex-post human rights impact assessments, which is crucial for evaluating and addressing any foreseeable effects of macroeconomic policies on human rights. This international standard imposes a procedural obligation, that is, a duty of due diligence, as a result of which the disproportional impact of economic reforms on women's shoulders would be exposed. A significant portion of this official document is dedicated to addressing the gendered impacts of structural adjustment programmes.

The IMF should prevent States from breaching their human rights duties, including CEDAW's legal obligations. The Fund is bound to establish due diligence procedures to assess the impact on human rights. While this constitutes a positive obligation challenging the prevailing political discourse (Kendrick, 2020: 12), it remains procedural. The IMF's bureaucrats should explore alternative economic rules and policies, incorporating empirical evidence and fostering a more transparent policy making process, when advising or imposing political conditionalities on member states.

The guiding principles' legal approach can contribute to shaping a more gender-responsive IEL. Human rights serve as a transformative tool in the fields of finance and the economy, offering a method to address complex objectives with broad consensus, such as reducing poverty, inequality, and combating climate change (Bohoslavsky and Cantamutto, 2022).

Despite facing institutional resistance, IOs in the financial and monetary domains have consistently engaged with human rights: the right to property, forming the basis of their mandate, is recognized as an essential human right (Koskenniemi, 2021). Integrating human rights more broadly, including women's rights, into the economic rationale of global rules and policies is an essential strategy for the foundation of a more inclusive and sustainable IEL.

Notes

[1] Remarks by Gita Gopinath, IMF First Deputy Managing Director, delivered at the Korea Gender Equality Forum. September 27–28, 2022, available at https://www.imf.org/en/News/Articles/2022/09/27/sp092722-ggopinath-kgef-gender-korea [last accessed on 30 November 2022]

[2] By bureaucrats, I refer to technical experts, mainly civil servants, working for government agencies (for example, central banks, treasuries and financial supervisor authorities) and IOs (for example, the IMF and the World Bank, among others) as nonelected specialists.

[3] Meaning-making is a process in which legal and economic categories are conceptually built inside IOs. They are then translated into rules and policies at national and global levels.

[4] This chapter is an updated and revised version of the following previous publication by the author: Camila Villard Duran (2021) 'The (in)visible woman at the International

Monetary Fund: Engendering national economic rule-making', *Journal of International Economic Law*, 24(4): 738–54, https://doi.org/10.1093/jiel/jgab037. The author would like to thank Julia L. Gomes Ferraz for her invaluable research assistance.

5   Liechtenstein applied to the IMF for membership in May 2023. Should it become a member, it would bring this number to 191.

6   The 'norm substitution' strategy was crucial in pursuing these institutional changes as it enabled 'the emergence and institutionalization of novel practices clandestinely, while maintaining the pretense that nothing has changed' (Kentikelenis and Babb, 2019, p 1727).

7   In 2017, the IMF sent a letter to the former UN Independent Expert on foreign debt and human rights, Mr Juan Pablo Bohoslavsky, stating that '[t]he IMF has not accepted the Declaration on Human Rights as the motivating principle of our operations. UN agencies have generally accepted our arguments as establishing the limits of our engagement and obligations on promoting human rights' (IMF, 2017: 2). However, several UN agencies, including CESCR, have argued precisely the opposite of that: 'international financial institutions and other international organizations are bound by any obligations incumbent upon them under general rules of international law, … They are therefore bound to comply with human rights' (CESCR, 2016: p 3).

8   Curiously, this paper on gender equality, contrary to other IMF publications, was written only by male academics.

References

Ali, K. (2003) 'Gender exploitation: from structural adjustment policies to poverty reduction strategies', *The Pakistan Development Review*, 42(4): 669–94.

Aslanbeigui, N. and Summerfield, G. (2000) 'The Asian crisis, gender, and the international financial architecture', *Feminist Economics*, 6(3): 81–103.

Barnett, M. and Finnemore, M. (2004) *Rules for the World: International Organizations in Global Politics*, Ithaca, NY: Cornell University Press.

Bedford, K. (2013) 'Economic governance and the regulation of intimacy in gender and development: Lessons from the World Bank's programming', in C. Gülay, E. Prügl and S. Zwingel (eds), *Feminist Strategies in International Governance*, New York: Routledge, pp 233–48.

Benería, L. (1992) 'The Mexican debt crisis: restructuring the economy and the household', in L. Beneria and S. Feldman (eds), *Unequal Burden: Economic Crises, Persistent Poverty and Women's Work*, Boulder, CO: Westview Press.

Berik, G. (2017) 'Beyond the rhetoric of gender equality at the World Bank and the IMF', *Canadian Journal of Development Studies*, 38(4): 564–9.

Bloom, D.; Kuhn, M. and Prettner, K. (2017) 'Invest in women and prosper', *IMF Finance and Development*, September.

Bohoslavsky, J.P. and Cantamutto, F. (2022) 'Not even with a pandemic: The IMF, Human Rights, and rational choices under power relations', *Human Rights Quarterly*, 44(4): 759–83.

Bohoslavsky, J.P.; Cantamutto, F. and Clérico, L. (2022) 'IMF's surcharges as a threat to the right to development', *Development*, 65(2): 1–9.

Bretton Woods Project (2017) '*The IMF and Gender Equality: A Compendium of Feminist Macroeconomic Reviews*', October.

Budgeon, S. (2019) 'The resonance of moderate feminism and the gendered relations of austerity', *Gender, Work and Organization*, 26(8): 1138–55.

Caglar, G. (2013) 'Feminist strategies and social learning in international economic governance', in G. Caglar, E. Prügl and S. Zwingel (eds), *Feminist Strategies in International Governance*, London: Routledge.

Calkin, S. (2018) 'The World Bank and the challenge of 'the business case' for feminist IPE', in J. Elias and A. Roberts (eds), *Handbook on the International Political Economy of Gender*, Cheltenham, UK and Northampton, US: Edward Elgar Publishing, pp 311–22.

Campbell, H. (2010) 'Structural adjustment policies: A feminist critique', *Journal of Political and International Studies*, 27(1): 1–14.

CESCR (United Nations Committee on Economic, Social and Cultural Rights) (2016) 'Public debt, austerity measures and the International Covenant on Economic, Social and Cultural Rights' (Statement, E/C.12/2016/1).

Chwieroth, J.M. (2010) *Capital Ideas: The IMF and the Rise of Financial Liberalization*, Princeton: Princeton University Press.

Coburn, E. (2019) 'Trickle-down gender at the International Monetary Fund: the contradictions of "femina economica" in global capitalist governance', *International Feminist Journal of Politics*, 21(5): 768–88.

Comenetz, J.; Bulir, A. and Brixiowl, Z. (2017) 'The gender gap in education in Eritrea in 1991–98: A missed opportunity?' (IMF Working Paper 01/94).

Cornia, G.; Jolly, R. and Stewart, F. (1987) *Adjustment With a Human Face, Volume 1:* Protecting the Vulnerable and Promoting Growth, Oxford: Oxford University Press.

Detraz, N. and Peksen, D. (2016) 'The effect of IMF programs on women's economic and political rights', *International Interactions*, 42(1): 81–105.

Donald, K. and Lusiani, N. (2017) 'The IMF, gender equality and expenditure policy', Bretton Woods Project.

ECOSOC (UN Economic and Social Council) (1997/2) 'Official Records of the General Assembly', Fifty-second Session, Supplement No. 3 (A/52/3/Rev.1), chap. IV, para. 4.

Elson, D. (1992) 'From survival strategies to transformation strategies: women's needs and structural adjustment', in L. Beneria and S. Feldman (eds), *Unequal Burden: Economic Crises, Persistent Poverty and Women's Work*, Boulder, CO: Westview Press.

Elson, D. and Cagatay, N. (2000) 'The social content of macroeconomic policies', *World Development*, 28(7): 1347–64.

European Commission; IMF; Organization for Economic Cooperation and Development; UN and World Bank (2008) 'System of national accounts'.

Gianviti, F. (2002) 'Economic, social and cultural rights and the International Monetary Fund', IMF Paper.

Giddings, A. and Blair, C. (2021) 'The adaptive mandate of the International Monetary Fund: challenges and opportunities in the time of COVID-19', *Rutgers International Law and Human Rights Journal*, 1: 130–200.

International Monetary Fund (2010) 'The Fund's mandate – the legal framework', IMF – Legal Department.

International Monetary Fund (2013) 'Jobs and growth: Analytical and operational considerations for the Fund', IMF Policy Papers.

International Monetary Fund (2015) 'Guidance note for surveillance under Article IV consultation', IMF Policy Papers.

International Monetary Fund (2017) 'The IMF and the human rights; Reports and materials on the social and human rights impact of fiscal consolidation policies ', IMF Letter to the Office of the High Commissioner for Human Rights, July 27.

International Monetary Fund (2018) 'How to operationalize gender issues in country', IMF Policy Paper.

International Monetary Fund (2019) 'Review of implementation of IMF commitments in support of the 2030 Agenda for Sustainable Development', IMF-SPR.

International Monetary Fund (2022) 'IMF strategy towards mainstreaming gender', IMF Policy Papers.

International Monetary Fund (2023). 'Gender Diversity in the Executive Board', Interim Report of the Executive Board to the Board of Governors.

Kendrick, A. (2020) 'Economic policy and women's human rights: A critical political economy perspective', *International Journal of Human Rights*, 24(9): 1353–69.

Kennedy, D. (2016) *A World of Struggle: How Power, Law, and Expertise Shape Global Political Economy*, Princeton: Princeton University Press.

Kentikelenis, A.E. and Babb, S. (2019) 'The making of neoliberal globalization: Norm substitution and the politics of clandestine institutional change', *American Journal of Sociology*, 124(6): 1720–62.

Keohane, R.O. (1988) 'International institutions: Two approaches', *International Studies Quarterly*, 32(4): 379–96.

Koskenniemi, M. (2004) 'Global governance and public international law', *Kritische Justiz*, 37(3): 241–54.

Koskenniemi, M. (2021) 'Prologue', in J.P. Bohoslavsky and F. Cantamutto (guest eds), 'SPEAK OUT! at the Laboratory for Advanced Research on the Global Economy: Special Issue on the IMF and Human Rights', LSE Human Rights.

Kunz, R. (2011) *The Political Economy of Global Remittances: Gender, Governmentality and Neoliberalism*, Abingdon: Routledge.

Kunz, R.; Prügl, E. and Thompson, H. (2019) 'Gender expertise in global governance: Contesting the boundaries of a field', *European Journal of Politics and Gender*, 2(1): 23–40.

Laframboise, N. and Trumbic, T. (2003) 'The effects of fiscal policies on the economic development of women in the Middle East and North Africa' (IMF Working Paper 03/244).

Lagarde, C. (2013) 'A new global economy for a new generation', in World Economic Forum Annual Meeting, Davos, Switzerland, January 23.

Lagarde, C. (2016) 'Women's empowerment: An economic game changer', Los Angeles, November 14, Available from: https://www.imf.org/en/News/Articles/2016/11/14/SP111416-Womens-Empowerment-An-Economic-Game-Changer

Linarelli, J.; Salomon, M.E. and Sornarajah, M. (2018) *The Misery of International Law: Confrontations with Injustice in the Global Economy*, Oxford: Oxford University Press.

Lingam, L. (2005) 'Structural adjustment, gender and household survival strategies: Review of evidences and concerns', CEW Center for the Education of Women, University of Michigan.

Mariotti, C.; Galasso, N. and Daar, N. (2017) 'Great Expectations: Is the IMF turning words into action on inequality?', Oxfam Policy Paper.

Mazzucato, M. (2018) *The Value of Everything: Making and Taking in the Global Economy*, New York: Hachette.

Neaga, D.E. (2012) '"Poor" Romanian women between the policy (politics) of IMF and local government', *European Journal of Science and Theology*, 8(1): 291–301.

Razavi, S. (2013) 'Governing the economy for gender equality? Challenges of regulation', in G. Caglar, E. Prügl and S. Zwingel (eds), *Feminist Strategies in International Governance*, Abingdon: Routledge.

Sadasivam, B. (1997) 'The impact of structural adjustment on women: A governance and human rights agenda', *Human Rights Quarterly*, 19(3): 630–65.

Sarraf, F. (2003) 'Gender-responsive government budgeting' (IMF Working Paper No 03/83).

Stotsky, J. (1996) 'Gender bias in tax systems' (IMF Working Paper No 96/99).

True, J. and Parisi, L. (2013) 'Gender mainstreaming strategies in international governance', in C. Gülay, E. Prügl and S. Zwingel (eds), *Feminist Strategies in International Governance*, Abingdon: Routledge, pp 59–78.

Tsounta, E. (2006) 'Why are women working so much more in Canada?: An international perspective' (IMF Working Paper No. 06/92).

United Nations (UN) (2018) 'Report of the Special Rapporteur on extreme poverty and human rights' (A/HRC/38/33), UN Human Rights Council, 18 June–6 July.

UN (2022) 'Mandates of the Independent Expert on the effects of foreign debt and other related international financial obligations of States on the full enjoyment of all human rights, particularly economic, social and cultural rights; the Special Rapporteur on the right to development; the Special Rapporteur on extreme poverty and human rights and the Working Group on discrimination against women and girls' (OL OTH 16/2022), Geneva, March.

Yoo, E. (2011) 'International human rights regime, neoliberalism, and women's social rights, 1984–2004', *International Journal of Comparative Sociology*, 52(6): 503–28.

Young, B. (2018) 'Financialization, unconventional monetary policy and gender inequality', in J. Elias and A. Roberts (eds), *Handbook on the International Political Economy of Gender*, Cheltenham, UK and Northampton, US: Edward Elgar Publishing,

Young, B. (2013) 'Structural power and the gender biases of technocratic network governance in finance', in G. Caglar, E. Prügl, and S. Zwingel (eds), *Feminist Strategies in International Governance*, Abingdon: Routledge.

10

Why are Neoliberal Policies Machistas?

Diane Perrons

1. Introduction

Neoliberal economic theory has dominated national and international policy making in all but a few countries in the last four decades even though it has led to increasing inequalities, existential threats to the environment, crises of care, comparatively low levels of economic growth and periodic economic collapses. While many critics see neoliberal economic policies 'as the root cause of these converging crises, it is the same neoliberal worldview that is shaping the response' (Action Aid International, 2022: 4).

Neoliberal economic policies appear to be technical and neutral, but in reality, they have unequal social content as well as unequal social impacts (Elson and Çağatay, 2000: 1362), both of which are gendered or machista, and this chapter aims to explain why, by focusing on neoliberal economic policy responses to public debt via austerity. Following a very brief discussion of austerity policies, the next section delineates the gendered social content of neoliberal economic theory and austerity policies; the subsequent section refers to their gendered impact, though these are interrelated.[1]

Neoliberal prescriptions were abandoned at the height of the 2008 financial crash and again in 2020 when the COVID-19 pandemic struck, as countries throughout the world engaged in high levels of public spending to prevent economic collapse and extremely high death rates. This abandonment was encouraged by the IMF in 2008 when it instructed States to 'follow whatever policies it takes to avoid a repeat of a Great Depression scenario' (Blanchard, 2008), and again in 2020 when the G20, backed by the IMF, urged States 'do what it takes' to minimize the economic and health impacts of COVID-19 (Wintour and Rankin,

2020). On each occasion, rather than thinking that as fiscal stimuli can be used to mitigate crises, they could also be used in a positive way to finance the Sustainable Development Goals, or gender inclusive and green development as many have recommended, or even to 'build back better' as many governments claimed they would, neoliberal policies were quickly restored, either voluntarily by nation states, or, in the case of low- and middle-income highly indebted countries, under IMF compulsion. Moreover, the vast amounts of public money that were spent in response to these crises was not used in a progressive way; rather, in both cases it was the banks and large corporations that received the bulk of the funds, while inequalities, including gender inequalities, increased and vast numbers of people throughout the world continue to face cost of living crises and declining health, care and educational services, and are predicted to do so until at least 2025 (Ortiz et al, 2015; Ortiz and Cummings, 2022).

Austerity can be defined as a conscious policy designed to reduce public deficits and debt by cutting public expenditure or raising revenue or both. It reflects a particular kind of masculinized free market thinking that prioritizes the health of the economy over and above social wellbeing, and, in practice, austerity policies have highly unequal gendered impacts with devastating consequences for those who experience multiple forms of discrimination and disadvantage. Although women (as well as men) are differentiated by social class, age, 'race', ethnicity, citizenship status, (dis)ability, sexuality and other markers of social distinction, as well as by their geographical location, State policies and occupations, all of which make the experience of austerity very different depending on who you are, where you are and what you do, the fact that neoliberal economic theory and related policies are gendered/ machista is not.

2. Gender biases in neoliberal economic thinking

Neoliberal economic theory sees the economy as an inanimate being, almost separate from society, and defined by abstract macroeconomic variables such as debt, deficit, inflation and interest rates, all of which need to be kept within certain boundaries to maintain the value of the currency, ensure economic stability and accomplish growth – the key objective. Indeed, the so-called 'gender strategy' of the IMF also tries to achieve this goal (see chapter 9). At the micro level, the focus is on scarcity and how to obtain the optimal allocation of resources, which is thought to follow from individuals buying and selling goods and services in the free market according to their own tastes and preferences and independently of others. This perspective is idealist because there are so many situations that do not meet the assumptions necessary for the free market to work according to the theory and relatedly because so many activities lie completely outside of the market – for example, most environmental issues are only considered as externalities and social reproduction, including unpaid care work, is not considered at all.

Feminist economists by contrast point out that a more effective and inclusive approach would be to think consciously about how people could organize and manage the economy in ways that would secure their economic, social and environmental goals (Nelson, 2019). These goals could centre on human rights, economic, social, gender and climate justice rather than focusing on maximizing output (GDP) as the goal of policy.

When public debt is considered to be too high, as it was after public funds were used to bail out the banks after the 2008 financial crash and to prevent the economic and health crises associated with the 2020 COVID-19 pandemic, neoliberals insisted on 'fiscal consolidation', that is, austerity policies to reduce this debt. After the 2008 financial crisis, for example, there was a widespread belief based on limited research (subsequently found to be flawed) that if public debt amounted to more than 90 per cent of GDP then the economy would be 'cut in half' (Reinhart and Rogoff, 2010: 573). So, the majority (115) of countries introduced austerity measures to cut the debt, in the belief that reducing government spending would generate economic growth (Ortiz et al, 2015). The resulting policy, termed 'austerity for prosperity' or 'expansionary fiscal contraction', assumes that by contracting fiscal space that is, the amount of money the government can spend, the public sector will stop crowding out the private sector, public sector deficits and debt will fall, the confidence of creditors will increase and interest rates will fall, conditions which neoliberals believe will stimulate investment and thereby regenerate economic growth.

This oxymoronic belief – that contraction of the public sector will lead to expansion – does not work in practice, and the idea that economic catastrophe will follow if public debt exceeds 90 per cent of GDP was proved to be incorrect when 193 countries introduced stimulus packages at the height of the COVID-19 pandemic, with some exceeding 90 per cent of GDP. However, in their loans to many low-income countries the IMF built in a requirement for 'fiscal consolidation' (IMF, 2020) once the immediate COVID-19 threat diminished and overall, 143 countries are practicing austerity until at least 2025 (Ortiz and Cummings, 2022). This illustration shows that while State finance is accepted as being critical at times of crises, as soon as these ease there is an immediate return to neoliberal orthodoxy and reliance on the private sector for overall wellbeing, even though this strategy has not been very effective in either restoring economic growth or reducing the debt owing to its deflationary impact which is also gender biased.

The neoliberal perspective portrays public spending as wasteful, unaffordable and damaging to the economy. It focuses on and favours private sector production and overlooks the productive roles of households and the State in producing both people and value to the economy. Using the ratio of debt to GDP to define the boundaries of the available fiscal space takes no account of what the expenditure is used for, which is myopic and fails to recognize that public investment can bring positive returns over time (Muchhala and Guillem, 2022).

Neoliberal economics has a supply side perspective and argues that national income or growth is propelled by private sector investment, which in turn is driven by the supply of savings. So, when growth is low, it is assumed that savings are too low because taxes on businesses and public expenditure are too high and crowd out the private sector, thereby impeding growth, and when unemployment is high it is assumed that this is because wages are too high. Consequently, policies are introduced to cut public expenditure, often by cutting wages of public sector employees, reducing public subsidies and sometimes by raising taxes, but if so, mainly through consumption taxes which can be introduced quickly but are regressive. In addition, public companies or utilities are often privatized to raise public funds, but this strategy often raises prices, decreases quality, depresses employment, wages and working conditions, increases costs and leads to falls in maintenance and renewal, as much of the profit made is distributed to shareholders rather than reinvested. All of these outcomes tend to disadvantage women to a greater extent than men as women are overrepresented in public sector employment, are more likely to be the direct service users (without which women's unpaid labour would increase given the contemporary gender division of labour) and are much less likely to be shareholders.

The overall effect of austerity policies in practice is to lower rather than raise economic growth and they lead to overall losses of employment, including losses in the private sector, reductions in tax revenue and in some cases increased spending on unemployment pay and social protection, so increasing public deficits and debts. By contrast, the more pragmatic IMF researchers argued that the intense fiscal consolidation policies that took place from 2010 was one of the factors holding down growth and encouraged States, especially the high-income ones, to engage more directly in the economy to restore growth, pointing out that fiscal multipliers are large in this circumstance, and more specifically that a 1 per cent reduction in State spending can result in a reduction of 1.7 per cent in growth (Blanchard and Leigh, 2013). Thus, the policy of expansionary fiscal contraction is in practice, as well as in language, oxymoronic and unlikely to lead to economic recovery, but rather lead to further debt and higher debt service charges, leading to a cycle of decline. As it has been argued, 'austerity is a dangerous idea because the way austerity is being represented by both politicians and the media – as the payback for something called the "sovereign debt crisis," supposedly brought on by states that apparently "spent too much" – is a quite fundamental misrepresentation of the facts' (Blyth, 2013: 4).

In neoclassical economic theory and policy there is an underlying assumption that it is the private sector that creates wealth while public expenditure is largely redistributive and inefficient. The possibility that public expenditure and social policies can be productive is rarely, if ever, contemplated. Yet public expenditure can boost rather than depress economic activity, as Keynes argued and past economic recoveries have demonstrated. This alternative approach is advocated by feminist and heterodox economists because they see the economy as demand rather than supply driven. So, in periods of recession or low growth they see the problem as one of insufficient demand in the economy and the role of the State is to step in and increase its expenditure and investment to expand employment and increase demand, which in turn will boost investment. Increasing demand from marginal groups and women who spend a high proportion of their incomes would be particularly effective and begin to address the current distributional crisis (UNCTAD, 2022). Therefore, by investing directly in the economy, State expenditure can have a positive multiplier effect and prevent the waste of idle resources and loss of human life that would otherwise follow from waiting for the market to right itself. As John Maynard Keynes (1924: 80) pointed out 'in the long run we are all dead', and it was these ideas that underpinned the initial IMF and State responses to the financial and COVID-19 crises before returning to neoliberal orthodoxy.

The neoliberal view is also very different from alternative perspectives that are evident in UN institutions as well as in left, green and feminist thinking. UN Women (2021) have put forward a plan for sustainability and social justice and the UN Conference on Trade and Development (UNCTAD, 2017; 2022) foresees a positive role for State finance in the form of a global new deal and investment in social and physical infrastructure, including green projects, to aid economic recovery and increase the likelihood of the Sustainable Development Goals being realized. These reports also commented favourably on an emerging body of feminist economic research that demonstrates that public investment in social infrastructure can be productive and lead to increased employment, economic growth, greater gender equality and help protect women's human rights. This evidence comes from various regions around the world, including the US, the Republic of Korea and Turkey (Antonopoulos and Kim, 2011; Ilkkaracan, Kijong and Kaya, 2015)

A simulation study by the UK's Women's Budget Group for the International Trade Union Confederation (ITUC) for seven Organization for Economic Co-operation and Development (OECD) countries (ITUC, 2016) investigated the employment impacts of investing in physical (construction sector) and social infrastructure (caring sector) and calculated the number of jobs that would be created in these sectors themselves (the direct jobs), the jobs created in sectors that supply goods and services to these sectors, such as beds or toys for the care sector or bricks for construction (that is, the indirect jobs), and the jobs created as a consequence of the newly employed workers spending their wages (that is, the induced effects). The study found that if the investment took place in caring, then women would take up the majority of jobs but, owing to expansion in other sectors, jobs in stereotypically male sectors would be created too. More specifically, while both forms of investment would generate increases in employment, investment in care would create substantially more jobs overall, and up to four times as many jobs for women in the majority of countries, and almost the same number of jobs for men owing to the indirect and induced jobs created as it would be if the investment took place in construction. This analysis is based on the current gender division of labour between construction and care but, ideally, if the predicted expansion of these sectors occurred and appropriate training was provided, then the pay and gendering might become more equal.

One criticism of this analysis is that the results are due to the lower pay in the care sector, but more recent analysis shows that, even if the pay levels were equalized, more jobs would still be created if the investment took place in care (De Henau and Himmelweit, 2021). An additional benefit of investing in care is that its initial effect is likely to be more carbon neutral than the initial effect of investing in physical infrastructure. A parallel study of six 'emerging' economies found broadly similar results (ITUC, 2017). Apart from creating new jobs and aiding economic recovery, investment in childcare and social care would help to resolve some of the central economic and social problems that confront contemporary societies: the deficit in care, declining fertility, demographic aging and continuing gender inequality. However, when governments do increase public investment to provide a fiscal stimulus, as in 2008 and 2020, they generally favour physical rather than social infrastructure investment – a further gender bias given current employment patterns.

3. Gender biases in neoliberal economic policy with reference to austerity

Austerity[2] is gendered because it creates a triple jeopardy for women (Fawcett Society, 2012; CESR, 2018). Women lose more jobs, more services and are less likely to receive social protection than men owing to the stereotypical and indeed real differences in the roles that women and men play in the economy and in the home, the social norms that sustain these gender differences and the failure of neoliberal macroeconomic policies to recognize the significance of these gender differentiated roles. The gender division of labour varies among countries and has changed over time, but even so it remains universal even in countries where there have been decades of equal opportunities policies. It represents one of the main and most enduring sources of gender inequality and injustice and undermines women's human rights.

In the labour market, women face segregation and discrimination as well as limited access. Paid work continues to be gender segregated: vertically by status and, horizontally, by sector, occupation and contract, and there are 18 countries where husbands can prevent their wives from doing any paid work, and 2.7 billion women are prevented by law from doing the same jobs as men (UN Women, 2019). Men are more likely to hold senior positions in finance and management while women are more likely to be found lower down the hierarchy, with lower pay, in more flexible and insecure jobs. In addition, women are overrepresented in the public sector, especially in caring, health and teaching, where they generally find more decent work; but in times of austerity, not only are they likely to lose jobs but also likely to face pay restraint leading some workers to leave the sector, causing a further deterioration in service quality and a vicious spiral of decline in public provision with women much more likely than men to pick up the resulting increase in unpaid domestic and caring work at home. Cutting these public services also contravenes international human rights (UN Independent Expert, 2018) because they cause undue harm and, as many feminist and heterodox economists would argue, even if reducing public debt was considered absolutely necessary there are alternative ways of doing so, such as raising the tax rate of people with high incomes, closing tax havens or introducing transaction taxes on financial services which would not cause undue harm, as required by international human rights law (see chapter 5).

Women are also overrepresented in the informal sector and in rural and agricultural communities and are more likely to be family helpers rather than registered as workers. Deep-seated gendered social norms also mean that when jobs are scarce, women are much more likely than men to lose theirs, and where there is social protection it is often based on the heads of households, disproportionately male, so even when available, women are less likely than men to receive social protection in their own right, which in turn not only affects income but also limits their opportunities, including their ability to escape from unsafe households.

This uneven distribution of caring and domestic responsibilities furthers women's disadvantage in the labour market, limiting the types of jobs they can do and the amount of time for which they can do them. Yet both domestic and care work are 'vital to individual socialization and the reproduction and maintenance of people upon which the economy depends' (King Dejardin, 2009: 3) and, if valued, these kinds of work would contribute between 10 per cent and 39 per cent of GDP (UN Women, 2019). Overall, women spend over 2.5 as much time as men on domestic and caring work (UN Women, 2019) and this work increased during the pandemic (WEF,

2020). This essential economic and social contribution is not recognized by neoliberal economists.

Unpaid care work constitutes a time tax on women and results in their having less access to money and finance, lower lifetime earnings and pensions and therefore fewer resources with which to withstand austerity. It also lowers women's independence, their voice in household and community decision making, their presence in positions of power and inclusion in political and economic policy making, and reflects and reinforces unequal power relations between women and men. While the presence of women in political and economic policy making would not inevitably change policies, widening representation to include people with more varied experiences of life would almost certainly lead to some different policy choices.

One of the most gendered and least visible cuts in public services is support for survivors and victims of violence against women and girls (VAWG), and this is a serious and pervasive human rights violation. VAWG affects all societies, social classes and cultures and impacts on women disproportionately (33 per cent for women and 5 per cent for men, UN Women, 2015) and these figures are likely to understate the true extent of violence, as many victims and survivors remain silent owing to male impunity, to women's economic dependency on their partners, and to the discriminatory and patriarchal attitudes in society that consider male violence to their female partners a normal part of everyday life. More recent figures find that there has been little change over the past decade and that, worldwide, 'more than five women or girls are killed every hour by someone in their own family' (UNODC and UN Women 2022: 5).

During the COVID-19 pandemic, VAWG increased in 80 per cent of the 49 countries surveyed by UN women, including increases in China and Somalia of up to 50 per cent and in Colombia of 79 per cent (UN Women, 2020). In the UK, femicide trebled in the first three weeks of the first lockdown and calls to helplines increased by 50 per cent. The risk of violence increased owing to the difficulties of escape, of contacting the services and refuges, but also because of the preceding periods of austerity which had dramatically reduced the services available. In Brazil, the 2015 austerity programme which led to a 58 per cent reduction in spending on services that specifically benefitted women included a 15 per cent cut in the support for survivors of sexual or domestic violence (David, 2018), and yet the femicide rate is the fifth highest in the world. In the UK, services for victims and survivors of VAWG were reduced considerably during the ten years of austerity between 2010 and 2020, and even though some funds were provided during the pandemic these were tiny compared to the preceding cuts. These cuts took place despite a study by UK government researchers that estimated the cost of domestic violence at £66 billion ($80 billion) per year when the physical and emotional harms (as far as it is possible to measure in monetary terms), lost output (as a consequence of days at work lost due to illness), and the costs incurred by health and victim support services, as well as by the police and the criminal justice system are taken into account (Rhys et al, 2019). Not only does this show that austerity programmes undermine women's wellbeing and rights, but also that neoliberal policies are male biased because in this case, the failure to fund these services is economically irrational.

Austerity increases joblessness and deprives people of the services and social protection that might otherwise have mitigated these effects, leading to a lowering of living standards especially for women, minority groups and those who are already poor. Legally, States are not committed to guaranteeing any particular standard of living; but austerity policies are incompatible with human rights obligations, if they mean that people are 'deprived of essential foodstuffs, [of] primary health care, of basic shelter and housing, or of the most basic forms of education' (CESCR, 1990: paragraph 10). Austerity policies signal that States are failing to discharge their obligations under the International Covenant on Economic, Social and Cultural Rights (ICESCR), which was signed and ratified by the majority of States, as well as under the Convention on the Rights of the Child (CRC) and the Convention on the Elimination of all forms of Discrimination against Women (CEDAW), which were signed by up to 187 States (see Bohoslavsky, 2020). These conventions recognize that resources are not unlimited, but they commit States to working progressively towards an environment that enables human flourishing and using all available resources to this end. When resources are limited, then priority should be given to the most deprived. If States fail to meet these obligations when they have the necessary resources, they are guilty of retrogression, in other words, they are choosing policies that move them away from rather than towards securing rights even though more progressive alternatives exist (Elson, 2012).

At present, conventions are only legally binding if they are implemented through national legislation, an issue currently under discussion. Nonetheless, States still have to report on the extent to which human rights are being secured or violated, and UN rapporteurs and treaty bodies monitor State performances. In effect, their reports serve to name and shame States that violate human rights or fail to move towards targets; and campaigners use these reports to press for progressive change. Rights conventions can also be used as yardsticks to evaluate proposed policy changes, but this is either not done or not done effectively.

The UN Special Rapporteur on extreme poverty and human rights described the UK's austerity programme as misogynist, chaotic and cruel (Alston, 2019). The UK government rejected the report's findings even though between 2010 and 2018 it had cut social protection by £37 billion while simultaneously lowering taxes by £57 billion (WBG, 2018). This policy violated the conventions, since not all available resources were drawn upon to ensure that existing rights were maintained. Far from everyone suffering austerity together as the government claimed, this was a clear illustration of how neoliberalism is machista, because the tax cuts benefitted the more affluent tax payers, disproportionately men, while the cuts in public sector employment and services and social protection disadvantaged those experiencing multiple forms of intersecting inequalities, especially women.

4. Conclusion

The world is in a state of almost permanent crisis; currently facing economic slowdown, a crisis in care, health, education and most recently the war in Ukraine which has led to massive increases in the prices of energy and food and resulted in rising global inflation and a cost of living crisis. Yet neoclassical economic thinking continues to dominate economic policy in the major financial institutions as well as many nation states and prioritizes economic stability over the wellbeing of people and the planet. The response to rising inflation is to allow interest rates to rise, which increases debt servicing charges including those for public sector borrowing, so increasing overall public debt. By so doing, the interests of creditors are prioritized while curtailing the ability of States to protect people from the rising costs of living by maintaining public services and employment and providing social protection. In short, this means a return to or a continuation of austerity which impacts most negatively on women, especially those facing multiple intersecting forms of discrimination, and undermines their rights. While there are many critiques of this perspective given its failure to reduce debt, as well as it leading to a wide range of social harms, neoliberals themselves would attribute the continuation of debt to the 'incomplete application of its principles' (Polanyi, 2001 [1944]: 149).

What is needed instead is a fundamental transformation that puts social wellbeing at the centre of economic policy making and ensures that the economy works for people rather than vice versa, as well as a radical redistribution of income by preventing profiteering and excessive dividend payments to shareholders, reversing labour's ever falling share of value added and rebalancing the world economy by cancelling much of the debt of low- and middle-income countries while ensuring that any new loans are subject to human rights – including gender and environmental – impact assessments. While these assessments are a legal requirement, it is important to ensure that these are carried out effectively by drawing on the expertise of feminist researchers.

Economic and social policies could work together to secure more sustainable outcomes. The international financial institutions and national governments should draw on the expertise of those who fully understand how to practice gender mainstreaming and have the competence to carry out gender impact assessments and gender-responsive budgeting effectively so as to ensure that, at the very least, their own policies do not lead to a retrogression of women's human rights. In addition, they should take note of the very many alternative policies – including global new deals (UNCTAD, 2017) and care (people and planet) centred economies (Action Aid, 2022; WBG, 2022) – that have been put forward and are much more likely to secure more sustainable and gender inclusive futures.

Notes

1 Note that this chapter is based on Perrons (2021).
2 See Elson and Çağatay (2000), who refer to the deflationary bias, the commodification bias and the male bias.

References

Action Aid International (2022) 'The care contradiction: The IMF, gender and austerity', [online] 10 October, Available from: https://actionaid.org/publications/2022/care-contradiction-imf-gender-and-austerity

Alston, P. (2019) 'Final report of the Special Rapporteur on extreme poverty and human rights visit to the United Kingdom of Great Britain and Northern Ireland', United Nations General Assembly [online] 23 April, Available from: https://undocs.org/A/HRC/41/39/Add.1

Antonopoulos, R. and Kim, K. (2011) 'Public job-creation programs: The economic benefits of investing in social care? Case studies in South Africa and the United States' (Working Paper No 671), Levy Economics Institute [online], Available from: https://www.levyinstitute.org/pubs/wp_671.pdf

Blanchard, O. (2008) 'IMF survey interview' in C. Andersen, IMF Survey: IMF Spells Out Need for Global Fiscal Stimulus, IMF [online] 29 December, Available from: https://www.imf.org/en/News/Articles/2015/09/28/04/53/soint122908a

Blanchard, O. and Leigh, D. (2013) 'Growth forecast errors and fiscal multipliers' (IMF Working Paper 13/1), Available from: https://www.imf.org/external/pubs/ft/wp/2013/wp1301.pdf

Blyth, M. (2013) Austerity: The History of a Dangerous Idea, Oxford: Oxford University Press.

Bohoslavsky, J.P. (2020) 'Complicity of international financial institutions in violation of human rights in the context of economic reforms', Columbia Human Rights Law Review, 52(1): 203–50.

CESCR [Committee on Economic, Social and Cultural Rights] (1990) 'General Comment No. 3: The nature of states parties' obligations', Office of the High Commissioner for Human Rights [online], Available from: https://www.refworld.org/pdfid/4538838e10.pdf

CESR [Center for Economic and Social Rights] (2018) 'Austerity in the midst of inequality threatens human rights: Fact sheet 18', [online] 1 October, Available from: https://www.cesr.org/austerity-midst-inequality-threatens-human-rights-south-africa/

David, G. (2018) 'The impacts of IMF-backed austerity on women's rights in Brazil', Bretton Woods Project [online] 29 March, Available from: https://www.brettonwoodsproject.org/2018/03/impacts-imf-backed-austerity-womens-rights-brazil/

De Henau, J. and Himmelweit, S. (2021) 'A care-led recovery from COVID-19: Investing in high-quality care to stimulate and rebalance the economy', *Feminist Economics*, 27(1–2): 453–69.

Elson, D. (2012) 'The reduction of the UK budget deficit: A human rights perspective', *International Review of Applied Economics*, 26(2): 177–90.

Elson, D. and Çağatay, N. (2000) 'The social content of macroeconomic policies', *World Development*, 28(7): 1347–64.

Fawcett Society (2012) 'The impact of austerity on women', [online] 19 March, Available from: https://www.fawcettsociety.org.uk/the-impact-of-austerity-on-women

Ilkkaracan, I.; Kijong, K. and Kaya, T. (2015) 'The impact of public investment in social care services on employment, gender equality and poverty: The Turkish case', Istanbul Technical University Women's Study Center in Science, Engineering and Technology and the Levy Economics Institute of Bard College [online] August, Available from: http://www.levyinstitute.org/pubs/rpr_8_15.pdf

IMF (2020) 'IMF executive board approves a US$739 million disbursement to Kenya to address the impact of the COVID-19 Pandemic', press release [online] 6 May, Available from: https://www.imf.org/en/News/Articles/2020/05/06/pr20208-kenya-imf-executive-board-approves-us-million-disbursement-address-impact-covid-19-pandemic

ITUC (2016) 'Investing in the care economy: A gender analysis of employment stimulus in seven OECD countries', [online] 29 February, Available from: https://www.ituc-csi.org/investing-in-the-care-economy

ITUC (2017) 'Investing in the care economy: Simulating employment effects by gender in countries in emerging economies', [online] 13 January, Available from: https://www.ituc-csi.org/investing-in-the-care-economy

Keynes, J.M. (1924) *A Tract on the Monetary Reform*, London: Macmillan.

King Dejardin, A. (2009) 'Gender (in)equality, globalization and governance' (Working Paper No 92), International Labour Office [online] March, Available from: https://www.ilo.org/wcmsp5/groups/public/---dgreports/---integration/documents/publication/wcms_108648.pdf

Muchhala, B. and Guillem, A. (2022) 'Gendered austerity and embodied debt in Ecuador: Channels through which women absorb and resist the shocks of public budget cuts', *Gender and Development,* 30(1–2): 283–309.

Nelson, J. (2019) *Economics for Humans*, 2nd edn, Chicago, IL: University of Chicago Press.

Ortiz, I. and Cummings, M. (2022) 'End austerity, a global report on budget cuts and harmful social reforms in 2022–25', Initiative for Policy Dialogue, Global Social Justice, ITUC, Public Services International, ActionAid International, Arab Watch Coalition, et al [online], Available from: https://assets.nationbuilder.com/eurodad/pages/3039/attachments/original/1664184662/Austerity_Ortiz_Cummins_FINAL_26-09.pdf?1664184662

Ortiz, I.; Cummings, M.; Capaldo, J. and Karunanethy, K. (2015) 'The decade of adjustment: A review of austerity trends 2010–2020 in 187 countries' (ESS Working Paper No 53), International Labour Office [online], Available from: https://www.social-protection.org/gimi/gess/RessourcePDF.action?ressource.ressourceId=53192

Perrons, D. (2021) *Is Austerity Gendered?*, Cambridge: Polity Press.

Polanyi, K. (1944) *The Great Transformation: The Political and Economic Origins of our Time*, repr 2001, Boston, MA: Beacon Press.

Reinhart, C. and Rogoff, K. (2010) 'Growth in a time of debt', *American Economic Review,* 100: 573–8.

Rhys, O.; Barnaby, A.; Roe, S. and Wlasny, M. (2019) 'The economic and social costs of domestic abuse' (Research Report 107), Home Office [online] January, Available from: https://assets.publishing.service.gov.uk/government/uploads/system/uploads/attachment_data/file/918897/horr107.pdf

UNCTAD (2017) 'Trade and Development Report 2017: Beyond austerity: Towards a global new deal', Available from: https://unctad.org/webflyer/trade-and-development-report-2017

UNCTAD (2022) 'Trade and Development Report 2022. Development prospects in a fractured world: Global disorder and regional responses', Available from: https://unctad.org/webflyer/trade-and-development-report-2022

UN Independent Expert on debt and human rights (2018) 'Impact of economic reforms and austerity measures on women's human rights' (A/73/179), Human Rights Council, 18 July.

UNODC and UN Women (2022) 'Gender-related killings of women and girls (femicide/feminicide)', [online], Available from: https://www.unwomen.org/sites/default/files/2022-11/Gender-related-killings-of-women-and-girls-improving-data-to-improve-responses-to-femicide-feminicide-en.pdf

UN Women (2015) 'Progress of the world's women, 2015–2016: Transforming economies, realizing rights', [online], Available from: https://www.unwomen.org/sites/default/files/Headquarters/Attachments/Sections/Library/Publications/2015/POWW-2015-2016-en.pdf

UN Women (2019) 'Facts and figures: Economic empowerment', [online], Available from: https://www.unwomen.org/en/what-we-do/economic-empowerment/facts-and-figures

UN Women (2020) 'Impact of COVID-19 on violence against women and girls and service provision: UN Women rapid assessment and findings', [online], Available from: https://www.unwomen.org/en/digital-library/publications/2020/05/impact-of-covid-19-on-violence-against-women-and-girls-and-service-provision

UN Women (2021) 'Beyond COVID-19: A feminist plan for sustainability and social justice', [online], Available from: https://www.unwomen.org/sites/default/files/Headquarters/Attachments/Sections/Library/Publications/2021/Feminist-plan-for-sustainability-and-social-justice-en.pdf

WBG [Women's Budget Group] (2018) 'The impact of austerity on women in the UK. Submission to the UNHRC', [online], Available from: https://www.ohchr.org/sites/default/files/Documents/Issues/Development/IEDebt/WomenAusterity/WBG.pdf

WBG (2022) 'A green and caring economy: Final report', [online], Available from: https://wbg.org.uk/wp-content/uploads/2022/11/A-Green-and-Caring-Economy-Report.pdf

Wintour, P. and Rankin, J. (2020) 'G20 leaders issue pledge to do 'whatever it takes' on coronavirus', *The Guardian* [online] 26 March, Available from: https://www.theguardian.com/world/2020/mar/26/g20-leaders-issue-pledge-to-do-whatever-it-takes-on-coronavirus

WEF [World Economic Forum] (2020) 'COVID-19: How women are bearing the burden of unpaid work', [online] 18 December, Available from: https://www.weforum.org/agenda/2020/12/covid-women-workload-domestic-caring/

11

Continuity of the IMF's Androcentric Policies Before, During and After the Pandemic: The Case of Latin America

Alicja Paulina Krubnik

1. Introduction

The clash of gender equity[1] and neoliberalism has been ongoing for decades, and an analysis of the International Monetary Fund's (IMF) practices is perhaps one of the most pertinent areas that begs for a critical analysis. The IMF's role in the neoliberalization of socioeconomic policies throughout Latin America has been well established to have created inequity across many lines of enquiry. Their impact has come from decades of conditional lending programmes, often in response to the already burdening effects of financial crises. This chapter begins with an analysis of the gendered effects of said conditionality throughout an era of successive debt crises in Latin America in the late 20th century by establishing the central tenets around which IMF conditions are structured: financialization and increasing corporatization, liberalization, deregulation and austerity. Since there is some debate on the influence that the IMF has had on social policy, this chapter examines evidence that makes this connection explicit.

In the contemporary context of the pandemic crisis, the IMF's role has been maintained and even heightened in some cases (Kentikelenis and Stubbs, 2022; Muchhala and Guillem, 2022). With many of the new funding arrangements being conditional, it is important to examine the IMF-backed policies. Though some notable changes are present, there are many androcentric continuities that are disconcerting for gender equity that are made apparent when analyzing the mechanisms of financialization and privatization (and corporatization), liberalization, deregulation and austerity.

Finally, this chapter presents an analysis of the broader 'IMF and Gender' efforts. The 'gender turn' since 2013 (post global financial crises, when gendered effects of crises were unignorable) is not insignificant, however it misses the fundamental calls from critical feminist thought. When gender-based analysis or engendering is done, it is done incompletely and thus insufficiently. Worse yet, the IMF tends to co-opt gender discourse and mould it to neoliberal policy aims. A fundamental paradigm reconceptualization is needed to address gender inequity.

2. IMF conditionality of crises past

Latin American countries had turned to the IMF after a particularly turbulent time in the late 1970s and 1980s. Borrowing-led development initiatives of the 1970s, marked by a context of military dictatorships that systematically and massively violated the human rights of the population, were not long after followed by steep increases in interest rates, declining commodity prices, droves of capital flight and panicked creditors. This contributed to the culmination of successive financial, particularly debt, crises throughout Latin America and the so-called 'lost decade'. The ramifications of debt crises are not gender neutral and this was no exception in Latin America. Structural constraints of informal norms and family structures as well as formal limits to labour markets, economic holdings like land, and politics to name a few (Kabeer, 2018) placed women in precarious positions to begin with and limited their ability to weather the crises.

At the same time, around the 1980s, a rise in market-led neoliberal economic ideas and pressure from Global North stakeholders contributed to the structural conditionality aspects of lending arrangements between the creditor and borrowing States. What had initially begun as the IMF's policy strategy to '[reduce] excess demand by cutting fiscal deficits and restricting the growth of the money supply', imposed into the avenues of 'the privatization of public enterprises, trade liberalization, the reform of banking and bankruptcy legislation, anti-poverty measures, and the prevention of money-laundering and terrorist financing' by the 1980s (Babb and Buira, 2005: 2). The structural adjustment policy packages fit into the neoliberal tenets of financialization or corporatization (beyond even privatization), liberalization, deregulation and austerity (Summers and Pritchett, 1993: 383).[2]

Largely, IMF conditions promote policies along the lines of said neoliberal tenets. These core aspects are found woven into most conditional programmes and are problematic for Marxist, feminist and postcolonial scholars alike. However, apart from these neoliberal tenets, and increasingly so as of the 1990s, lending arrangements included conditions geared toward poverty reduction, including social safety net development. According to the IMF, 'under IMF-supported programs, the Fund helps governments to protect and even increase social spending' (IMF, 2015 as cited in Kentikelenis et al,

2016: 564). Some research into this claim has, however, found conflicting outcomes; social policy conditions in lending arrangements were highly stringent and had eligibility criteria that were outdated for the poverty profiles (Kentikelenis et al, 2016: 564). This would have implications for the ability of women at the intersection of marginalizing systems based on class, 'race', ethnicity, sexual orientation and ability to weather crises. Social programmes would also compensate for household economic loss that tends to result in less money invested into woman members during financial crises.

Poverty reduction-oriented conditions are expected to have different effects on gender than conditions surrounding financialization and corporatization, liberalization, deregulation and austerity. This calls for further analysis on the overall impact of IMF conditionality on inequality. One such way to do this is to examine whether IMF conditions have a redistributive effect where they are implemented; this can be achieved by analyzing the change in the strength of national social protection programmes (though other levels of analysis would also prove to be very telling). This is particularly important since social protection programmes

> are a critical source of financial resources for low-income women due in large part to the enduring gender pay gap and other factors which concentrate women more heavily in lower-income deciles, are often the first services to be reduced [in times of financial crisis], even in countries that suffer extreme poverty. (Razavi, 2016 as cited in Muchhala and Guillem, 2022: 287)

Of course, one can look at the overall effects of conditional lending programmes (that is, by the number of conditions) on social spending, but since different conditions' effects can counter one another, it is more useful to examine how disaggregated conditions impact social spending. Kentikelenis (2016) and Kentikelenis and Stubbs (2023) have usefully examined conditional programmes during this era (from the 1980s until the early 2000s around the time of the global financial crisis) and found that they largely fit into 12 categories of policy areas: external debt issues; financial sector, monetary policy and central bank issues; fiscal issues; external sector (trade and exchange system); revenues and tax issues; labour issues (public and private sector); State-owned enterprise (SOE) reform and pricing; SOE privatization; social policy (restrictive or neutral); redistributive policies; institutional reforms; land and environment; as well as a residual category for conditions regarding things like national accounts framework, balance of payments reporting and household surveys (see Kentikelenis and Stubbs (2023) for detailed descriptions of each category).

Disaggregated by policy area, an analysis of conditionality throughout Latin America between the 1980s until 2009 by Krubnik (2021) found that social services and welfare spending overall was significantly and substantially negatively impacted by conditions pertaining to the external trade and exchange system sector and public and private sector labour issues, which can be categorized as liberalization and deregulation conditions, respectively. Most interestingly, redistributive conditions had the substantively largest negative impact on social services and welfare spending. This may at first appear nothing short of bizarre, seeing as how Kentikelenis et al (2016) and Kentikelenis and Stubbs' (2023) categorization includes conditions on poverty reduction measures, including Poverty Reduction Strategy Paper development and implementation, increases in social sector spending, and minimum employment in social protection programmes, and excludes any restrictive policy. The estimated average 12.3 per cent decrease in social services and welfare spending year-over-year calls for further investigation (Krubnik, 2021). In addition to accounting for theoretically supported potential confounding variables, the use of instrumental variable analysis in the study ruled out potential unobserved factors so that the results can be attributed to the impact of conditions. This seemingly counterintuitive result points to the issue that even when redistributive conditions make the cut for lending arrangements, they are likely to still uphold the central tenets of neoliberalism that have contractionary effects. Additionally, it is important to recognize that financialization and increasing privatization and corporatization, liberalization, deregulation and austerity work simultaneously, a point that will be revisited.

A deeper look into social protection programmes

In the earlier analysis, social services and welfare broadly include social protections that are direct to beneficiaries, both social insurances (contributory) and safety nets (non-contributory) (Krubnik, 2021; Kentikelenis and Stubbs, 2023). Education and healthcare spending, relating to the 'administration, management, inspection, and operation of' facilities, belong to their own categories of social spending (Segura-Ubiergo, 2007: 129–30, as cited in Krubnik, 2021). Non-contributory safety nets are of particular importance for poverty reduction purposes as they are targeted at populations living in poverty (Cecchini and Atuesta, 2017: 25), whereas contributory social insurance can also be helpful for inequality reduction in the best cases, but are more preventative.

It is important to recognize that social protection programmes come in different forms, some more or less helpful for gender equity gains. Contributory insurance programmes are built on top of structures that constrain women to begin with, though 'the degree of gender inequality reproduced by contributory insurance (such as formal pensions tied to employment conditions) in the labour market generally depends on the relationship between entitlements to a pension and employment history' (Becerra Moro, 2011: 3). Women tend to already occupy labour roles valued less in the economy to begin with, due to the 'gender-typing' of work (Rubery, 2013: 18) that prevents the equalization of education from translating into the equalization of value-added to the labour market (Becerra Moro, 2011: 3), pointing to the undervaluing of women's work. Unvalued women's work, that is domestic care work, pushes women into flexible, non-regular and often informal and/ or precarious work, which also creates inequality in the eligibility for and benefits derived from contributory insurance schemes.

Even non-contributory social safety net programmes have gendered effects, and a look into the social safety nets considered by the World Bank (WB) reveals the nature of this. They consider six types of social safety net programmes: unconditional cash transfers (UCTs), conditional cash transfers (CCTs), school feeding programmes, unconditional in-kind transfers, public works and fee waivers (WB, 2015: 8). Under the description of CCTs, conditions are explained to ensure child school attendance or visits to health facilities (in addition to attendance of skills training programmes). UCTs are 'targeted to particular categories of people' (WB, 2015: 8), including the elderly, families with children or other dependants. School feeding programmes are targeted toward school-age children. Lastly, unconditional in-kind transfers tend to also be targeted at specific populations; the World Bank has specifically outlined in-kind transfers programmes for children and pregnant people (WB, 2015: 8). What each of these targeted programmes shows is women tend to be covered insofar as they are caretakers, but women without said responsibilities are a much lesser focus. While these safety net targeting strategies may have counterbalancing effects in reducing some care responsibilities for women, they do not fundamentally aim to restructure care constraints from their gendered domains, and can instead re-entrench gender structural constraints for women facing poverty, even encouraging labour market exits (Becerra Morro, 2011: 4). And, even though it has been shown that cash transfers made directly to women have positive impacts on family wellbeing, several studies on the distribution of income within households show that this money tends to be usurped away from investment in women, especially during times of financial crisis when household expenditures are rationed (Blanton et al, 2019).

3. IMF conditionality in the contemporary context

The previous arguments have pointed to issues whereby IMF conditions in Latin America throughout the crisis periods between the 1980s and the post-2008 financial crisis era have inequality-increasing impacts through encouraging and even impelling national governments toward financialization and increasing corporatization, liberalization, deregulation and austerity. The result is that even those conditions pertaining to redistributive social protection policies have had contractionary effects on social services and welfare. What, though, are the continuities and differences in the context of the current global pandemic crisis?

IMF conditions and advice throughout the pandemic

Austerity

The effects of conditionality policies that affect gender and social protection policies do not remain in the past. For one, the effects of past conditions described earlier 'have put vulnerable groups, and women especially, in an unfavourable position to face the health crisis and its direct and indirect impacts' (Bohoslavsky and Rulli, 2021: 100). However, even beyond the lasting effect of past conditionality, conditionality itself has extended through in the case of the most recent two global crises (not to mention national level crises within Latin America). During the COVID-19 pandemic, loans (concessional and non-concessional) had been approved for Argentina, Bolivia, Chile, Colombia, Costa Rica, Ecuador, El Salvador, Honduras, Mexico, Nicaragua, Panama and Peru with specifically conditional loan arrangements for Argentina, Costa Rica, Ecuador, Honduras and Panama. Conditionality is thus still relevant, though as mentioned earlier, surveillance results and social policy advice outside of conditional loans is also a way in which the IMF can exert influence.

Though conditions and advice generally recommended increasing expenditure on healthcare and non-contributory social safety nets, 'the most recurrent policy recommendation was to begin or resume fiscal consolidation as soon as the conditions created by the health and economic crisis of the COVID-19 pandemic alleviate' (Razavi et al, 2021: 15). Based on the IMF's October 2020 World Economic Outlook data, the proportion of countries contracting expenditure in Latin America and the Caribbean was 76 per cent (Ortiz and Cummins, 2021: 7). Social safety nets mentioned frequently by the IMF should not go unnoticed as they do make evident a more prominent focus to shelter people experiencing poverty from the effects of the crisis through 'provisions to maintain or even moderately increase social spending' (Kentikelenis and Stubbs, 2022: 11). About half of the country reports by the IMF discussed social spending and general poverty-reducing spending floors (Razavi et al, 2021: 17). However, it is unsurprising that on average nearly 40 per cent of overall reviews indicated these targets were unmet given the combination of other policies prescribed (Razavi et al, 2021: 17). Even more, in the vast majority of cases where social protections and poverty reduction spending floors were not reached, fiscal consolidation was still recommended by the IMF (Razavi et al, 2021: 17).

So, advice and conditions tend to point toward austerity when pandemic issues have alleviated (though likely not from a gender inequity standpoint), but what was also found in analyses of COVID-19 conditions was a concern for fiscal space, 'macro-criticality' or the degree to which they affect macroeconomic stability (Razavi et al, 2021: 17). Interestingly enough, gender-equality is also considered macro-critical by the IMF (IMF, 2022b). While macro-criticality also involves spending efficiency and can thus have the aim of ensuring government spending actually reaches those experiencing poverty, it also often involves preventing growth of social protection programmes and reducing spending. Thus, 'the criteria by which social spending is assessed by the IMF (sustainability, adequacy, efficiency), in other words, can pull in different directions' (Engström, 2023: 1140). Though the IMF may aim to reconcile instrumental and intrinsic benefits of gender equality, the result is one that privileges the former and, in many ways, takes away from pursuing gender equity on intrinsic grounds, especially where it clashes with neoliberal institutions.

Additionally, where external debt issues are higher, primarily in middle-income countries, 'the IMF is calling for greater austerity ... and is consistent with concerns from the international community that debt service is being prioritized over social spending and, more broadly, the health and wellbeing of populations' (UNICEF, 2021 as cited in Kentikelenis and Stubbs, 2022: 11). As Engström has pointed out, the concern for fiscal space and austerity rests uneasy with rights-based discourses of social protections (2022: 10). These can very well be seen as policies that have consistently been used by the IMF that end up preventing 'approaches that seek to help countries build up universal provision of basic social protection services' (Kentikelenis and Stubbs, 2022: 11).[3]

By not engendering social protection programmes and by retrenching them, the IMF, and States with whom they have agreements, place women, especially those at the intersection of class, 'race', ethnicity, sexual orientation and/or ability-based systems of marginalization, in a position to have their equity further hampered and even worsened.

Financialization and privatization (and corporatization)

Forms of financialization and privatization have also continued to play a prominent role in the pandemic policy advice and conditions of the IMF to Latin American countries. For one, in consultations regarding flexible credit line arrangements (Table 11.1), countries were explicitly judged on their external position, 'a capital account position dominated by private flows and a track record of steady sovereign access to international capital markets on favourable terms, among others' (Razavi et al, 2021: 43), and few made the cut (Table 11.2). Public private partnerships (PPP) and privatization have been identified as recurrent policy advice and conditionality targets throughout the pandemic era (Razavi et al, 2021: 10), in continuance with IMF and World Bank pushes for PPPs in the health sector, but also in energy and public utilities and housing, among other essential goods and services (Bohoslavsky and Rulli, 2021). The IMF-backed reductions in corporate income taxes (CITs) are also an example of encouraging not just privatization, but corporatization in many Latin American countries. In low- and middle-income countries (not Latin American specific), about 32 per cent of recommendations regarding CIT were to reduce them (Razavi et al, 2021: 36).[4]

Privatization, corporatization and the financialization that tends to follow also works for austerity; though a number of countries in Latin America have privatized pensions as a result of structural adjustment policies from the IMF and World Bank (which have taken extensive effort in many cases to be partially reversed [Ortiz et al, 2018]), the former has recommended the further privatization of subnational pension schemes to cut public costs, such as in consultations for Brazil arrangements (IMF, 2020; Razavi et al, 2021: 30).

What is more is that social protection 'has been characterised as a matter of "risk management", adding macroeconomic concerns and financial market development to social protection programmes' (Engström, 2023: 1144), thereby tying social protection to financialization.

The gendered issues previously mentioned with regard to contributory social protection point to the fact that the equalizing rhetoric of market participation misconstrues actual inequities in how women and their labour is under- and unvalued. Financial liberalization is tied to a greater macroeconomic volatility, which burdens women without financial resources in times of crisis and pushes women 'into the labor force to take on more precarious forms of work' when their households lose employment (Seguino, 2021: 347). Seguino also importantly points to the macroeconomic effects that financial liberalization has on creating deflationary bias and resulting contraction which has negative employment effects felt by women (2021: 347).[5] Also, on a more basic level, the ability to capitalize on markets is of course lower for those with less investible financial assets who face 'higher fees and interest rates in order to access credit [thereby] accumulating lower gains from investment' (Iversen and Rehm, 2019 as cited in Huber et al, 2022: 6; Iversen and Rehm, 2022).

Liberalization

Though also included in advice and conditions during the pandemic, investment and trade liberalization were less featured. There was some mention of amending foreign investment agreements for the purposes of increasing market friendliness (Razavi et al, 2021). However, the lack of information regarding private debt to external creditors is also telling, since private (creditor) external debt makes up the vast majority of debt for middle-income (many Latin American) countries; an average of about US$2.5 billion out of well over US$3.5 billion of overall external debt (Kentikelenis and Stubbs, 2022: 9). This form of debt, however, is not a part of the Debt Service Suspension Initiative; 'the recent experience of countries that undertook restructurings with private creditors – like Argentina and Ecuador – shows that such "case-by-case" approaches minimize their negotiating power and lead to the adoption of harsh austerity measures' (ECLAC, 2021, as cited in Kentikelenis and Stubbs, 2022: 15).

So, one can see the complex yet intimate connection between macro-liberalization and debt. In terms of trade and export-oriented liberalization, Elson and Pearson (1981) and many feminist scholars since have for a while now established that 'women were being absorbed as workers in labor intensive export manufacturing industries in the Global South due to their relatively low wages ... Standing (1989) later dubbed this process the "global feminization of labor"' (as cited in Seguino, 2021: 346–7). On the other hand, investment and 'trade liberalisation is associated with increases in women's labour force participation worldwide' (Peterson, 2005: 510), though the gendered implications are complicated by whether the industry is vertical and the quality of labour regulations. As Seguino aptly points out, 'there is thus no one-size-fits-all trade or investment policy that can be counted on to promote gender equality in all countries' (Seguino, 2021: 347). Since numerous studies 'have found that gender wage gaps have either widened, or if they have narrowed, the discriminatory portion of the wage gap has increased' (Menon and Rodgers, 2009 as cited in Seguino, 2021: 347), the structural component of women's equity needs in-depth case analysis that also takes into account personal empowerment from potential increased employment opportunities. In analyzing local structural inequity, one should also consider which women have access to increased opportunities and whether the divide is equitable for low income and racialized women or whether opportunity for more underprivileged women is lesser and/or more precarious.

Deregulation: spotlighting labour flexibilization

Several accounts of conditions and review advice from the IMF's COVID-19 lending arrangements have mentioned cuts to operational expenditures of public services and 'the implementation of labour market reforms, or their continuation, to make them "more flexible"' (Razavi et al, 2021: 33).[6] This again has been particularly applied to middle-income countries by the IMF. By flexibilization, the IMF and debtor States have typically relied on 'relaxing dismissal regulations; restraining minimum wages; limiting salary adjustments; decentralizing collective bargaining; and making it easier to hire workers on temporary and non-standard contracts' with the aim of supporting business growth, despite a lack of empirical connection (Razavi et al, 2021: 33).

The neoliberal mechanisms of 'fragmentation, segmentation and precariousness of employment' (Fernández, 2022: 46), stemming from deregulation and flexibilization, result in the dispossession of, especially racialized and low-income, women. Furthermore, 'to the extent that this leads to the informalization of employment, it could have an effect on fiscal balances by reducing social security contributions and possibly taxes' (Razavi et al, 2021: 8; Ortiz and Cummins, 2019). One promising development is that, with regard to labour market flexibilization reforms, 'the IMF (2019) has identified the need to promote consultations with trade unions and civil society organizations in its new Social Spending Strategy' (Razavi et al, 2021: 34). As the International Labour Organization's work around 'decent work' suggests, this could enable alternate means to increase protections for those in informal labour situations and limit dispossessive impacts.

The simultaneity of neoliberal mechanisms

As this analysis has shown, the neoliberal mechanisms of past crises have continued and a feminist lens uncovers that IMF macro policy prescriptions of financialization and privatization, liberalization, labour deregulation and austerity have regressive gendered impacts. As suggested by Peck (2013) and Seguino (2021), this chapter analyzed neoliberal policies as explanatory variables. It is important to note that the 'myriads [of] impacts also do not function in isolation, but rather interact and compound one another' (Bürgisser, 2019: 8). These policies should be analyzed in order to identify each one clearly in operation and find its pathways of operation (Seguino, 2021: 346), but the ways in which they are intertwined and uphold each other need to be understood too. Additionally, 'cumulative gendered impacts of an entire reform programme [are] really required to inform policy' (Bürgisser, 2019: 8).

4. Discussion: 'The IMF and gender'

The previously mentioned findings of the most recent COVID-19 arrangements would suggest that the IMF have not taken a genuine gendered approach to their advice and conditions in Latin America, thereby circumventing their responsibility in terms of human rights. This is puzzling, though, given the significant focus on gender that the IMF signals. Especially since 2013, somewhat of a structural break time, 'the IMF's publications about gender equity have grown exponentially, creating a rich textual universe about the productive, even virtuous role of women in the world economy' (Coburn, 2019: 777), citing both instrumental and intrinsic benefits to incorporating women further into the (global) economy. More recently, the IMF's focus on women has been ramping up; 'as of June 2018, the Fund had published more than 2,900 documents and videos about women' (Coburn, 2019: 777) and this commitment can be seen in their 'Gender and the IMF' web page (IMF, 2022a). The IMF's spending floors discussed earlier are an example of the focus that is being placed on protecting vulnerable groups and indicates that the IMF is 'engaged with rights-based concerns, albeit without explicitly adopting that vocabulary' (Engström, 2022: 11).

However, a deep examination from a feminist political economy perspective reveals that structural constraints and gender relationships impacted by them are not well understood. Regarding social protection concerns, the IMF's advice is too narrow; 'gender concerns commonly [enter] as a labour force participation question, or a question of access to finance' (Engström, 2023: 1143). Gender equality as instrumental for macro-criticality is still featured in the rhetoric (Sayeh, 2021; IMF, 2022b)

The IMF's 2018 'How to operationalize gender issues in country work' document had some promising aspects to it in addition to a major focus on women's labour participation and its macro-criticality (IMF, 2018). Paragraph 25 recognized how laws can create structural inequities for women and paragraph 26 importantly notes that cuts to public services and employment can be gendered, and in such cases mitigating factors or alternate policy mixes should be considered. Also notable was that 'gender budgeting' was a focus, which recognizes that government policies have gender differential impacts that institutionalize and constitutionalize inequity (IMF, 2018: 15). Nevertheless, vague outlines leave unanswered what the IMF specifically understands as inequality-generating and which policies might mitigate or replace inequality-generating ones (Bürgisser, 2019: 6). The more recently published 'IMF Strategy Toward Mainstreaming Gender' (IMF, 2022b) also has encouraging aspects. Inequality is recognized and there is a step toward recognizing the myth of a formal–informal economy binary (Peterson, 2010, 2012 as cited in Martín de Almagro and Ryan, 2019); the 'formal economy relies on the unwaged labour of the informal sector, and formal/informal economic activities ... bleed together and cannot be differentiated' (Martín de Almagro and Ryan, 2019: 1064). Though the focus on gender still surrounds primarily the macro-criticality of women's human capital and social policies that relate to women's roles as carers, there is limited mention of active labour market policies and public infrastructure to support formal economy participation, as well as legalizations of inequality that should be remedied (IMF, 2022b).

The main issues that remain with the IMF's gender practices are that entire policy packages in arrangements need to be engendered. In gender budgeting terms, this means 'the whole budget is addressed, not just those expenditures that are explicitly targeted to gender equality' (Elson, 2021: 465). Elson (2021) points to another important issue, and one that has been alluded to throughout this chapter: the mechanisms of neoliberal macroeconomic policies pursued by the IMF, which I have identified here as financialization and privatization (or corporatization), liberalization, deregulation of labour and austerity work to uphold one another's gendered effects. I go as far as to argue that the 'Women in Development' (WID) approach of approximately the 1970s until the 1990s is still operational as it realizes a women's unequal access to resources but does not question the underlying gendered relations that continue to challenge equity (Miller and Razavi, 1995), as is evidenced by continued conditions and recommendations for social protection programmes throughout Latin America. Just as trickle-down economics does not solve issues of class inequality, neither would these policies trickle-down to solve gender issues observed in Latin America (Coburn, 2019). As Coburn has articulated, 'the discursive construction of "femina economica", an elastic and contradictory figure, [is] symptomatic of broader tensions within the IMF and the world capitalist economy' (Coburn, 2019: 769).

Fundamentally, gender has just been incorporated selectively into the existing neoliberal paradigm proven problematic across Latin America and in a way that obscures the need for a paradigmatic shift in line with feminist insights. The use of a critical feminist lens, and especially an intersectional one, uncovers the problems with operations that 'tack on' gender analysis to problematic neoliberal policies. It makes apparent the contradictions of financialization and corporatization, liberalization, deregulation and austerity and the fact that these contradictions will not be rid of their dispossessive power by incorporating neoliberal ideas of women's empowerment. A fundamental paradigm shift is needed to address the androcentricity of the IMF's policies – one that values all forms of gendered labour and recognizes the contradictions of neoliberal capitalist 'solutions' to gender inequity.

Appendix

Table 11.1: COVID-19 approved IMF emergency financing in Latin American countries

	Type of emergency financing	Amount approved in SDR (million)	Date of approval
Argentina	Extended Fund Facility (EFF)	31,914	25 March 2022
Bolivia	Rapid Financing Instrument (RFI)	240.1	17 April 2020
Chile	Flexible Credit Line (FCL)	17,443	29 May 2020
	*Flexible Credit Line (FCL)	*13,954	*29 August 2022
Colombia	Flexible Credit Line (FCL)	7,849.6 (12,267 on IMF, 2022d)	1 May 2020
	Augmentation of FCL	4,417.4	25 September 2020
	*Flexible Credit Line (FCL)	*7,155.7	*29 April 2022
Costa Rica	Extended Fund Facility (EFF)	1,237	1 March 2021
	Rapid Financing Instrument (RFI)	369.4	29 April 2020
Ecuador	Rapid Financing Instrument (RFI)	469.7	1 May 2020
	Extended Fund Facility (EFF)	4,615	30 September 2020
El Salvador	Rapid Financing Instrument (RFI)	287.2	14 April 2020

(continued)

Table 11.1: COVID-19 approved IMF emergency financing in Latin American countries (continued)

	Type of emergency financing	Amount approved in SDR (million)	Date of approval
Honduras	Stand-by Arrangement (SBA) and Stand-by Credit Facility (SCF)	149.9	Sep 13, 2021
	Augmentation of SBA and Augmentation of SCF	162.37 (96.36 and 66.01, respectively)	1 June 2020
Mexico	Flexible Credit Line (FCL)	35,650.8	19 November 2021
Nicaragua	Rapid Financing Instrument (RFI)	86.67	20 November 2020
	Rapid Credit Facility (RCF)	43.33	
Panama	Rapid Financing Instrument (RFI)	376.8	15 April 2020
	Precautionary and Liquidity Line (PLL)	1,884	19 January 2021
Peru	Flexible Credit Line (FCL)	8,007	28 May 2020
	**Flexible Credit Line (FCL)	**4,003.5	**27 May 2022
Suriname	Extended Fund Facility (EFF)	472.8	22 December 2021

* Information listed on IMF, 2022c, but not IMF, 2022d

** Information listed on IMF, 2022d, but not IMF, 2022

Sources: IMF, 2022c; IMF, 2022d

Table 11.2: Description of social service and welfare social protections

Category of social spending	Description
Social services and welfare	'Social security includes transfer payments, including payments in kind to compensate for reduction or loss of income or inadequate earning capacity; sickness, maternity, or temporary disablement benefits; old age, disability, or survivor's pensions; pro-poor programs; unemployment compensation benefits; family and child allowances; and welfare services for children, old persons, and the handicapped' (Segura-Ubiergo, 2007: 130).
Education	Education includes 'pre-primary, primary, secondary, and tertiary educational affairs. Expenditures related to the administration, management, inspection, and operation of pre-primary, primary, secondary (i.e., high school level), and tertiary (i.e., university level) educational affairs' (Segura-Ubiergo, 2007: 130).
Healthcare	Healthcare includes 'hospital affairs and services (i.e., general and specialized hospital and services, medical and maternity centre services, nursing and convalescent home services, clinics, and paramedical practitioners) and public health affairs and services (e.g., the administration, management, operation, and support of disease-detection services such as laboratories and population-control services)' (Segura-Ubiergo, 2007: 130).

Table 11.3: Types of IMF COVID-19 arrangements

Financing facilities	Conditionality	Duration/delivery
Non-Concessional (General Resource Account)		
Stand-by Arrangement (SBA)	Ex-ante prior actions can apply, ex-post (IMF, 2023a)	Up to three years (IMF, 2023a), tranched (Kentikelenis and Stubbs, 2022)
Extended Fund Facility (EFF)	Ex-post structural reform focus, ex-ante prior actions can apply (IMF, 2023a)	Typically three years, can be up to four years (IMF, 2023a) with 'deep and sustained structural reforms' (IMF, 2023c); tranched (Kentikelenis and Stubbs, 2022)
Rapid Financing Instrument (RFI)	Ex-ante prior actions can apply, no ex-post, no reviews (IMF, 2023a)	Outright (IMF, 2023a); rapid (tranched Kentikelenis and Stubbs, 2022)
Flexible Credit Line (FCL)	Ex-ante qualification criteria, ex-post annual reviews can apply (IMF, 2023a)	One or two years (IMF, 2023a); tranched (Kentikelenis and Stubbs, 2022)
Short-Term Liquidity Line (SLL)	Ex-ante qualification criteria, no ex-post (IMF, 2023a)	12 months, successive SLLs possible (IMF, 2023a); tranched
Precautionary and Liquidity Line (PLL)	Ex-ante qualification criteria, ex-post (IMF, 2023a); non-binding (Kentikelenis and Stubbs, 2022)	Six months, or one to two years (IMF, 2023a); tranched (Kentikelenis and Stubbs, 2022)
Concessional Loans (Poverty Reduction and Growth Trust)		
Stand-by Credit Facility (SCF)	Ex-ante prior actions can apply, ex-post (IMF, 2023a)	One to three years (IMF, 2023a); tranched (Kentikelenis and Stubbs, 2022)
Extended Credit Facility (ECF)	Ex-post structural reform focus, ex-ante prior actions can apply (IMF, 2023a)	Three to four years, fifth year extension can apply (IMF, 2023a); tranched (Kentikelenis and Stubbs, 2022)
Rapid Credit Facility (RCF)	Ex-ante prior actions can apply, no ex-post, no reviews (IMF, 2023a)	Outright (IMF, 2023a); rapid (Kentikelenis and Stubbs, 2022)
Grant (CCRT and Initially PCDR)		
Catastrophe Containment and Relief Trust (CCRT)	No (Kentikelenis and Stubbs, 2022), though 'to qualify for the support, the afflicted country should put in place appropriate macroeconomic policies' (IMF, 2021: 8) can apply	Two years, immediate (IMF, 2023b); rapid (Kentikelenis and Stubbs, 2022)
Non-Financial/Signalling Instruments (N/A Financing)		
Staff Monitored Program (SMP) (including Program Monitoring with Board (PMB) involvement)	Ex-post, ex-ante can apply (IMF, 2023a)	6–18 months, longer durations can apply (IMF, 2023a)
Policy Coordination Instrument (PCI)	Ex-post, ex-ante can apply (IMF, 2023a)	Six months to four years (IMF, 2023a)

Notes

[1] Readers will notice that I use 'equity' throughout this chapter, even when referring to IMF documents or other analyses that focus on 'equality', purposefully, with the aim of redirecting the conversation toward one of equity with the view that normative concerns are inescapable with scholarship that focuses on the intrinsic benefit of gendered analyses.

[2] It is important to note that while conditionality is the most outwardly evident way that the IMF can exert its influence, it is not the only way. The institution holds both formal and informal power and a privileged position in the international economic (even political) thought and policy making. It can thus influence national monetary and fiscal policies, but also a host of other governance policies outside of those domains through surveillance and internationally salient advice for low- and middle-income countries. Information regarding compliance with policies they support can impact national policy makers through the threat of signalling to investors, which is exacerbated when there is between-country competition for external finance.

[3] Clarke and Newman argue that 'at the heart of this austerity strategy is a belief that strategies of fiscal constraint can, counter-intuitively, produce expansionary effects in national economies, increasing private consumption and investment and producing growth in Gross Domestic Product (GDP)' (2012: p 301). However, as will be demonstrated by the scholarship of various feminist and other critical heterodox (political) economy scholars, there are several mechanisms that operate to further create dispossessive effects for women at the intersection of identities impacted by austerity. Furthermore, even in engaging in this growth over redistribution and equity argumentation, Guajardo et al have convincingly dispelled this tickle-down-esque belief in austerity; they have found that 'a 1 percent of GDP fiscal consolidation reduces real private consumption by 0.75 percent within two years, while real GDP declines by 0.62 percent' (Guajardo et al, 2011: p 29; Guajardo et al, 2014). Even in the cases where domestic demand is expected by this logic to increase, Guajardo et al found fiscal consolidation to be contractionary (Guajardo et al, 2011: p 29; Guajardo et al, 2014). If spending were to increase, it would likely do so in a highly inequitable way, as we have seen happen with luxury economy spending recently (Garelik, 2021; Indvik, 2022). The other more common outlook, and more probable cause for austerity-driven policy by the IMF (and other Global North IFIs), is that 'low- and middle-income countries have no alternative than to introduce austerity as a prerequisite for gaining access to international financial assistance, lest 'moral hazard' problems emerge' (Kentikelenis and Stubbs, 2022: p 6). Perhaps, however, the larger point is to look away from perpetual debt-inducing arrangements to gain external funding and further integrating into global financial markets that have, if one recalls the late 20th century, contributed in no insignificant way to debt and economic issues across Latin America to begin with.

[4] Broadening value-added tax (VAT), which pushes expenses to consumers, including those in poverty or at risk of being in poverty (especially since exceptions were recommended to be reduced), were mentioned in more reports than 'recommendations to improve revenue collection from more progressive direct forms of taxation, such as personal income taxes (PITs), corporate income taxes (CITs) and wealth taxes' (Razavi et al, 2021: p 36).

[5] This is because 'central banks in countries with liberalized capital accounts feel pressure to keep inflation low, since wealth holders avoid inflation as it reduces the real rate of return on their financial investments. This has contributed to central banks adopting contractionary monetary policies with negative employment effects, and thus exacerbating gender job competition' (Seguino, 2021: p 347).

[6] For about 38.5 per cent of upper-middle-income countries, 14.3 per cent of lower-middle-income countries and just 2.3 per cent of reports on low-income countries (Razavi et al, 2021: p 33).

References

Babb, S. and Buira, A. (2005) 'Mission creep, mission push and discretion: The case of IMF conditionality', in Ariel Buira (ed) *The IMF and the World Bank at Sixty*, London: Anthem Press, pp 59–84.

Becerra Moro, M.J. (2011) 'Engendering social security and protection: The case of Latin America' Friedrich-Ebert-Stiftung: International Policy Analysis.

Blanton, R.; Blanton, S. and Peksen, D. (2019) 'The gendered consequences of financial crises: A cross-national analysis', *Politics & Gender*, 15(1): 941–70.

Bohoslavsky, J.P. and Rulli, M. (2021) 'Bretton Woods' pandemic policies: A gender equality analysis – perspectives from Latin America', *Development*, 64(1–2): 97–106.

Bürgisser, E. (2019) 'The IMF and Gender Equality: Operationalising Change', The Bretton Woods Project [online], Available from:https://www.brettonwoodsproject.org/wp-content/uploads/2019/02/Operation alising-Change.pdf

Cecchini, S. and Atuesta, B. (2017) 'Conditional cash transfer programmes in Latin America and the Caribbean: Coverage and investment trends', ECLAC, United Nations.

Clarke, J. and Newman, J. (2012) 'The alchemy of austerity', *Critical Social Policy*, 32(3): 299–319.

Coburn, E. (2019) 'Trickle-down gender at the International Monetary Fund: The contradictions of "femina economica" in global capitalist governance', *International Feminist Journal of Politics*, 21(5): 768–88.

Elson, D. (2021) 'Gender Budgeting', in Günseli Berik and Abru Kongar (eds) *The Routledge Handbook of Feminist Economics,* Abingdon and New York: Routledge, pp 459–67.

Elson, D. and Pearson, R. (1981) '"Nimble fingers make cheap workers": An analysis of women's employment in third world export manufacturing', *Feminist Review*, 7: 87–109.

Engström, V. (2023) 'Social protection in the mandate of the IMF', *The International Journal of Human Rights*, 27(7): 1–21.

Fernández, D.C. (2022) 'Development model, labour precariousness and new social inequalities in Latin America', *Cepal Review*, 2022(136): 46–61.

Garelick, R.K. (2021) 'How luxury survived the pandemic', *The Washington Post Magazine* [online] 17 November, Available from:https://www.washingtonpost.com/magazine/2021/11/17/how-luxury-survived-pandemic/

Guajardo, J.; Leigh, D. and Pescatori, A. (2011) 'Expansionary austerity? New international evidence' (WP/11/158), IMF Working Paper [online], Available from: https://www.imf.org/external/pubs/ft/wp/2011/wp11158.pdf

Guajardo, J.; Leigh, D. and Pescatori, A. (2014) 'Expansionary austerity? international evidence', *Journal of the European Economic Association*, 12(4): 949–68.

Huber, E.; Petrova, B. and Stephens, J.D. (2022) 'Financialization, labor market institutions and inequality', *Review of International Political Economy*, 29(2): 425–52.

Indvik, L. (2022) 'What 2022 holds in store for luxury', *Financial Times* [online] 6 January, Available from: https://www.ft.com/content/2beb4 15c-156c-4b8b-8384-101a0b13a3d8

IMF (2015) 'Protecting the most vulnerable under IMF-supported programs', International Monetary Fund Factsheet, Available from: https://www.imf. org/external/np/exr/facts/protect.htm

IMF (2018) 'How to operationalize gender issues in country work', *IMF Policy Papers* [online] 13 June, Available from: https://www.imf.org/en/ Publications/Policy-Papers/Issues/2018/06/13/pp060118howto-note-on-gender

IMF (2020) 'Brazil: 2020 Article IV Consultation-Press Release; Staff Report; and Statement by the Executive Director for Brazil', IMF Country Report No. 20/311.

IMF (2021) 'Catastrophe containment and relief trust – fifth tranche of debt service relief in the context of the COVID-19 pandemic', (Policy Paper No 2021/074), *IMF Policy Papers* [online] 20 December, Available from: https://www.imf.org/en/Publications/Policy-Papers/Issues/2021/ 12/17/Catastrophe-Containment-and-Relief-Trust-Fifth-Tranche-of-Debt-Service-Relief-in-The-511094.

IMF (2022a) 'Gender' [online], Available from: https://www.imf.org/en/ Topics/Gender

IMF (2022b) 'IMF strategy toward mainstreaming gender', IMF [online] 28 July, Available from: https://www.imf.org/en/Publications/Policy-Papers/Issues/2022/07/28/IMF-Strategy-Toward-Mainstreaming-Gen der-521344

IMF (2022c) 'COVID-19 financial assistance and debt service relief', IMF [online] 9 March, Available from: https://www.imf.org/en/Topics/imf-and-covid19/COVID-Lending-Tracker#ftn

IMF (2022d) 'Active IMF lending commitments as of [28 February 2022 and 31 October 2022]', IMF [online], Available from:https://www.imf. org/external/np/fin/tad/extarr11.aspx?memberKey1=ZZZZ&date1 key=2022-02-28;https://www.imf.org/external/np/fin/tad/extarr11. aspx?memberKey1=ZZZZ&date1key=2022-10-31

IMF (2023a) 'IMF lending instruments' in 'IMF lending', *International Monetary Fund – Factsheets* [online], Available from: https://www.imf.org/ en/About/Factsheets/IMF-Lending

IMF (2023b) 'Catastrophe containment and relief trust', *International Monetary Fund – Factsheets* [online], Available from: https://www.imf.org/en/About/ Factsheets/Sheets/2023/Catastrophe-containment-relief-trust-CCRT

IMF (2023c) 'The extended fund facility', *International Monetary Fund – Factsheets* [online], Available from: https://www.imf.org/en/About/Fac tsheets/Sheets/2023/Extended-Fund-Facility-EFF

Iversen, T. and Rehm, P. (2022) 'Information and financialization: credit markets as a new source of inequality', *Comparative Political Studies*, 55(14): 2349–81, Available from: https://doi.org/10.1177/0010414022 1074286.

Kabeer, N. (2018) 'Gender, livelihood capabilities and women's economic empowerment: reviewing evidence over the life course', London: Gender and Adolescence: Global Evidence (GAGE).

Kentikelenis, A. and Stubbs, T. (2022) 'Austerity redux: The post-pandemic wave of budget cuts and the future of global public health', *Global Policy*, 13(1): 5–17.

Kentikelenis, A. and Stubbs, T. (2023) *A Thousand Cuts: Social Protection in the Age of Austerity*, New York: Oxford University Press.

Kentikelenis, A.E.; Stubbs, T.H. and King, L.P. (2016) 'IMF conditionality and development policy space, 1985–2014', *Review of International Political Economy*, 23(4): 543–82.

Krubnik, A.P. (2021) 'IMF conditionality, social programmes, and the impact to women's welfare: An empirical analysis of historical policy responses to financial crises in Latin America and their gendered effects', Thesis, *LSE Economic History*, 1–58.

Martin de Almagro, M. and Ryan, C. (2019) 'Subverting economic empowerment: Towards a postcolonial-feminist framework on gender (in) securities in post-war settings', *European Journal of International Relations*, 25(4): 1059–79.

Miller, C. and Razavi, S. (1995) 'From WID to GAD: Conceptual shifts in the women and development discourse' (Occasional Paper 1), United Nations Research Institute for Social Development.

Muchhala, B. and Guillem, A. (2022) 'Gendered austerity and embodied debt in Ecuador: Channels through which women absorb and resist the shocks of public budget cuts', *Gender & Development*, 30(1–2): 283–309.

Ortiz, I. and Cummins, M. (2019) 'Austerity: The new normal – a renewed Washington Consensus 2010–24' (Working Paper), Initiative for Policy Dialogue (IPD), International Confederation of Trade Unions (ITUC), Public Services International (PSI), European Network on Debt and Development (EURODAD), The Bretton Woods Project (BWP) [online], Available from: https://dx.doi.org/10.2139/ssrn.3523562

Ortiz, I. and Cummins, M. (2021) 'Global austerity alert: Looming budget cuts in 2021–25 and alternative pathways', Initiative for Policy Dialogue (IPD), Global Social Justice (GSJ), International Confederation of Trade Unions (ITUC), Public Services International (PSI), Arab Watch Coalition (AWC), The Bretton Woods Project (BWP), Third World Network (TNW).

Ortiz, I.; Durán-Valverde, F.; Urban, S.; Wodsak, V. and Yu, Z. (2018) 'Reversing pension privatization: Rebuilding public pension systems in Eastern European and Latin American countries (2000–18)', *International Labour Office*, 63: 1–58.

Peck, J. (2013) 'Explaining (with) neoliberalism', *Territory, Politics, Governance*, 1(2): 132–57.

Peterson, S.V. (2005) 'How (the meaning of) gender matters in political economy', *New Political Economy*, 10(4): 499–521.

Razavi, S.; Schwarzer, H.; Durán Valverde, F.; Ortiz, I. and Dutt, D. (2021) 'Social policy advice to countries from the International Monetary Fund during the COVID-19 crisis continuity and change', International Labour Organization.

Rubery, J. (2013) 'From "women and recession" to "women and austerity"', in *Women and Austerity: The Economic Crisis and the Future for Gender Equality*, Routledge IAFFE Advances in Feminist Economics 11, Abingdon: Routledge, pp 18–34.

Sayeh, A.M. (2021) 'A new agenda for macro stability: Opening remarks at the Harvard Growth Lab's Development Talk by Deputy Managing Director Antoinette M. Sayeh', IMF [speech] 21 September, Available from: https://www.imf.org/en/News/Articles/2021/09/21/sp092121-a-new-agenda-for-macro-stability-dmd-sayeh

Seguino, S. (2021) 'Gender and Economic Growth', in *The Routledge Handbook of Feminist Economics* (1st edn), Routledge, pp 341–9.

Segura-Ubiergo, A. (2007) *The Political Economy of the Welfare State in Latin America: Globalization, Democracy, and Development*, Cambridge; New York: Cambridge University Press.

Summers, L.H. and Pritchett, L.H. (1993) 'The structural-adjustment debate', *American Economic Review*, 83(2): 383–9.

World Bank (ed) (2015) 'The state of social safety nets 2015', World Bank Group.

PART IV

IMF, Women and Diversities in Latin America and Argentina

12

Life Sustainability and Debt Sustainability: Care in the Centre

María Nieves Rico

'It is time to aim at the heart of the present'
The Philosophical Discourse of Modernity
Habermas, 1985

1. Introduction

Public indebtedness and its consequences has a more complex meaning when analyzing how it appears and operates in the daily life of people, politicizing and reflecting on its relation with the non-monetary economy; the guarantee and exercise of human rights, particularly economic, social and cultural rights; as well as the increase of economic and social vulnerability of communities that are abandoned so that they can individually solve, if they can, their needs and reach a certain welfare level, but dismissing that in fact this is a collective challenge.

In the last decades, Latin American countries have suffered the asphyxiating pressure of the external debt taken by governments. Evidence shows that debt has been an instrument that serves as an excuse to cut budgets and public services so as to structurally reform and adjust the monetary economy, as well as to reduce fiscal deficit. At the same time, these orthodox policies appeal to an allegedly necessary 'austerity' in terms of expenses and public investment, as well as to the obligation to a timely and 'disciplinary' repayment of debt services, regardless of the consequences that this has or may have for the population, particularly for women and their rights.

Moreover, indebted countries have their capacity to comply with their obligations undermined and have their possibilities to act limited in at least two ways: (1) the provision of goods and services to the population to protect their rights, especially to those who live in poverty or who are in a major situation of economic vulnerability; and (2) the implementation of public policies that lead to a higher level of welfare and contribute to processes of substantive equality.

In this chapter, life and care sustainability, rooted themselves in a time and space of extreme structural inequalities, are analytically linked to the scenario of questioning the so-called debt sustainability. Incorporating this perspective refers to the question of *'who owes to whom?'* (Federici, Gago and Cavallero, 2021), evidencing the loss of purchasing power of household income (salaries, pensions and subsidies) and the increase of private indebtedness in households that has a major impact on women and that is strongly linked to the unfair distribution of unpaid care tasks between men and women. It is essential to take into account that care involves two scarce resources: money and time, and nowadays women and their care tasks inside their households subsidize the economic system and the State as there are virtually no public policies of care and there is a strongly biased market offer, while they strongly contribute to the development of countries through an invisibilized non-monetary economy that is not part of the national system of accounts.

The daily life of women becomes more paradoxical than ever: they work more both in paid and unpaid jobs, and they are more indebted. In the words of a woman: "I work to pay". What happens at country level is also paradoxical: the environmental and care crises, along with the economic recession, which jeopardize life sustainability, come with huge profits for the local and international financial system, along with currency devaluation and capital flight.

Cutbacks in the public sector have effects on women that deepen at least three risks: they reduce or directly lose access to existing public services; have fewer opportunities to generate income or find a decent job; and they feel obliged socially, culturally and economically to accept the increasing burden of unpaid care jobs.

Thus, the elements of public and private debt that replicate and even deepen asymmetries among actors are added to the unfair and imbalanced social organization of care (SOC): State, market, families and civil society (Razavi, 2007). At the same time, the negative effects on women of the rigid gender division of work within and outside households, care debts that do not appear on traditional economic data, and the non-compliance of the right to receive care of large human groups are intensified.

The analysis of the chapter evidences the lack of gender neutrality and blindness of country indebtedness and the implications of cutbacks in social policies on the guarantee and effectiveness of the right to care that is specifically being developed in the present in the countries of the region.

2. Life sustainability

Care, apart from the polysemy of the concept, has an essential and systemic role, and is a critical element to ensure the life and functioning of societies. Addressing the requirements for life sustainability leads to an assessment of care, a material and symbolic process (Rodríguez Enríquez and Partenio, 2020) that is essential for human existence to continue in an independent way at an individual, social and ecological-environmental level, in which the biological and social reproduction of the population is guaranteed, while bases are built to achieve an acceptable life quality 'that deserves to be lived' (Pérez-Orozco, 2006). However, its invisibility 'has hidden one of the mechanisms that enable ways of distribution of income, wealth and time' (Carrasco, 2016: 41).

The current care organization in Latin America, supported by the gender division of work in the public and private sectors, shows a large imbalance and an unfair distribution of responsibilities, resources and assessments among its four pillars, or diamond tips (Razavi, 2007: 21): State, market, civil society and families, a euphemism for 'women'. In this context, life sustainability in our societies is built day after day in households through direct and indirect care, and its management that women provide in an unpaid way, sometimes in a voluntary and loving manner, while on other occasions they provide it in an unwanted, obliged and even coercive form, whether due to prevailing cultural mandates or power relations and conflicts that are triggered within households (Rico, 2011: 109).

Evidence provided by surveys of time use in the region clearly suggests that another unfair and asymmetric relation is added to the aforementioned imbalance among institutional actors: women devote three times the amount of time men devote to unpaid care tasks. This has significant costs on their health, their opportunities to generate their own income, their freedom and their decisions on their life goals. This is even more exacerbated in the case of women who live in rural areas and who devote a larger amount of time to reproductive work than women from urban areas due to the burden of tasks to survive, a State that is less present as a provider of care services and the lack of development of the service market in these areas (Marco Navarro and Rico, 2013).

This reality is unavoidable when prioritizing, designing and financing policies and programmes, as well as defining where cutbacks are made in the public budget, as if it is considered that care is a service and it is impossible to generate stock because it is produced and consumed in the same place, as María Ángeles Durán (2018) states, care policies will always have an important economic basis, not only in terms of financing and money, but also in terms of time that is outside the market. Time as an articulating axis of human experience is currently in dispute because different areas and activities of daily life, the labour market and the public world compete for this resource, appealing to the need for policies with redistributive effects of time and care responsibilities.

In accordance with Joan Tronto (2017), the current crisis is no longer a work crisis and became a crisis of social and capitalist reproduction, which operates against its supporting basis; in other words, today the conflict is 'capital-life'. In this context, the so-called crisis of care and its social organization (Rico, 2011: 108; Pérez-Orozco, 2006) in the four dimensions of care – the material dimension that implies a job, the economic dimension that involves costs and contributions, the psychological dimension that refers to the creation or maintenance of an affective bond (Batthyány, 2004), and the human rights dimension (Pautassi, 2007) – are strongly linked to time poverty that mainly affects women.

Time poverty, in terms of care tasks, limits the opportunities to enter the labour market, and if women can enter this market, they focus on part-time jobs and unregistered economic activities so as to comply with the responsibilities they have. It also hinders their possibilities to pay for care services in the market. The vicious circle among care, poverty and inequality disproportionately affects women, especially those without their own income, those who live in a single-parent household with children under 15 years old, as well as those who are in a poverty situation, whether a monetary or multidimensional one.

Not only does life sustainability focus on people care, but it also focuses on ecosystem care and maintenance, particularly those renewable and non-renewable natural resources that are extremely degraded and those that are threatened by extractivism and overexploitation in the interests of production (see chapter 4). In this respect, the goal is to strengthen daily activities that people, especially women, do for the environmental sustainability of households and communities, as well as to regulate or directly eliminate those business investments and activities, either private or public, which contribute to the climate crisis and the deterioration of the planet, while they put people under risk. Life sustainability involves not only a higher level of equality, but also, and fundamentally, a change of paradigm.

Considering this perspective, taking care of the environment and acknowledging the existing ecological debt in countries refer people to other ways of producing, consuming and distributing, and lead to debate on specific issues, such as the impacts of the external debt (and the economic policies implemented based on it) on the population and related natural and built habitat, the unfulfilled growth promises, and the violation of rights that involves the deepening of a development model that damages life in all its dimensions.

International instruments of human rights, such as the Convention on the Rights of Persons with Disabilities (2008) and the Inter-American

Convention on Protecting the Human Rights of Older Persons (2015), lay the legal basis to put care at the centre of the development of countries and establish the universal and interdependent right to care, while highlighting the responsibility of the State in that process. Thus, life sustainability has a great analytic validity and requires a human rights-based approach, while it strongly compels research, politics and civil service. This way of carrying out impact assessments of the economic policies that are implemented is essential (Bohoslavsky and Cantamutto, 2022) when considering unpaid care tasks and housework as an economic category. However, reality is very different, as the UN Independent Expert on external debt and human rights, Attiya Waris, stated: 'Unfortunately, there is no debt in the world that is renegotiated with a human rights perspective' (Deutsche Welle, 2022), let alone specifically considering women's human rights.

Nowadays, complex social and economic contexts are found in Latin America which complicate facing the care crisis and life sustainability, but that does not imply postponing debates and actions aimed at overcoming structural inequalities that affect countries and proposing new ways to grow and develop. Crises are not new to the region, but the situation after the COVID-19 pandemic has aggravated them and has made them evident.

3. Austerity: it never rains but it pours

Not only does the International Monetary Fund (IMF) grant loans to countries, but it also supervises and gives technical–political advice so that the policies and programmes implemented by governments can contribute to the repayment and fulfilment of debt services within the agreed deadlines, negotiate refinancing, as well as result in macroeconomic stability and greater growth, but without considering that wealth is distributed with extreme inequality (Bohoslavsky and Cantamutto, 2022). This introduces ethical, political and ideological dimensions to debt sustainability.

Among the most common suggestions, the one called 'austerity' can be found, which entails the pressure of increasing financial costs, and consequently a set of measures with significant cutbacks of public expenses and budget for social policies, especially the wage costs of the health and education sectors, as well as the services of social security and protection, all of which are fields where the guarantee of the human right to care, to be cared and to self-care (Pautassi, 2007; 2018) is evident. For example, in October 2022, the IMF board suggested to Argentina a greater adjustment of basic service fees, the reduction of subsidies and a strong reduction of social expenses, which was expressed in agreements made at the executive branch level, supported by the Argentine Parliament, in line with Law No. 27612, 'Strengthening of Public Debt Sustainability', which intends to put paid to the idea that external debt is illegal and that it is negotiated without transparency.

As Budgeon (2019) mentions, austerity also refers to a cultural policy, an implicit ideological tool that arises regarding the implementation of governmental policies designed to discursively address the negative consequences on the population of the political decisions that are made due to the financial pressure under orthodox economic and clearly androcentric approaches (Bohoslavsky and Rulli, 2021). This perspective ignores that austerity intensifies many of the neoliberal policies in place prior to the debt, that this is not a *'necessary'* approach because there are other mechanisms, and that it has consequences on gender equality and women's rights.

Life sustainability and equality are two goals connected to a new social organization and *'another'* economy, one that is transformative and whose main goal is to sustain life, and where progress goes beyond GDP growth and macroeconomic balance, positioning human rights and care, as well as the coordination between the productive and reproductive systems, with traditional economic indicators. All of which implies prioritizing life sustainability over capital accumulation as a strategy to achieve welfare for the population as a whole, not only individually at each country level, but also from a global perspective as care becomes a public asset and crosses borders creating global chains (Pérez-Orozco, 2016) of care led by women that usually migrate, driven by the indebtedness in their households and countries.

One of the major direct or indirect consequences of the measures taken due to the agreements with the IMF is the replication and deepening of gender inequalities. In this regard, it can be observed that, along with stopping wage increases in labour environments that are already characterized by low salaries and unregistered jobs, such as paid domestic and care services in households, the hiring of fewer woman nurses, caregivers and teachers, jobs that are purely feminized, is induced (ActionAid International, 2022). OIT (2019) estimates that 249 million out of 381 million workers dedicated to the provision of care at a global level are women and 132 million are men, and in the region the monthly average salary of domestic workers represents 44.7 per cent of the average salary that other remunerated people receive (OIT, 2021). All those jobs clearly proved to be central and essential during the COVID-19 pandemic.

In this respect, the health crisis joined the debt and care crises and established synergies that boosted gender inequalities. For instance, during the first year of the pandemic, the closure of schools, and the reduction of the service offer caused by the lockdown and social distancing aggravated gender inequalities as mostly women lost their paid jobs. The Economic Commission for Latin America and the Caribbean (ECLAC, 2021) indicated that the severe exit of women from the labour market represented an 18-year setback for Latin America in this period in terms of their labour participation, showing a very slow recovery in the present. At the same time, for many households the pandemic brought new debts connected to domestic equipment or for labour and study purposes, together with the increase of care tasks that mainly women performed, resulting in *more work and more debts*.

Although the IMF adopted a (self-denominated) strategy of gender mainstreaming in July 2022, it does not assume any responsibility for the consequences of the policies it promotes on gender gaps, and regression is not considered in the guarantee and exercise of human rights, particularly economic, social and cultural rights (ESCR). On the contrary, instead of performing an ex ante assessment on the potential negative impacts of its recommendations in terms of social and gender equality, as well as in terms of autonomy and women's rights, so as to avoid any setback, the strategy focuses on limited and insufficient compensatory actions of social protection after austerity policies have already made damage.

Echoing two phenomena, that is, political pressure to include a gender perspective and the importance of having more persons generating income for households to support the growth of countries, recently the IMF has explicitly considered the incorporation of women into the labour market, even if this happens with bad conditions (even dangerous conditions for their physical integrity) due to the ambiguity of human rights in the economic field (Elson and Rodríguez Enríquez, 2021). This is an example of how feminist demands to the IMF are ignored and end up being what is called a *pink wash* (ActionAid International, 2022), which is the process used by an institution to improve its reputation by adopting certain orders and commitments that make it more *modern*, for that specific period, and addressing concerns from the civil society; in this case, the feminist economy and women's organizations, such as the letter sent to the IMF by more than 500 institutions and persons (LATINDADD, 2020).

The implementation of integrated care systems and tools to overcome poverty and inequality, found in the present in social conversation and political debate in several countries of the region, requires infrastructure works for care, such as the construction of child centres, centres for long-term care and day care centres for persons with functional dependency. However, this is not specified in the agreements made with multilateral credit agencies, while other sectors of the economy do appear in them and are prioritized (along with their financing sources), evidencing what the priorities are.

4. Private debt in family management of care

The society, market/capital, countries and world are in debt to women for historically taking care of life, persons, households and environments without remuneration, valuation, prestige and in an invisible way. From this perspective, women are creditors. However, everyday reality in Latin America shows that women experience a huge pressure due to the existing indebtedness in households. This indebtedness is no stranger to country situations as progressively, external debt with international banks is linked to the debts families take, while it impoverishes people and makes them more vulnerable and penetrates the economic life of households. The number of women among loan borrowers is significant; for instance, in Brazil in December 2019, 41 million out of the total number of borrowers were men and 44 million were women (Rodríguez, 2020).

Women face survival and daily work costs to optimize resources, they reduce regular expenses and take loans and formal and informal debts so as to fulfil basic needs, and these are mechanisms with a short-term benefit that end up contributing to replicating inequalities. Debts that are accumulated to access the most basic goods and services – food, medicine, energy and the urban services of water and electricity, as well as education and health – impact on care and its quality. Thus, household indebtedness has a predominant role in care management, along with precariousness management. In this context, despite the growing and promoted bancarization, interpersonal networks of solidarity, whether family, neighbourhood or friendship ones, are crucial, mainly, but not exclusively (Cosacov, 2022: 34), in popular sectors.

The National Indebtedness and Care Survey (*Encuesta Nacional de Endeudamiento y Cuidados*, ENEC) carried out in Argentina in 2021 showed that different loan instruments, whether formal or informal, are used to pay daily expenses, such as food and medicine (about 46.8 per cent of households), pay taxes, services and condominium fees (33.2 per cent), pay rent (about 20.8 per cent) and pay education and health costs (16.8 per cent), and it is worth mentioning the effect of taking debt to pay other debts: loans (32.5 per cent), purchases on tick (31.5 per cent) and credit cards (28.8 per cent) (Wilkis and Tumini, 2022: 22). At the same time, its conclusions are unquestionable in terms of higher levels of indebtedness in households where women are the head of the family, with care demands and low income.

> Households that are more exposed to indebtedness are those where care implies fulfilling changing combinations of needs and demands of children and adolescents, elderly people and disabled people. In these households, critical cases can be found where the high level of exposure to indebtedness is three times the one in households without care demands. (Wilkis and Tumini, 2022: 47)

This way, what Federici (2021: 20) calls *reproduction financialization* is created.

The weakness of limited public care policies currently comes with a growing, though scarce, presence of business provision; while this is biased as to the cost of services, it is expanding its offer to sectors with a lower income. This commercialization process of care appears as a solution to the needs of households, and usually women decide to become indebted and find time to work in a paid job in order to have access to income and the benefits of social security if they have a decent job, knowing that the movement is partial as they will still perform care tasks before and after the hours of service.

Today, being indebted to live and becoming indebted for care purposes are everyday experiences of many women in some Latin American countries. But this is not just an individual and private experience, even if it is experienced in isolation and even with guilt from their own subjective view. As a study carried out in Argentina (Luzzi, 2022) showed, women are the ones in charge of the monetary management of care. Thus, most of them assume a particular type of commitment linked to care values, obligations and practices within households, called *care debts*, which are feminized debts (Wilkis, 2021, quoted in Luzzi, 2022) that are part of their permanent contributions to life sustainability.

5. Final conclusions

The UN Secretary-General, António Guterres, during the sessions of the ECLAC carried out in Buenos Aires in October 2022, requested international financing institutions to reduce the public debt of several countries of Latin America and the Caribbean, providing more favourable financing conditions, because if they do not restructure the debt, poverty will increase significantly. Among the mechanisms to reduce debt, the conversion of debt into a project of climate adaptation is mentioned. In this context, it is necessary to reflect on the possibility that the strengthening of care services and the creation of a comprehensive care system are also proposed as mechanisms of debt reduction. *Why not?*

Certainly, States play a crucial role in the implementation of comprehensive care systems; therefore, they must guarantee resources through their budgets. This implies finding ways to make their financing feasible and sustainable, but not from an isolated perspective, as part of the debates and agreements regarding the universalization of the social protection pillars – education, health, social security and care – but also with respect to the necessary financing, without regression, in order to guarantee the exercise of people's human rights, including the right to care. Thus, debt management could be considered as an element that, without damaging life sustainability in the present, could contribute to life sustainability instead. Transforming the vicious circle of debt, inequality and poverty into a virtuous and transformative circle through the multiple positive effects and return generated by investing in comprehensive care systems is not only necessary, but an intelligent strategy to recover and achieve fairer and thriving societies (Bango, Campanella and Cossani, 2022).

Processes regarding resistance and resilience against the external and internal debt of countries, and the creation of comprehensive care systems, must be carried out along with a cultural policy of the deconstruction of the gender division of work and the naturalized assignment of care tasks to women. As Federici (2021) states, this is not only about fighting the debt, but also and simultaneously about changing labour relations and encouraging a reappropriation process of social wealth together with the valuation of reproduction and care work so that life sustainability is not an illusion.

References

ActionAid International (2022) 'The care contradiction: The IMF, gender and austerity'.

Bango, J.; Campanella, J. and Cossani, P. (2022) 'Financiamiento de los sistemas integrales de cuidados Propuestas para América Latina y el Caribe', ONU Mujeres, October.

Batthyány, K. (2004) *Cuidado infantil y trabajo: ¿un desafío exclusivamente femenino?; una mirada desde el género y la ciudadanía social*, Montevideo: CINTERFOR.

Bohoslavsky, J.P. and Rulli, M. (2021) 'Bretton Woods' pandemic policies: A gender equality analysis – perspectives from Latin America', *Development*, 64(1): 1–10.

Bohoslavsky, J.P. and Cantamutto, F. (2022) 'Not even with a pandemic: The IMF, human rights, and rational choices under power relations', *Human Rights Quarterly*, 44(4): 759–83.

Budgeon, S. (2019) 'The resonance of moderate feminism and the gendered relations of austerity', *Gender, Work and Organization*, 26(8): 1138–55.

Carrasco, C. (2016) 'Sostenibilidad de la vida y ceguera patriarcal. Una reflexión necesaria' *ATLÁNTICAS – Revista Internacional de Estudios Feministas*, 1(1): 34–57.

Cosacov, N. (2022) 'Deudas, cuidados y vulnerabilidad. El caso de las mujeres de hogares de clases medias en la Argentina', Documentos de Proyectos, Santiago: CEPAL.

Deutsche Welle (DW) (2022) 'Experta de ONU pide un mecanismo de la 'verdad' sobre endeudamiento argentino', [online] 5 October, Available from: https://www.dw.com/es/experta-de-onu-pide-un-mecanismo-de-la-verdad-sobre-endeudamiento-argentino/a-63349435

Durán, M.Á. (2018) *La riqueza invisible del cuidado*, Valencia: Universitat de València.

ECLAC (2021) 'La autonomía económica de las mujeres en la recuperación sostenible y con igualdad' (*Informe Especial COVID-19 No 9*), Santiago.

Elson, D. and Rodríguez Enríquez, C. (2021) 'Del Dicho al Hecho: la Narrativa de Género del FMI y los Derechos Humanos de las Mujeres', *Revista Derechos en Acción*, 18: 275–310.

Federici, S. (2021) 'Mujeres, dinero y deuda. Notas para un movimiento feminista de reapropiación', in S. Federici, V. Gago and L. Cavallero (eds) *¿Quién le debe a quién? Ensayos transnacionales de desobediencia financiera*, Buenos Aires: Tinta Limon Ediciones, pp 19–41.

Federici, S.; Gago, V. and Cavallero, L. (eds) (2021) *¿Quién le debe a quién? Ensayos transnacionales de desobediencia financiera*, Buenos Aires: Tinta Limón and Fundación Rosa Luxemburgo.

LATINDADD, Red Latinoamericana por justicia social y económica (2020), 'Carta al FMI', [online] 5 October, Available from: https://www.latind add.org/2020/10/05/carta-al-fmi-en-contra-de-las-politicas-de-austeri dad-de-sus-programas-de-recuperacion-covid-19/

Luzzi, M. (2022) 'Deudas, cuidados y vulnerabilidad: interacciones de las mujeres con organizaciones financieras y no financieras en la Argentina', Documentos de Proyectos, Santiago: CEPAL.

Marco Navarro, F. and Rico, M.N. (2013) 'Cuidado y políticas públicas: debates y estado de situación a nivel regional' in L. Pautassi and C. Zibecchi (coords) *Las fronteras del cuidado. Agenda, derechos e infraestructura*, Buenos Aires: ELA-Editorial Biblios.

OIT (2019) *Perspectivas sociales y del empleo en el mundo – Tendencias 2019,* Geneva.

OIT (2021) 'El trabajo doméstico remunerado en América Latina y el Caribe, a 10 años del Convenio núm. 189', Lima: International Labour Organization, Oficina Regional para América Latina y el Caribe.

Pautassi, L. (2007) 'El cuidado como cuestión social desde un enfoque de derechos' (LC/L.2800-P), serie Mujer y Desarrollo, No 87, Santiago de Chile: Comisión Económica para América Latina y el Caribe (CEPAL).

Pautassi, L. (2018) 'El cuidado como derecho. Un camino virtuoso, un desafío inmediato'. *Revista de la Facultad de Derecho de México*, LXVIII(272): 717–42.

Pérez-Orozco, A. (2006) 'Amenaza tormenta: La crisis de los cuidados en la reorganización del sistema económico', *Revista de Economía Crítica*, 5(1): 7–37.

Pérez-Orozco, A. (2016) *Desigualdades a flor de piel: cadenas globales de cuidados. Concreciones en el empleo de hogar y articulaciones políticas*, ONU Mujeres.

Razavi, S. (2007) 'The Political and Social Economy of Care in a Development Context: Conceptual Issues', *Research Questions and Policy Options*, Geneva: UNSRID Gender and Development Programme Paper Number 3.

Rico, M.N. (2011) 'Crisis del cuidado y políticas públicas: el momento es ahora', in M.N. Rico and C. Maldonado Valera (eds), *Las familias latinoamericanas interrogadas. Hacia la articulación del diagnóstico, la legislación y las políticas*, Serie Seminarios y Conferencias 61, Santiago: CEPAL.

Rodríguez Enríquez, C. and Partenio, F. (2020) *Sostenibilidad de la vida desde la perspectiva de la economía feminista*, Buenos Aires: Madreselva.

Rodríguez, G. (2020) 'O sistema financeiro e o endividamento das mulheres', Río de Janeiro: Instituto EQUIT [online] March, Available from: https://www.equit.org.br/novo/wp-content/uploads/2020/06/O-sistema-financeiro_web.pdf

Tronto, J. (2017) 'Hay una alternativa: los homines curans y los límites del neoliberalismo', *Revista Internacional de cuidados*, 1(1): 27–43.

Tumini, L. and Wilkis, A. (2022) 'Cuidados y vulnerabilidad financiera: un análisis a partir de la Encuesta Nacional de Endeudamiento y Cuidados en la Argentina (ENEC)', Documentos de Proyectos, Santiago: CEPAL.

13

Where a Right Fails, a Debt Increases: Gender Inequalities and Economic Vulnerability of Women and LGTBQ+ Groups

Florencia Partenio and Ariel Wilkis

1. Introduction

Since at least a decade ago, the academic and activist literature, as well as the literature of human rights organizations and agencies, has started to pay attention to the transformations of social protection and their impact on household indebtedness, whose widespread dynamics put women and LGTBQ+ groups at risk of a greater economic vulnerability (Wilkis and Partenio, 2010; Carrasco and Tello, 2011; Callegari et al, 2019; Cavallero and Gago, 2019; Bohoslavsky, 2021; Federici, 2021). In the context of the COVID-19 pandemic, these inequalities were deepened and evidenced the pre-existing multidimensional crisis (Pérez Orozco and Fernández Ortiz de Zárate, 2021), as well as the impacts of the economic recession on human rights (Bohoslavsky, 2020; Bohoslavsky and Rulli, 2020).

During the health crisis, the care crisis was not only intensified (Arza, 2020; Rodríguez Enríquez, 2020; Pautassi, 2021), but also the dynamics of private indebtedness related to care, generating an overload of unpaid work and an increase of time poverty for women, lesbians and trans femininities (Partenio, 2021; Tumini and Wilkis, 2022). In the case of Argentina, their role in supporting homes has been key for the daily functioning of life. In terms of food provision and preparation, the early strategies in popular neighbourhoods enabled a 'neighbourhood quarantine' that allowed for circulation outside homes and that was coordinated in those geographies (Bustos and Villafañe, 2020: 15). Moreover, the role of community women workers was essential to support the network of care in the most affected sectors (Fournier and Cascardo, 2022). Furthermore, the pandemic intensified monetary management that helped to guarantee the care of children and adolescents, elder people and/or disabled people. However, the situation for low-income sectors was already critical before the pandemic in terms of an increase of the indexes of poverty, indigence and the level of indebtedness of households (INDEC, 2019) due to the impact of structural adjustment policies and reforms implemented between the end of 2015 and 2019 that seriously affected the levels of social protection, as well as labour, economic, social and cultural rights of women and LGTBQ+ groups (CELS, 2018; Partenio, 2018). In 2017, the percentage of Argentine households that requested any type of loan and at the same time sold their goods or used their savings was less than 20 per cent, while in 2019 that same percentage rose to 27.4 per cent (Wilkis, 2020). In this respect, the private debt of households acts as an interface between inequality and sovereign debt (Bohoslavsky, 2016), which during that period rose considerably in Argentina through the 'Stand By' agreement entered into with the International Monetary Fund (IMF).

In the pandemic context, the measurement and prediction of the social inequalities created by private indebtedness using an index of household financial vulnerability (Wilkis, 2020) has helped bring to notice multiple sources of such fragility. In the particular case of the Buenos Aires Metropolitan Area, the 'bubbles' of indebtedness that families more exposed to financial vulnerability have created to deal with their daily expenses are evidenced (Wilkis, 2020: 18). In the case of households more prone to indebtedness, they are more likely to default on payments of services, taxes and debts, and as a result there is an increase of financial dependency through informal loan instruments (purchases on tick, employers' loans, lenders). In addition, they turn to relatives and friends to ask for loans. As to how these loans are used, during the pandemic, the main purpose of loans was to pay daily expenses (for example, food and health) and previous debts. Households with persons who receive social security benefits (for example, Universal Child Allowance) and emergency income were more prone to indebtedness than those who do not receive these benefits (Wilkis, 2020; Partenio, 2022a).

During the pandemic, our studies show there is a clear difference in terms of exposure to indebtedness between households with care tasks and households without care tasks. Private indebtedness was used to finance expenses and consumption to support daily care tasks. About 47 per cent of households took loans to pay for food and medicines, house maintenance (33 per cent of households used the borrowed money to pay taxes, services and condominium fees, and about 21 per cent used the money to pay rent), a previous loan (32 per cent), debts related to purchases on tick (31 per cent), and 29 per cent used the money to pay other credit card debts (their own or borrowed ones), expenses of house or car maintenance (20 per cent), and school fees and health insurance coverage (17 per cent) (Tumini and Wilkis, 2022). Besides, when care needs are the main reason for which households take loans, they tend to use multiple sources to get money, combining circuits of formal and informal loans. In this regard, the notion of banking or financial exclusion does not include the ways in which the most economically vulnerable sectors relate with multiple instruments of formal loans, as in many cases they have access to them through friends or relatives (for example, through the circuit of borrowing credit cards).

This chapter focuses on the households of popular classes and addresses two key questions in order to understand the connection between the increase of private indebtedness and the deepening of inequalities. The questions are: 'What is the relation between social protection and household indebtedness? What is the impact of the dynamics of a greater tendency to economic vulnerability of women and LGTBQ+ groups? Using the intersection between feminist economy and money sociology, this chapter explains three dynamics rooted in the daily lives of women, lesbians and transgender persons that live in Argentina, whose impact on gender inequalities is linked to the principle of 'where rights fail, debts increase'. These dynamics are explained by analyzing labour and linking paths, monetary management and social care organization. This explanation has reinforced one of the main findings of our joint work for more than ten years: monetary debts are the other side of social and economic rights.

The reflections presented in this chapter are based on a qualitative and quantitative study focused on analyzing the relations between the care crisis and the increase of economic vulnerability during the COVID-19 pandemic in Argentina. Field work was outlined using deep interviews in an intentional-type sample that took place in two stages in 2021 in the same households and geographic areas of Greater Buenos Aires. The sample was made of 47 interviews of women from popular classes (Partenio, 2022a; 2022b). A design of semi-structured interviews was used, which analyzed the socio-labour and budget situation, as well as the care organization of households and the situation of interviewed women. This analysis resumed the findings of the National Indebtedness and Care Survey (Encuesta Nacional de Endeudamiento y Cuidados, ENEC) with national representation (Tumini and Wilkis, 2022). Both researchers were sponsored by the Project 'Socioeconomic recovery after the crisis generated by Covid-19 from a gender perspective: promoting economic autonomy of women and care of elder and disabled people in Argentina' of the Economic Commission for Latin America and the Caribbean (ECLAC).

The rest of the chapter is organized into four sections. In section 2, the situation before the pandemic is explained and a dynamics that sheds light on how economic vulnerability of women may be created when the coverage of social protection benefits fails – or are reduced – is presented. Section 3 shows the analysis of other dynamics that boost economic vulnerability when protection mechanisms of labour rights fail. Section 4 presents a dynamics that enables us to unravel how economic vulnerability is deepened when rights are paradoxically recognized in an individual manner. Finally, section 5 presents some final thoughts as to the relation among indebtedness, care crisis and lack of access to rights.

2. Social vulnerability and private indebtedness on the verge of the pandemic

In the context of an unprecedented situation like the pandemic, studies in Latin America and the Caribbean noticed the deepening of the exclusion of disabled people and their families, posing a series of recommendations and strategies in the areas of health, education, labour inclusion and social protection, and care (Meresman and Ullmann, 2020). Due to the economic situation resulting from the crisis, many households decreased 'the expenses related to therapeutic services and pedagogical supports they had accessed prior to the pandemic. These tasks ... are now [the] responsibility of the members of the household, particularly, women, increasing gender gaps related to domestic work and unpaid care work' (Meresman and Ullmann, 2020: 39).

This regional situation is reflected in the local scene, but it is particularly in the households of popular classes where the daily care organization is aggravated by structural issues prior to the pandemic, such as the low urban infrastructure, the inadequate access to public services and the decrease of income (Partenio, 2022a). However, the most critical cases took place in households where disabled people live, whose dependency was intensified due to the closing of health care facilities and therapeutic centres. The story of Luz (a 38-year-old unemployed woman who lives in a biparental house) is presented later; she is in charge of three children, and two of them are disabled. Her situation is similar to that of other interviewed households, where 22 disabled persons live, almost half of which do not receive allowances from the social security system. Here is where a dynamics that sheds light on how the economic vulnerability of women may be created when the coverage of social protection benefits fails – or are reduced – is presented.

In accordance with our study, the budgets of households where disabled people live were more affected during the pandemic, although their situation was already fragile. Luz has a 16-year-old daughter with a severe disability and she is under a specific treatment with medications and requires help with washing and feeding tasks because she has celiac disease. Her 14-year-old son has autism and has gone through different education facilities with a therapeutic assistant. She also has a six-year-old son with her current partner. The most important change in terms of care organization during the pandemic was the fact that their children remained in their house without in-person (school and therapeutic) activities.

But the situation of care overload existed prior to the pandemic. Luz had her first two children when she was very young and her husband abandoned her during her second pregnancy. She had to leave her paid job as a teacher to take care of her daughter. Since their two children were born, she has not received economic support from the father, who "to the present does not understand he has children with special needs" (interview with Luz, in Partenio, 2022a). Due to the father's history of gender violence, Luz avoids his visits in her house and it is very difficult for her to negotiate the payments of child maintenance.

The budget situation of Luz's household got worse in the years prior to the pandemic, when the access to a right included in social security benefits for disabled persons was reduced. In fact, her budget was affected because in 2019 her son's allowance was rejected[1] and she has been following the appropriate proceedings to obtain it for more than two years. Despite the fact that autism is recognized as an intellectual disability, and from the moment it is diagnosed they suggest obtaining the Unique Certificate of Disability (Certificado Único de Discapacidad, CUD), Luz must resume countless online proceedings to update the certificate that expired during the pandemic. Luz could not find another job as a payroll employee and always tried to get unregistered jobs (sell food, and so on) from her house to get an income and keep performing her care tasks. Although she manages to get money when there is an emergency, the pandemic jeopardized her daily organization.

Every day Luz has to juggle multiple tasks to ensure there is food and medications and manage medical appointments: "I am responsible for my three children and also my mother" (interview with Luz, in Partenio, 2022a). As the results of ENEC at a national level show (Tumini and Wilkis, 2022), Luz – as do many other women – had to take care of elder persons that do not even live in the same house, in this case, her 68-year-old mother, whose pension was seized due to a loan prior to the pandemic. Not only does Luz ensure direct care (prepare food, go with her to her medical appointments), but she must also 'manage' her mother's budget threatened by new indebtedness.

During the pandemic, Luz felt she "was going crazy" considering the bills of her house she could not pay (debts of water, electricity and mobile phone services), the late payment of fees for her children's school, the loan payment of the National Administration of Social Security (Administración Nacional de la Seguridad Social, ANSES)[2], the purchases on tick in the grocery store, the debts she accumulated and the concern for the income decrease of her partner who is an independent worker (interview with Luz, in Partenio, 2022a).

Negotiations with former partners and the resulting conflicts as to the responsibility to provide *money for care* (Wilkis, 2013; 2017) increased in the pandemic (school fees, psychological care coverage, health insurance coverage, appropriation of family allowances, non-compliance with child maintenance). Women frequently express how tired they are due to these conflicts and, in certain situations, they end up not claiming monthly child maintenance in exchange for a health insurance coverage that ensures services that the public sector cannot guarantee. These negotiations may include issues as to who receives family allowances. This happened to Luz who had to start the proceedings to receive the allowances of the Unique System of Family Allowances (Sistema Único de Asignaciones Familiares, SUAF)[3], which was affected by the labour changes of her former partner before the pandemic.

> 'For my two oldest children I receive a family allowance because their dad has a registered job; I may say that I played the mother role because some months he gave me the family allowance, but some other he did not, so I got furious and I told him: No! You know what? I will receive it.' (Interview with Luz, in Partenio, 2022a)

However, these negotiations are exhausting for her and she prefers to keep the health insurance of her former husband that covers the therapeutic centre, transport and medications that her oldest daughter with a disability needs, instead of insisting on the compliance for child maintenance for her two children.

In this way, the analyzed dynamics reflects not only the effects of the interruption of social security benefits, but also a method of organization complicated by gender relations that obliges women to give up part of their rights in exchange for receiving 'something' (in this case, health insurance coverage). For Luz, this resulted in not only increasing monetary management to ensure childcare, but also a greater indebtedness to cover the lack of services and the payment of child maintenance by the father. In this regard, women seem to be the ones that must 'arbitrate' which rights are monetarily recognized and which one are not, resulting in having less money for care and more debts to pay.

3. Labour vulnerability and deepening of economic vulnerability

Qualitative studies have shown the critical situation that sectors with inadequate social and labour protection went through in the pandemic in

Argentina, specifically women domestic workers (Partenio, 2022b) and the members transgender groups (Fournier and Cascardo, 2022). In these cases, the greatest exposure to indebtedness is not only evidenced in households with children, adolescents and persons with disabilities (mostly single-parent households and with female heads of the household in unregistered activities), but also in the households of trans femininities, who are victims of multiple forms of exclusion (housing, education, health) and sexual discrimination.

The critical profiles are those where a structural situation, poor labour experiences, a stay in unregistered jobs and high demand of care in the household are combined. The most urgent situations are in almost all the houses where women are the heads of the household and are unemployed or work in unregistered jobs, without receiving child maintenance from fathers. However, the situation is critical in households with persons with disabilities. The story of Mónica, a 46-year-old domestic unregistered worker, is presented now.

Mónica is the head of her household consisting of six daughters; the oldest one is 25 years old and the youngest one is four years old. Her 20-year-old daughter has a severe disability and requires permanent care. Due to the fact that she has an unregistered job, Mónica worked during the social and compulsory lockdown because she "went to fulfil" the labour needs of her employers that did not comply with the government regulations during the pandemic. As it is evidenced in women single-parent and extended households with similar characteristics (Partenio, 2022b), the presence of teenager and young daughters has been key – before and after – the pandemic to manage the care of their siblings, while their mothers "went to work" in the houses of other people. In the case of Mónica, her daughter has schizophrenia and needs full care, so when Mónica goes to work "her other daughters take care of her". The network of care is formed by her oldest daughters. "We have no relatives nearby, there are no grandparents, uncles, aunts or someone else, there are no friends or neighbours, no one. We have lived like this all our lives", Mónica explains (interview in Partenio, 2022b).

Despite the fact that she has a disability allowance, the monthly budget for her daughter's health needs exceeds the amount she receives. Her daughter's medication is one of the most important *money management of care* aspects for Mónica, and at many times this is the main reason for her indebtedness. During the lockdown, she kept managing prescriptions (for example, paying for a courier service) and sacrificing hours of paid work to take her daughter to her weekly appointments. Although that management does not exempt her from paying the medication, at least these prescriptions allowed her to buy them. She spent all her time managing the money from the Universal Child Allowance (AUH), "reducing expenses" and "working more hours" to pay for these proceedings as she no longer has health insurance coverage. Her labour and non-labour income is not enough and, as she mentioned in the interview, "I can borrow money … if I have to buy medication for [her daughter] … because imagine that she is already unstable taking her medication, without it she turns into a person who needs a straitjacket and be sent into a mental health institution". This priority order relegates other payments in her household that turn into debts in arrears, such as the ones she already had before the pandemic (electricity bills and taxes). Considering this desperate situation, sometimes she has to ask for "advance payments" from her women employers, which translates into a new source of debt that many times is paid by working more hours in the same day. She also needed to ask for an ANSES loan "to pay for electricity" because, as she explains, "no institution gives me anything [a formal loan] as I am an unregistered employee and my Veraz credit score[4] is not good". The burden of these debts, even the ones from her former husband (who was reported for gender violence) that she had to assume, makes her express how tired she is in different parts of the interview ("I am sick of this", "I am exhausted") (interview with Mónica, in Partenio, 2022b). This situation of economic vulnerability not only exposes her to a larger mental burden, but also to physical risks.

Not only has her very poor labour situation, without the minimum protections required, intensified her working day (working in more houses to generate more income), but it has also forced her to work in risky situations for her own health, even during the pandemic, when she went to an emergency centre with her "gallbladder to the limit". Mónica delayed health appointments for several months as well as the surgery because she was afraid of losing her job, until she had to go to a hospital for an emergency surgery.

In this analyzed dynamics, economic vulnerability gets worse when registration and labour protection policies fail. However, Mónica's history reflects both labour and financial precariousness, and this obliges her to resort to the informal circuit as she has a bad Veraz credit score. In the case of the women of this sector, the financial histories that included Veraz credit scores before the pandemic determined the access to loans during the pandemic, regardless of the registration status of their jobs. In fact, during the pandemic, Mónica took debt from her women employers, asking for advance payments to pay for her daughter's medication; she turned to her oldest daughter to borrow money; and house bills and taxes accumulated, including an interruption of the service because of her non-payment. In these cases, the lack of *money for care* (due to low income, non-compliance with child maintenance, inadequate social protection) is the immediate prelude to indebtedness because of *care debts*.

Mónica's household situation is not very different from the one in other single-parent households. In accordance with the qualitative study (Tumini and Wilkis, 2022), the main financing source of houses with a female head of the household and care responsibilities are family and friends (60 per cent of these households resorted to these loans, compared to 45 per cent of houses with a male head of the household). Another very important financing source is nearby stores through purchases on tick (40 per cent of houses with a female head of the household resort to them, compared to 30 per cent of houses with a male head of the household), although findings also show that women-headed houses are more exposed to lenders and financial institutions (one out of four households turned to them in the pandemic).

4. Care paradoxes and deepening of economic vulnerability

Social security benefits have been one of the main objects of dispute in care monetary management, as their claim or management has turned into multiple sources of conflict (in general with fathers) and proceedings that women start to ensure *money for care*. Unlike male beneficiaries, women that manage those State monetary benefits are judged for the handling of these pieces of money (Wilkis and Partenio, 2010) and tensions are created as to the economic control men try to have over women (Kreutzer, 2004). Conflicts for the management of these benefits may even arise when parents do not live together, but both are beneficiaries of these payments. The years women spend disputing for these benefits translate into new indebtedness dynamics. This is how Mirta lived during the years prior to the pandemic (she is 51 years old, she is part of a single-parent household, she has seven children and she is a domestic worker), asking for advice in ANSES to recover her children SUAF. Although she receives an allowance for being a mother of seven children, she tried to manage the SUAF ownership her former partner received every month, but it was difficult for her to continue the administrative proceedings during the pandemic. She even became aware that her former husband had managed ANSES loans with this allowance without telling her or their children. Due to income decrease during the pandemic and the lack of access to these benefits, Mirta experienced debt distress and assumed risky commitments with a lender (to buy food and clothes for her children), a financial institution (for daily expenses), and unpaid electricity, water and internet bills accumulated. As she had a delinquency background in the Veraz credit report, she turned to her boyfriend to borrow his credit cards to buy a mobile phone and pay it in instalments for her children so they could study remotely. When a series of public offices reopened, Mirta asked for a wage garnishment against the father of the four of her children who were still minors and she managed to receive payments in the middle of 2021. Her budget situation did not improve automatically, but she quickly started to determine payment priorities and she used the first SUAF payments she received to pay the lender.

At the same time, women are the ones who must report to other relatives how they used the money from the government and they must solve how to survive day by day. In general, family men both ignore the value of the care monetary management women perform and they do not comply with their care obligations.

To show the ambivalence and contradictions of the relation between law and debts, this chapter presents a dynamics that explains how economic vulnerability may arise when rights do not fail or are present, but when they are recognized, paradoxically, in an individual way. For that purpose, Mabel's story, a 59-year-old woman, is told. She lives in a house built in a settlement with her former husband (63 years old) and her three adult children. Mabel takes care of her 38-year-old daughter who has a psychomotor impairment. She also keeps taking care of her former husband as she monitors his pension proceedings and controls the health management programme for his cardiovascular problems.

In her house, the sources to obtain *money for care* are her daughter's disability allowance and the convenience store located in her house where she works with her former husband. Her 31-year-old daughter gets income for taking care of her nephews and nieces. Services and food are mainly paid with money earned in the convenience store, where they also 'take bets', as a lottery agent outside the official circuit.

For more than three decades, Mabel could not access a registered job in the labour market, but she always tried to combine informal activities with home care, particularly, taking care of her daughter. With regards to monetary and non-monetary management of her daughter's care, Mabel says "I feel alone in this struggle, you know", and that makes her tell her family story:

> 'I mean, I have always put up with many things despite the fact he beat me at the beginning, you know. We have always had money problems, you know, and problems with my daughter. I have always taken care of her alone, he was never there for me with my daughter's problems.' (Interview with Mabel, in Partenio, 2022a)

For Mabel, the income they get from the family business must be allocated to the house where the children they have in common live. But she recognizes there is an unequal management of money and excessive withdrawals from the funds of the convenience store (the common 'savings') by her former husband. This is not new to her because when he was her husband he "always lied" to her as to the money he earned (interview with Mabel, in Partenio, 2022a).

During the pandemic, the difficulty in accessing public offices of the health system and social security – along with the change to online help desks – complicated the proceedings regarding social benefits, certifications, prescriptions, and medical appointments. The failure of several sectors in the context of the lockdown (transport services, communication with special schools, in-person proceedings that turned into online ones) resulted in greater costs and a time increase for these proceedings. In these households, mothers were fully in charge of these proceedings, not fathers, regardless of whether they were living together or not (Partenio, 2022a; 2022b).

During the pandemic, both direct care of her daughter and care prerequisites were intensified. The management Mabel made multiplied in the pandemic, including communications to guarantee 'day medical centre videoconferences', receiving schools supplies, health insurance proceedings and the claim for 'safe' transport after the special school reopened (Partenio, 2022a). In the case of care monetary management, one of the most complex issues was to guarantee the regular receipt of medications.

From the beginning of social, preventive and compulsory lockdown, Mabel – all on her own – each month managed her daughter's costly medication because, as she and other mothers say, "if we do not act, nobody gives you anything". She could not pay for the medication with the allowance; for that reason, she made multiple proceedings to get it, but "it was all very complex, and obtaining the [circulation] permit, you know, that sometimes was also difficult to get ... and I used the allowance money for transport". However, these proceedings were not exempt from objections. The management of the allowance money results in a source of conflict with her former husband and her other children, who questioned how that money was used. Not only is she the 'representative' who receives the allowance, but she also assumes full responsibility for delayed payments and debts (food, health, services, taxes) that exceed the household income. Without being the individual beneficiary of this social benefit, Mabel tried to get loans through the social security system to guarantee some of her daughter's needs, but she could not obtain them. She even resorted to the formal circuit, but they asked her for 'a pay stub'. She borrows credit cards to guarantee "important purchases" (household appliances, clothes for her daughter) despite the fact that her other children "throw this in her face" (interview with Mabel, in Partenio, 2022a).

In this case, the care paradox is reflected in the blindness of policies targeted at the dependent population, where the role of those who daily perform several care prerequisites (including the care monetary management) remains invisibilized. In this way, it is possible to tell the stories of mothers who are in charge of their disabled children for all their lives and who not only had difficulties to access a job, but also to get loans in the formal circuit, seriously undermining their economic autonomy.

5. Final thoughts

Women, lesbians and trans femininities of popular classes – including those who perform domestic work in other houses and those who work in community organizations – in Argentina live *encuentadas* (drowning in bills) (Wilkis, 2017) because they go through indebtedness cycles as part of their regular financial practices and they have to use their labour and non-labour income to pay consumption loans. Most of these loans come from the informal sector under highly unfavourable conditions in terms of interest rates and repayment. Previous experiences in the banking and financial system affect their credit history as a significant number of them end up with a delinquency background (Partenio, 2022a).

In the households of popular classes, the care crisis is much more evident. Using the dynamics presented, it is possible to notice how the overload of unpaid care work is linked to debt distress and the lack of access to social protection for women, lesbians and trans persons.

The collaborative work carried out for more than ten years enabled the development of a perspective on debts, care and rights that links the feminist economy with money sociology. The conclusion this chapter offers is 'where rights fail, debts increase'. This conclusion, as presented, is not gender neutral. On the contrary, debts that increase when rights fail are connected to an unequal distribution of care. *Care debts* are a clear consequence of an unfair social protection system in terms of gender. Focusing on these debts as a privileged indicator of unfairness is one of the main contributions of our current and future work.

Notes

[1] For the 2018–19 period, the government alliance called Cambiemos rejected hundreds of disability allowances without any reason (CELS, 2018).

[2] A programme of personal loans launched in 2018 for beneficiaries of retirement pensions, pensions and child allowances.

[3] In accordance with ANSES, those who are employees on payroll, independent workers, seasonal workers, employees who receive workers' compensation and those who are beneficiaries of unemployment insurance receive a family allowance per child for each one of their children under 18 years old or with a disability, in which case there is no age limit.

[4] It refers to the name of the private company with one of the largest databases on credit history and track record of individuals and companies in Argentina.

References

Arza, C. (2020) 'Familias, cuidado y desigualdad' in *Cuidados y mujeres en tiempos de COVID-19: la experiencia en la Argentina*, Documentos de Proyectos (LC/TS.2020/153), Santiago: Economic Commission for Latin America and the Caribeean (ECLAC), pp 45–66.

Bohoslavsky, J.P. (2016) 'Economic inequality, debt crises and human rights', *Yale Journal of International Law*, 41(2): 177–99.

Bohoslavsky, J.P. (2020) 'COVID-19, economía y derechos humanos', *Sur – Revista Internacional de Derechos Humanos*, 30(17): 85–99.

Bohoslavsky, J.P. (2021) 'The explosion of household debt: Curse or blessing for human rights?', *Human Rights Quarterly*, 43(1): 1–28.

Bohoslavsky, J.P. and Rulli, M. (2020) 'COVID-19, instituciones financieras internacionales y continuidad de las políticas androcéntricas en América Latina', *Revista Estudios Feministas*, 28(2): e73510.

Bustos, J.M. and Villafañe, S. (2020) 'Introducción' in *Cuidados y mujeres en tiempos de COVID-19: la experiencia en la Argentina*, Documentos de Proyectos (LC/TS.2020/153), Santiago: Economic Commission for Latin America and the Caribeean (ECLAC), pp 11–28.

Callegari, J.; Pernilla, L. and Kullberg, C. (2019) 'Gendered debt – a scoping study review of research on debt acquisition and management in single and couple households', *European Journal of Social Work*, 23(5): 742–54.

Carrasco, C. and Tello, E. (2011) 'Apuntes para una vida sostenible', in M. Freixanet (coord), *Sostenibilitats. Polítiques públiques des del feminisme i l'ecologisme*, Barcelona: Institut de Ciències Polítiques i Socials.

Cavallero, L. and Gago, V. (2019) *Una Lectura Feminista de la Deuda. ¡Vivas, Libres y Desendeudadas Nos Queremos!*, Buenos Aires: Fundación Rosa Luxemburgo.

CELS (2018) *La situación de los derechos económicos, sociales y culturales en la Argentina*, Buenos Aires: Centro de Estdudios Legales y Sociales [online], Available from: https://www.cels.org.ar/web/wp-content/uploads/2018/09/informesDESC.pdf

Federici, S. (2021) 'Mujeres, dinero y deuda. Notas para un movimiento feminista de reapropiación', in S. Federici, V. Gago and L. Cavallero (eds), *¿Quién le debe a quién? Ensayos Transnacionales de Desobediencia Financiera*, Buenos Aires: Tinta Limon Ediciones.

Fournier, M. and Cascardo, F. (2022) 'Deudas, cuidados y vulnerabilidad: el caso de las organizaciones comunitarias y los espacios asociativos de cuidado en la Argentina', Documentos de Proyectos (LC/TS.2022/52, LC/BUE/TS.2022/4), Santiago: Economic Commission for Latin America and the Caribeean (ECLAC).

Kreutzer, S. (2004) 'Una mujer con dinero es peligrosa. Cuestiones de género en el manejo del dinero y la deuda a nivel familiar' in M. Villarreal (coord), *Antropología de la deuda: crédito, ahorro, fiado y prestado en las finanzas cotidianas*, México: CIESAS/Miguel Ángel Porrúa.

Meresman, S. and Ullmann, H. (2020) 'COVID-19 y las personas con discapacidad en América Latina: mitigar el impacto y proteger derechos para asegurar la inclusión hoy y mañana', Serie Políticas Sociales, No 237 (LC/TS.2020/122), Santiago: CEPAL.

National Institute of Statistics and Census (INDEC) (2019) *Encuesta Nacional de Gastos de los Hogares 2017–2018: Informe de gastos*, Buenos Aires.

Partenio, F. (2018) 'Cambiemos en el poder: la experiencia de perder derechos. Un análisis feminista de las reformas del gobierno de Mauricio Macri', in R. Flores, N. Brenta, M. De Miguel, F. Partenio and M. Schorr (eds), *La economía argentina a dos años de gobierno de Cambiemos* (Análisis No 26), Buenos Aires: Fundación Friedrich Ebert-Stiftung.

Partenio, F. (2021) 'Ofensiva corporativa sobre los cuidados: el caso de las plataformas de cuidado en América Latina' in A. Pérez Orozco and S. Piris (coords), *Megaproyectos, herramienta corporativa al asalto de la vida*, Bilbao: OMAL [webinar] June.

Partenio, F. (2022a) 'Deudas, cuidados y vulnerabilidad: el caso de las mujeres de hogares de clases populares en la Argentina', Documentos de Proyectos (LC/TS.2022/56-LC/BUE/TS.2022/2), Santiago: Economic Commission for Latin America and the Caribeean (ECLAC).

Partenio, F. (2022b) 'Deudas, cuidados y vulnerabilidad: el caso de las trabajadoras de casas particulares en la Argentina', Documentos de Proyectos (LC/TS.2022/53, LC/BUE/TS.2022/3), Santiago: Economic Commission for Latin America and the Caribeean (ECLAC).

Pautassi, L. (2021) 'El trabajo de cuidado no remunerado en salud en el contexto de América Latina. La centralidad durante la crisis de COVID-19', *Estudios Sociales del Estado*, 7(13): 108–44.

Pérez Orozco, A. and Fernández Ortiz de Zárate, G. (2021) *¿Y si el hámster dejara de mover la rueda capitalista?*, Bilbao: Paz con Dignidad-OMAL-Colectiva XXK.

Rodríguez Enríquez, C. (2020) 'Elementos para una agenda feminista de los cuidados', in K. Batthyány (coord) *Miradas latinoamericanas a los cuidados*, Buenos Aires and México: CLACSO-Siglo XXI.

Tumini, L. and Wilkis, A. (2022) 'Cuidados y vulnerabilidad financiera: un análisis a partir de la Encuesta Nacional de Endeudamiento y Cuidados (ENEC) en la Argentina', Documentos de Proyectos (LC/TS.2022/61-LC/BUE/TS.2022/1), Santiago: Economic Commission for Latin America and the Caribeean (ECLAC).

Wilkis, A. (2013) *Las sospechas del dinero*, Buenos Aires: Paidós.

Wilkis, A. (2017) *The Moral Power of Money. Morality and Economy in the Life of the Poor*, Stanford: Stanford University Press.

Wilkis, A. (2020) *Radiografía social de la vulnerabilidad financiera de las familias en contexto de pandemia en el AMBA*, San Martín: EIDAES.

Wilkis, A. and Partenio, F. (2010) 'Dinero y obligaciones generizadas: las mujeres de sectores populares frente a las circulaciones monetarias de redes políticas y familiares', *La Ventana, Revista de Estudios de Género*, 4(32): 177–213.

14

Debt and the Right to Education in Latin America and the Caribbean

Francisco Cantamutto and Agostina Costantino

1. Introduction

The State is the main guarantor of the human right to education. It is responsible for providing public, free, inclusive and quality education for everyone throughout life. Ilias Bantekas argues that this is a legacy of liberal – as a way to guarantee capable individuals – and socialist – as it understands the importance of education as a common asset – traditions. However, neoliberal schools do not necessarily support this same idea (Bantekas, 2018). They do believe education is important, but they understand that ultimately this is a responsibility of individuals or their environment. How to obtain resources for education is an individual problem, and there exists an excessive confidence in the market to find a solution, both for the provision of education and its financing, for instance, through loans.

Neoliberal policies have affected education in several ways, including their own conception as a good and not as a right. In that respect, they promoted – and promote – a lack of distinction among the ways of providing it, eventually considering the different providers as a part of the aggregation of a market offer. Privatization is the last form of this boost to commercialization. Thus austerity policies and structural reforms undermine the human right to education by not ensuring decent conditions of access and permanence. As it will be explained here, this affectation is not gender neutral, as it tends to exclude girls, adolescents and women, limiting their careers, overloading them with tasks and exposing them to other forms of discrimination or violence.

The State shift as education provider implies a growing pressure on household income in order to keep access to education. This pressure has been combined with a widespread reduction of the income of households that live off their ability to work, which seems to lead to household indebtedness processes. In this case, there are also differential effects on women, who often make decisions to cover the expenses related to domestic and care tasks.

These changes came along with a reconfiguration of capitalism on a worldwide scale since the 1970s. After breaking the Bretton Woods Agreements, a class offensive was deployed and its political-economic programme was neoliberalism (Block, 1989; Harvey, 2007). Neoliberal reforms drove financialization, which is a prevailing trait of our era. This is the control of finances over economies, produced due to the preponderance of both financial actors and their functioning logics (Palley, 2021). Today this affects different aspects of daily life, both in the construction of subjectivities and the access to goods and services.[1] In particular, the spreading of indebtedness as the way to deal with a lack of resources has resulted in a double violation of human rights: first, because it does not guarantee their fulfilment and it depends on indebtedness; and second, because the very dynamics of debt jeopardizes the fulfilment of those same rights in the future. Thus financialization violates the respect for human rights.

This chapter analyzes the impacts of public debt on the human right to education, focusing on Latin America and the Caribbean (LAC), although many of its conclusions may become more generalized outside the region. The next section presents recent trends of public finance for education, and their effects are analyzed in a gender-responsive way. The lack of attainment of investment goals in education is particularly damaging for the rights of girls, adolescents and women, excluding them from access and permanence in the education system, blocking training and job opportunities and exposing them to other forms of discrimination and segregation. The third section analyzes the relation between these investment deficits and public indebtedness.[2]

2. The deficit of State financing to education and its differential impact by gender

As we mentioned, neoliberal reforms tended to understand education as a good. Thus the 'market' started to be assessed as a market with different providers, without a very clear distinction between public and private institutions, which were treated as simple service providers. In some cases, neoliberal reformers started to believe that it could be less costly for the State to partially finance private entities to cover educational needs, with better results. Privatization is also promoted in delegating the provision of textbooks, the design of learning software, the building and maintenance of infrastructure, the training offer for teachers and tools of school management, among others, to companies. The fewer fiscal commitments of the State in this respect tend to defund public entities. This produces pressure on household finances, which increases their exposure to indebtedness. As women tend to be responsible for domestic and care tasks, the education-related debt often impacts on them. Moreover, due to the fact that women's income tends to be more irregular, they are more exposed to indebtedness to keep access and permanence in the education system.

However, evidence shows that private education does not always get better results. Instead, it does promote several ways of segregation (Malouf and Farr, 2019). Privatization has been even higher in early childhood education and tertiary education, which has affected particularly the access and permanence in the education system of women. Due to the fact that at the same time they carry the burden of care tasks (Ambrose and Archer, 2020), difficulties may arise over competing demands on their time, which results in different education paths. In fact, when there are limitations to access or permanence in the education system, girls, adolescents and women tend to be the ones who drop out of education to focus on domestic and care tasks. This limits the currency of their training and thus their access to other cultural resources that help undermine the forms of social discrimination they suffer. Not only this, but with fewer educational credentials, their future access to jobs may be more precarious than that of their male peers. Besides which, nowadays, the lack of public resources in education limits job opportunities in this particularly feminized sector.

In general, the trend is that States finance education by considering supply and demand. In the case of the demand subsidy, money goes from the State to households so that they decide where they will study. These resources reach beneficiaries in a direct way by means of a State allocation or by educational institutions (with an item that belongs to the institution or funds provided by the State). This transfer may be made as grants, assigned by criteria of academic performance or economic needs. However, in some cases, this transfer is made through loans given by the very same educational institutions, banks or the State. This is especially true in the case of higher education – in the region, the most important example is Chile, but Colombia and Brazil also use this system in a widespread way. This alternative takes the financing problem to households, pushing their income and generating a damaging dynamics of indebtedness.

If the offer is kept, the State often provides resources to educational institutions through budget items that are planned annually. Even though the priority is allocating resources to public institutions, in the last decades, the allocation of public resources to private institutions also became more widespread, directly financing their operations.[3] Furthermore, States have incorporated new ways of resource allocation (García de Fanelli, 2019). On the one hand, formulas with several indicators of supplies and results are used (such as enrolment and graduation rates, number of teachers, and so on) to determine the resources to be allocated. On the other hand, contracts with specific purposes have become more widespread, where funds are made available for an investment or specific task (such as the construction of certain infrastructure or internationalization through the exchange of teachers). These mechanisms are presented as more suitable ones to assess management, and often they are part of the loans of multilateral agencies that try to assess specific results. This logic makes educational institutions compete with each other and usually generates damaging incentives that affect quality (for instance, the need to increase the graduation rate may encourage less demanding methods of evaluation).

At the same time, the programmes to finance specific goals often operate against the general financing of education: fewer general funds are available for the free determination of institutions and they are replaced by funds with specific purposes, which do not always satisfy the needs of educational communities. The institutions with a greater ability to capture these funds are more likely to achieve improvements in infrastructure, scientific promotion programmes, internationalization and so on. The main problem of this logic is that it tends to reinforce asymmetries: institutions with a better ability to capture funds – regardless of the reason – may have access to them and raise their own abilities investing them, thus they have more chances to obtain new financing. In consequence, institutions with certain disadvantages are more and more excluded from financing.

It is worth highlighting that this does not necessarily happen due to a mismanagement of resources. For instance, smaller entities from isolated areas may have fewer institutional capacities to make allocations in response to these types of calls, thus they are left out and inequality is fed back. In general, we find that education results depend largely on the social position of origin of educational communities (wealth and parental education level are the main characteristics). Thus, poorer communities need additional support to reach the same baseline conditions as other schools that start with a more favourable social capital. The logic of supposing that baseline conditions to capture additional funds are the same only reinforces origin inequalities. This effect is particularly significant to identify intersectional forms of discrimination against women, whose opportunities may be more affected when they start from a vulnerable social context.

It is worth highlighting that these trends are contrary to a wide group of obligations of States, which must ensure public, free, quality and inclusive education for everyone throughout life, as well as regulate the offer of private education and even limit it when it violates the right to education. These obligations are contained in the Universal Declaration of Human Rights of 1948 and developed in the International Covenant on Economic, Social and Cultural Rights (ICESCR) of 1966. They are also mentioned in the Convention against Discrimination in Education (1960), the International Convention on the Elimination of All Forms of Racial Discrimination (1965), the Convention on the Elimination of All Forms of Discrimination against Women (1979), the Convention on the Rights of the Child (1989), the Convention on the Rights of Persons with Disabilities (2008) and in regional frameworks, such as the Charter of the Organization of American States (1948).

They are also set forth in the Sustainable Development Goal 4 (SDG 4), which urges States to ensure inclusive and equitable quality education. The 2015 Report on the Protection of the Right to Education against Commercialization, by the former United Nations (UN) Special Rapporteur on the human right to education, Kishore Singh, is precisely focused on the limits that may be drawn to the presence of private capital in education due the risks it poses (A/HRC/29/30).[4] Finally, they are also contained in a similar way in the Abidjan Principles,[5] adopted in 2019 by international experts on human rights, including Dr Kombou Boly Barry, a UN Special Rapporteur on the right to education.

How much should States invest to ensure the fulfilment of the human right to education? The United Nations Educational, Scientific and Cultural Organization (UNESCO) is the responsible agency in this matter. In accordance with its 2030 Education Agenda,[6] its recommendation is to invest at least 4 to 6 per cent of GDP or 15 to 20 per cent of public expenditure in education to achieve SDG 4, which aims at ensuring inclusive and equitable quality education and promoting lifelong learning opportunities for all. These values specify the commitments set forth in the meetings in Oslo (Ministry of Foreign Affairs of Norway, 2015) and Addis Ababa (2015)[7] to increase financing so as to achieve SDG 4. The education ministers of LAC indicated in section 20 of the Declaration of Lima (2014) the willingness to achieve this higher guideline (UNESCO, 2014). Even more: along with LAC heads of delegation, they committed – after the Incheon Declaration (2015) – that these will be the *minimum* levels of investment (CLADE, 2015). This is a possible way to bridge the gaps with respect to more developed nations.

Has this investment been achieved? Considering that the parameters were established in 2015, 30 countries of the region were compared in accordance with their performance between 2015 and 2020 as to the previous trend from the beginning of the century, through the investment indicator in education with respect to GDP. The report highlights that there are 14 countries that do not comply with the suggested minimum investment. Nine out of the 16 complying countries reduced their investment in the last five years, instead of increasing or maintaining it. Only four of them exceeded the 6 per cent commitment; the rest of the countries comply with the minimum investment

(4 per cent). Doing the same exercise for the indicator that compares the importance of the investment for education and public expenditure, again there are 14 countries that did not reach the suggested minimum (15 per cent). Seven out of the 16 that comply with the minimum goal exceeded the higher percentage of the recommendation (20 per cent). In other words, the commitments agreed at an international level to ensure the human right to education have not been fulfilled in a systematic and widespread way by LAC countries.

The lack of enough investment in education by States allows different forms of privatization, commercialization and financialization. Specifically, if the State does not commit sufficient resources to finance education, the – actual or perceived – deterioration of the sector leads some companies to offer education services to those who can afford them, whether as a formal provision or even as extra-institutional tutoring. This creates cost-effective investment niches that do not necessarily imply a total privatization of the sector, although they do imply a growing penetration of private businesses in the education sector.[8] As we mentioned before, private provision does not seem to have the goal or expected result of reducing the several forms of discrimination and segregation – considering private provision's high level of connection with inequality of origin income. As we suggested, this phenomenon is not gender neutral.

Moreover, the lack of public finance in education has several negative impacts. Without enough funds, damaged infrastructure or existing equipment cannot be replaced, and the needs resulting from the expansion of the population that attend educational institutions cannot be satisfied. This was particularly evident during the COVID-19 pandemic, when LAC faced several problems in efforts to continue with education in a virtual way. It is worth highlighting that, as was evident during the pandemic, the inability to keep connection between students and their educational institution increases the exposure of girls, adolescents and women to gender violence, limiting prevention and care tools.

The lack of investment makes sustaining the quality of teacher training difficult, as well as a decent salary for their work, which is impossible to pay without resources. Incidentally, the lack of a decent salary for the non-teaching support personnel affects attendance conditions – such as health and safety – in the institutions. These institutions may influence the flow of persons that decide to work as teachers by creating problems of adverse selection (qualified personnel decide not to work in this activity due to bad salaries) or lack of personnel.[9] Without a doubt, this leads to legitimate union claims. As education is a sector where the labour participation of women is particularly high, the lack of resources especially affects their opportunities.

Thus the lack of enough public investment in education has a sixfold negative impact on women, adolescents and girls. First, because they are more likely to be excluded from access to the education system when there is underinvestment, as the access of the men of households is often prioritized. Second, because this exclusion conditions the future career, by blocking job opportunities that require certain credentials. Third, it also limits current job opportunities as work in the education sector is highly feminized, so women lose decent job opportunities in the public sector. Fourth, as the income gap in the public sector tends to be smaller than in the rest of the economy, this loss of jobs widens the gap at an aggregated level. Fifth, the education system not only guarantees certain knowledge, but it also provides care conditions, which gives free time to responsible adults, who are then available to work, learn or rest. When these conditions are not available or are poor, the overload of care tasks falls on women, adolescents and girls. Sixth, the education system also gives support and prevention tools as to safety in cases of gender violence. The lack of sufficient resources limits the ability to deal with this specific type of violence.

3. Public debt and education financing

Although complying with education investment commitments has several determinants, here we emphasize its connection with public indebtedness. Neoliberal reforms made States lose several sources of collection by eliminating taxes – especially progressive ones – and other non-tax revenues (such as those from public companies). The policies of opening and liberalization increased the exposure of peripheral economies to external shocks, which reduced available resources during crises. Furthermore, along with labour reforms, they reconfigured economies with higher levels of precariousness in the labour market, which also reduced access to the resources of States.

These losses of fiscal resources came with a higher access to loans as a financing alternative. In fact, States of peripheral countries took more and more debt (Cantamutto and Castiglioni, 2021). Since the mid-1990s, LAC States have rapidly taken debt (Figure 14.1). Although at the beginning of the 21st century the dynamics were the opposite, largely thanks to a favourable situation of international prices, the 2008 crisis set a limit to this path: from that moment, Latin American public debts grew again. Munevar calculates that public debt in the region reached 78 per cent of GDP in 2020, when US$95,000 million were allocated to the repayment of debts (Munevar, 2021a).

Indebtedness may cover fiscal needs in a certain period of time as it provides liquidity. The problem is that, in subsequent periods of time, when such debt must be paid, it turns into a source of resource loss. This implies a systematic exit of money as interest, whose importance may jeopardize other items, such as those that guarantee the human right to education. During 2020, 108 out of 116 peripheral economies were witnesses of an

Figure 14.1: Debt of the central government as a GDP proportion, simple average of 28 LAC countries

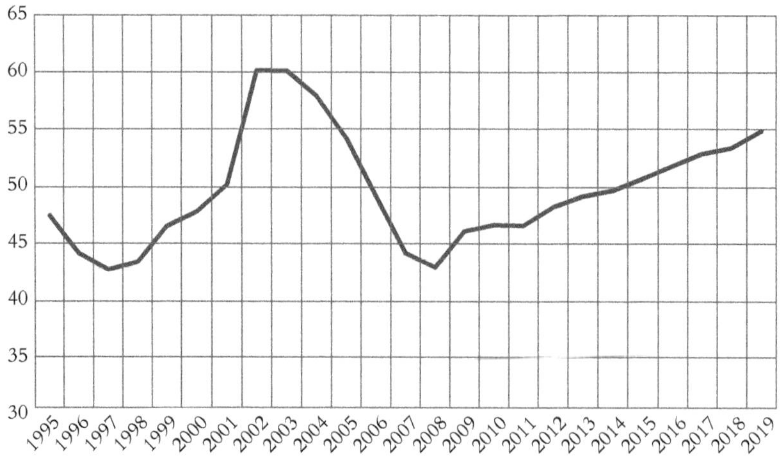

Source: Own creation with data of the International Monetary Fund (IMF)

increase of their public debts, by a total of US$1,900,000 million (equivalent to 8.3 per cent of their GDP). At the same time, these countries paid about US$194,000 million to creditors. Instead of using these funds to deal with the crisis, they were used to repay debt: in 62 of these countries, these types of payment exceeded the investment in health, and in 36 they exceeded the funds for education (Munevar, 2021b).

Figure 14.2 shows the evolution the services of the total public debt and the debt with multilateral agencies (which is part of the previous one), both compared to the investment in education for the entire region as a whole, and as an average for all LAC countries. The chart shows the public debt kept its high importance until 2007 and fell from that moment until 2014, when it started to grow again. The services of the multilateral debt accounted for more than one third of the total services at the beginning of the period. Their values fell until 2011, and they have slightly grown since then. Their importance in total services increased. In contrast, investment in education is more stable in time, which evidences a low correlation among these variables. If we look at the situation since 2014, investment in education shows a slight fall, while the total repayments of debts grew more than the repayments of the multilateral debt.

Mechanical analyses should be avoided: there are contexts where States may repay debt without necessarily diverting financing from education. This happened during the first decade of the 21st century, under a context of high international prices and growth. In a context of high dynamism, the contradiction is not evidently shown: it seems possible to invest in education

Figure 14.2: Services of public debt, multilateral debt and investment in education as a proportion of the total public expenditure, an average for LAC

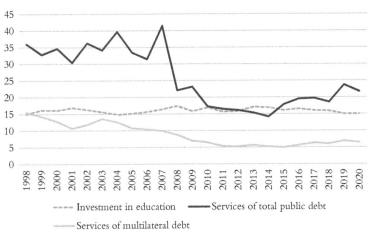

Source: Own creation with data of the World Bank

at the same time as debt is paid. The contradiction arises more clearly when such economic growth slows down: in the last seven years, it is evident that the rise of the services of debt – the total debt and, to a lesser extent, the multilateral debt – replaces the investment in education. Thus precisely when life conditions become more vulnerable, the shift from human rights in favour of creditors becomes clearer. In 2019, Haiti, Guyana and El Salvador paid more debt than the amount they invested in a combined way in education, health and social protection (Agg, 2021).

During the pandemic, the burden of debt limited the options of States when they had to take action. Considering the procyclical nature of public expenditure in the region, the GDP fall in 2020 caused an estimated fall of 9 per cent of investment in education (ECLAC and UNESCO, 2020). The impact of this shift had immediate and long-term effects on the deterioration of the conditions of education systems (Ledoux and Koffi Segniagbeto, 2020; World Bank, 2021).

In Table 14.1, the tension between the expenses related to public debt and the investment in education is shown in another way, comparing the two indicators previously used – its burden for the total public expenditure and for the GDP – with their equivalents as to debt (frequently used as sustainability indicators). The table shows the percentage variation of indictors in the last five years with respect to the previous five-year period for the countries that have enough data. The main result is that there exists a negative correlation among these indicators in the region: when increasing the expenditure in one item, it decreases in other. In the region taken on average, the burden

Table 14.1: Variation of debt and education indicators, 2016–20 period compared to 2011–15 period

Country	With respect to GDP		Country	With respect to total public expenditure	
	Debt	Education		Debt	Education
Argentina	180%	–5%	Argentina	185%	–10%
Honduras	133%	–17%	Honduras	156%	–10%
Ecuador	115%	–11%	Ecuador	104%	–3%
Brazil	109%	5%	Brazil	98%	3%
Colombia	99%	–2%	Nicaragua	79%	–3%
Nicaragua	97%	–5%	Colombia	79%	–5%
Grenada	87%	–21%	Mexico	66%	–5%
Mexico	63%	–10%	Paraguay	49%	6%
Haití	59%	–14%	Haití	48%	8%
Paraguay	57%	–24%	Jamaica	48%	–8%
Dominica	41%	53%	ALYC	30%	–4%
Jamaica	33%	–12%	El Salvador	8%	–6%
ALYC	31%	–2%	Costa Rica	7%	9%
El Salvador	12%	–5%			
Costa Rica	6%	3%			
Dominican Rep.	4%	26%			
Panamá	–2%	–6%	Dominican Rep.	–8%	14%
Guyana	–3%	42%	Perú	–18%	13%
Perú	–3%	18%	Guatemala	–21%	7%
Belize	–19%	12%	Panamá	–26%	–13%
Guatemala	–21%	4%	Belize	–27%	–2%
Correlation		–43%			–44%

Source: Own creation with data of the World Bank

of debt has increased when the two periods 2011–15 and 2016–20 are compared (31 per cent if it is measured with respect to the GDP, and 30 per cent with respect to public expenditure). This has resulted in a reduction of investment in education (2 per cent in the indicator compared with the GDP, and 4 per cent with respect to total public expenditure).

Few countries in the region do not have this general behaviour, which is not found when comparing with the average of the rest of the world. The three most dynamic countries in this indebtedness process are Argentina, Ecuador and Honduras. The size of these economies is very different, with different productive specializations, so it does not seem that the cause is related to a problem of this type. In the three cases, they were under liberal-conservative governments for the most part of the last five years, but they were not the only countries with this type of government. An exclusive characteristic of this group is that the three of them had an agreement with conditionalities in force with the IMF. This is an interesting and distinctive finding as the IMF is seldom considered in relation to education because its agreements do not have mandates in this regard. Development banks and institutions – the World Bank, Inter-American Development Bank (IDB), Corporación Andina de Fomento (CAF, currently called Development Bank of Latin America) – invest in education issues, and have received relatively more attention.

This is because the impact of debt does not end with repayment. Its growing magnitude gives an even more leading role to creditors in the determination of public policies on a wide range of issues. Sometimes this role is surreptitious, made through capital movements that destabilize economies. A capital exit creates fiscal problems, as well as uncertainty in the exchange and financial market, and it worries the population. Governments try to avoid these type of events because then they are presented as the responsible parties of a crisis. The power of creditors is structural, and therefore they do not always need to present themselves in a public and explicit way. For that purpose, they have mediators in the public debate who introduce themselves as interpreters: the mass media, private consulting firms that provide allegedly aseptic – technical – analyses, and risk rating agencies, through their recommendations. All these actors, who have a strong presence in the public scene, tend to emphasize the importance of maintaining well-organized finances. It is very important to emphasize that they do not know the other obligations that States have with their citizens (Bonet de Viola, Delfor and Fernández, 2020; Koskenniemi, 2021), such as ensuring quality education.

The IMF particularly became the agency in charge of translating creditors' demands into programmes of specific public policies. The 'correct' or 'appropriate' policies for the countries are considered in the annual reviews that this agency makes on the member countries, and that are considered as a valid assessment of the economy. Other assessments, such as the ones of the World Bank in its report *Doing Business*, act in the same sense.[10] Thus, loan agencies, protected by their interstate nature, appear validating the vision of creditors through their reports.

The IMF is focused on solving financial, monetary and exchange imbalances, and initially it does not have a direct connection to the human right to education. However, due to its increasing emphasis on fiscal consolidation and the opening of economies, it has an impact on the ability of States to invest in education. The IMF understands that the main source of instability is fiscal deficit and, therefore, it needs to rapidly advance towards its reduction. For this agency, the way to do this is through the reduction of certain public expenses – but it never proposes to reduce debt services – therefore, it insists on reducing expenditure, even if it is already below the average of similar countries (Ambrose and Archer, 2020). Of course this affects sensitive areas, such as public employment, protection and social security. In fact, this emphasis on the reduction of fiscal deficit through limitations to personnel hiring or the salaries paid in the public sector, even without having a direct destination in terms of education, negatively impacts this sector (Ambrose and Archer, 2020; Stubbs and Kentikelenis, 2021).[11]

The areas of health and education are often the heaviest ones in the total wage bill, so expenditure limitations and wage ceilings or hiring restrictions affect those areas in a special way. In fact, the IMF recognized that very indebted countries end up making adjustments in education and health, the areas that suffer the most during financial crises (Bantekas, 2018). This way, teachers end up working more hours, having more students or working for lower salaries. These are basic functions of the State that are affected when cutbacks are made, but also in dynamic terms because they expel qualified personnel or they prevent them from being interested in participating in the sector. These are often highly feminized areas of the labour market, so cutbacks have an unequal effect on women, who find fewer jobs or, if they get them, they receive a lower salary. Within the public sector, the pay gap between men and women is usually about 10 per cent lower than the one in the private sector, so when its scope is limited, the pay gap extends as a consequence. Even more: as we have already explained, cutbacks in education imply limitations in ensuring universal access to education, which often particularly affect women and girls.

There are other international agencies that act together with the IMF, but they are less focused on current problems because they are focused on development loans. The World Bank, CAF and IDB have a strong presence in the region. They also use conditionalities in their loans (Moreira Martins, 2021a, 2021b). Their vision is imposed because they have the ability to unlock donations and international cooperation, mainly for vulnerable countries. Although in the last decade the number of required conditions per agreement decreased, their influence has been key when prioritizing macroeconomic stability as a policy goal, so that States often limit public expenditure – even in education (Brunswijck, 2019). The incentive to privatization and to several forms of public–private association has also been present in the last decades. Although their projects account for only 0.2 per cent of the regional public debt, its influence in education is relevant, determining the creation of indicators, goals and technical resources.

4. Final remarks

The State is the main guarantor of the human right to education. It is responsible for providing public, free, inclusive and quality education for everyone throughout life. Neoliberal policies have affected education in several ways, including their own conception as a good and not as a right. In that sense, there is a distinction between the private and public provision forms, blurring the obligations of the State. Commercialization and privatization derived from a change of the priorities of States when choosing the destinations of public expenditure, imposing the burden of gaining access to education on the income of households. This change of priorities is not gender neutral because it particularly affects girls, adolescents and women, who are the first ones to abandon the education system, limiting their access to care and protection from forms of violence, as well as current and future job opportunities.

Neoliberal structural reforms deprive States of tools of economic policy, contributing to a change of priorities in favour of creditors. In fact, we discovered that LAC States have had very limited compliance with their own international commitments in terms of investment in education. This has at least six types of negative impact on women, adolescents and girls. First, because they are more likely to stop having access to the education system as households tend to prioritize the access of men. Second, this same exclusion limits the access to certain job opportunities that require credentials, so their future careers are conditioned. Third, it also limits current job opportunities as the education sector has a particularly high participation of women. Women are the first ones that lose decent job opportunities in the public sector. Fourth, as in this sector the income gap tends to be smaller, the loss of jobs tends to widen the gap at an aggregated level of the economy. Fifth, the insufficient or poor provision of care conditions by the education system overloads (even more) girls, adolescents and women with care tasks. Sixth, the lack of sufficient resources limits the ability of the education system to give support and prevention tools as to safety in cases of gender violence.

The burden of the debt has changed over time, but its impact goes beyond the existing level. The payment of debt services may replace other expenses, such as the ones used to invest in education. The data that is presented here shows that the contradiction arises more clearly when economic growth slows down, which is when the rise of debt services – the total debt, and to a lesser extent, the multilateral debt – replaces investment in education. Thus precisely, when life conditions become more vulnerable, the shift from human rights in favour of creditors becomes clearer.

In the region, in the last five years, debt growth happened as a result of the fall of public investment in education. The three countries that stand out the most in this trend have a particular characteristic: they have been under programmes with conditionalities with the IMF. Although more attention is often given to development banking entities when analyzing the impact of multilateral financing on education, it seems that the IMF has a relevant role. As the IMF is the agency that provides resources in situations of crisis, its impact is key. However, its action is coordinated with the other development banking entities. Its conditions tend to be focused on price stability and fund release for the repayment of debts as main goals, which reduces the ability of the State to fulfil other rights, such as the human right to education. This shift of priorities is against sustained development in the medium term, as well as the possibility to do economic politics in the interest of other goals, such as a decent life or the fulfilment of human rights.

International agencies understand that the main source of instability is fiscal deficit and that, in consequence, it should be reduced through cutbacks of public expenditure. This affects sensitive areas, such as public employment, protection and social security and education, even when this sector does not appear explicitly as a target. The limitations to the hiring of personnel or the salaries paid in the public sector affect the areas of health and education because they are the most important ones in the total wage bill. In this way, teachers end up working more hours, having more students or working for lower salaries. These are basic functions of the State that are affected when cutbacks are made, but also in dynamic terms because they expel qualified personnel or they prevent them from being interested in participating in the sector. The lack of enough public investment in education damages infrastructure, equipment and support personnel. This enables the emergence of different forms of privatization whose goals are not oriented to the reduction of different forms of discrimination and segregation.

Notes

[1] The connection between financialization at a structural level, the effects on daily life and resistance has been comprehensively introduced in Cavallero and Gago (2019).

[2] This chapter recovers the findings of the report titled 'Impactos del endeudamiento en la realización del derecho humano a la educación', by the Latin American Campaign for the Right to Education (Campaña Latinoamericana por el Derecho a la Educación, CLADE), available from: https://redclade.org/wp-content/uploads/Impactos_endeudamiento_LATAM_completo.pdf

[3] For instance, in Costa Rica, Mexico and Peru, more than 90 per cent of public funds for institutions of private education are given as direct allocations. See Arias et al (2021).

[4] See the report at https://www.right-to-education.org/node/1187.

[5] See the report at https://www.abidjanprinciples.org/.

[6] The 2030 Education Agenda explains these values in sections 14 and 105. It is available here: https://unesdoc.unesco.org/ark:/48223/pf0000245656. The UNESCO guide Unpacking Sustainable Development Goal 4: Education 2030 contains the same guideline (p 23); it is available at https://unesdoc.unesco.org/ark:/48223/pf0000246300.

[7] The Addis Ababa Declaration (see especially sections 12, 20 and 78) is available at https://unctad.org/system/files/official-document/ares69d313_es.pdf. The Oslo Declaration

emphasizes the movement of resources to finance education. It is available at https://www.regjeringen.no/globalassets/departementene/ud/dokumenter/oslo-summit-on-education-for-development--chairs-statement.pdf.

8   See UNESCO (2015; 2021) and A/HRC/29/30 to know more about commercialization and privatization trends, as well as related risks. For an analysis of the Argentinean case, see Feldfeber et al (2018).

9   To know more about the aforementioned effects of underinvestment in education, see Archer and Saalbrink (2021), and Marphatia (2010).

10   This report has caused great unrest at an international scale due to its accusations of data distortion to favour or damage countries. For instance, see El País (2021).

11   Due to the pressure of the civil society, in 2007, the IMF stopped imposing wage ceilings in its recommendations. However, a recent report suggested that this practice has returned to the uses of the agency, which included it in most of its agreements. See Archer and Saalbrink (2021).

References

Agg, C. (2021) 'COVID-19 and the looming debt crisis', Unicef [online] April, Available from: https://www.unicef-irc.org/publications/pdf/Social-spending-series_COVID-19-and-the-looming-debt-crisis.pdf

Ambrose, S. and Archer, D. (2020) 'Who cares about the future. Finance gender responsive public services!', ActionAid [online] 13 April, Available from: https://actionaid.org/publications/2020/who-cares-future-finance-gender-responsive-public-services

Archer, D. and Saalbrink, R. (2021) 'The public versus austerity. Why public sector wage bill constraints must end', Education International, Action Aid and Public Services International [online], Available from:https://actionaid.org/sites/default/files/publications/The_public_vs_austerity.pdf

Arias Ortiz, E.; Elacqua, G.; López Sánchez, Á.;Téllez Fuentes, J.; Peralta Castro, R.; Ojeda, M. et al (2021) 'Educación superior y COVID-19 en América Latina y el Caribe: Financiamiento para los estudiantes', Instituto Internacional de la Unesco para la Educación Superior en América Latina y el Caribe (IESALC), Banco Interamericano de Desarrollo (IDB) and Asociación Panamericana de Instituciones de Crédito Educativo (ÁPICE). Available from: https://unesdoc.unesco.org/ark:/48223/pf0000378257

Bantekas, I. (2018) 'Sovereign debt and the right to education', in I. Bantekas and C. Lumina (eds), *Sovereign Debt & Human Rights*, Oxford: Oxford University Press, pp 233–47.

Block, F. (1989) *Los orígenes del desorden económico internacional*, Buenos Aires: Fondo de Cultura Económica.

Bonet de Viola, A.; Delfor, A. and Fernández, J. (2020) 'Crisis económica, deuda externa y realización de los derechos humanos. Análisis de la colisión jurídica entre las obligaciones fiscales internacionales y el pacto de los derechos económicos, sociales y culturales', Cuadernos de la Facultad de Humanidades y Ciencias Sociales, 58: 181–208.

Brunswijck, G. (2019) 'Flawed conditions: The impact of the World Bank's conditionality on developing countries', Eurodad Briefing Paper [online] 9 April, Available from: https://www.eurodad.org/flawed-conditions

Cantamutto, F. and Castiglioni, L. (2021) 'El primer año de la pandemia y, ¿una crisis de deuda en el horizonte?', in Silvia London (ed), *La investigación en ciencias sociales en pandemia, un año después*, Bahía Blanca: Documentos de Trabajo del IIESS, pp 267–84.

Cavallero, L. and Gago, V. (2019) *Una lectura feminista de la deuda*, Buenos Aires: Fundación Rosa Luxemburgo.

CLADE (2015) 'En comunicado, países de América Latina y el Caribe presentes en el Foro se comprometen a un 'esfuerzo sin precedente' para mejorar la educación', *¡La Educación como Derecho Humano se Defiende!* [online] 21 May, Available from: http://haciacoreapost2015.blogspot.com/2015/05/en-comunicado-paises-de-america-latina.html

ECLAC and Unesco (2020), 'La educación en tiempos de la pandemia de COVID-19', [online] August, Available from: https://repositorio.cepal.org/bitstream/handle/11362/45904/1/S2000510_es.pdf

El País (2021) 'El brutal escándalo en el Banco Mundial que terminó con la eliminación de un informe', [online] 16 September, Available from: https://bit.ly/3KM9AkG

Feldfeber, M.; Puiggrós, A.; Robertson, S. and Duhalde, M. (2018) *La privatización educativa en Argentina*, Confederación de Trabajadores de la Educación de la República Argentina, Available from: https://www.ei-ie.org/es/item/25693:la-privatizacion-educativa-en-argentina

García de Fanelli, A. (2019) 'El financiamiento de la educación superior en América Latina: Tendencias e instrumentos de financiamiento', *Propuesta Educativa*, 28(52): 111–26.

Harvey, D. (2007) *Breve historia del neoliberalismo*, Madrid: Akal.

Koskenniemi, M. (2021) 'Foreword', in J.P. Bohoslavsky and F. Cantamutto (eds), *SPEAK OUT! at The Laboratory for Advanced Research on the Global Economy*, LSE Human Rights [online], pp 3–6, Available from: https://bit.ly/3CGLLbn

Ledoux, B. and Segniagbeto, K. (2020) '¿Qué precio pagará la educación por la COVID-19?', International Institute for Educational Planing – UNESCO [online] 27 April, Available from: https://www.buenosaires.iiep.unesco.org/es/portal/que-precio-pagara-la-educacion-por-la-covid-19

Malouf, K. and Farr, J. (2019) 'False promises: How delivering education through private schools and public-private partnerships risks fueling inequality instead of achieving quality education for all', Oxfam Briefing Paper.

Marphatia, A. (2010) 'The adverse effects of International Monetary Fund programs on the health and education workforce', *International Journal of Health Services*, 40(1): 165–78.

Moreira Martins, E. (2021a) 'Banco Interamericano de Desarrollo: Lineamientos para educación y proyectos financiados en América Latina y El Caribe,' CLADE [online], Available from: https://redclade.org/wp-content/uplo ads/BID-estudio-Erika6.pdf

Ministry of Foreign Affairs of Norway (2015) 'The Oslo Declaration', Available from: https://www.regjeringen.no/globalassets/departement ene/ud/dokumenter/oslo-summit-on-education-for-development--cha irs-statement.pdf

Moreira Martins, E. (2021b) 'Banco Mundial: Lineamientos para educación y proyectos financiados en América Latina y El Caribe', CLADE [online], Available from: https://redclade.org/wp-content/uploads/CLADE_Ba nco-Mundial_v9.pdf.

Munevar, D. (2021a) 'La pandemia de la deuda en América Latina y el Caribe', *Cuadernos de Economía Crítica*, 7(14): 157–61.

Munevar, D. (2021b) 'A Debt Pandemic. Dynamics and Implications of the Debt Crisis of 2020', Eurodad Briefing Paper.

Organization of American States (1948) 'Charter of the Organization of American States', Available from: http://www.oas.org/dil/1948%20char ter%20of%20the%20organization%20of%20american%20states.pdf

Palley, T. (2021) 'Financialization revisited: The economics and political economy of the vampire squid economy' (Working Paper 2110), Post-Keynesian Economics Society.

Stubbs, T. and Kentikelenis, A. (2021) 'Condicionalidad y deuda soberana: Un panorama general de sus implicancias en los derechos humanos', *Derechos en Acción*, 6(18): 173–215, Available from: https://revistas.unlp.edu.ar/ ReDeA/article/view/12006/10863.

Unesco (2010), "Addis Ababa Declaration". Available from: https://unes doc.unesco.org/ark:/48223/pf0000187149

Unesco (2014) 'Education for All (EFA) in Latin America and the Caribbean: assessment of progress and post-2015 challenges: Lima Statement'. Available from: s://unesdoc.unesco.org/ark:/48223/pf0000230628_eng

Unesco (2015) 'Replantear la educación. ¿Hacia el bien común global?', [online], Available from: https://unesdoc.unesco.org/ark:/48223/pf000 0232697;

Unesco (2021) 'Global education monitoring report 2021/22. Non-state actors in education: Who chooses? Who loses?'.

United Nations (1960), "Convention against Discrimination in Education". Available from: https://www.ohchr.org/en/instruments-mechanisms/inst ruments/convention-against-discrimination-education

United Nations (1965), "International Convention on the Elimination of All Forms of Racial Discrimination". Available from: https://www.ohchr. org/en/instruments-mechanisms/instruments/international-convention-elimination-all-forms-racial

United Nations (1979), "Convention on the Elimination of All Forms of Discrimination against Women New York". Available from: https://www.ohchr.org/en/instruments-mechanisms/instruments/convention-elimination-all-forms-discrimination-against-women

United Nations (1989), "Convention on the Rights of the Child". Available from: https://www.ohchr.org/en/instruments-mechanisms/instruments/convention-rights-child

United Nations (2006), "Convention on the Rights of Persons with Disabilities". Available from: https://www.un.org/development/desa/disabilities/convention-on-the-rights-of-persons-with-disabilities/convention-on-the-rights-of-persons-with-disabilities-2.html

World Bank (2021) 'Actuemos ya para proteger el capital humano de nuestros niños. Los costos y la respuesta ante el impacto de la pandemia de COVID-19 en el sector educativo de América Latina y el Caribe', [online], Available from: https://openknowledge.worldbank.org/handle/10986/35276?locale-attribute=es

PART V

Gender Impact Analysis: Frameworks and Experiences

15

Debt Sustainability Analysis: Life After Capital – A View from Feminist Economics

Patricia Miranda and Verónica Serafini Geoghegan

1. Introduction

The return of the debt in most countries of the Global South while a crisis of social reproduction and care is deepening has evidenced the need of feminist economics to address the analysis of the connections between both processes; plus the challenges related to the climate crisis, with differential impacts on women and historically unprotected groups, and the effects of the war between Russia and Ukraine on the prices of food and energy at a global level, which have also affected the increase of the interest rate to control inflation, which has resulted in the increase of the cost of debt.

Indebtedness and its resulting crises had significant consequences in the past for the life of people, even putting survival and welfare at risk during the whole vital cycle. Women were particularly affected by this phenomenon because they are at a disadvantage in almost any field, mainly as to the unpaid work resulting from the gender division of work.

This chapter analyses debt sustainability in the light of the assumptions of feminist economics. Countries that receive financing and technical advice from financial agencies, such as the International Monetary Fund (IMF) and the World Bank (WB), have driven analysis frameworks and tools for debt management that prioritize capital flows and their return in the name of financial and macroeconomic stability over human rights and the wellbeing of people.

From the view of feminist economics, this represents a contradiction with the goals of economic performance, whose main concern should be to maintain and reproduce life. Although the calculation of debt sustainability is made using a number of economic assumptions from the neoclassical school in order to provide a technocratic veil, its consequences extend to an ethical–political field as their clear purpose is to favour capital over life.

This chapter presents a critical look at the debt sustainability analysis from feminist economics. Following this introduction, the second section presents the analytical categories of feminist economics that are useful for this debt analysis. The third section presents the theoretical structure of the economic orthodoxy to address debt sustainability and its consequences for the population and particularly for women. Finally, the last section presents the conclusions.

2. Life sustainability: feminist economics

'Life sustainability is understood as a historical process of social reproduction, a complex, dynamic, and multidimensional process of need fulfilment in continuous adaptation of individual identities and social relations' (Carrasco, Borderías and Torns, 2011: 60). According to Bosch, Carrasco, and Grau (2005: 2), this process

> not only refers to the actual possibility that life continues – in human, social, and ecological terms –, but to the fact that such process implies developing acceptable life levels, life standards, or life quality for all the population. This sustainability then implies a harmonic relation between humanity and nature, and between sisters and brothers.

In the idea of 'sustainability', feminist economics is part of the criticism to the economic orthodoxy, the use of analytical categories that characterizes this approach to analyze the condition of women, the intersectional look, and the multidisciplinary wealth for its interrelation with other disciplines, such as the environmental ones.

The emphasis put on maintaining life can be explicitly found in the classical authors of economics, such as Adam Smith, David Ricardo and even Karl Marx, who propose the need of a subsistence salary that includes the costs of maintaining life considering social needs.

Smith recognizes the role of women in social reproduction through the care and upbringing of children that then will be 'productive' workers and will contribute to the 'wealth of nations'. This author also refers to the existence of needs that arise from culture and customs, so they go beyond biological reproduction. This is not a minor aspect as it has consequences for the subsistence salary in the microeconomic field and, at a macroeconomic level, production should provide the 'necessary and convenient' things for life.

However, classical authors do not refer to the value of social reproduction work or include in their analysis the existence of inequalities between men and women in the labour market and different salaries based on sex that are not explained by the market, productivity or specialization.

With the arrival of the neoclassical school, which was the prevailing paradigm both among scholars and in the international economic agencies during the 20th century, social reproduction work disappears from the theoretical structure of the economic sciences. This fact invisibilizes an important proportion of the effort made to guarantee the economic results generally measured by the Gross Domestic Product (GDP), national revenue or wealth in an economy.

The focus of neoclassical or marginalist scholars became the mechanism to determine efficiency prices through the balance between supply and demand. With this approach, social relations and needs disappear, and any possibility to include social reproduction work is lost.

This doctrine divides the economic activity in dichotomic areas – public/private fields, market/family, productive/reproductive work – that do not connect with each other; the first ones are the object of study, where the monetized economy prevails.

The private/family/reproductive areas are kept subordinated and their content is undervalued. When they are considered, the analysis uses the same assumptions and theories as in the private sector; therefore, it does not recognize or explain the problems that affect women or inequalities.

The theorem of the 'representative economic agent' or 'homo economicus', on which the neoclassical structure is based and that aims at explaining market relations, is also assumed in the family with some changes that recognize the existence of different conducts; however, in essence the idea of profit maximization remains. For instance, women 'choose' combinations of time to work and leisure, goods and services based on prices and opportunity costs defined in the market. The inequalities resulting from the gender division of work or the inequalities generated by the market and that are not explained by supply and demand are not considered, against the definitions of neoclassical theories.

This way, spaces, activities, economic flows and production where women participate are invisibilized. The work considered is the one that goes through the market and is paid.

The existence of a 'representative' agent whose main interest is to optimize her budget restriction hides inequalities and the consideration of social needs. Even though this representative agent is supposed to have neutral characteristics in terms of gender, she actually takes the role socially assigned to men as providers in a family, with a woman devoted to domestic and unpaid work.

At a macroeconomic level, adding the maximization of profits (consumption) and benefits (production) generates income flows that ignore the effect of unpaid (domestic and care) work that happens in households and communities in economic aggregates. Social reproduction work, as it is largely done for free, is not included in the costs or in salaries.

Feminist economics, with the contributions of Antonella Picchio, Nancy Folbre, Cristina Carrasco and Susan Himmelweit, among other economists, incorporates social reproduction work, extending the income flow as the amount of work included in economic activities increases. The working population includes those who perform unpaid work, regardless of what they do in the labour market or if they receive remuneration, and the concept of welfare is expanded to go beyond education and health – components of human capital for the neoclassical school – and to include daily care.

With the incorporation of social reproduction in the theoretical structure, feminist economics reshapes the microeconomic and macroeconomic analysis, forcing the redefinition of the analytical and indicator categories, and the epistemological and methodological transformations of economics. This alternative approach enables us to understand reality and influence on proposals of change that contribute to an emancipatory economy for women.

Not only does feminist economics challenge the assumptions of the 'representative economic agent' that do not distinguish differences between men and women, but it also assumes the existence of differences among women, many of which become inequalities when social class, ethnicity, sexual orientation and nationality, among others, are considered. One example is domestic and care work.

The hiring of these services by persons or households is marked by inequalities among women. Migrant, Black and rural women are the ones hired for these occupations, generally with lower salaries and in precarious conditions, both in their own communities or countries and when they participate in the so-called global chains of care.

In this respect, the idea of 'accumulation for dispossession' proposed by David Harvey (2005), to which Silvia Federici (2010) adds dispossession 'of the reproduction work', helps to understand the process by which capitalism maintenance is supported with the appropriation of the free work of women both within countries and among them.

Country indebtedness, especially in Latin America, took place to guarantee growth models that mainly benefited private capital. The lack of interest in benefiting work and salaries is reflected in the unequal access to assets, such as land, forests or water, the appropriation of retirement funds, the precariousness of the labour market and the persistence of poverty, the subordination conditions of women, the migrations generated due to the removal of farmers and indigenous people from their original territories, and unfair tax structures.

In debt crises, these problems are deepened and other problems are added, such as the liberalization of markets or the privatization of public or common goods, measures that ended up being beneficial for capital and aggravating the unpaid work of women.

The gender division of work implies not only exclusion from the labour market or inclusion with many obstacles, but also a subordinated social position due to the devaluation of unpaid work.

According to Federici (2010), women were forced to chronic poverty, economic dependency and their invisibility as workers, while for male workers, their product, the labour force, was devalued (Federici, 2010).

Thus 'the invisibility of housework hides the secret of all capitalist life: the source of social surplus – unwaged labor – must be degraded, naturalized, made into a marginal aspect of the system' (Caffentzis, 1999: 14).

The divergent paths of life sustainability and debt sustainability are understood by analyzing the capital–life conflict in the context of the capitalist development. Ensuring life sustainability requires focusing on social reproduction due to its importance for the life of people and for being a determinant factor of capital accumulation possibilities. Ensuring debt sustainability – from the orthodox perspective – requires focusing on capital and the accumulation requirement; one of its mechanisms is the dispossession of social reproduction work.

In the following section, the meaning and the way of calculating debt sustainability frequently used by credit international institutions and governments are presented so as to evidence the contradiction between both goals and the need to include deep changes in the conceptual and methodological framework of the debt analysis.

3. Debt sustainability: the economic orthodoxy

Debt sustainability has a positive meaning in terms of economic performance from most of the economic doctrines, and even using common sense. Being against debt that is sustainable is very difficult. However, if the principles used for the calculation and the measures involved in ensuring a positive outcome are analyzed, the costs in terms of welfare and human rights of people end up with a negative balance.

Capital over people

The concern over the analysis of debt sustainability became stronger in the debate at the beginning of the new millennium after recurring crises and in an international context where globalization forecasted an increasing economic unpredictability.

Debt management from the economic orthodoxy, as indicated by the IMF and the WB, is based on the analysis of the costs and risks of the loan portfolio, whose main goal is to ensure the ability to pay the public debt.

The analysis focuses on the needs of new financing, the profile of maturity of the debt balance, the interest rates, the exchange rates and the currencies of the new and taken debts, as well as the evolution of the non-financial variables that affect the generation of currency, such as commodity prices.

With this information, public institutions responsible for debt management, in general ministries of finances, are often in charge of defining and creating a 'debt profile' that considers current indebtedness and ideally future indebtedness projections, which in turn enables them to estimate the burden of debt payment and non-payment risks.

This analysis is not only made by the public sector. Private risk rating agencies, such as Moody's, Standard & Poor's and Fitch, also assess the quality of the sovereign debt and they become signallers for international financial markets.[1] Therefore, governments not only look for good ratings by those agencies, but also pay for getting those assessments. The goals of these ratings are to generate information that proves or guarantees the payment of principal and reveals potential related risks (Delgado, 2006: 304).

From this perspective, the goal of the institutional structure is to guarantee favourable conditions for capital. The experience of the recent debt crises shows that governments and financial agencies have also chosen to comply with loan agreements and to transfer the costs of the crisis to the population at the time of debt repayment. The ultimate goal of debt sustainability is to ensure the conditions that national and international financial flows require for the repayment of the principal and the payment of interest, and for that purpose countries need proper procedures of risk management.

Debt sustainability: frequently used (androcentric) indicators

According to the IMF, the public debt of a country is considered sustainable if the government can comply with all its current and future payment obligations without exceptional financial aid or default.

The methodology the IMF uses and that, in general, is used by countries and even other creditors, is classified into two types: Debt Sustainability Analysis (DSA) for low-income countries (LIC DSA) and Debt Sustainability Analysis for international market-access countries (MAC DSA). The use may vary considering that there are low- and middle-income countries that are assessed with the DSA for low-income countries.

In the first case, indebtedness thresholds or limits are used as solvency and liquidity indicators in accordance with the ability to manage debt (low, moderate and high); the more management ability a country has, the higher the margin of indebtedness limit (IMF, 2018). In the second case, thresholds are not applied because a framework of sovereign risk with several sustainability criteria is used, which adjust to the context and the size of economy of the countries.

Generally used public debt indicators give initial information about fiscal sustainability. They are usually ex-post indicators, in other words, they present facts. The indicators with sustainability thresholds are:

- Solvency:
  - current value of the external public debt as a GDP percentage;
  - current value of the external public debt as a percentage of the export of goods and services.

Other indicators are also used, such as the indicator of total public debt (internal and external) of the non-financial public sector (NFPS) as a GDP percentage. However, there is no general agreement on what level of debt is 'dangerous'. Critical values vary significantly in accordance with the type of economy and the methodology applied. A value considered acceptable for industrialized countries is considered too dangerous for developing countries. For instance, one of the criteria of the Maastricht Treaty for the adoption of a common currency in the European Union was to have a public debt under 60 per cent of the GDP.

- Liquidity:
  - total public debt service as a proportion of public revenue: repayment capacity;
  - external public debt service as a proportion of exports.

In general terms, the data of indicators from the current year or previous years are public information. However, for the purposes of analyzing debt sustainability, it is essential to count and clearly spread the projections of stock, service, GDP, public revenue and so on for a period of time of at least ten years. This way the government, as well as the members of parliament and other actors of a country, have the necessary information to assess the burden and cost of a certain loan in the social debt for future generations, with the risk of deepening existing gaps if the destination of those resources does not generate transformations towards the reduction of inequalities.

Debt sustainability: austerity versus tax justice

In accordance with the orthodox vision, the debt origin is public deficit, which is generated when revenue is lower than expenditure. Therefore, deficit reduction is the first goal in the agreements with international agencies, such as the IMF. For that purpose, the first response has been to limit the necessary resources for the implementation of public policies or implement regressive taxes that enable a faster tax collection, which in general is unfair and generates inequalities.

Besides this, when a country plans a project of great magnitude, such as an infrastructure project, in general, the country turns to indebtedness as a way of bringing to the present the fiscal revenue from the following years. Therefore, the financial conditions of this indebtedness are also a risk factor for medium and long-term sustainability.

Apart from the fact that the repayment capacity is a priority in this approach, the analysis of debt sustainability may have very optimistic projections and give a wrong impression about future sustainability, as well as the difficulty to include the evolution of different types of debt that countries have today in scenarios of risk, and other exogenous factors that may affect repayment capacity. In this respect, this tool is not appropriate for the financial strategies that a country needs to be able to guarantee rights and achieve development goals.

As to the destination of the resources obtained through indebtedness, the works carried out in the context of gender-responsive budgets evidence the low fiscal priority that policies whose goal is to ensure women's rights have had. In most Latin American countries, the resources allocated to prevent gender violence and implement care policies are scarce, and many times they are subject to budget cutbacks.

In consequence, austerity not only has the goal of addressing a debt crisis, but it also precedes it. Debt crisis is postponed at the expense of women, but at the same time there are other expenses that are continuously generated whose importance is above the ones needed to ensure women's rights (Serafini and Fois, 2021: 16–17).

Blanchard (1990) and Buiter (1985) defined two conditions for a public debt sustainability based on the intertemporal budget restriction of the government: i) the debt/GDP relation should converge in the long term to its initial level after a period in which it has significantly grown, and this requires the generation of a primary surplus after the growth period of the debt/GDP ratio; and ii) for a fiscal policy to be sustainable, the government with a pending debt should execute the primary budget surplus.

The widespread option has been to generate this surplus by reducing expenses, not by increasing revenue, despite the fact that the analytical framework includes this possibility. Box 15.1 shows the main indicators, including the 'tax gap' indicator.

Box 15.1: Indicators of debt sustainability

Primary gap (Blanchard, 1990): This indicator warns about the primary balance required to stabilize the debt/GDP ratio, given the projected paths of the actual interest rate and the GDP.

Thus, this indicator reflects the difference between the value of future primary balances required to stabilize the debt/GDP ratio and the initial primary balance.

$$Dt + 1 = (1 + rt) Dt - Bt$$

where Dt is the public debt in the t period, rt is the interest rate of the debt, and Bt is the primary fiscal balance (without including the payment of interest).

Debt mismatch (Calvo, Izquierdo and Talvi, 2003): owing to the high volatility of macroeconomic variables and capital flows in Latin America, a crucial element for debt sustainability is its composition (what currencies and in which proportion form such debt) based on the composition of the (tradable and non-tradable) national production. The external debt proportion over the internal debt is compared to the proportion of the production of tradable goods over the production of non-tradable goods in the economy. This is a perfect match (indicator=1) when tradable goods participate in the GDP in the same proportion in which the external debt participates in the total public debt. The other end is the perfect mismatch with the indicator 0.

Croce and Juan-Ramón (2003): the authorities determine the maximum level of debt/GDP and the primary surplus to achieve is calculated.

The tax political gap (Blanchard, 1990): proposes a sustainability indicator that considers the consistency or gap in the current tax policy while keeping the debt/GDP ratio constant. This is the indicator tax gap that measures the difference between the existing tax burden and the 'sustainable' tax burden.

This indicator shows the level of tax burden required to stabilize the debt/GDP ratio, with a level of expenditure, a path of GDP growth and an initial debt stock. If the ratio is negative, the indicator shows that the tax pressure of the economy is too low to stabilize the debt/GDP ratio.

The creation of fiscal space through the increase of tax resources is not often considered as a strategy of debt sustainability. On the contrary, one of the main pillars of the Washington Consensus implemented to face the debt crisis in the 1980s was tax reduction. The outcome was the so-called 'lost decade' in the 1980s and it even continued far beyond the 1990s for some countries.

As evidenced, the decisions about debt sustainability, apart from their technical-economic content, imply to prioritize debt repayment and a clear stance as to the sectors that benefit from debt – capital holders and beneficiaries of infrastructure works – and the general population that will suffer the effects of adjustments when funds have to be repaid.

The instrumental role of women in the analyses of debt sustainability

The analysis of debt sustainability ex-ante provides the magnitude of the necessary and permanent fiscal adjustment so that debt can become sustainable. There are three groups of variables. As explained in the previous paragraphs, the control of the primary deficit is the first and most important group, which involves measures from the expenditure side and from the revenue side.

Besides, the planned outcomes in the debt sustainability indicators can be ensured through GDP growth. However, growth is not neutral to women and gender inequalities as certain patterns of growth may be useful for debt sustainability, but they do not necessarily contribute to the economic autonomy of women. Economic growth is sustained, without including it in its measurement, in unpaid and care work that mainly women perform.

GDP performance in Latin America has not benefited men and women alike. A key outcome is the divergence between growth rates and the feminization of poverty. Latin America shows that as the GDP grew, so did the index of feminization of poverty in all the countries of the region, evidencing that benefits were not equally distributed.

Another indicator that shows the insufficiency of growth to improve opportunities and the economic autonomy of women is the persistence of the income gap between men and women, who receive about 20 per cent less than men.

This lower remuneration ends up being a subsidy for the activities and economic branches that benefit from women's work. This subsidy increases if the high burden of unpaid work is considered, estimated at 15 per cent of the GDP in the region, along with its role in the reduction of the costs of the food basket. Ultimately, GDP growth that contributes to improve the indicators of debt sustainability does not necessarily translate into something beneficial for women.

A variable that also affects debt sustainability in a positive way is the input of capital flows because it enables the interest rate and the exchange rate to be sustained, and it eases the problem of currency mismatch. Also, this flow is not gender neutral because family remittances, tourism and *maquila* intervene with a high proportion of women due to their participation in the global chains of care or their high labour participation in precarious jobs with wage discrimination.

Finally, it is also relevant to analyze debt financing processes along with the demographic structure and the life cycle of countries. Sustainability calculations are made to 20 years at most, while refinancing may obtain longer terms, which may have impacts on intergenerational and gender equity. In the future, whenever it would be necessary to increase taxes to repay the debt, women who could not save enough money in social security or who do not have assets (because they are outside the labour force) will need non-contributory policies to finance their lives when they get older, and in turn will be affected by the restrictions of the fiscal policy.

Fiscal rules and their blindness to women's rights and gender inequalities

The analysis of debt sustainability goes hand in hand with the existence of the fiscal rules that have been implemented since 1985 and a recent boost for the implementation of fiscal councils, promoted by the IMF. Arguments in favour of fiscal rules and fiscal councils include the need to avoid a deficit bias and to establish a depoliticized framework for the fiscal policy (Braun and Gadano, 2007), and to look for an alleged independence similar to the one expected from central banks with the monetary policy.

For the IMF,

> fiscal rules are long-lasting constraints on fiscal policy aimed at providing a credible commitment to fiscal discipline. They set numerical limits on a budgetary aggregate (e.g. level of public debt, deficit, growth of public expenditures). These constraints are useful to address deficit biases (that can lead to excessive debt levels) and procyclical policies (exacerbating economic cycles), ultimately helping promote more prudent and stabilizing fiscal policies. (IMF, 2022: 1)

There exist four types of fiscal rules used in the context of debt sustainability: budget balance rules (BBR), debt rules (DR), expenditure rules (ER) and revenue rules (RR) that are applied to the central or general government, or the public sector. The rules have information on their legal basis, coverage, escape clauses and stabilization features, as well as the application procedures, and they balance the existing key support characteristics, including independent control agencies and laws of fiscal accountability.

Although there are four types of rules, the most common ones have been a combination of a debt rule along with operating limits of expenditure or budget balance. Davoodi et al (2022: 7) state that in 2021 about 70 per cent of the countries with fiscal rules had a debt rule combined with another aggregate. One third had a debt rule together with a deficit limit and an expenditure ceiling, while another quarter had a debt rule combined with a budget balance rule. According to these authors, expenditure rules are more and more common and they are often set as a maximum limit to the annual growth of expenditure. Revenue rules are less used under the argument that governments have less control over annual revenue.

Fiscal rules also have gender biases:

- Some countries have as a rule a debt or deficit 'golden rule' only for physical investment, as human capital investment is considered in the national accounts as a current expense (Truger, 2016), which would also include care. De Henau and Himmelweit (2020), and Himmelweit and Perrons (2006) reject this assumption stating that investment in care has high levels of return, even higher than physical investment due to the effect on the expansion of labour opportunities for women.
- The return of the investment on human capital and care is not considered in GDP or the tax system, but international agencies (IMF and WB) do include the incorporation of women to increase GDP (without taking into account the excess of hours they already have) and reduce the debt burden.
- As no fiscal rules are incorporated on the side of revenue and as rules are stated on the side of expenditure or balance, the basic principles of human rights, such as progressiveness, non-discrimination or the use of the maximum available resources are not guaranteed and the 'austerity' goal is placed as a priority.
- The rules applied in Latin American countries – as well as in the rest of the world – are designed to limit social expenditure and promote austerity:
  - Expenditure rules: Peru, Paraguay, Grenada, Argentina, Costa Rica, Ecuador, Panama, the Bahamas, Honduras, El Salvador, Brazil, Mexico and Jamaica.
  - Debt rules: Argentina (subnational), the Bahamas, Brazil (subnational), Ecuador, El Salvador, Grenada, Jamaica, Peru, Panama and Uruguay.
  - Balance rules: Brazil, Ecuador, El Salvador, Grenada, the Bahamas, Honduras, Jamaica, Panama, Paraguay, Peru, Mexico, Chile and Colombia.
  - Revenue rules: El Salvador.
- Dondo and Oliva (2021) propose other types of rules, such as:
  - When the budgets for Health and Education do not reach at least 4 per cent of the GDP, or show annual increases lower than 0.25 per cent of the GDP, the government will automatically charge an extraordinary tax to large fortunes.
  - When certain sectors have extraordinary profits, an additional tax rate will be automatically applied to their income tax, which could have a specific allocation.
  - To limit tax expenses (resources that the State stops collecting when it grants any preferential tax treatment). For instance, the tax expense generated by the subsidies and benefits granted to large economic groups cannot exceed 1 per cent of the GDP.

4. Debt sustainability: life after capital

The debt process is part of a system that includes all the economic sectors (real, monetary, public and external) where women are invisibilized or considered as an instrument. Indebtedness is part of the fiscal policy;

therefore, it cannot be separated from the other components, such as expenditures or the tax system.

The analysis and the calculation of debt sustainability are not gender neutral and threaten life sustainability by prioritizing capital interest over the rights and needs of the population.

Debt sustainability is a political fact, more than a technical and economic calculation, as it implies to value and then decide over whom falls the burden of the financial and fiscal consequences. This decision focuses on women as the main responsible ones for the social reproduction of life and as generators of flows of material and symbolic resources that contribute to guarantee sustainability.

Budget restrictions that result from the need to reduce deficit or guarantee debt repayment prevent the financing of policies that ensure rights and satisfy women's needs. These same restrictions do not affect capital because they enable increasing debt to continue to keep the conditions its continuous accumulation requires, such as through investment in infrastructure (that often includes care infrastructure).

The priority given to the financial protection of the interest of financiers over the interest of the population of the borrower countries, including women, deepened a condition and position that was already subordinated prior to indebtedness or the debt crisis.

The consequences of ensuring debt sustainability from an androcentric perspective promote a greater pressure over the work of women, either paid or unpaid. The shrinkage of the State in public services generates indebtedness of households and overloads women with work, aimed at providing these services in a private or family way. Thus, debt sustainability is based on the self-exploitation of families and women that are part of them, deepening the social reproduction and care crisis.

Not including the debt impact on women's rights in the analyses of debt sustainability is not a universally valid technical criterion, but a political decision with deep legal implications: it is a way of creating the conditions to perpetuate the violations of the human rights of women.

Acknowledgements
The authors thank Rodolfo Bejarano, Daniela Berdeja and Carola Mejia for their feedback.

Note
[1] Risk rating agencies were the target of criticism and even lawsuits and fines after the 2009 financial crisis due to their role in favourable ratings that generated excessive indebtedness of families and companies, and that finally ended up in default, which caused the global financial crisis. The conflicts of interest generated were the main focus of criticism, because certifications are hired by the same parties to be rated. Besides, under an oligopoly, risk rating agencies may have simultaneous access to the information of the public and private

sector, in other words, information about creditors and debtors. With the informational advantage (information asymmetries), benefits and incentives are generated that may distort ratings (as in 2008–09). Criticism has already led to the proposal that these private risk rating agencies disappear and that public ones are created.

References

Blanchard, O. (1990) 'Suggestions for a New Set of Fiscal Indicators' (OECD Economics Department Working Papers No. 79), OECD [online] 1 April, Available from: https://www.oecd-ilibrary.org/docserver/435618162862. pdf?expires=1671474569&id=id&accname=guest&checksum=02C9B B8498F7929BD66C1DF1D42350FC

Bosch, A.; Carrasco, C. and Grau, E. (2005) 'Verde que te quiero violeta. Encuentros y desencuentros entre feminismo y ecologismo', [online], Available from: https://www.fuhem.es/media/cdv/file/biblioteca/Bolet in_ECOS/10/verde_que_te_quiero_violeta.pdf

Braun, M. and Gadano, N. (2007) '¿Para qué sirven las reglas fiscales? Un análisis crítico de la experiencia argentina', *Revista de la CEPAL*, 91(April): 53–65.

Buiter, W. (1985) 'A guide to public sector debt and deficits', *Economic Policy*, 1(1): 13–79

Caffentzis, G. (1999) 'On the notion of a crisis of social reproduction: A theoretical review', in M. Dalla Costa and G. Dalla Costa (eds), *Women, Development and Labor of Reproduction*, Eritrea: Africa World Press.

Calvo, G.; Izquierdo, A. and Talvi, E. (2003) 'Sudden stops, the real exchange rate and fiscal sustainability: Argentina's lessons', Inter American Development Bank.

Carrasco, C.; Borderías, C. and Torns, T. (2011) 'Introducción: El trabajo de cuidados: antecedentes históricos y debates actuales', Catarata, Available from: https://www.fuhem.es/media/cdv/file/biblioteca/Economia_crit ica/El-trabajo-de-cuidados_introduccion.pdf

Croce, E. and Juan-Ramón, H. (2003) 'Assessing fiscal sustainability: A Cross-Country Comparison', IMF Working Papers Working, 3(145), Available from: https://doi.org/10.5089/9781451856569.001

Davoodi H.R.; Elger, P;. Fotiou, A.; Garcia-Macia, D.; Han, X.; Lagerborg, A.; et al (2022) 'Fiscal rules and fiscal councils: Recent trends and performance during the pandemic' (Working Paper No 22/11), IMF.

De Henau, J. and Himmelweit, S. (2020) 'The gendered employment gains of investing in social vs. physical infrastructure: evidence from simulations across seven OECD countries' (IKD Working Paper No 84), The Open University [online] April, Available from: https://www.open.ac.uk/ikd/sites/ www.open.ac.uk.ikd/files/files/working-papers/DeHenauApril2020v3.pdf

Delgado, A. (2006) 'Calificadoras y costos asociados con la calificación riesgo-país', in E. Correa and A. Girón (2006) *Reforma Financiera en América Latina*, CLACSO [online], Available from: http://bibliotecavirtual.clacso. org.ar/ar/libros/edicion/correa/guzman.pdf

Dondo, M. and Oliva, N. (2021) '¿Qué son las reglas fiscales?', CELAG blog [online] 27 September, Available from: https://www.celag.org/nuevo-enfoque-en-el-diseno-de-reglas-fiscales/

Federici, S. (2010) *Calibán y la bruja. Mujeres, cuerpo y acumulación primitiva,* Madrid: Traficantes de sueños, Available from: https://traficantes.net/sites/default/files/pdfs/Caliban%20y%20la%20bruja-TdS.pdf

Harvey, D. (2005) 'El 'nuevo' imperialismo: acumulación por desposesión', CLACSO [online], Available from: http://biblioteca.clacso.edu.ar/clacso/se/20130702120830/harvey.pdf

Himmelweit, S. and Perrons, D. (2006) 'Gender and fiscal rules: how can we afford the rising cost of care?', [online], Available from: https://www.levyinstitute.org/pubs/CP/May2006_symposium_papers/paper_Himmelweit_Perrons.pdf

IMF (2018) 'The Debt Sustainability Framework for Low-Income Countries', [online] 13 July, Available from: https://www.imf.org/external/pubs/ft/dsa/lic.htm

IMF (FMI) (2022) 'Reglas fiscales, cláusulas de escape y shocks de gran magnitud', Fiscal Affairs, Available from: https://www.imf.org/-/media/Files/Publications/covid19-special-notes/Spanish/spspecial-series-on-covid19fiscal-rules-escape-clauses-and-large-shocks.ashx

Serafini, V. and Fois, M. (2021) 'Mujeres, deuda y desigualdades de Género', Latindadd [online], Available from: https://www.latindadd.org/wp-content/uploads/2021/08/Mujeres-deuda-y-desigualdad-Final-1.pdf

Truger, A. (2016) 'Reviving fiscal policy in Europe: towards an implementation of the golden rule of public investment', *European Journal of Economics and Economic Policies: Intervention*, 13(1): 57–71.

16

Measuring and Managing Gender Equality: The Case of Gender Budgeting in Austria

Ulrike Marx

1. Introduction

Numbers are powerful. They determine who holds power, they operate as diagnostic instruments within liberal democracies, they make modern modes of government both possible and judgeable, and they are crucial techniques for modern government and therefore are indispensable to the complex technologies through which government is exercised (Rose, 1999). However, numbers are not merely technical achievements: quantification carries a form of political rationality (Alonso and Starr, 1987; Rose, 1991; Hopwood, 1992; Porter, 1996; Rose, 1999; Desrosières and Naish, 2002; Porter, 2004).

Previous research has demonstrated a constitutive relationship between numbers and politics: the exercise of politics depends upon numbers, but the very act of social quantification is itself political in two ways. On the one hand, 'political judgements are implicit in the choice of what to measure, how to measure it, how often to measure it and how to present and interpret the results' (Alonso and Star, 1987: 3, cited in Rose, 1999), so that our political imaginary is shaped by statistical representation. On the other hand, numbers create the appearance of a neutral, depoliticized judgement because quantification appears to act as an automatic, technical and objective mechanism for prioritizing problems and allocating resources (Rose, 1991). This is nowhere clearer than in the rise of the New Public Management (NPM), where quantified performance indicators have come to dominate in the delivery and governance of public services (Mennicken and Espeland, 2019). This quantification and economization of political decision making and the allocation of resources, often through quasi-marketized mechanisms concerned with economic value, has resulted in a fundamental shift 'from "government by democracy" towards "governance by numbers"' (Mennicken and Salais, 2022: 1) that simultaneously embeds a political agenda and renders that agenda invisible by giving it the appearance of a politically neutral technology and objectivity.

In this sense, quantification is not bad but dangerous. It can be powerful as a way of 'counter accounting' (Gallhofer et al, 2006), for example, 'counter accounting is here constituted by information and reporting systems employed by groups such as campaigners and activists with a view to promoting their causes or countering or challenging the prevailing official and hegemonic position' (Gallhofer et al, 2006: 681). Thus, quantification and the development of, for example, indicators are always already political (1) in the priorities (what is counted and made visible); (2) in that when we create visibilities that draw attention to specific priorities we always create invisibilities to other aspects at the same time (we can never represent everything in its complexity); (3) as quantification is performative (Chiapello, 2008) so it does not just 'represent reality' but 'creates' reality. For example, Chiapello (2008) argues that 'accounting helps to make economics performative, being one of the instruments through which economics can make the world conform more closely to its descriptions' (Chiapello, 2008: 12). And finally, (4) research in accounting as practice often show limits of quantification to represent complex relations, for example, in practice people count what is relatively easy to count.

Therefore, work on debt sustainability and its implication on human rights will benefit from previous research in social studies of accounting beyond uncovering political bias.

This chapter discusses a related example, namely the emergence and implementation of gender budgeting during an NPM reform in Austria.[1] Gender budgeting is an internationally recognized strategy for implementing gender equality, especially in governmental and public organizations. The concept is based on the idea that gender relations influence the economic and social reality of women and men. These gender relations are understood as social constructions that are fundamentally changeable but assign different social and economic roles to men and women (Sharp, 2000). Thus, Sharp (2000) argues, women and men are affected differently by budget policies of the State. Gender budgeting initiatives, which have emerged worldwide since the 1990s, essentially pose the question of the distribution of financial resources and their impact on gender equality (Elson, 2002), thereby promising to make visible the political and gendered implications of seemingly neutral and technical matters of budget allocations. Gender budgeting initiatives develop and use a variety of different tools to assess the impact of public revenue and expenditure on gender relations, as well as strategies to ensure a gender-equitable distribution of resources (Sharp, 2003: 3). They thereby promise to make the political visible through a counter-quantification process that highlights the gendered nature of a seemingly neutral technology. In this light, it was an apparently radical move when gender budgeting became part of a budgetary law reform in Austria. As a result, all public institutions were required to implement gender budgeting and develop equality indicators to governmental policies and practices.

However, the implementation of gender budgeting is anything but a straightforward process. Gender budgeting can rather be understood as a hybrid of different discourses (such as discourses on human rights, gender equality, modernization of public service delivery or value for money) and technologies (Kurunmäki, 2004; Kurunmäki and Miller, 2006; Miller et al, 2008; Kurunmäki and Miller, 2011). In previous work (Marx, 2019) I have argued that the discourse of gender budgeting in Austria was characterized, on the one hand, by a radical feminist critique of the State and national budgets that made the political nature of budgeting more visible. On the other hand, it simultaneously depoliticized gender by operationalizing gender equality through technologies of performance such as key performance indicators (KPIs), audits and impact assessments that rendered 'gender' as a matter of calculation based on binary-sexed bodies, thereby closing off any space for a broader political discussion of gender. As such, the practice of gender budgeting can be understood as embodying the contradictory processes outlined earlier: simultaneously making political inequalities visible, while depoliticizing the actual construction of core political categories, and the ways in which those categories can enter into political debate, by delimiting the space of appearance of gender *as a political category* to numbers.

This chapter extends our understanding of gender equality initiatives by theorizing this ambivalent relationship between feminist politics and accounting. In feminist political discourse, calculative practices like cost/benefit calculation, performance evaluation and the quantification of difference are a matter of political concern. While quantification is understood to depoliticize feminism, translating political demands into matters for technocratic management (Budgeon, 2011), we should not lose sight of the fact that quantification is a powerful way to make feminist concerns visible and give them a form of political legitimacy (Bergmann, Gubitzer et al 2004, Klatzer, 2008). Over the past decades, gender equality has moved from the margins to the centre of political debate, partly because of the visibility given to it by quantification and techniques like gender pay gap analysis.

I will discuss the link between feminism and 'managing by numbers', drawing upon governmentality studies to theorize the emergence and implementation of gender budgeting in Austria between 2009 and 2012. The remainder of the chapter is structured as follows: first, I will briefly review how gender budgeting and gender mainstreaming are localized in a feminist discourse, then I will briefly introduce governmentality studies with a particular focus on numbers, quantification and accounting. Afterwards, drawing on governmentality studies as a conceptual framework, I will discuss the ambivalent character of numbers in the emergence and implementation of gender budgeting and show how gender budgeting was linked to an NPM reform where a reliance on SMART indicators (specific, measurable, achievable, relevant and time-bound) became a suggested solution to questions of gender equality. In this case, I take up the feminist critique of gender budgeting as a neoliberalization of feminist agendas into a top-down technocratic management concept, and thus a de-democratization and domestication of feminism (Squires, 2005; 2007; McRobbie, 2009; Budgeon, 2011).

2. Organizing feminism and the emergence of gender budgeting

Feminism is organized in diverse forms. In her analysis of third wave feminism, Budgeon (2011) points out that feminism is characterized by diversity, fragmentation and internal contestation, which produces a series of historically unique contradictions. One the one hand, third wave feminism is characterized by a movement of feminist values and practices into mainstream social institutions and popular consciousness, leading to a broad acceptance of gender equality and empowerment in practice as well as in theory. Walby (2011) points out that contemporary feminism has gone beyond protest and is now embedded in different organizational forms including projects in civil society, where they shape political discourse and social goals, and in governmental programmes, where they are institutionalized as sets of policies in governmental departments and ministries. She argues that feminism is no longer only a protest movement but is now organized within, as well as outside, the State and is therefore increasingly embedded in institutions. Such institutionalized forms of feminism are often not recognized as feminist, because the dominant understanding of feminism is narrowly limited to protest and popular culture. 'Feminism can be less visible but no less significant when it forms coalitions with other social forces and joint projects, which are not explicitly labelled feminist' (Walby, 2011: 24). One domain where the institutionalization of feminism is proceeding is the economy. In contrast to the situation of the 1970s, when feminist strategies often involved separate women's committees to give women an independent voice, feminist strategies today have shifted from women's issues to an analysis of gender power relations. In 1995, governments across the world signed the Beijing Platform for Action. Along with their endorsement of the Plan of Action went a commitment to achieve gender equality and the empowerment of women. Gender mainstreaming was identified as the most important mechanism to reach this ambitious goal. It is defined as:

> Mainstreaming a gender perspective is the process of assessing the implications for women and men of any planned action, including legislation, policies or programmes, in all areas and at all levels. It is a strategy for making women's as well as men's concerns and experiences an integral dimension of the design, implementation, monitoring and evaluation of policies and programmes in all political, economic and societal spheres so that women and men benefit equally and inequality is not perpetuated. The ultimate goal is to achieve gender equality. (Moser and Moser, 2005: 12)

Despite concerns that institutionalization may lead to feminists 'abandoning their original radical ideas and demands' (Walby, 2011: pos. 501), feminism has become increasingly influential through stronger coordination via coalitions and networks. With the mainstreaming of feminist aims, gender equality has become widely accepted as a social good and has been institutionalized through quotas, State strategies and equality acts, and has become a symbol of modernity (Budgeon, 2011). Radical feminists are concerned that gender equality is increasingly framed as central to the realization of both modernization and economic efficiency and its achievement is presented as a key to good governance (Squires, 2007).

Before gender budgeting entered the Austrian political discourse it emerged in broader debates in global economic governance discourses. For example, Çağlar (2009) shows how 'gender' was framed in relation to 'the economy' through two different story lines in discourses on global economic governance. The first story line asked how economic measures impact women specifically, and often disadvantageously when compared with the impacts on men. The second story line explored how asymmetrical gender relations negatively impact economic growth and therefore women's integrations into the labour market become a major economic and political objective. This focus on the economic impact of gender inequality has two effects, according to Çağlar (2009). First, it creates a desire to measure impact to create 'correct facts' and more accurate economic measures. Second, gender relations become an object for political intervention, to address the problems that these 'more accurate' measures render visible. On the one hand, reproductive labour becomes economically relevant and the care economy is recognized; on the other hand, women are discovered as economic subjects who should be relieved from their care responsibilities. In both cases the result is a marketization of care, and the incorporation of social reproduction ever more into the formal (or often informal) economy, albeit with significant inequalities structured through class and race (Ehrenreich and

Hochschild, 2002). Thus, different combinations of economic and gender knowledge lead to different rationalizations and different forms of gender responsive global economic governance. In other words, gender equality approaches such as gender mainstreaming and gender budgeting have made equality become part of governance structures which are organized through the normalization and institutionalization of a neoliberal economic agenda.

In Austria, the concept of gender budgeting was first taken up by a group of economists and social scientists (BEIGEWUM, 2002). They fundamentally criticized State budget policy and budgeting practices, arguing that: (a) budgets are instruments of domination that obscure patriarchal power structures; (b) this obfuscation is facilitated by the apparent technical neutrality of budgets; and (c) budgeting is a technology of exclusion that systematically excludes lay people, that is, citizens, from the budgeting process (BEIGEWUM, 2002). At the beginning of the 2000s, therefore, the social and economic effects of the State budget on the reproduction of gender relations were the focus of attention in the context of gender budgeting. A discourse analysis (Marx, 2019) has shown that gender budgeting was understood as an emancipatory strategy concerned with distributive justice, transparency, accountability and participation. Accordingly, specific technologies for the implementation of gender budgeting ideals were proposed, which aimed at the critical data-supported economic analysis of the effects of politics on gender relations, and on strategies to activate women (and men) and enable them to participate in budgeting processes, thereby opening up the scope for political action (BEIGEWUM, 2002). However, these critical feminist concepts of gender budgeting were not implemented in this form in Austria. They failed in an almost paradoxical way because of the success of feminist politics.

In 2009, equality between women and men gained constitutional status as a central objective of the Austrian State budget (Article 13, paragraph 3 B-VG). It is therefore binding for all local authorities and the Confederation. The budgetary law reform came into force in 2013 (Article 51, paragraph 8 BV-G) and makes 'equality' an integral part of the principle of 'impact orientation in financial management'. All public institutions in Austria are thus obliged to develop and apply instruments that enable an analysis and management of gender-related effects in budgeting. Thus, gender budgeting in Austria seems to be an extremely ambivalent phenomenon. On the one hand, it is enshrined in the Austrian federal constitution, on the other hand, its practice seems far removed from the radical feminist ideas that inspired it. Critics of gender mainstreaming raise concerns that this approach is a top-down technocratic advocacy (McRobbie, 2009) that translates gender equality into technocratic processes, reducing 'feminism' to a series of procedures, such as impact assessments, that eschew both political participation and normative contestation in their reliance upon professional expertise and evidence-based indicators. This does little to challenge the dominant, neo-liberal institutional logic (Squires, 2007). In this sense, gender budgeting provides an ideal case to explore processes which explicitly connect gender equality with economic governance. The example of gender budgeting in Austria thus seems to support the rather critical diagnoses of the success of third wave feminism, as formulated by Squires (2007), McRobbie (2009) and Gill and Scharf (2011).

In the following section, I will introduce an analytical framework to help us understand how gender budgeting is transformed into something it was not.

3. Governmentality and social studies of accounting

The management of social issues increasingly draws upon accounting and auditing technologies such as cost-benefit analysis, impact audits, performance indicators and rankings (Deegan, 2017). In her analysis of the measurement and management of human rights, gender violence and sex trafficking, Merry (2016) points out that 'quantification is seductive'. The use of numbers to describe social phenomena in countable and commensurable terms promises concrete information that allows easy comparison, facilitation of decision-making in the absence of more detailed and contextualized knowledge and conveys 'an aura of objective truth and scientific authority despite the extensive interpretative work' that goes into the construction of numbers (p 126). Merry (2016) argues that indicators are appealing 'because they claim to stand above politics, offering rational, technical knowledge that is disinterested and the product of expertise. ... They address a desire for unambiguous knowledge, free from political bias' (175–82). The impact of quantification and accounting in forms of governance needs to be understood more comprehensively, and particularly the role of quantification in governing equality in the operationalization of feminist politics.

In research on accounting in its social and institutional context, accounting and calculative practices are intrinsic to and constitutive of social relations.

> From such a perspective accounting can no longer be regarded as a neutral device that merely documents and reports 'facts' of economic activity. Accounting can now be seen as a set of practices that affects the type of world we live in, the type of social reality we inhabit ... the way in which we administer the lives of others and ourselves. (Miller, 1994: 1)

This understanding of accounting is inspired, at least in part, by Foucauldian studies of governmentality. For Foucault 'government' does not refer to *the* State or *the* government of a state but rather to those activities that aim to shape the conduct of others (and/or the self) in a certain direction. Strategy plays a crucial role in 'the art of government', however, paradoxically, governmentality rejects any top-down, centralized notion of power and strategy. Governmentality has four principles:

First governmentality involves the development and deployment of specific strategies and forms of knowledge [e.g. about the economy and about the reproduction of gender] to tackle particular problems [e.g. gender equality and economic growth]. Governmentality is practical: how to think about and improve, if not solve, a given social problem. Second, governmentalist strategies are predicated upon increasing individual freedom while reducing the role of, say, the state or management. Third, governmentalist strategies are legitimized to the extent that they are rendered neutral, rather than furthering a particular vested interest. Fourth, governmentalist strategies develop credible ways to define, monitor, and assess a population so that specific types of individuals can be targeted for intervention. The efficiency and effectiveness of representation and intervention has to be open to evaluation and contestation (Foucault 1980). (McKinlay and Pezet, 2017: 3–4)

Thus, an analysis of government, as 'conduct of conduct', starts from practices not institutions. These calculated and rationalized activities are understood to be undertaken by a multiplicity of agencies employing a variety of techniques and forms of knowledge to shape conduct by working through desires, aspirations and beliefs for definite but shifting ends, with a diverse set of relatively unpredictable effects (Dean, 2009). Practices that contest and call into question the 'art of government' are referred to as 'problematizations': sets of questions from which actions on individuals and the social can be understood, legitimized and contested. According to McKinlay and Pezet (2017), action is structured across three dimensions:

the representation of the individual or of the social, the knowledge that underpins this representation and the expert debates that legitimize this knowledge. Only through knowledge can the social be described. To problematize is to give knowledge the status of truth. And only through this truth can practices be directed at the individual or the population be legitimised. (McKinlay and Pezet, 2017: 11)

To put this differently, the emergence of different accounting phenomena, such as gender budgeting (Marx, 2019), can be understood as the outcome of historical contingent processes. New accounting constellations (Miller, 1991) appear because different groups of people, vocabularies and technologies are temporarily linked together in a particular moment of time, rather than resulting from linear, rational improvements or functional adaptation in a changing environment. From this perspective, accounting techniques are understood as technologies of government that make it possible to translate political ideals of government into practice. Miller and Rose (1990) distinguish three aspects of the governmentality:

- Political rationalities are 'ways of thought' within which conceivable problems and conceivable solutions to problems as well as those responsible for them can be defined. In the context of NPM and gender budgeting, for example, equality is conceptualized as a technical optimization and efficiency problem that can be dealt with within the framework of impact-oriented budgeting.
- Government technologies refer to, for example, actual control instruments. The translation of impact targets into quantitatively measurable indicators is a concrete example of such a technology. These technologies are in a reciprocal constitutional relationship with political rationality; their existence enables and materializes political rationality, which in turn legitimizes and motivates the technologies.
- Expertise includes specialized knowledge associated with the technologies and rationality of government, and the social authority attributed to those who possess the expertise. They are considered 'authorized problem solvers'. It is now the management accountant and specialists for impact orientation in the federal ministries who are responsible for the feminist agenda of gender equality. This, too, recursively reinforces the construction of equality as a technical problem.

With the help of the analytical instruments of social studies of accounting and governmentality analysis, I will now offer a discussion of gender budgeting in the course of a NPM reform with some concluding remarks.

4. Discussion and conclusion

In the perspective of governance analysis, gender budgeting is understood as a set of instruments through which the stated goal of equality between women and men is to be articulated and operationalized. However, this is anything but self-evident, since it cannot be assumed that the entity to be controlled (to be 'governed') – the gender relations – would be given without problems. Rather, gender relations as an object of government had to be historically 'problematized' and thus made visible through feminist discourse and studies of gender. At the same time, this problematization includes a critique of State budget policy and the underlying economic models, which systematically cannot 'see' these gender relations (Çağatay, Elson and Grow, 1995).

It is precisely this critical problematization that underlies the analyses and concepts of the BEIGEWUM Group (2002), which makes the concept of gender budgeting known in Austria. The authors criticize the ideological and dominating character of State budget policy as well as the exclusion of citizens from a gender-theoretical perspective. Gender budgeting as a political programme aims at a transformation of national budgets as technologies of power. Programmatic ideals and aspirations aim at: (a) increasing the transparency of political priorities in income and expenditure (BEIGEWUM, 2002: 86, 112, 180); (b) representing the budget's impact on women, children and men, especially the impact on unpaid work and the care economy (10, 16, 17, 189); (c) transforming the bureaucratic, hierarchical and male-dominated budgeting process towards transparency and participation (18, 19); (d) ensuring the application of gender expertise in the budgeting process (18, 19), and (e) monitoring the government's accountability and commitment to gender equality. This problematization is rationalized as an emancipatory and participatory political strategy. It is about the transformation of gender relations through the analysis of current conditions and the gender equality effects of the State budget as well as empowerment and participation in budget design. Accordingly, fundamental economic analyses are required at the level of technologies, and technologies of agency, such as the establishment of interministerial working groups with civil society participation and gender experts (BEIGEWUM, 2002).

This problematization could not prevail in Austria because it was not compatible with the prevailing political discourses. However, it was later possible to connect feminism, gender mainstreaming and gender budgeting to the NPM discourse in Austria. This resulted in a more functionalist discourse on gender equality, in which the economic and budgeting instruments of the NPM are regarded as suitable technologies for changing gender relations. Equality thus becomes a technical optimization and efficiency problem in the context of results-oriented budgeting, and the original more radical feminist critique of gender responsive budgeting is translated into the framework of NPM managerialism.

Despite being very brief in my explanations, I suggest that a governmentality analysis allows us to systematically and critically analyze the concrete form of gender budgeting in Austria and to better understand how a technocratic shortening of the originally comprehensive ideas came about. The result of this development is ambivalent. On the one hand, it is an undoubted success of feminist politics that gender mainstreaming and gender budgeting are an obligatory part of State action in a generally politically very conservative state like Austria. On the other hand, the governmentality analysis also shows that the logic of quantification associated with impact-oriented budgeting has significantly changed the gender equality policy agenda and practice and deprived it of its fundamentally critical impetus.

The reduction of feminist politics to gender mainstreaming and gender budgeting within the framework of the NPM thus entails, firstly, the danger that essential emancipatory goals and agendas will be marginalized because they are not accessible to the instruments of impact-oriented governance. Secondly, gender equality policy goals are mobilized through a neoliberal efficiency-oriented control logic, which can ultimately only conceptualize equality as an instrument of economic efficiency. Therefore, feminist research and practice today must critically examine the calculative practices of NPM. I argued elsewhere (Marx, 2019) that gender budgeting in the context of Austrian budgetary law reform appears as a case where feminist ideals are co-opted by a neoliberal policy reform. When national budgets became a feminist concern in Austria, budgets were framed as technologies of domination and exclusion that needed to be transformed to become more inclusive, democratic and emancipatory. One prominent issue of problematization was a critique of the apparent neutrality and objectivity of numbers. It is thus surprising that with the operationalization of gender, statistics and performance indicators became the preferred technologies to manage gender equality. Gender equality and how it is framed in Austrian budgetary law reform can be understood as neoliberal governmentality because it is presented as a strategy of need formation (Yeatman, 1994), where women are framed as clients or customers of the State. A fair distribution of resources appears to be informed by 'user needs' and evidenced through the quantification of those needs by means of accounting and audit technologies such as gender impact assessment. Calculative practices enabled a neoliberal government of gender equality because gender equality performance is based on ideas of efficiency, optimization and competition. Gender equality is framed as modern and incentive systems are put in place to integrate women into employment. Gender equality issues are increasingly tackled with calculative, managerial technologies that are transplanted from the private sector, such as SMART indicators (specific, measurable, achievable, relevant and time-bound), benchmarks and audits.

Note

[1]   This chapter is based on earlier work published in GWO: Marx, Ulrike (2019) 'Accounting for equality: Gender budgeting and moderate feminism', *Gender, Work and Organization*, Available from: https://doi.org/10.1111/gwao.12307

References

Alonso, W. and Starr, P. (1987) *The Politics of Numbers*, New York, NY: Russell Sage Foundation.

BEIGEWUM (2002) *Frauen macht Budgets: Staatsfinanzen aus Geschlechterperspektive*, Vienna, Austria: Mandelbaum.

Bergmann, N.; Gubitzer, L.; Klatzer, E.; Klawatsch-Treitl, E. and Neumayr, M. (2004) *Gender Budgeting. Handbuch zur Umsetzung geschlechtergerechter Budgetgestaltung*, Vienna, Austria: Attac Österreich.

Budgeon, S. (2011) *Third Wave Feminism and the Politics of Gender in Late Modernity*, Basingstoke: Palgrave Macmillan.

Çağatay, N.; Elson, D. and Grow, C. (1995) 'Introduction', *World Development*, 23(11): 1827–36.

Çağlar, G. (2009) *Engendering der Makroökonomie und Handelspolitik: Potenziale transnationaler Wissensnetzwerke*, Wiesbaden: VS Verlag für Sozialwissenschaften.

Chiapello, Eve (2008) 'Accounting at the heart of the performativity of economics', *economic sociology_the European electronic newsletter*, Cologne: Max Planck Institute for the Study of Societies (MPIfG), 10(1): 12–15.

Dean, M. (2009) *Governmentality: Power and Rule in Modern Society*, London, UK: Sage.

Deegan, C. (2017) 'Twenty five years of social and environmental accounting research within Critical Perspectives of Accounting: Hits, misses and ways forward', *Critical Perspectives on Accounting*, 43: 65–87.

Desrosières, A. and Naish, C. (2002) *The Politics of Large Numbers: A History of Statistical Reasoning*, Cambridge, MA: Harvard University Press.

Ehrenreich, B. and Hochschild, A. (2002) *Global Woman: Nannies, Maids and Sex Workers in the Global Economy*, London: Granta.

Elson, D. (2002) 'Gender responsive budget initiatives: Key dimensions and practical examples', *Gender Budget Initiatives*, 16: 15–29.

Gallhofer, S.; Haslam, J.; Monk, E. and Roberts, C. (2006) 'The emancipatory potential of online reporting: the case of counter accounting', *Accounting, Auditing & Accountability Journal*, 19(5): 681–718.

Gill, R. and Scharff, C. (2011) 'Introduction' in R. Gill and C. Scharff (eds), *New Femininities: Postfeminism, Neoliberalism and Subjectivity*, Houndsmills: Palgrave Macmillan, pp 1–17.

Hopwood, A.G. (1992) 'Accounting calculation and the shifting sphere of the economic', *European Accounting Review*, 1(1): 125–43.

Klatzer, E. (2008) 'The integration of gender budgeting in performance-based budgeting', presented at the conference Gender Public Budgeting Responsible To Gender Equality (Presupuestación Pública Responsable con la Igualdad de Género), 9–10 June, Bilbao.

Kurunmäki, L. (2004) 'A hybrid profession – The acquisition of management accounting expertise by medical professionals', *Accounting, Organizations and Society*, 29(3–4): 327–47.

Kurunmäki, L. and Miller, P. (2006) 'Modernising government: The calculating self, hybridisation and performance measurement', *Financial Accountability & Management*, 22(1): 87–106.

Kurunmäki, L. and Miller, P. (2011) 'Regulatory hybrids: Partnerships, budgeting and modernising government', *Management Accounting Research*, 22(4): 220–41.

Marx, U. (2019) 'Accounting for equality: Gender budgeting and moderate feminism', *Gender, Work & Organization*, 26(8): 1176–90.

McKinlay, A. and Pezet, E. (2017) *Foucault and Managerial Governmentality: Rethinking the Management of Populations, Organizations and Individuals*, New York, NY: Taylor & Francis.

McRobbie, A. (2009) *The Aftermath of Feminism: Gender, Culture and Social Change*, London: Sage.

Mennicken, A. and Espeland, W.N. (2019) 'What's new with numbers? Sociological approaches to the study of quantification', *Annual Review of Sociology*, 45: 223–45.

Mennicken, A. and Salais, R. (2022) *The New Politics of Numbers: Utopia, Evidence and Democracy*, Cham: Springer Nature.

Merry, S.E. (2016) *The Seductions of Quantification: Measuring Human Rights, Gender Violence, and Sex Trafficking*, Chicago, IL: University of Chicago Press.

Miller, P. (1991) 'Accounting innovation beyond the enterprise: Problematizing investment decisions and programming economic growth in the U.K. in the 1960s', *Accounting, Organizations and Society*, 16(8): 733–62.

Miller, P. (1994) 'Accounting as social and institutional practice: An introduction', in A. Hopwood and P. Miller, *Accounting as Social and Institutional Practice*, Cambridge: Cambridge University Press, pp 1–39.

Miller, P. and Rose, N. (1990) 'Governing economic life', *Economy and Society*, 19(1): 1–31.

Miller, P.; Kurunmäki, L. and O'Leary, T. (2008) 'Accounting, hybrids and the management of risk', *Accounting, Organizations and Society*, 33(7–8): 942–67.

Moser, C. and Moser, A. (2005) 'Gender mainstreaming since Beijing: a review of success and limitations in international institutions', *Gender & Development*, 13(2): 11–22.

Porter, T.M. (1996) *Trust in Numbers: The Pursuit of Objectivity in Science and Public Life*, Princeton, NJ: Princeton University Press.

Porter, T.M. (2004) 'The culture of quantification and the history of public reason', *Journal of the History of Economic Thought*, 26(2): 165–77.

Rose, N. (1991) 'Governing by numbers: Figuring out democracy. Accounting', *Organizations and Society*, 16(7): 673–92.

Rose, N.S. (1999) *Powers of Freedom: Reframing Political Thought*, Cambridge: Cambridge University Press.

Sharp, R. (2000) 'The economics and politics of auditing government budgets for their gender impacts', Hawke Institute, University of South Australia.

Sharp, R. (2003) *Budgeting for Equity: Gender Budget Initiatives within a Framework of Performance Oriented Budgeting*, New York: United Nations.

Squires, J. (2005) 'Is mainstreaming transformative? Theorizing mainstreaming in the context of diversity and deliberation', *Social Politics: International Studies in Gender, State & Society*, 12(3): 366–88.

Squires, J. (2007) *The New Politics of Gender Equality*, Houndsmills: Palgrave Macmillan.

Walby, S. (2011) *The Future of Feminism*, Cambridge: Polity.

Yeatman, A. (1994) *Postmodern Revisionings of the Political*, New York, NY: Psychology Press.

17

Rights, Gender and Progress Indicators: The Debts of Democracy

Flavia Marco Navarro and Laura Pautassi

1. Introduction

The lack of a gender-based approach on core issues, such as public and private indebtedness, and its consequences for people, appears over and over again as the effects of such lack become evident in our lives. This chapter analyzes the intrinsic and instrumental value of a gender-based approach in the field of financial obligations of States (public debt) and of women and sexual diversities (private debt), as well as in relation to the standards and principles connected to the protection of persons and their relation with the development and implementation of progress indicators.

These indicators are a solid tool from a number of aspects (design and assessment of policies of the three branches of the State, international supervision and monitoring, citizen empowerment and the disclosure of public information among several State agencies), and, at the same time, as long as they are incorporated into the set of State actions, they will enable greater institutionality and guaranties for exercising the rights of women and sexual diversities.

Particularly, in relation to the impact of public and private indebtedness, in section 2 of this chapter we focus on some elements that have characterized the economic processes in Latin America that, far from being neutral, have clearly had gender biases. In section 3, progress indicators are presented that are used in current international monitoring mechanisms in the region and their potential to measure State obligations linked to debt with a gender-based approach is considered. In section 4, the economic autonomy of women is addressed as a category of explicative and aspirational content, which at the end creates a fiction, where both deficits in the exercise of rights and the different impacts of public policies are evidenced, including those related to debt and the access to loans by citizens. In section 5, final conclusions are presented that highlight the need to promote the recognition of a life free of indebtedness that enables women and sexual diversities to have economic autonomy in all its dimensions.

2. Incorporating approaches in indebtedness

Among the many contributions that feminism has made, the concept of 'approach' can be found, which relates to the claim of power asymmetry that structures societies and considers sexual differences and identities as pillars of hierarchization, and caused the incorporation and implementation of the powerful formula of *gender mainstreaming*. The concept summarizes one of the main strategies in the field of public institutionality, which is the idea of transversality. That is to say, the only way to transform structural inequalities requires going through all the areas of society that produce and reproduce them. This methodology challenged State theories, the economy, politics and subjectivities with a very important development at a global, interdisciplinary and regional level that enabled the visualization of the asymmetric relations between genders and to determine when a different treatment is legitimate and when it is discriminatory.

Precisely the gender-based approach produced a paradigm change as it developed a set of ideas, methodologies and techniques that questioned and analyzed the ways through which social groups have created and allocated responsibilities, activities and conducts to women, men and sexual diversities. This is not only a concept, but also an intervention strategy. It is worth remembering that, as early as in the 1990s, the feminist movement raised at a global level, but particularly in Latin America, that the effects of the macroeconomic policies implemented in the context of the structural adjustment in peripheral countries (today the Global South) have not been neutral in terms of gender. The emphasis was on the fact that the macroeconomic policies applied in the region in the last decades of the 20th century did not clearly recognize the implications of gender relations; even further, women were considered as an economic resource (Birgin, 1992).

First, in the diagnoses before the application of neoliberal policies, the existing relation between productive sectors, linked to the traditional economy, and residual or unproductive sectors, where essential services were included, particularly all care activities, whether paid or unpaid ones, was shown. Second, short-term austerity measures were implemented that aimed at maintaining added demand under control to lower inflation and reduce fiscal deficits. Also, long-term policies were implemented in order to liberalize trade, deregulate and privatize, considering the effects of macroeconomic policies in the lives of women as they received the impact of the adjustment by working harder inside and outside households (Birgin and Pautassi, 2001). The inequality pattern is transformed into a structural pattern, and its approach, far from being a goal of public policies, was systematically invisibilized in the governmental agendas of Latin America.

It is worth mentioning that the pioneering contribution of feminism, along with the activism of women's movements, achieved its incorporation in the Platform of Action of the World Conference on Women in Beijing (1995) and, at a regional level, in the Conference on Women in Latin America and the Caribbean.[1] In each one of the countries of the region, transversality has been a direct mandate for the mechanisms for the advancement of women (from ministries or undersecretariats) that generally plan their actions considering national plans for equal opportunities and treatment. However, transversality did not reach the 'hard' areas of State decisions, such as the economy, budget, treasury or institutional affairs, and in general there have been few times when women heads of ministries have been regularly integrated into presidential cabinets, much less been included in the debate on public indebtedness in these institutional areas.[2]

At the beginning of this century and in this context, the Millennium Declaration (2000) included the human rights approach as a core strategy, which consisted of highlighting the bonding nature of the State obligations contained in international covenants and treaties of human rights and how these rules must go through the action of the State in all its areas, jurisdictions, rules and actions (Pautassi, 2021). Without explicitly recognizing that this is a feminist strategy, the implementation of the human rights approach involved a significant scene change, especially for social policies at a regional level, and it provided an important action framework for many of the political leaders at the beginning of this century in Latin America (Abramovich and Pautassi, 2009). The principles of universality, equality, interdependence and indivisibility of human rights, as unavoidable guiding principles on human rights, are included as action standards for States, accordingly. Both approaches (gender and human rights) thus include transversality as their pillar of action and empowerment of persons as objective. In the case of Latin America, sectors of the feminist movement claim emancipation as a collective process (Lamas, 2020).

The actual implementation of this approach does not end in a political declaration, but it creates a methodology for the implementation of public policies with territorial implications and in all the levels of public institutionality. In particular, although a gradual achievement of rights content is included in international covenants and treaties, especially considering the restrictions resulting from the limitation of the available resources, its fulfilment is unavoidable. Furthermore, the human rights approach imposes numerous obligations with an immediate effect that are related to the connected standard of using the maximum of available resources,[3] the standard of progress and the standard of non-regressiveness. In fact, when States ratify international instruments on human rights, States commit to make periodic reports before treaty bodies on the progressive measures to ensure the compliance of committed obligations.

It should be asked if among those mandates gender equity is included as a core element for accountability or if it is included through a narrative path. In other words, how much has been introduced in specific indicators that reflects if and how debt affects women and dissidences in a disproportionate way, and thus if measure scales have been established to determine the connection between public indebtedness and the achievement of equality and non-discrimination standards, especially with respect to the economic autonomy of women. As it will be explained in the following sections, the gender-based approach is not part of the approaches on debt yet.

3. Progress indicators: obligation on data

The accountability process is remarkably useful from a rights-based approach as it enables and requires the State to make diagnoses of the situation, identify implementation deficits, establish pending agendas and produce updated information that enables society to control State actions. This is how monitoring systems were introduced at the level of the system of United Nations (UN) High Commissioner for Human Rights (HCHR, 2012) and the Organization of American States (OAS) based on progress indicators for monitoring the Protocol of San Salvador by the Working Group for the analysis of national reports contained in the Protocol of San Salvador (WGPSS, 2015) and the Belém do Pará Convention (MESECVI, 2015). Progress indicators have the particularity that when measuring the obligations contained in human rights they include quantitative (structural, process and result) indicators, as well as qualitative indicators or qualitative progress signs.

In fact, the importance of introducing quantitative data and information, but mainly qualitative ones, is justified by the fact that these approaches assume that persons and their rights must be at the centre of the policies that the State creates, and, therefore, it would be a contradiction to assess or monitor policies with this approach without listening to the very beneficiaries of rights (Abramovich, 2021). Likewise, it has been warned that while the feminist and human rights perspectives are not included in the production of indicators for decision making and economic policies, it would be impossible to make progress on structural inequalities (Bohoslavsky, 2018).

The particularity of these type of indicators is that, unlike socioeconomic data that accounts for the development level achieved, progress indicators measure if the fulfilment of what was committed to for each right has effectively been achieved. In contrast to development policies or the 2030 Agenda and the 17 Sustainable Development Goals (SDG), indicators take the obligation included in each treaty as the unit of measurement, and based on this they determine the most suitable tools for its verification. Therefore, an important number of progress indicators have been defined that seek to assess State conduct regarding the compliance of obligations, which integrates and specifies the sustainable development agenda. This accountability and monitoring process by States is generating a large corpus of information and interpretation of the scope of rights. As an example, in the context of the indicators created by the WGPSS and approved by the OAS General Assembly in 2015, using three cycles of periodic reports,[4] States have been

Table 17.1: Type of indicators

Conceptual category	Type of indicator		
	Structural	**Process**	**Result**
Right reception	Incorporation of the obligation in the legislation	Human rights perspective in public policies	Guarantee situation in the main components of the law
Financial and budget commitment	Legal provisions that set forth resources to be allocated	Process relevance and efficiency to implement public policies	Availability (level and format) of invested resources
State abilities	Institutional structure of the State and legal system	Acceptability, adaptability and quality of efforts of budget programmes	Results on which the State has direct influence
Equality and non-discrimination	Institutionality to ensure equality, identification	Incorporation of the equality principle in actions, programmes and/or policies	Gaps in the guarantee of rights by groups or regions
Access to justice	Judicial and administrative resources for enforcement	Resource efficiency and procedural guaranties	Efficiency of judicial resources
Access to information and participation	Basic conditions for the access to information on the institution for the design, follow-up and assessment of public policies for citizens	Characteristics of public policies for access and guarantee of transparency and participation	Advance on information availability for the law, citizen empowerment and effective participation

Source: Own elaboration based on Pérez Gómez, Pérez Molina, Loreti, Pautassi and Riesco, 2022 (*based on WGPSS (2015)*)

developing systems of public information based on indicators and using the following categories.

As shown, due to the existence of budget commitments as transversal categories and financial resources that each State allocates, along with State abilities which refer to the specific ways in which the inside power of a State is organized, together with the principle of equality and non-discrimination, among others, the bases to measure the scope of compliance of State obligations using indicators are established. Although in the case of the monitoring of the Protocol of San Salvador no indicators have been defined in relation to public and private debt, the matrix in progress enables the WGPSS to include them using the aforementioned categories.

It is worth mentioning that the first two cycles of reports assessed determined the bases for measuring rights, and during the third cycle the WGPSS starts to measure progressiveness as to the fulfilment of economic, social and cultural rights (ESCR). When assessing States that have submitted reports, WGPSS experts state that '... progressiveness cannot be assessed exclusively in terms of allocations of resources, let alone only in terms of budgets. Moreover, progressiveness goes beyond mere marginal advances in quantitative indicators as the execution of clear actions to improve the living standards of persons is needed ...' (WGPSS, 2020). They add that the assessment is based on

> a multidimensional valuation that considers the evolution of the situation about the compliance with ESCR in a longitudinal way, assessing the changes of the different variables that form the core of the rights and considering a dynamic horizon, in accordance with the social changes that establish the essential requirements of population, defined using decent living standards for all persons without discrimination. For that purpose, the WG has applied a qualitative and quantitative method through which both information on right fulfillment using established indicators and observable trends in such level of fulfillment are processes, which is the basis to assess their progressiveness, considering the set of established indicators. (WGPSS, 2020)

This in turn includes an approach of gender, diversity and multiculturalism.

In the case of States and civil society, it has implied an unprecedented exercise as they have no experience in these types of accountability mechanisms or in the periodic production of information. However, there is not a wide-ranging transformation yet and a greater breakdown of data is required by sex or gender identity, age, level of education, ethnicity and 'race' (Pautassi, 2018). In turn, using three cycles of report analysis based on progress indicators and qualitative progress signs, the inseparable relation between the quantitative data and the qualitative perspective has been strengthening.

But how can indebtedness' impact on the level of human rights fulfilment be measured? Are there obligations to ensure a life free of debts? Which are the rights that should be measured? The answers to these questions are of paramount importance. Although standards related to the concept of a decent life, rights interdependence and debt have been established,[5] they still need a greater conceptualization and to claim the consideration of indebtedness as a regressive measure in relation to the life conditions of the population and the guaranty of the access to ESCR. Therefore, in order to advance in this linking of obligations, standards and indicators, we start with the concept of economic autonomy of women and diverse sexual identities, so that from that point we can identify elements to be considered for future interventions both for public policies and for international monitoring.

4. The fiction of economic autonomy of women

According to the Economic Commission for Latin America and the Caribbean (ECLAC), autonomy is understood as 'the ability of persons to make free and informed decisions about their lives, so that they can be and make considering their own aspirations and wishes in the historical context that makes them possible' (ECLAC, 2022). Considering precisely gender inequalities, this institution identified three interrelated dimensions of women's autonomy: physical, economic and in political decision making (ECLAC, 2022).

Economic autonomy is understood as the ability of women to generate their own income and resources with access to paid work with equal conditions compared to men. It considers the use of time and the contribution of women to the economy (ECLAC, 2022). Autonomy implies exercising human rights and in particular economic autonomy requires exercising ESCR. All dimensions of women's autonomy are interdependent, like human rights.

Reflecting on economic autonomy and the exercise of citizenship, from a rights-based approach, allows visualizing the differences between what we request and what we aspire to as goals of equity and equality, as well as the complexities we must consider, many of them linked to power relations between women and men, which are present at the moment of proposing, designing and analyzing gender-based indicators (Rico and Marco Navarro, 2010).

Many times, we have claimed that having a paid job is not a synonym for economic autonomy for women, both due to the circumstances in which the job is given, usually without access to social security coverage, and in relation to the amounts of money women receive as remuneration. It is worth mentioning that women use their salary for different purposes, as they prioritize health and education costs of the family and they leave almost no margin to use their salary freely for what they want. Also, the low time availability of women must be added due to domestic work and unpaid care work. Life is time, and if we do not have time at our disposal, we do not have our lives at our disposal. On top of that, the private indebtedness of women must be also added as another limitation of economic autonomy.[6] Then paid work is a necessary requirement, but it is not enough for this dimension of women's autonomy and probably it is not for diverse sexual identities either.

The economic autonomy of women is without a doubt a very important conceptual category to account for the different realities of women, the gaps and gender inequalities compared to men, but also among women. Women's autonomy, in all its economic, physical and political dimensions, is an aspiration, a must. However, today this is a fiction for two reasons. First, due to the lack of resources as even in the case of women with their own income, in general they have taken private debts; therefore, they are not necessarily free to use their income. This is a practical reason; economic autonomy results in a fiction due to an overwhelming reality.

Second, due to the fact that this autonomy, which has been so demanded by feminists, presents certain (apparent) contradictions with the theory of care, which is also feminist. Then the change of paradigm that we expect that places care at the centre of life (and of economy and policies) implies that women accept themselves as vulnerable, as opposed to the fully independent person that is supposed to function in societies and markets, and who is in charge of dependent populations (both in terms of economy and care). We propose to accept ourselves considering human fragility and interdependence. This is a theoretical reason that, in a nod to Nancy Fraser (Fraser, 1997), could be called the dilemma of care and autonomy.

Our interest focuses on the first reason that makes economic autonomy a fiction for women and how it relates to indebtedness, both at a micro and macro level.

Women's indebtedness

Access to loans is something desirable and promoted by several international bodies and cooperation agencies, even by numerous women's organizations. This is an area where women face particular obstacles related to the absence of collaterals and formal jobs, often required for loan granting in the formal financial system.

Then when does loan access become a limitation instead of promoting the economic autonomy of women? First, when due to the obstacles to access formal loans, women turn to informal lenders for money, or even to institutions of the financial system specializing in microloans with a very high interest rate compared to the ones of traditional banking.

A study on women's indebtedness performed in the city of Tarija, Bolivia (ECAM, 2021), shows that almost one fifth of surveyed women became indebted to satisfy health and educational needs; in other words, these are consumption loans, which are the ones with the highest interest. It also shows that physical and emotional health is modified after these loans due to the stress generated when they are repaid (or not repaid) and the family conflicts that this situation creates.

What was mentioned has resulted in an international tendency of financial civil disobedience, the so-called 'who owes to whom', which evidences the women's claims regarding what States, markets, men and the capitalist system owe. This tendency also questions the idea that women are good payers, which is considered as an advantage to receive loan programmes because payments made in a timely manner hide countless personal and family sacrifices (Equipo de Comunicación Alternativa con Mujeres – ECAM, 2021).

Moreover, it is undeniable that exercising financial civil disobedience leaves activists outside the financial system. However, the fact is that many women, especially entrepreneurs, craftswomen and women workers from the gastronomy sector and others, want to access financing and they needed it even more after the pandemic, when many of them used their capital and ran out of stock of their products. For instance, this was confirmed by a case study of women that work in tourism in two districts of the Chiquitania region in Bolivia (Knaudt et al, 2021). Another recent study by UN Women also shows that loans are a demand from businesswomen and women entrepreneurs who have the motivation to start and maintain a business, which in turn relates to the motivation to consolidate their autonomy. In addition, the study evidences that 99 per cent of loans granted to women in Bolivia are microloans. (Marconi et al, 2022).

Then, what can be done? How should the indebtedness issue be addressed? At first, policies and strategies that are deployed must understand that the purpose is to improve the situation of women, increase their income and their freedom of action, and not to restrict them.

The advice that could be offered is key. In this respect, a study carried out in Bolivia shows weak advice is given by financial entities as they do not believe this is their responsibility (ECAM, 2021), but this provision of information and advice can come from other sources, including the State and the women's movement.

The regulation of financial entities is also important, not only to make transparency measures compulsory with respect to the citizens that use their services, but also to limit the interest and to apply it properly. Also, the Bolivian case shows that many women workers who invest the amount of their loans in their business obtained them as consumption loans with a very high interest, but with fewer requirements (Knaudt et al, 2021; Marconi et al, 2022). This phenomenon, also identified in other cases, as happened in the past in Chile, for instance, can be reversed with the necessary willing and appropriate supervision by banking entities and States.

For the Bolivian case, it is worth mentioning the proposal of a common fund of guaranties and the creation of a trust for loans for businesswomen and women entrepreneurs that attracts both investors and cooperation funds (Marconi et al, 2022). In the case of Argentina, the several studies performed that link indebtedness, gender and care, especially the qualitative approaches, are very interesting (Partenio, 2022), and for the case of women workers in the health sector see Castilla (2022).

Country indebtedness and the differential impact on women

Gender studies has plenty of evidence on the differential impact that the situations of fiscal vulnerability due to debt distress and the resulting fiscal austerity measures applied in countries have on women. A milestone in this regard were the programmes of structural adjustment applied in the region during the 1980s and 1990s. More recently, even during and after the pandemic, the management of external debt has also led to measures of the same type due to the conditions of credit agencies.

With the financial crisis of 2008, the United Nations Human Rights Office of the High Commissioner (OHCHR) had already warned about the fact that, in developing countries, the adjustment measures resulting from the crisis had an impact on structural inequalities, deepening them, in general, in the exercise of rights (United Nations Human Rights Office of the High Commissioner, 2013).

In a recent study (Geoghegan and Fois, 2021), the effects that the consequences of indebtedness in Latin America had on women and gender inequalities were analyzed, putting into perspective the risks faced by the region due to an increase of public debt, a problem that worsened with the pandemic. The authors make a call to Latin America not to repeat past mistakes and not to repay the debt that limits the fulfilment of human rights or the goals to reduce inequalities.

The conclusions of the aforementioned study highlight the fact that the impact of public debt distress is transmitted to citizens through jobs, public services, food security and private indebtedness. These effects are separated by sex and in most cases women disproportionately suffer, among other causes, due to the gender division of work as the job crisis and the shrinkage of the State result in an increase of the total work burden. The study concludes that, in contexts of tax inequality, public debt in the end is repaid by the sectors that benefited the least from the resources obtained with it.

The study by Giacometti et al (2019) evidences the differential impacts that austerity measures implemented by the Argentine government had on women, at least in the exercise of the right to health, education, work, social security and a life free of violence, as well as the evident effect among indigenous people and migrants, of which, it is worth recalling, half of them are women. The previously mentioned study, which covers the period of 2015–19, evidenced a deficit in the exercise of long-standing ESCR, but it also showed how these needs have emphasized and even generated new deficits in the exercise of rights as a result of the crisis and the austerity measures applied. These are regressive measures that violate the principle of progressiveness in terms of human rights.

Moreover, the study shows the violation of several principles of international human rights law through sectorial policies, whether through action or omission. In other words, there are resources, but the State neither promotes effective policies of expenditure allocation nor guarantees coverage in social areas, or their distribution. The Argentine State is aware of these situations as they were mentioned by the mechanisms of international monitoring, among others, by the International Covenant on Economic, Social and Cultural Rights (ICESCR) Committee and by the WGPSS. Afterwards, (Bohoslavsky et al, 2020) it has been proved that, despite the fact that the Argentine State made a significant fiscal effort during 2020 to try to minimize the social and economic effects of the pandemic and the resulting recession, rights deficits persist and again affect women in an intersected way.

At the beginning of the pandemic, this larger public expenditure financed a number of measures whose goal was to quickly strengthen the health system; help workers and companies; make unconditioned monetary transfers to the most vulnerable persons; protect the rights of women, children, adolescents, elder persons and disabled persons; as well as a broad range of measures of emergency to minimize the economic and social impact of the pandemic, the social and compulsory lockdown (*aislamiento social y obligatorio*, 'ASPO') and the recession. These policies were implemented in the context of a recession and fiscal deficit and marked by the debt restructuring with private creditors and, most recently (2021), with the IMF. Despite the debt relief with private creditors, due to the drop of tax collection as a result of the economic collapse, the State increased public expenditure and for such purpose it turned to further monetary issuance. Even so, a considerable deterioration of ESCR can be observed in Argentina, and the rates of poverty, extreme poverty and unemployment are their most brutal expressions, along with the heterogeneous nature of a federal country, and of course with the differential impact among women and diverse sexual identities.

In Latin America, the right to care, to be cared and to self-care were gradually recognized in this context and, without a doubt, this was something that the pandemic accelerated (Pautassi, 2007), a formula resulting from applying the rights-based approach in the context of the Regional Conference on Women in Latin America and the Caribbean, which took place in Quito in 2007.[7] This recognition of care as a human right, among many other effects, separates care from the need or the status (formal paid worker), which were the reasons why it was provided for years. The change occurred after it was identified as a right that integrates the corpus of human rights and that established obligations for the State, companies, social and community organizations and families, where men have a significant debt with women. While it has been recognized, to date its jointly responsible exercise has not been made effective and the debt that society as a whole has with women has not been collectively assumed.

5. Final reflections

Whether we call it economic autonomy or not, it is clear that we, as the authors and also as women, advocate for women's freedom to decide about their economy (apart from their bodies) and this requires certain conditions to become possible. These conditions are the exercise of ESCR, which States have the obligation to respect, protect and fulfil. In particular, recognizing the right to care, as a process that combines historical feminist demands and current State obligations, creates an unprecedented space to coordinate among sectorial policies, administration levels of the State and between the State and civil society. In that respect, we especially highlight progress indicators and monitoring mechanisms established at a regional level, as they show the value of empirical evidence and the frequency of data production as a key to verify compliance with State obligations. Although they require greater dissemination and appropriation, the potential they have with respect to the indebtedness of women and sexual diversities is extremely important.

It is clear that policies must address the several limitations that women face today to have enough and regular income, and to be able to use it; these limitations are linked to, among other things, private indebtedness and the differential consequences of public debt policies in the countries. Including progress indicators to measure State obligation compliance in relation to indebtedness patterns must be a regular and frequent action that, among other functions, enables the measuring of principles such as the progressiveness principle and regressiveness prohibitions, along with the principles of equality and non-discrimination, among other core principles of human rights. These actions are already in progress at a regional level, we only need to promote their incorporation and appropriation at State level to encourage the State's effective compliance.

In turn, while the right to care is not recognized as a universal, comprehensive and interdependent right with civil, political and ESC rights, structural inequalities cannot be reduced or eliminated. In the same vein, we must promote the recognition of a life free of indebtedness secured by guaranties (and the provision of goods and services) to fully exercise economic autonomy. In the context of a law or institutional mechanisms, along with universal public policies, it is possible that the debts democracy has with women can be identified, measured and solved in an equal way.

Notes

[1] These conferences have taken place since 1977 every three years and they generate agendas and regional gender political agreements.

[2] On this matter, see chapter 20 by Magalí Brosio and Mariana Rulli in this book.

[3] This is how the Committee on Economic, Social and Cultural Rights has considered it, 'General Comment No. 3. The nature of States parties' obligations (paragraph 1 of Article 2 of the Covenant)', 14 December 1990.

[4] PSS monitoring reports are available at: https://www.oas.org/es/sadye/inclusion-social/protocolo-ssv/

[5] On this matter, see chapter 5 by Juan Pablo Bohoslavsky and Julieta Rossi in this book.

[6] In agreement with several chapters of this book, particularly chapter 12 by M. Nieves Rico and chapter 13 by Ariel Wilkis and Florencia Partenio.

[7] In the following conferences that took place in Brasilia (2010), Santo Domingo (2013), Montevideo (2016), Santiago de Chile (2020) and Buenos Aires (2022), the recognition of care as a human right has been ratified and an agenda to promote care societies has been opened, https://conferenciamujer.cepal.org/15/es/documentos/compromiso-buenos-aires

References

Abramovich, V. (2021) 'Los derechos humanos en las políticas públicas', in L. Pautassi and F. Marco Navarro (eds), *Feminismos, cuidados e institucionalidad. Homenaje a Nieves Rico*, Buenos Aires: Fundación Medife, pp 375–92.

Abramovich, V. and Pautassi, L. (2009) 'El enfoque de derechos y la institucionalidad de las políticas sociales', in V. Abramovich and L. Pautassi (eds), *La revisión judicial de las políticas sociales*, Buenos Aires: Del Puerto editores, pp 279–340.

Barbery Knaudt, R.; Marco Navarro, F. and Subirana Osuna, J. (2021) *El turismo: Una apuesta por el desarrollo con rostro de mujer. El caso de la Chiquitania en Bolivia*, Santa Cruz de la Sierra, Bolivia: CEPAD.

Birgin, H. (1992) 'La reformulación del orden mundial: el lugar de las mujeres en las estrategias de desarrollo', in R. Rodriguez (ed) *Fin de siglo: Género y cambio civilizatorio*, Ediciones de las mujeres, No 17, Santiago: Isis International, pp 7–20.

Birgin, H. and Pautassi, L. (2001) '¿Género en la reforma o reforma sin género?. Desprotección social de las leyes previsiona-les en América Latina', *Serie Mujer y Desarrollo*, No 36.

Bohoslavsky, J.P. (2018) *El impacto de las reformas económicas y las medidas de austeridad sobre los derechos de las mujeres*, Buenos Aires: Friedrich Ebert Stiftung.

Bohoslavsky, J.; Marco Navarro, F. and Pautassi, L. (2020) *De la crisis de la deuda a la crisis del COVID 19 y su impacto en los derechos económicos, sociales y culturales en Argentina*, Buenos Aires: Mimeo.

Castilla, M. (2022) 'Deudas, cuidados y vulnerabilidad: el caso de las trabajadoras de la salud en la Argentina', Documentos de Proyectos (LC/TS.2022/41, LC/BUE/TS.2022/5), Santiago: Comisión Económica para América Latina y el Caribe (CEPAL).

ECLAC (2022) 'Observatorio de igualdad de género en América Latina y el Caribe', United Nations [online], Available from: https://oig.cepal.org/es/autonomias/autonomia-economica

Equipo de Comunicación Alternativa con Mujeres (ECAM) (2021) 'Mujer y endeudamiento', Tarija, Bolivia: ECAM-MISEROR.

Fraser, N. (1997) '¿De la redistribución al reconocimiento?. Dilemas en tomo a la justicia en una época 'postsocialista', in N. Fraser, *Iustitia Interrupta: Reflexiones críticas desde la posición 'postsocialista'*, Bogota, Colombia: Siglo del Hombre Editores, pp 17–54.

Giacometti, C.; Marco Navarro, F. and Pautassi, L. (2019) *Los impactos de las medidas de austeridad en los DESC en el corto y mediano plazo en Argentina*, Buenos Aires: Mimeo.

Lamas, M. (2020) *Dolor y política. Sentir, pensar y hablar desde el feminismo*, Mexico: Océano.

Marconi, R.; Prado, M.; Quelca, G. and Sánchez, C. (2022) *Inclusión financiera de las mujeres. Hacia la igualdad de género en los servicios financieros: Diagnóstico y propuesta*, La Paz, Bolivia: ONU-Mujeres.

MESECVI (2015) *Guía para la aplicación de la Convención Interamericana para Prevenir, Sancionar y Erradicar la Violencia contra la Mujer*, Washington, DC: OEA.

Partenio, F. (2022) 'Deudas, cuidados y vulnerabilidad: el caso de las trabajadoras de casas particulares en la Argentina', Documentos de Proyectos (LC/TS.2022/53, LC/BUE/TS.2022/3), Santiago: Comisión Económica para América Latina y el Caribe (CEPAL).

Pautassi, L. (2007) 'El cuidado como cuestión social desde un enfoque de derechos' *Serie Mujer y Desarrollo*, No 57.

Pautassi, L. (2018) 'Access to Justice in Health Matters: An Analysis Based on the Monitoring Mechanisms of the Inter-American System', *Health and Human Rights Journal*, 20(1): 185–97.

Pautassi, L. (2021) 'La agenda de género a nivel regional: prácticas, enfoques y estrategias', in M. Herrera, N. De La Torre and S. Fernandez, *Tratado de Géneros, Derechos y Justicia*, Buenos Aires: Rubinzal Culzoni, pp 21–40.

Pérez Gómez, L.; Pérez Molina, I.; Pautassi, L.; Loreti, C. and Riesco, R. (2022) 'Indicadores de progreso para el derecho a la alimentación adecuada en ocho países de América Latina', in L. Pautassi and M. Carrasco (eds) *Derecho a la alimentación adecuada en América Latina y el Caribe: desafíos y claves para su garantía, protección y realización*, Buenos Aires: Eudeba, pp 73–154.

Rico, M. and Marco Navarro, F. (2010) 'Autonomía económica y derechos del trabajo. Implicancias para el diseño y análisis de indicadores de género' in V. Abramovich and L. Pautassi, *La medición de derechos en las políticas sociales,* Buenos Aires: Editores del Puerto, pp 233–64.

United Nations Human Rights Office of the High Commissioner (2012) 'Indicadores de derechos humanos. Guía para la medición y aplicación', Geneva: United Nations.

United Nations Human Rights Office of the High Commissioner (2013) 'Report on austerity measures and economic and social rights', Geneva: United Nations.

WGPSS (2020) 'Examen de los Informes presentados por los Estados Parte al Protocolo Adicional a la Convención Americana sobre Derechos Económicos, Sociales y Culturales 'Protocolo de San Salvador'. Observaciones recomendaciones finales a la República de El Salvador' (OAS/Ser.L/XXV.2.1 GT/PSS/doc.2/20), Grupo de Trabajo para el análisis de los informes nacionales previstos en el Protocolo de San Salvador, September.

Working Group for the analysis of national reports contained in the Protocol of San Salvador (WGPSS) (2015) *Indicadores de progreso para la medición de derechos contemplados en el Protocolo Adicional a la Convención Americana sobre Derechos Humanos en materia de Derechos Económicos, Sociales y Culturales - Protocolo de San Salvador,* Washington DC: OAS.

PART VI

Work Agenda
for Egalitarian Transformations

18

A Gender Lens for the International Monetary and Financial System: Truly Feminist Reforms Needed

Christina Laskaridis

1. Introduction

The international monetary and financial system (IMFS) is used to describe the institutions and practices that govern international monetary and financial affairs. Fundamental shortcomings in this system become overwhelmingly apparent time and time again after large crises, such as the global financial crisis and the COVID-19 pandemic. The IMFS increases financial imbalances, boom and busts in credit and asset prices with significant consequence for the macroeconomy (BIS, 2015). This is largely the result of its haphazard evolution, resulting in the disproportionate dominance of finance (Mader et al, 2019) and institutions whose governance reproduces power imbalances between countries. The global financial safety net, comprised of international reserves, central bank swap lines, regional financing arrangements and International Monetary Fund (IMF) resources, is supposed to underpin and provide a backstop to the IMFS during a crisis, but has proven woefully inadequate to shelter citizens from the storm.

In recent years, institutions that are fundamental to shaping global economic governance, such as the IMF, World Bank, G-20 and the Organization for Economic Co-operation and Development (OECD), have introduced a number of initiatives to mainstream gender across their activities (World Bank Group, 2015; OECD, 2016; Thomas et al, 2018; IMF, 2022b). Despite this growing interest towards gender equality, little is done to ensure that inequality is tackled on a structural level and that commitments are in fact reflected in gender equality on the ground. Instead, global economic and financial governance remains characterized by a 'strategic silence', masking the ways in which the IMFS reinforces gender and other inequalities (Young et al, 2011). This supposed gender-neutrality of the IMFS and the international financial architecture (IFA) has been challenged by feminist scholars who examine the gendered organization and restructuring of the global economy (Griffin, 2015; Mezzadri et al, 2022). As the IMFS shapes and is shaped by the macroeconomic environment overall, it is critical for women's rights and gender equality. With women's paid and unpaid work a cornerstone of economic life, the organization of social reproduction sustains the current structure and governance of the IMFS.

As this chapter will argue, failure to adopt a gender lens to the structural aspects of the IMFS is a failure to tackle the roots of gender inequality. It also leaves the efforts for mainstreaming gender rhetorical and remote from the problems that plague it. These include addressing the immediate impact on women and children caused by global shocks (Azcona et al, 2020), in a context in which developing countries keep providing net financial resources, as a group, to developed countries. Sections 2 and 3 further the gender-critique of two institutions central to the IMFS: the Group of 20 (G-20) and the IMF. The IMF is mandated to promote international monetary cooperation, and address international balance of payments problems. Through a gradual 'mission creep' it has positioned itself as crisis manager, and bears colossal weight over how international monetary and financial crises are addressed (Boughton, 2000; Babb and Buira, 2005). Financial crises, and subsequent domestic adjustment programmes adopted in their wake, including IMF surcharge policy, have high political, economic and social impacts that lead to further destabilizing dynamics: higher inequality, spiralling public finances, income collapses and debt deflationary cycles (Furceri and Zdzienicka, 2011; Guzman et al, 2016), with grave gendered impacts (Ghosh, 2010; 2021). The G-20 has emerged as a focal point for the world's largest countries to address international economic and financial stability. Both these institutions therefore are integral to decisions around addressing financial crises, with power to shape international monetary and financial affairs, and promote an enabling macroeconomic environment for women's rights.

Section 4 examines key structural issues of the IMFS and how they perpetuate gender inequalities. Characteristics of the IMFS, whose gendered dimension has hitherto received less attention, include global liquidity cycles, currency hierarchies and elements of sovereign debt 'architecture'. The chapter concludes with an examination of the IMFS through the prism of a rights-based economy identifying a range of feminist reforms.

2. G-20

The G-20 brings together finance ministers and central bank governors from 19 countries and the European Union. It was established in the aftermath of the Asian financial crisis, explicitly recognizing the financial turbulence that results from globalization, and was thus mandated to strengthen international financial architecture. While broader than the Group of 7, it is an informal forum for global economic governance, as well as highly unrepresentative of the vast majority of UN member states, and according to Hopkins and Bürgisser (2020), was elevated into the limelight of international financial economic governance as a counterweight to the more representative UN process.[1]

The G-20 meets annually, and its meetings are aimed at producing negotiated outcome documents. The G-20 finance ministers and their working groups produce a number of documents each year that feed into the G-20 process and several communiqués. Over the course of 1999 to 2022, twenty-five countries have hosted the G-20, during which finance ministers and central bank governors and deputies produced a number of communiqués. Figure 18.1 summarizes the references to gender and women's rights in the final communiqués. The topic of gender inequality and women's rights are largely absent.[2] Clearly visible is the lack of any reference for the first period of the G-20's existence. The earlier mentions of women and gender in G-20 communiqués focus heavily on women's financial inclusion and greater labour market participation. The source of gender inequality can be seen to stem from labour market discrimination, disconnected from a sense of understanding of how micro-level processes aggregate into international macroeconomic issues such as gendered global supply chains (Mezzadri et al, 2022). Gender goals for the G-20 were initiated in 2014 during the Australian presidency's commitment to reducing the gender gap in labour market participation. The first Women's Summit (W20), in 2015, put forward a set of policy recommendations for the G-20 to consider, focusing on labour market issues (for example, participation and entrepreneurship), labour market discrimination and associated occupational segregation, and issues of social protection (W20, 2015). The sentiment around the goal of women's empowerment is orientated around the 'double dividend' of increasing productivity and growth that may arise from more women entering the labour force, rather than the intrinsic value of equality. Since the pandemic, the G-20 has made explicit reference to the disproportionate impact that economic crisis and COVID-19 related crises have had on vulnerable social groups, including women and children. There remains however a disconnection between the wide-ranging issues addressed, such as financial instability, sovereign debt repayment problems and creditor participation, the problems of capital flow volatilities and

Figure 18.1: Annual mentions of women and gender-related topics in G20 Finance Ministers and Central Bank Governors Communiqués, 1999–2022

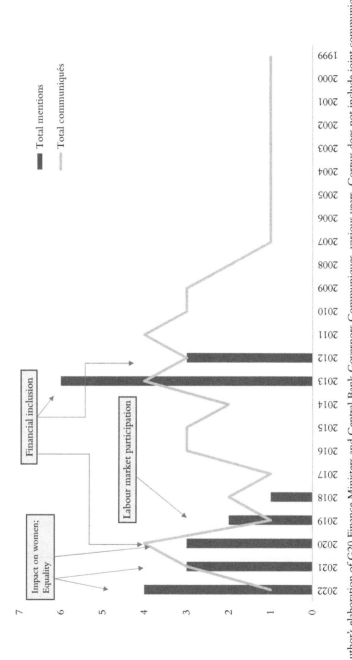

Source: Author's elaboration of G20 Finance Ministers and Central Bank Governors Communiques, various years. Corpus does not include joint communiques with other ministers' meetings, appendices or working group documents.

international spillovers of monetary and exchange rate policies, and a gendered understanding of the IMFS. The references to women and gender in G-20 communiqués do not reflect an understanding of how its subject matters are mediated by and through gender. Instead, they focus on a narrower understanding of women's role in the economy, similar, for instance, to the view of instrumentalization of gender that has been documented by the IMF (Bohoslavsky and Rulli, 2021). Little is done to connect this disproportionate gendered impact of crises to the overarching characteristics of the global economy. None of the G-20 communiqués communicate a message that substantive equality needs to be driven by fundamentally addressing the reasons behind why inequalities are entrenched at the global level. Nor do G-20 communiqués address structural barriers that arise from the role of women in the economy and social reproduction. A gender lens to examine the international financial architecture reveals how the policies and processes that take place in the IMFS are conditional on women's paid and unpaid care activities, as well as being highly impactful on the progress of women's rights. By overlooking women and girls, the G-20 finance ministers reveal the exclusionary character of their responses. Structures of international economic governance, by failing to adequately incorporate a gender lens into their core practice, fail to mitigate risks and appropriately address systemic risks when they arise. A gender-neutral view of international financial architecture masks the ways in which unequal institutions, processes and practices reproduce at the local, national and international level, and unequally distribute gains and losses of economic life. At each successive meeting, commitments fail to address the interlinked nature of gender relations in international financial architecture and global economic governance structures. Strengthening the substantive links with a gender analysis would enable a clear documentation of how commitments on advancing the rights of women and children, and commitments for gender equality, are part of reform of the IMFS.

3. IMF

The IMF provides financial assistance to countries with balance of payment problems, often disbursed in tranches over a multi-year period, subject to conditionalities of macroeconomic austerity – policies that aim to shrink public expenditures and control sovereign debt, as well as liberalization and privatization programmes – which lead to a host of well-known, devastating impacts, such as greater inequality, poverty and deeper recessions, adversely affecting a variety of human rights (Lusiani and Saiz, 2013; Bohoslavsky, 2018; Lusiani and Chaparro, 2018) (see chapter 10 by Diane Perrons and chapter 11 by Alicja Krubnik). Concessional or non-concessional terms accompany IMF financial assistance, with the General Resource Account providing the latter, which arises in most part through the IMF quota system, reflecting imperfectly the relative global economic position of the country. Access by each country is governed by limits in terms of the size of the loan vis-à-vis the country's quota. A primarily low-income criterion determines whether countries can access IMF concessional financing, from lending facilities that are supported via voluntary contributions of richer countries (IMF, 2022a).

Sovereign debt crises have direct adverse impacts on the realization of human rights, given the diversion of resources from essential social services to debt service, through numerous policy conditionalities, and ineffective, unfair, inefficient debt relief and restructuring processes (Herman et al, 2010; Bueanaventura et al, 2017; Bantekas and Lumina, 2019). Given the weaknesses in the global financial safety net and the enlarged role of the IMF as crisis manager, the IMF has ended up with an integral role in sovereign debt workouts (Hagan, 2020), despite longstanding demands for the UN to be the core facilitator. The IMF has contributed to delays in restructuring through the reliance on overoptimistic baselines in Debt Sustainability Analysis (DSA), that lead to less debt relief by creditors and the placement of adjustment burdens on the debtor (Laskaridis, 2021a). Using optimistic assumptions about growth, debt sustainability is predicated on dramatic fiscal adjustments, implying less need for debt relief (Laskaridis, 2020). Given multiple forms of gender discrimination, there is a disproportionate impact on women of the impacts of debt crises, debt servicing and IMF policy conditionality associated with qualifying for debt relief or restructuring. This is for a number of reasons, including women's role in care responsibilities (children, elderly and the sick), as food and water providers in the context of subsistence agriculture, and due to constrained access to land, property, social security and independent finances (Lumina, 2012).

Women's rights are enshrined in numerous human rights legal frameworks.[3] The IMF includes conditionalities that affect all spheres of the economy – privatization, taxation, expenditures, user fees for education, health, access to water utilities and liberalization of trade and investments. These policies have been shown to negatively impact equality, poverty, unemployment and social safety nets, leading to rising prices for food and medicine and the marginalization of the poor in many debtor countries (Weeks and McKinley, 2006). Women's right to health, education, water and work suffer as women bear the brunt of the economy contracting. Shrinking public services are substituted through women's unpaid time; if access to medical care or pensions disappear, women and girls are the first to leave school or work to provide for other family members (Lumina, 2012). IMF policies worsen the education gap between women and men, as increased tuition fees may force families to prioritize boys' education. IMF privatization policies may affect access to water and waste-collection services, affecting fees and distance travelled for free water, with implications for contaminated water which would affect health spending. IMF policies systematically constrain fiscal space, and fail to support social and economic policies that would support women's and gender rights (Burgisser and Nissan, 2017).

IMF non-concessional loans are subject to interest on which the IMF may levy further surcharges. Surcharges are additional costs, over and above normal interest payments and other fees. There are two types of surcharges: those that relate to the size of the loan and those that relate to the length of time that the loan is still outstanding. Countries in a prolonged downturn, characterized by a deep crisis, usually face greater capital flight, which – absent capital controls – is typically financed from ever larger loans from the IMF. With surcharges, countries in greater need ultimately end up paying more to borrow from the Fund. Together with the standard headline borrowing rate, when one incorporates surcharges, the borrowing costs constitute a severe and punitive cost for borrowing countries (Arauz et al, 2021; Bohoslavsky et al, 2022; Stiglitz and Gallagher, 2022). The precise application of surcharge fees is opaque, yet recent estimates suggest that surcharges constitute close to half of non-principal debt service to the Fund by its five largest, outstanding borrowers (Argentina, Ecuador, Egypt, Pakistan and Ukraine) (Arauz et al, 2021). The same five countries constitute up to 95 per cent of surcharge income in 2021 – a very significant source of operating income for the IMF as a whole. In 2021, surcharge income constituted approximately half of the Fund's operating income (IMF, 2021).

There are several reasons why the Fund ostensibly applies surcharges: first, to disincentivize large or prolonged use of Fund credit; second, to encourage early repayment; third, to manage its own credit risk; and fourth to build up precautionary balances for the Fund. As examined in Laskaridis (2022), these do not hold up to scrutiny. First, surcharges are not needed to disincentivize a country's borrowing from the fund. Access to IMF assistance is highly conditional on measures that are procyclical and contractionary, bringing a loss of domestic control over policy and high political, social and economic costs. Given the inadequacy of the global financial safety-net, when countries in crisis need to borrow from the Fund, they face few other options for liquidity to tide them over (Stubbs et al, 2021). The negative social, economic and political consequences of borrowing from the IMF are a sufficient disincentive to not require additional punitive surcharges. Second, there is little basis for the argument that surcharges provide a disincentive to prolonged use of IMF resources and hence encourage early repayment. There are few examples where countries repaid the Fund early – only eight since 2009, and the primary reason in these instances were to avoid the stigma associated with IMF programmes and costs of conditionality (Arauz et al, 2021). More problematic is the understanding of 'prolonged' use, arbitrarily defined as the middle of loan durations. Early repayment does not constitute a source of available firepower for the Fund, which is sourced from quotas, new arrangements to borrow and bilateral borrowing agreements. Third, the IMF contends that surcharges are needed to manage the Fund's credit risk. Application of punitive additional costs as a means to manage risk makes little sense in the existent dysfunctional sovereign debt architecture, in which IMF loans are always repaid, ranking primus inter pares among other creditors due to its preferred creditor status (Li, 2021). Fourth, and finally, the IMF argues that surcharges are indispensable to accumulating precautionary balances. Yet this is disputed in the IMF's own account, where regular interest and fee charges are sufficient to cover operating income, and increases in revenue in the near term are only partly due to the surcharge revenue (IMF, 2021). Furthermore, relying on those in deep crisis to earn additional charges as an income generator, to accumulate a buffer and to manage credit risk, is deeply unethical, and contrary to the IMF's own mission.

In creating a gender lens across all lending, surveillance and technical assistance operations, but one that does not address the overarching macroeconomic environment that is built upon the structural and intersectional roots of gender inequality, the IMF's gender lens can be criticized for leaving inequalities' root causes unchanged (Bueanaventura et al, 2017). Furthermore, by failing to revoke and abolish its surcharge policy, the IMF fails to understand how women face significantly disadvantaged labour market conditions, especially during a crisis. Despite progress being made by the IMF on researching gender inequality, including operationalizing – if only minimally – gender-based policy advice, austerity and fiscal consolidation remain the IMF's go-to staple advice. While the IMF prepares its strategy for mainstreaming gender work in the IMF (IMF, 2022b) (see chapter 9 by Camila Villard Duran), it should consider that its objective to not harm the rights and wellbeing of women and girls directly conflicts with its surcharge policy.

There is no shortage of evidence that conditionality associated with IMF programmes, specifically, cuts to public sector employment positions, have disproportionately gendered negative impacts, as jobs in health, education and public services are occupied by women (Bueanaventura et al, 2017; Women's International League for Peace and Freedom, 2017). There are several direct and indirect channels through which IMF conditionality and its surcharge policy are not gender neutral. Public expenditure is often the target of IMF conditionality and its reduction greatly impacts upon unpaid labour and women's 'time poverty' (Ghosh, 2021). Surcharges are procyclical – meaning they worsen the downturn and deepen a crisis. Their use exacerbates gendered impacts of crises with negative consequences on women and girls (Grantham et al, 2021). Conditionality of IMF programmes negatively affect childcare provision, and the removal of subsidies increases prices of basic goods including food and medicines (Thomson et al, 2017;

Daoud, 2021). As informal workers, women lack benefits arising from social and legal protections. Performing the majority of unpaid domestic household care work, any reductions in provision of child or elderly care, or difficulties in accessing care facilities, leads to greatly expanded unpaid female household labour. Policies, including the surcharge policy, that divert valuable resources from the public budget, lead to reduced access to healthcare facilities, clean water, sanitation, education and any further public service provision, and directly impact upon child and maternal mortality rates. Despite facing a devastating war, over the period of 2021 to 2023, Ukraine will spend approximately a quarter of its total spending on healthcare during the pandemic on surcharges, reaching approximately US$423 million in surcharges (Eurodad, 2022). Surcharges policy drains resources from the provision of social protection and the spending needed to guarantee access to essential services. In the context of a sovereign debt crisis, the negative gendered impacts of IMF surcharges also arise from the erosion of a borrower's ability to pay. Surcharges exacerbate a debt burden which can constrain a country's development prospect (Harris and Lane, 2018), and during a debt crisis severely undermine a State's capacity to enable the realization of economic, social and cultural rights, and the right to development. Debt repayment ends up taking a precedent over and above the primacy of human rights and is often carried out at their expense (United Nations, 2011). Surcharges leave debt-ridden countries with less funds for regular debt service, for expenditure on essential services and exacerbate the negative spiral of a crisis. When a country faces unsustainable debt burdens, prolonged crises and repeated debt restructuring are more likely, as resources are taken out of the country and debt restructurings remain 'too little too late' (Guzman et al, 2016).

4. Structural characteristics and policy proposals for the IMFS

As developed by theorists of social reproduction (Federici, 2004; Mezzadri et al, 2022), women's paid and unpaid labour time constitute the fundamental premise of economic and social activity. This has taken place in the context of historical patterns of inequality both within and between countries, through colonial histories of development. This has led to structural asymmetries of power and representation in institutions of global governance, such as the G-20 and the IMF. Figure 18.2 outlines a gendered map of certain elements of the international monetary and financial system. It shows how certain structural features of the global economy are constituted through gendered relations, and how specific policies could have gendered consequences.

Structural features of the IMFS are the result of a long-standing process of liberalization of financial markets, begun in the 1970s and 1980s, that led

Figure 18.2: A gender lens and feminist reforms for the international financial and monetary system

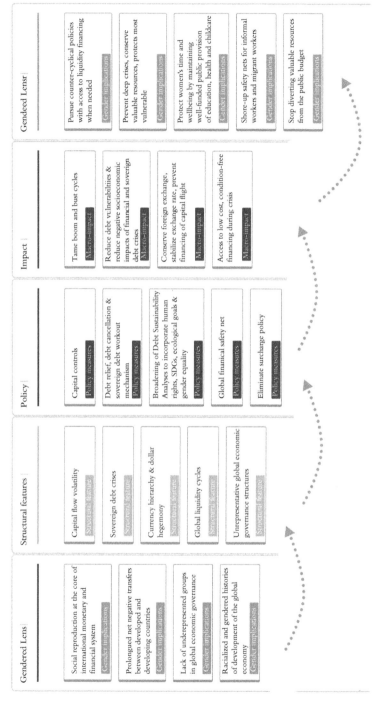

Source: Author's elaboration of how the IMFS is shaped by gender and how policies of IMFS can have gendered impacts

to the dramatic expansion of cross-border financial instruments and rapid growth in private credit markets (Blankenburg, 2019). While capital markets became increasingly globalized, the result was greater volatility, contagion and increases to financial instability. After the global financial crisis, while Global North countries attempted to shore up their economies through unconventional monetary policies, developing and especially low-income countries, traditionally excluded from global capital markets and reliant on official sources of foreign funds, have been increasingly able to access private capital markets. The debt profiles of developing countries have shifted significantly, leading to concerning growth of sovereign debt levels and an increasing number of countries in debt distress and risk of debt distress (Bonizzi et al, 2020; Laskaridis, 2021b). The fate of countries' borrowing, and the refinancing risks countries face, are a product not only of domestic policy, but rather of the common dynamics in global financial markets affected by the way countries have integrated into global financial markets.

'Global liquidity', defined as the 'ease of international financing in the international financial system' (BIS, 2015), explains fluctuations in global financial flows and borrowing costs (Cerutti et al, 2017). As shown in Bonizzi et al, (2019; 2020), global liquidity cycles drive debt dynamics and country issuance, which exposes countries to vulnerabilities and instabilities that arise when global liquidity shrinks and the risk appetite of global lenders changes (Akyüz, 2017; UNCTAD, 2019a; 2019b). The lack of regulation of global liquidity, and aversion towards capital flow management, means that fluctuations of global liquidity, and the actions of central banks and large financial private actors, bear heavily on the macroeconomic environment of low- and middle-income countries. Lack of reserves to support the exchange rate, sudden withdrawals of foreign capital, interest rate increases as part of quantitative tightening, and more broadly the consequences of surges and shrinkages in global liquidity, disproportionally impact women and girls.

Structural inequalities in the IMFS are constituted through international currency hierarchies. Rather than fiscal profligacy being the source of debt repayment problems, the monetary sovereignty of a country is a key determinant of the degrees of freedom a country's authorities have when faced with financial turbulence (Kaltenbrunner, 2015; Bonizzi et al, 2019; Patricio Ferreira Lima, 2022). These issues are interlinked, as the strength of the US dollar, currently at a high, is associated with global liquidity, and procyclically affects the ability of countries to service their debts. The implication of unequal integration in the global economy is that access to liquidity is a binding constraint for low- and middle-income countries which face fewer options through the global financial safety net during a crisis. As most of developing country debt is priced in dollars, a strong dollar increases the cost of debt service to developing countries. Global liquidity conditions are predominantly determined through the actions of private and public actors in high-income countries. These features are important from a gender perspective, as they link the gendered impacts of financial crisis to structural issues in the global economy.

These structural features of the IMFS lead to increased sovereign debt and other financial crises. The international debt architecture for dealing with sovereign debt distress however is not only broken, ineffective, unfair and inefficient (Guzman et al, 2016; Li, 2021); the IMF centres on domestic adjustment to resolve debt crises whose origins lie in external causes. Its reliance on problematic DSAs introduces a structural bias into the restructuring process via overoptimism in baseline growth forecasts, which is paid for by excessive fiscal adjustment instead of greater creditor debt relief (Laskaridis, 2021a). Along with the long-called for need for an independent sovereign debt workout process is the need for credible and independent assessments of debt sustainability that incorporate spending for meeting SDGs, realization of human rights and gender implication of the trajectories of fiscal and debt paths.

Several policies could help tame fluctuations in international monetary and financial conditions. Financial and sovereign debt crises need a fair and credible debt workout mechanism that works for debtor countries, mediated by independent assessments of debt sustainability, and integrates debt standstills, cancellations and capital flow management. Policies such as central bank swap lines, regional financing arrangements and the creation of Special Drawing Rights should be greatly expanded to shore up the Global Financial Safety Net. After much campaigning, the IMF agreed to a new allocation of SDRs, but given the lack of meaningful quota reform, the countries that need it the most receive the least (Eichengreen, 2021). Surcharge policy needs to be terminated. Diachronic debates about reforming the international financial architecture have in each iteration raised many possible areas for improvement, often pointing to greater representation and inclusiveness beyond the G7, G-20 and G24 (Aslanbeigui and Summerfield, 2000). The call for more representation of low- and middle-income countries in decisions about the international financial architecture dovetail with the need for greater women's representation. One way to do this has been through the mainstreaming of gender in international financial institutions. Yet, gender-focused understanding of the IMFS must go beyond the potted mention of gender equality in communiqués and the superficial box-ticking gender assessment of financial policies. The disproportionate impact that crises have on women, children, low-income families and migrants needs to be centred into discussions of reform of the IMFS. Social reproduction underpins the IMFS and unequal integration into the global economy creates the conditions that directly affect State's ability to promote gender equality.

5. Conclusion

The G-20 has developed a gender-blind approach to its role in overseeing the IMFS and international financial architecture. The vulnerabilities of the IMFS, such as sovereign debt crises, disruptive capital flows, volatilities in global liquidity and the inadequacies of the Global Financial Safety Net, need to be connected to a gendered understanding of the global economy as well as to the gendered impacts of policies related to these issues. The G-20 has failed to promote policies that would shore-up low and middle-income State fiscal capacity by supporting a generous write-down of debts. This perpetuates and exacerbates debt vulnerabilities, which are mostly afforded by sacrificing even further the legal obligation – that applies to both sovereign debtors and all creditors – of progressively promoting gender equality.

The IMF's economic adjustment programmes have sustained prolonged negative impacts on women's rights, by worsening access to public provision of education, health and childcare and care responsibilities that women take on, and by worsening economic macroeconomic prospects with less support for informal labour, especially of migrant, vulnerable and other social groups. In addition, its surcharge policy exacerbates the disproportionate costs of crises that are borne by women that compensate for falling domestic incomes and failing public provision of social services.

Policy measures need to recognize how the IMFS shapes and is shaped by women's paid and unpaid work. Some of the key reforms that have been proposed to address the IMFS need to be seen from a gender perspective. Given the negative implications of debt and financial crises on women and girls, policies are needed that regulate capital flows, smoothen fluctuations in global liquidity and provide low-cost unconditional liquidity to countries in need during a crisis. A better functioning Global Financial Safety Net, increased allocations and redistribution of SDRs, reforms to international debt architecture, independent and realistic DSAs that include gender, and SDG and environmental expenditures would tame boom and bust cycles, conserve foreign exchange, protect public resources to support domestic social infrastructures that can enhance women's rights, and protect women's time and wellbeing.

States, the organizations they are part of, members of the UN system and the IMF, are all bound by international human rights law. Thus, whether facing a crisis, or being in a position to shape the macroeconomic environment of other States, States must ensure respect, protection and fulfilment of human rights in their conduct of macroeconomic policies (Bohoslavsky, 2019, especially Principles 11 to 15). Therefore, achieving substantive equality by removing the intersectional barriers women and girls face is a legal mandate – and not a choice. Despite the G-20's and IMF's commitments to upholding women's rights, they have failed to create clear operational guidance that fulfil the promise of developing truly gender-sensitive policies and strategies.

Notes

[1] Its objective, as stated in the first communiqué: 'The G-20 was established to provide a new mechanism for informal dialogue in the framework of the Bretton Woods institutional system', (Group of 20, 1999: p 1).

[2] While not representative of the entirety of G-20 input documents and activities of the working groups, the main Communiqués of Finance Ministers and Central Bank Governors are representative of the core of G-20 outputs and viewpoint. The corpus covered in Figure 18.1 includes all communiqués, with searches for mentions of 'gender', 'women' and 'girls'. For a broader examination see Kulik (2021).

[3] These include the Universal Declaration of Human Rights, the International Covenant on Economic, Social and Cultural Rights, the Convention on the Rights of the Child and the Convention on the Elimination of all Forms of Discrimination against Women (CEDAW). SDG5 on gender equality as with all the 2030 Agenda on Sustainable Development goals are anchored in several international and regional human rights instruments, labour standards and other instruments with human rights dimensions.

References

Akyüz, Y. (2017) *Playing with Fire Deepened Financial Integration and Changing Vulnerabilities of the Global South*, Oxford: Oxford University Press.

Arauz, A.; Weisbrot, M.; Laskaridis, C. and Sammut, J. (2021) 'IMF surcharges: counterproductive and unfair', Center for Economic Policy Research [online] 28 September, Available from: https://www.cepr.net/report/imf-surcharges-counterproductive-and-unfair/.

Aslanbeigui, N. and Summerfield, G. (2000) 'The Asian crisis, gender, and the international financial architecture', *Feminist Economics*, 6(3): 81–103.

Azcona, G.; Bhatt, A.; Encarnacion, J.; Plazaola-Castaño, J.; Seck, P.; Staab, S. and Turquet, L. (2020) 'From insight to action: Gender equality in the wake of COVID-19', New York: UN Women.

Babb, S. and Buira, A. (2005) *Mission Creep, Mission Push and Discretion: The Case of IMF Conditionality. In the IMF and the World Bank at Sixty*, London: Anthem Press.

Bantekas, I. and Lumina, C. (eds) (2019) *Sovereign Debt and Human Rights*, Oxford: Oxford University Press.

BIS (2015) 'The international monetary and financial system', BIS Annual Economic Report, Bank for International Settlements [online] 28 June, Available from: https://www.bis.org/publ/arpdf/ar2015e5.htm.

Blankenburg, S. (2019) 'The unfolding debt crisis in developing countries revisited: Overview and recent trends', 12th UNCTAD Debt Management Conference, 18–20 November, Geneva.

Bohoslavsky, J.P. (2018) 'Impact of economic reforms and austerity measures on women's human rights' (UN Doc. A/73/179), United Nations [online], Available from: https://documents-dds-ny.un.org/doc/UNDOC/GEN/N18/229/04/PDF/N1822904.pdf?OpenElement

Bohoslavsky, J.P. (2019) 'Guiding principles on human rights impact assessments of economic reforms' (Human Rights Council, Fortieth Session A/HRC/40/57), United Nations [online], Available from: https://digital library.un.org/record/1663025?ln=en

Bohoslavsky, J.P. and Rulli, M. (2021) 'Bretton Woods' pandemic policies: A gender equality analysis – perspectives from Latin America', *Development*, 64(1): 97–106.

Bohoslavsky, J.P.; Cantamutto, F. and Clérico, L. (2022) 'IMF's surcharges as a threat to the right to development', *Development*, 65(2): 194–202.

Bonizzi, B.; Laskaridis, C. and Toporowski, J. (2019) 'Global liquidity, the private sector and debt sustainability in sub-Saharan Africa', *Development and Change*, 50(5): 1430–54.

Bonizzi, B.; Laskaridis, C. and Griffiths, J. (2020) 'Private lending and debt risks of low-income developing countries', Overseas Development Institute (ODI).

Boughton, J.M. (2000) 'From Suez to Tequila: The IMF as crisis manager', *The Economic Journal*, 110(460): 273–91.

Bueanaventura, M.; Chen, M.; Donald, K.; Lusiani, N.; Miranda, C. and Moussié, R. (2017) *The IMF and Gender Equality, A Compendium of Feminist Macroeconomic Critiques,* Bretton Woods Project [online], Available from: https://www.brettonwoodsproject.org/wp-content/uploads/2017/10/The-IMF-and-Gender-Equality-A-Compendium-of-Feminist-Macroe conomic-Critiques.pdf

Burgisser, E. and Nissan, S. (2017) 'Positioning women's rights and gender equality in the macroeconomic policy environment', in *The IMF and Gender Equality: A compendium of Feminist Macroeconomic Critiques*, Bretton Woods Project.

Cerutti, E.; Claessens, S. and Ratnovski, L. (2017) 'Global liquidity and cross-border bank flows', *Economic Policy*, 32(89): 81–125.

Daoud, A. (2021) 'The International Monetary Fund's intervention in education systems and its impact on children's chances of completing school', SocArXiv, Available from: https://doi.org/10.31235/osf.io/kbc34.

Eichengreen, B. (2021) 'This SDR allocation must be different', *Project Syndicate* [online] 10 September, Available from: https://www.project-syndicate.org/commentary/how-to-get-new-imf-sdrs-to-poor-countr ies-by-barry-eichengreen-2021-09

Eurodad (2022) 'Eliminate IMF surcharges immediately!', *Global Action for Debt Cancellation* [online] 7 April, Available from: https://debtgwa.net/statements/eliminate-imf-surcharges-immediately?utm_source=emailmarketing&utm_medium=email&utm_campaign=bretton_woods_news_lens_14_april_2022&utm_content=2022-04-14

Federici, S. (2004) *Caliban and the Witch: Women, the Body and Primitive Accumulation* (illustrated edn), New York: Autonomedia.

Furceri, D. and Zdzienicka, A. (2011) 'How costly are debt crises?' (WP/11/280), IMF Working Paper [online] 1 December, Available from: https://www.imf.org/en/Publications/WP/Issues/2016/12/31/How-Costly-Are-Debt-Crises-25400

Ghosh, J. (2010) 'Financial crises and the impact on women', *Development*, 53(3): 381–5.

Ghosh, J. (2021) 'Gender concerns in debt relief', International Institute for Environment and Development [online] December, Available from: https://www.iied.org/20691iied.

Grantham, K.; Rouhani, L.; Gupta, N.; Melesse, M.; Dhar, D.; Mehta, S.K. and Kingra, K.J. (2021) 'Evidence review of the global childcare crisis and the road for post-covid-19 recovery and resilience', International Development Research Centre [online], Available from: https://idl-bnc-idrc.dspacedirect.org/handle/10625/59915.

Griffin, P. (2015) 'Crisis, austerity and gendered governance: A feminist perspective', *Feminist Review*, 109(1): 49–72.

Group of 20 (1999) Communique – G-20 Finance Ministers and Central Bank Governors, [online] 15–16 December, Available from: . http://www.g20.utoronto.ca/1999/1999communique.pdf.

Guzman, M.; Ocampo, J.A. and Stiglitz, J.E. (2016) *Too Little, Too Late: The Quest to Resolve Sovereign Debt Crises*, New York: Columbia University Press.

Hagan, S. (2020) 'Sovereign debt restructuring: The centrality of the IMF's role', Peterson Institute for International Economics Working Paper, No 20–13 [online], Available from: https://doi.org/10.2139/ssrn.3667881

Harris, E. and Lane, C. (2018) 'Debt as an obstacle to the Sustainable Development Goals', United Nations, UN Department of Economic and Social Affairs [online], Available from: https://www.un.org/sw/desa/debt-obstacle-sustainable-development-goals

Herman, B.; Ocampo, J.A. and Spiegel, S. (eds) (2010) *Overcoming Developing Country Debt Crises*, Oxford, New York: Oxford University Press, Available from: https://find.library.duke.edu/catalog/DUKE005382580

Hopkins, E. and Bürgisser, E. (2020) 'Rethinking the global financial system for gender-equal economies', Women's Budget Group.

IMF (2021) 'Review of the adequacy of the Fund's precautionary balances', International Monetary Fund [online] 18 February, Available from: https://www.imf.org/en/Publications/Policy-Papers/Issues/2021/02/18/Review-of-the-Adequacy-of-the-Funds-Precautionary-Balances-50105

IMF (2022a) 'Factsheet – IMF support for low-income countries', IMF [online], Available from: https://www.imf.org/en/About/Factsheets/IMF-Support-for-Low-Income-Countries

IMF (2022b) 'IMF strategy toward mainstreaming gender' (Policy Paper No 2022/037), IMF [online] 28 July, Available from: https://www.imf.org/en/Publications/Policy-Papers/Issues/2022/07/28/IMF-Strategy-Toward-Mainstreaming-Gender-521344

Kaltenbrunner, A. (2015) 'A post Keynesian framework of exchange rate determination: A Minskyan approach', *Journal of Post Keynesian Economics*, 38(3): 426–48.

Kulik, J. (2021) 'G20 performance on gender equality', The Global Governance Project [online] 20 October, Available from: https://www.globalgovernanceproject.org/g20-performance-on-gender-equality-4/julia-kulik/

Laskaridis, C. (2020) 'More of an art than a science: The IMF's Debt Sustainability Analysis and the making of a public tool', *Œconomia. History, Methodology, Philosophy*, 10(4): 789–818.

Laskaridis, C. (2021a) 'Debt sustainability: A history of theory, policy and measurement', PhD thesis, SOAS University of London.

Laskaridis, C. (2021b) 'When push came to shove: COVID-19 and debt crises in low-income countries', *Canadian Journal of Development Studies / Revue Canadienne d'études Du Développement*, 42(1–2): 200–20.

Laskaridis, C. (2022) 'The gendered impacts of the IMF's harmful surcharges policy', Center for Economic and Policy Research [online] 15 April, Available from: https://cepr.net/the-gendered-impacts-of-the-imfs-harmful-surcharges-policy/

Li, Y. (2021) 'International debt architecture reform and human rights' (UN Doc A/76/167), United Nations [online], Available from: https://undocs.org/Home/Mobile?FinalSymbol=A%2F76%2F167&Language=E&DeviceType=Desktop&LangRequested=False

Lumina, C. (2012) 'Report of the Independent Expert on the effects of foreign debt and other related international financial obligations of States on the full enjoyment of human rights, particularly economic, social and cultural rights' (A/67/304), United Nations, p 23.

Lusiani, N. and Saiz, I. (2013) 'Safeguarding human rights in times of economic crisis' [Issue paper], Council of Europe, Commissioner for Human Rights, [online], Available from: https://rm.coe.int/safeguarding-human-rights-in-times-of-economic-crisis-issue-paper-publ/1680908dfa

Lusiani, N. and Chaparro, S. (2018) 'Assessing austerity: Monitoring the human rights impacts of fiscal consolidation [Briefing], Center for Economic and Social Rights [online], Available from: https://www.ssrn.com/abstract=3218609

Mader, P.; Mertens, D. and Van der Zwan, N. (eds) (2019) *The Routledge International Handbook of Financialization*, Abingdon, UK and New York, NY: Routledge.]

Mezzadri, A.; Newman, S. and Stevano, S. (2022) 'Feminist global political economies of work and social reproduction', *Review of International Political Economy*, 29(6): 1783–1803.

OECD (2016) '2015 OECD Recommendation of the Council on Gender Equality in Public Life', OECD [online] 8 March, Available from: https://www.oecd.org/governance/2015-oecd-recommendation-of-the-council-on-gender-equality-in-public-life-9789264252820-en.htm

Patricio Ferreira Lima, K. (2022) 'Sovereign solvency as monetary power', *Journal of International Economic Law*, 25(3): 424–46.

Stiglitz, J.E. and Gallagher, K.P. (2022) 'Understanding the consequences of IMF surcharges: The need for reform', *Review of Keynesian Economics*, 10(3): 348–54.

Stubbs, T.; Kring, W.; Laskaridis, C.; Kentikelenis, A. and Gallagher, K. (2021) 'Whatever it takes? The global financial safety net, Covid-19, and developing countries', World Development, 137: 105171.

Thomas, M.; Novion, C.; de Haan, A.; de Leon, G.; Forest, M. and Iyer, S. (2018) 'Gender Mainstreaming: A Strategic Approach', G20 Insights [online], Available from: https://www.cippec.org/wp-content/uploads/2018/09/TF4-4.5-Final-Gender-Mainstreaming-Policy-Brief-6-21-18-1.pdf

Thomson, M.; Kentikelenis, A. and Stubbs, T. (2017) 'Structural adjustment programmes adversely affect vulnerable populations: A systematic-narrative review of their effect on child and maternal health', *Public Health Reviews*, 38(1): 13.

UNCTAD (2019a) 'External shocks and financial stress post the global financial crisis', United Nations [online], Available from: https://unctad.org/en/PublicationsLibrary/gds2018d1_en.pdf

UNCTAD (2019b) 'Trade and development report 2019: Financing a global green new deal', United Nations.

United Nations (2011) 'Guiding principles on foreign debt and human rights' (A/HRC/20/23), United Nations General Assembly [online], Available from: https://primarysources.brillonline.com/browse/human-rights-documents-online/promotion-and-protection-of-all-human-rights-civil-political-economic-social-and-cultural-rights-including-the-right-to-development;hrdhrd99702016149

W20 (2015) Women's Summit Communique, Turkey 2015 G20 [online] October, Available from: http://www.g20.utoronto.ca/2015/151017-w20.html

Weeks, J. and McKinley, T. (2006) 'Does debt relief increase fiscal space in Zambia? The MDG Implications', International Policy Centre for Inclusive Growth (IPC-IG), Research Report/5 [online], Available from:http://ipcig.org/publication/27347?language_content_entity=en

Women's International League for Peace and Freedom (2017) 'Ukraine: The impact of interventions by international financial institutions on women' (UN Doc A/HRC/35/NGO/68), United Nations [online], Available from: https://documents-dds-ny.un.org/doc/UNDOC/GEN/G17/146/21/PDF/G1714621.pdf?OpenElement

World Bank Group (2015) 'World Bank Group Gender Strategy (FY16–23): Gender equality, poverty reduction and inclusive growth', World Bank [online], Available from: https://openknowledge.worldbank.org/handle/10986/23425

Young, B.; Bakker, I. and Elson, D. (2011) *Questioning Financial Governance from a Feminist Perspective* (1st edn), Abingdon, England; New York, NY: Routledge, Taylor & Francis Group. https://www.routledge.com/Questioning-Financial-Governance-from-a-Feminist-Perspective/Young-Bakker-Elson/p/book/9780415676700

19

Gender Bonds: Do They Leverage or Threaten Women's Rights?

Juan Pablo Bohoslavsky and Lena Lavinas

1. Introduction: the emergence of 'sustainable and fair finances'

As a financial sub-product of both the idea that the private sector can and should finance the Sustainable Development Goals (IMF, 2019: 81–92), and the more general phenomenon of the so-called 'financialization' (Fine, 2020; Braun and Koddenbrock, 2023), in the last years there has been a boom in the market of what was termed as 'sustainable bonds'. This market has grown by 2,000 per cent in the last five years (BIS, 2022), forecasting a growth of US$53 trillion by 2025 (Bloomberg Intelligence, 2021). This trend includes the bonds issued by the States, reaching US$1 trillion in 2021 with a growth expectation that ranged between 20 and 50 per cent by the end of 2022 (Moore, 2022).

The theoretical justification of this financial engineering consists of the possibility and convenience of strengthening the financial markets so that they encourage borrower States to make reforms and projects aimed at achieving sustainability, inclusion and governance (UNEP and UN Global Compact, 2021a) and, more recently and specifically, strengthening a gender-responsive economic recovery (Vaeza, 2021). The almost absolute prevalence of the financial markets in this process is unambiguous. The environmental, social and governance (ESG) factors, as components of the new sustainability framework, emerged in the first decade of the 2000s and have fully reshaped the logic that guides financial investments in virtually all sectors. The underlying idea of that framework is that it is possible to establish a common language shared by all actors involved in initiatives whose goal is to combine 'to do good' with the possibility of obtaining financial gains. This language is based on the definition of the standards expressed most often as indicators of goals to achieve, and that, therefore, enable the measurement of the impacts of these actions and determine if they have strengthened responsible environmental, social or corporate conducts.

Behind such principles, there exist two assumptions. The first one establishes that there is a convergence between goals and methods that will guide the actions and purposes of transnational corporations, institutional investors, civil society and all those that somehow are affected by investments that seek benefits (predominantly private gains) that will by far exceed any setback. This is as if the contradictions that imply different perspectives, concerns and values were a priori eliminated. The second assumption is the need to transform the content of the public policy into a financial investment. In other words, into a type of asset that improves the opportunities to generate financial profits.

The first wave of innovative financial products aimed at offering financial returns 'to do good' in austerity times. They were the 'social impact bonds' (SIBs) which became popular in developing countries and opened new paths to all sorts of investors (private investment funds, pension funds, banks, private equity firms and so on), facilitating even more the expansion of global financial markets and rent-seeking in the periphery of capitalism. SIBs and 'social benefit bonds' (SBBs) have been introduced as contemporary forms of humanitarian efforts, contributing to the creation of 'missing' markets that could provide social services in key areas that before were considered as public, so their provision was expected to be guaranteed by the State (education, health, occupational training, social rehabilitation of persons deprived of their liberty, infrastructure and homelessness, just to name a few). The idea is that investors will ensure an up-front funding to develop social programmes for which there are no sufficient public resources. If the pre-established goals are achieved, then 'the government repays the investments and provides a return based on the cost of savings realized from reduced future demand on public services' (Williams, 2020: 287). This is evidently a privatization strategy of public services.

Since then, similar initiatives have proliferated and, if no changes are made, they will continue developing as the trend is to permanently create new asset-classes,[1] in other words, specific groups of tradable products, such as equities and bonds, in order to improve the channels of new investments and drain-off surplus capital through them. Even so, as Langley (2020) argues, considering Muniesa et al (2017: 5), 'the transformation of a thing into an investible asset requires that it is "neatly delineated" in sovereign legal and juridical terms as a property that is detachable from its socio-material context'. This process is called 'asset codification' (Pistor, 2019).

This assetization process (Adkins et al, 2020; Birch and Muniesa, 2020; Langley, 2020) – that is turning everything into assets, including social rights – has gained traction and space among other trends such as the financialization of philanthropy, characterized as impact investment initiatives that align the interests of financial capital and the super-rich with community and international development issues (Sklair, 2022). In both cases, the assets logic and the rise of philanthrocapitalism are deployed in synchrony with the expansion of institutional investors and the continuous process of fictitious capital creation.[2] This indicates that assetization refers to a process in which any type of thing can be controlled, traded and capitalized so as to capture future flows of revenue, and it is primarily concerned with the promotion of a very particular type of ownership, the institutional or corporate ownership of assets.

Thus instruments that originally only financed projects and policies with environmental impacts ('green bonds') extended their goal to include social goals (so they are called 'social bonds'), including critical areas such as gender equality, health, labour rights and education. The goal of these bonds may also be to promote and facilitate the generation of renewable energy, the reduction of unemployment, the reduction of economic inequality (measured using the Gini index) or the salary gender gap that exists in the countries where those bonds are issued, or to improve social, green or governance indicators that certain companies specifically have (International Regulatory Strategy Group, 2021).

These bonds may be issued by States (both at national and subnational levels) or by private companies. With respect to the financial investment in the private sector, in March 2022, there were 67 countries with capital markets with specific regulations on the criteria of risk assessment in social, environmental and governance terms (Sustainable Stock Exchanges Initiative, 2022). This trend includes a growing issue of corporate gender bonds in Latin America (Núñez, Velloso and Da Silva, 2022). As an illustration, it is worth mentioning the case of the Brazilian Stock Exchange (B3), the first one in the world to issue (in 2021) $700 million in Sustainability-linked Bonds (SLBs), committed to the creation of a diversity index and the increase of women's leadership in capital markets (Bolsa de Valores do Brasil, 2021). This SLB is a ten-year fixed-income bond with an annual return of 4.25 per cent, designed exclusively for qualified institutional investors resident abroad, who are precisely the most interested ones in this type of investment with high risks in the countries of the Global South. In accordance with environmental, social and governance principles, if sustainability goals are not achieved as planned, the interest rate will be increased by 12.5 basis points (or 0.12 per cent). Against transparency assumptions, the identity of those investors cannot be disclosed as the custody position of any investor is protected by the law of banking secrecy.

Likewise, the alliance among the International Finance Corporation (IFC), UN Women and other UN agencies has been producing studies and creating guides on financial investment in private corporations that include gender-responsive commitments (Sustainable Stock Exchanges Initiative, 2022).

There are self-regulation codes created by investors, such as the 'Principles of Social Bonds' (2022), an initiative of the International Capital Market Association (ICMA). Those Principles offer guidelines on the destination of financing, the selection and evolution of projects, the management of financing, the provision of information and reports. At the European level, in 2018 the European Commission adopted a Sustainable Finance Action Plan, regulating aspects linked to the financing of activities and projects that seek to achieve 'social' or 'green' goals (European Commission, 2018). Clearly there exists an external stimulation in the development of markets of sustainable debt.

In this chapter, we will analyze a specific type of social bond: 'gender bonds' issued by States that are based on previous programmes of microloans and microfinance for women, especially in the Global South (AWID, 2023). They are financial instruments that finance projects[3] or public policies that – theoretically – aim to reduce gender inequalities and promote women's rights, while they generate gains for investors. The noncompliance of such 'social promises' of greater equality results in certain financial penalties, such as the payment of fines or higher interest rates by the States that issue the bonds. In other words, their structure consists in adding a provision to the bonds that includes a social goal as to gender (whether a project, policy, law or economic or social indicator) to be achieved by the borrower State, which is added to the financial obligations related to the very repayment of the principal and the payment of periodic coupons (Inderst and Stewart, 2018).

The chapter is organized as follows: after this introductory section, section 2 describes what existing guides are and how they work, as well as what actors promote State gender bonds. Section 3 presents and analyzes a series of limitations, contradictions and problems that this type of bond has. Section 4 presents the final remarks of the chapter.

2. Public bonds and gender equality

The ICMA, UN Women and the IFC of the World Bank – its private sector branch, which is committed to creating markets and attracting private investments – have forged a flourishing alliance as to gender bonds that may announce a greater promotion of these instruments in the coming years. This alliance has been unambiguous as to the role it expects financial markets to play in the reduction of gender inequalities in the world:

> The sustainable finance market has grown significantly, and investor appetite is high for products that address social issues. Social, Gender, Sustainability, and Sustainability-linked Bonds and Loans provide

avenues to direct capital towards reducing the inequalities that persist between women and men; yet they are not being used to their fullest potential. This note provides guidance to the market of how sustainable debt instruments could be used to advance gender equality in both the public and private sectors. We hope it encourages stakeholders across capital markets to go beyond business as usual in addressing gender inequalities and unlock the funding opportunities that sustainable instruments present. (ICMA, UN Women and IFC, 2021: 20)

In fact, in 2021 ICMA, UN Women and the IFC issued a practical detailed guide so as to use the notion of debt sustainability to specifically promote greater gender equality. Not only does this guide offer guidelines for the gender-responsive investment in companies or private endeavours, but also for the purchase of bonds issued by State authorities. For instance, it proposes that public bond holders request that the borrowed funds are used as a priority for a) the creation of an action plan for gender equality; b) the implementation of international frameworks for gender equality, such as CEDAW[4] and the Beijing Declaration and Platform[5]; c) laws and policies with a transformative potential as to gender equality, related to infrastructure, agriculture, energy and financial services; and d) tools for the gender-responsive budget (ICMA, UN Women and IFC, 2021: 8–9).

The guide proposes that gender bonds issued by States establish, for instance, the following goals. In the area of so-called 'entrepreneurship', tools should be developed in the labour market that are specific to women entrepreneurs, which facilitate digital platforms so that women cooperatives can sell their production, and improve women's access to information in relation to potential financing sources. In terms of public hiring, the gender-based perspective should be developed in contracting companies of the State and a database in this respect should be created. In the area of decent jobs and leadership opportunities, initiatives to facilitate that women can advance in the fields of science, technology, engineering, and maths, for instance, through grant and internship programmes, should be developed.

It is worth highlighting that the guide also includes goals related to unpaid care and domestic work, proposing the establishment of goals as to investment in the care economy, including taking care of children and elder people. Also, salaries and other benefits for the workers of the care sector should be increased, who are mostly women and frequently the ones who receive the lowest salaries. Likewise, the goal is to develop and improve the use of disaggregated data by gender in relation to unpaid care work and domestic work.

Finally, the guide establishes goals related to gender violence: improve the knowledge and access to services that respond to and prevent violence against women, girls and dissidents; establish a comprehensive national system to report gender-violence cases; develop a strategy to ensure women's safety in transport and public spaces; and create channels in social media to inform citizens about their rights and procedures they should follow in cases of abuse (ICMA, UN Women and IFC, 2021: 13).

In short, and as was explained earlier, all the topics highlighted by ICMA, UN Women and IFC so as to leverage women and reduce gender inequalities are based on the agenda largely defined by feminist and women's movements in their interactions with the State. Except one that today is crucial and decisive for women's struggles for their personal and economic autonomy, both in developed nations and in emerging economies or less developed countries: sexual and reproductive rights. This topic, which is very sensitive and now fiercely contested by groups of the far right and social and religious conservatism, has been excluded from this roadmap that is taking women's demands from the domain of rights claimed from the State to the field of business investments. This exclusion delegitimizes an essential dimension of women's autonomy by ignoring their rights to decide about their sexuality and reproduction, which has immediate and long-range consequences in each aspect of their productive and reproductive lives. At the same time, it is revealing as to how priorities and goals are defined by the investors' logic when issuing gender bonds.

The aforementioned guide suggests that public issuers should use disaggregated indicators by gender at the time of reporting on the impact of bonds. Both quantitative and qualitative indicators may be used to reflect the improvement in the areas covered by the bonds that are analyzed here. While interested readers will be able to refer to the guide for more details, we would like to highlight here the key performance indicators that have been proposed to measure if and how much of the burden of unpaid care work and domestic work has been redistributed in the country: 1) the number of policies adopted to ensure that workplaces are family-friendly, that is, to subsidize the care economy (of children and elder people); 2) the number of high-quality and affordable care services for girls and elder people; and 3) the number of weeks of maternity and paternity leave (ICMA, UN Women and IFC, 2021: 9, 18–19).

As it was warned, in general terms, these credit guides do not focus on the results linked to the wellbeing of women or aspects connected to labour conditions or levels of unionization (Durano, 2022). Besides, it is clear that those bonds are thought to consider the idea of entrepreneurship, assumed as a straightforward demand of the women's movement, when in fact this vision of the labour world is strongly disputed by several social movements, particularly by critical feminist movements. Little by little, with the creation of those new instruments to promote financial gains on the pretext of reducing gender inequalities, the ambiguity and the elusiveness of what truly transforms the relations between men and women are magnified, as well as what can effectively contribute to the reduction of gender asymmetries.

Thus it can be stated that, from the very beginning, these initiatives try to erode the strength of women's movements with the promise of solutions that would only be assessed in accordance with their merits and effectiveness at the time of bond maturity. It seems like, in the name of pragmatism, new interest alliances are forged based on the logic and dynamics of expropriation, and not on rights and actual equality. The definition of what should be a priority so as to build a path towards gender equality and how to achieve those goals is now beyond the reach of social movements and their relationship with the State, and is then typified in financial contracts. As a result, the struggle for equality exits the arena of the dispute over the public budget and enters the balance sheets of financial institutions.

This virtual privatization of certain essential social goals, epitomized through the promotion of gender bonds, happens in a context of austerity policies, shrinkage of the fiscal space and social repression, as well as high tax evasion, all costs that defund the State and favour financial wealth accumulation without even generating returns for the real economy.

As was mentioned earlier, the stock market has accepted the idea of gender bonds with an unprecedented confidence. It is worth remembering that the first bonds of this class were issued in 2013, when the IFC presented the programme called 'Banking on Women Bonds' for US$268 million, whose goal was to promote the financing of entrepreneurial women by financial entities. This programme was later incorporated into the programme of social bonds of the IFC. In 2017, QBE Insurance Group of Australia was the first private bank to issue bonds targeted at investors who were willing to allocate their resources to companies with plans to reduce gender inequalities. In Latin America, the issue of bonds by banking entities, such as in Panama and Colombia, also happened (Almeida Sánchez, 2021).

As to State issuers, the Bank of the State of Chile issued three 'Woman Bonds' in international markets (the first one in 2016 and the last one in 2020), whose collection would be used to finance projects in the charge of women (in the context of the programme 'Grow Entrepreneurial Woman'). The National Development Bank of Trust Funds for Rural Development (Fideicomisos Instituidos en Relación con la Agricultura, FIRA) in Mexico issued 'gender bonds' in the Institutional Stock Market of that country, aimed at increasing the available financing for women's projects in rural areas.

3. Limitations, contradictions and problems of gender bonds

Despite the increasing issuance of social impact bonds and the generation of more and more financial incentives that tend to assetize a number of economic and social rights, gender equality has been to this date a minor component in the environmental, social and governance strategies, 'still a drop in the bucket of the impact investment industry' (AWID, 2023: 8): about US$5 billion for gender impact out of a total ranging US$630–US$715 billion for the overall impact investment heading. Considering the evidence, in the investor assessment, the expected returns from the inclusion of the gender-based perspective in the investments are not working as their capitalization does not meet the expectations. Therefore, there is a need to continue struggling even more for the valuation of gender bonds through a well-crafted and coordinated strategy among international organizations, financial institutions and national States with the growing support of women's groups co-opted by the neoliberal mindset. Again, Brazil serves as an example. At the beginning of 2023, the largest bank of the country, Itaú, also prominent in the field of private philanthropy, managed to collect BRL 2 billion (about US$400 million) in the market to strengthen women's entrepreneurship, especially in poor areas. This was the greatest issuance of social financial securities (LF) ever made in the country. The IFC, which belongs to the World Bank Group, contributed with 50 per cent of the total, showing a strategy of mutual support between big private finance and one of the most influential multilateral organizations responsible for promoting what Daniela Gabor (2021) called the 'Wall Street Consensus', in other words, 'to escort global (North) institutional investors and the managers of their trillions into development asset-classes' (p 1).

A year later, in January 2024, it is the Brazilian government's turn to launch a special bond exclusively for women. The aim is to bring women into the capital market, where they are still a minority (around 1/4 of all retail investors). The bond is sold by Banco do Brasil, the country's largest public bank. A minimum investment of R$35 per month (US$7) ensures a return based on annual inflation (well below the Selic prime rate) plus a percentage, yet to be defined and which will vary according to the maturity of the investment. This bond offers legal and psychological support in the event of domestic violence and also life insurance of R$15,000.00 (US$3,000). Children will be entitled to receive food parcels for 12 months in the event of the death of the insured mother (Cardoso, 2024).

It is not an investment with an interesting return, far from it. Its appealing nature may lie, maybe, in the fact that femicide rates have been rising in the country since 2015, when the Feminicide Law was enacted. In 2022 alone, out of a total of almost 4,000 intentional murders against women, 1,400 were registered as femicides, when the offense was committed because the victim was a woman. The number of rapes is also growing steadily, with almost 75,000 cases formally registered in 2022. Not to mention that, according to the same source (The Brazilian Public Security Yearbook, 2023), more than 50,000 women face some kind of violence every day in Brazil.

The most disturbing fact is that the government is putting the burden of preventing the consequences of gender-based violence on the backs of the poorest women, those on low incomes and with no assets, by encouraging them to take out a kind of insurance policy to guarantee that in case they suffer any kind of domestic violence they will be covered by their own efforts, thereby ensuring some immediate means of survival for their children.

It is bewildering to see a centre-left government promoting financial products that call into question its obligation to make the public defender's office work by offering free, quality protection to those who cannot afford paying for it. Moreover, poverty and deprivation continue to be addressed with basic food baskets, as if temporary and partial food relief were a satisfactory and sufficient compensatory measure for the dramatic and devastating experience of violence.

Given the gigantic scale of gender-based violence in Brazil, one can imagine that the demand for this 'unconventional' bond might reach a large number of women, enabling the financial system to further expand its sources of profit, with the State's blessing.

The complexity of the weighing of the financial risk that environmental, social and governance factors pose has been increasing. For instance, a series of 269 indicators related to those three factors has been taken, covering 67 countries in the 2015–20 period, and evidenced that credit risk follows (although in a differential manner, based on the level of countries' revenues) the evolution of environmental, social and governance metrics (Semet, Roncalli and Stagnol, 2021). More specifically, discrimination against women, evidenced for instance in the lower levels of empowerment, higher salary gaps and unemployment rates, compared to those of men, is related to lower returns of public bonds (Semet, Roncalli and Stagnol, 2021: 18–19). This means that social inclusion affects fiscal sustainability.

Even so, it should be considered what investors assume their main obligation with their clients is: to generate profits. Thus investors are interested in social bonds if they generate additional financial returns and if they operate under lower risks. In fact, statistics show that investors rarely reduce loan costs in instruments of sustainable debt (Affirmative Investment Management Partners Limited, 2021; UNDP, 2022).

In a lengthy report on the implications of the so-called 'Principles for Responsible Investment', made in 2021 by the Financial Initiative of the UN Environment Programme (UNEP) and the UN Global Compact (2021b), titled 'The environmental, social and governance engagement for sovereign debt investors', the social factors related to gender inequality and the situation of women are not even mentioned. This data makes us question the level of international consensus that there exists around the recognition of the link between public finance sustainability and social inclusion.

Besides, it has been noted that one of the problematic aspects of gender bonds is the relation that exists between international finances and the regulatory sovereignty of countries. The more public bonds are used for goals related to specific policies and reforms, the more intervention power investors would have in domestic policies (Lupo-Pasini, 2022). In other words, this form of private conditionality could transform investors into regulators (Park, 2018), although regulation precedes the issuance of a bond.

However, when we look closely at the contractual infrastructure of social bonds, including gender bonds, we note additional complexities that make us doubt not only the level of actual intervention of investors in domestic policies, but also the incentives that both investors and States that issue bonds have to achieve the goals that these financial instruments create.

If we focus not on the obligation to repay the loan but on the legal and financial consequences resulting from the noncompliance of the obligation to achieve the 'social goal' (the gender one in our case), whether it involves the performance of a specific and concrete project or the attainment of a metric related to a social indicator, it is obvious that this is not considered as a serious breach, an event similar to a default that justifies the termination of the contract. This means that, by maintaining the contract, greater incentives are created, pushing the issuing State to achieve the social goal previous set (Cheng, Ehlers and Packer, 2022: 54). In any case, such noncompliance is expected to increase the interest rate of the contract, but this is not key for the continuation of the agreement, despite the fact that they are precisely 'sustainable bonds'.

Issuing States do not have incentives to stipulate that not achieving the social goal results in default.[6] Governments are reluctant to accept higher levels of intervention on domestic policies and regulations, and the fulfilment of the goals contained in the bonds often implies engaging numerous public agencies (even the Congress), which leads to bureaucratic complexities and additional policies (Lupo-Pasini, 2022: 693–4).

The verification of the (non)compliance of the provisions that contain social goals, including those related to gender, is outsourced to private companies, which are the ones that eventually decide if they attach the 'sustainability' stamp to the bonds. This activity is virtually deregulated. These private verifiers intervene in the stage prior to the issuance of bonds so as to verify if they have been elaborated following the framework of sustainable bonds and then during the execution of the contract verifiers audit the reports that issuing States have to release periodically as to the attainment of the committed social goals.

As with risk rating agencies, verifying companies of sustainable bonds are subject to significant conflicts of interest (Lupo-Pasini, 2022: 693–4). The price of the service provided by those companies is paid by both parties of the transaction that are certainly interested in having the sustainability of the bond certified (Gaillard and Waibel, 2018).

Another significant challenge faced by the development of sovereign gender bonds comes from not only the lack of recognition and expertise, but also the deliberate disregard of the financial sector (private investors of any type, risk rating agencies, ministries of finances, central banks) for the feminist economy and the gender-based perspective when thinking about the origins of discrimination against women and which projects and policies should be financed to effectively fight against it.

Ultimately, and as it was recently explained, 'The ecosystem supporting sustainable bonds is built only to increase the cosmetic appeal of those instruments to retail investors but with minimal prospect of promoting any real sustainability change' (Lupo-Pasini, 2022: 682).

4. (Concerning) conclusions

From a historical perspective, gender bonds can be deemed as the most recent invention of financial capitalism, and they can be placed in the progression that started with the dismantling of the welfare state and the debt crisis at the end of the 1970s and the beginning of the 1980s, continued with the privatization of public services, structural reforms and a higher commercialization of economic and social rights, the Washington Consensus, adjustment plans and other delicatessen of the economic orthodoxy, the Wall Street Consensus and the assetization of the world, which tries to put a price on and obtain financial gains from everything, including the demands of feminist movements.

When we put gender bonds under a microscope, as to their contractual infrastructure, we can argue that there is no actual incentive either in institutional investors or in the States that issue gender bonds to effectively implement changes at the level of domestic policies to achieve higher social inclusion through the reduction of gender inequalities. The 'gender' label seems to be more a 'pink wash' strategy designed to attract investors interested in supporting (or pretending to support) noble causes, but without much reflection (or transformative action) about the origin of gender structural inequalities and the policies mostly recommended by feminist scholars and the civil society to promote women's rights in an effective way and without being subordinated to claims and financial interests.

In the context of promoting 'good' finances as a solution to all contemporary challenges, women's struggles to revert the patriarchy's control on power structural relations in capitalist societies is actually being used to create more financial wealth, outside the real economy, and even more in the hands of huge asset management funds. Thus interest-bearing capital invades another dimension of the social reproduction sphere, basically the social battlefield for agency and collective power in society. With the same idea, it instrumentalizes the positive agenda of gender equality, making the logic of capital valuation prevail over the logic of the values of freedom, solidarity, autonomy and human rights. It is important to draw attention to the existence of a disguised conflict where 'valuation' is opposed to 'values': the valuation of capital through the capitalization of equality claims, now transformed into assets, thus ensuring future income resulting from the ownership of securities expropriates and reshapes feminist values, and bundles them to global debt markets. Because emancipatory dynamics have now been rooted in indebtedness and dependency, the very essence of the meaning of living a life free of restrictions and oppression no longer makes any sense (Honneth, 2014).

The mandates of international human rights law, which require States to protect particularly those groups exposed to higher social vulnerability, move the maximum available resources to ensure the fulfilment of economic, social and cultural rights for all, and ensure the enforcement of the prohibition to discriminate based on gender, are sacrificed in the financial jungle. In turn, this phenomenon of assetization of gender policies deeply compels issues related to democracy as the determination of the goals and the means to fully attain the fulfilling of women's rights is no longer subject to public and democratic debates between the State and interested persons and groups (including social movements), but now exclusively depends on valuation and market decisions.

Finally, similar to what happened with public–private Partnerships (PPP), gender bonds carry a heavy political-cultural cost as they consolidate the idea that interventions that tend to reduce gender inequalities are only legitimate if they generate financial returns; States tend to reproduce this logic when determining their budget priorities. This is one more brick on the neoliberal wall.

Acknowledgements

The authors thank Flavio Gaitán, Leda Paulani, Luiz Macahyba, and Corina Rodríguez-Enríquez for their critical feedback to the drafts of this work.

Notes

[1] In accordance with Greer, this indicates 'a set of assets that bear some fundamental economic similarities to each other, and that have characteristics that make them distinct from other assets that are not part of that class' (1997: 86).

[2] Drawing on Karl Marx´s concept of fictitious capital (third volume of *Das Kapital*), French economist Cédric Durand summarizes the concept as 'an incarnation of [a form of] capital which tends to free itself from the process of valorisation-through-production. ... Capital is fictitious to the extent that it circulates without production yet being realised, representing a claim on a future real valorisation process.' (2017: 57). Therefore, fictitious capital contrasts with the notion of real capital (invested in the real economy) as long as it relates to the phenomenon of capitalization of ownership. It is worth remembering the forms of fictitious capital: public debt, bank credit and company shares and bonds.

[3] See, for instance, the green bonds issued in 2019 by the City of Minneapolis to build an ecological centre of public services, which required that at least 20 per cent of employed persons were women and 32 per cent minorities. Specifics of the bond issue available at https://www.icmagroup.org/Emails/icma-vcards/Minneapolis_External%20Review%20 Report.pdf

[4] The Committee on the Elimination of Discrimination against Women (CEDAW) is the body of independent experts that monitors the application of the Convention on the Elimination of All Forms of Discrimination against Women.

[5] It was a resolution adopted by the United Nations (UN) in the Fourth World Conference on Women, carried out in Beijing in 1995. This declaration presents 12 critical areas that

create obstacles for gender equality and identifies the measures governments, international agencies and the social society should adopt to promote the autonomy and human rights of women and minorities.

[6] Not achieving the social goal set forth in the bond first should cause its anticipated settlement, in other words, the State should 'repay' the debt with the investors.

References

Adkins, L.; Cooper, M. and Konings, M. (2020) *The Asset Economy. Property Ownership and the New Logic of Inequality,* Cambridge: Polity Press.

Affirmative Investment Management Partners Limited (2021), 'Greenium—Fact or Fiction?', [online] 4 May, Available from: https://affirmativeim.com/greenium-fact-or-fiction/

Almeida Sánchez, M.D. (2021) 'La política fiscal con enfoque de género en países de América Latina', Serie Macroeconomía del Desarrollo, No 217, ECLAC.

AWID (2023) 'Gender impact investing & the rise of false solutions. An analysis for feminist movements', AWID.org January.

Birch, K. and Muniesa, F. (2020) 'Introduction', in K. Birch and F. Muniesa (eds), *Assetization: Turning Things into Assets in Technoscientific Capitalism,* Cambridge, MA: The MIT Press, pp 1–41.

BIS (2022) 'Challenges and new options', *BIS Quarterly Review,* No 47.

Bloomberg Intelligence (2021) 'ESG assets may hit $53 trillion by 2025, a third of global AUM', 23 February.

Bolsa de Brasil (2021) 'B3 lança título sustentável de US$ 700 mi atrelado a metas de diversidade', [online] 16 September, Available from: https://www.b3.com.br/pt_br/noticias/b3-lanca-titulo-sustentavel-atrelado-a-metas-de-diversidade.htm

Braun, B. and Koddenbrock, K. (eds) (2023) *Capital Claims: Power and Global Finance,* London: Routledge.

Cardoso, L. (2024) 'Tesouro lança título exclusivo para mulheres', *O Globo,* 17 January, p 12.

Cheng, G.; Ehlers, T. And Packer, F. (2022) 'Sovereigns and sustainable bonds: challenges and new options', *BIS Quarterly Review* 47(September), pp 1–10.

Durand, C. (2017) *Fictitious Capital. How Finance is Appropriating Our Future,* New York: Verso Books.

Durano, M. (2022) 'Injuring the care economy with private finance', Social Watch [online] 26 September, Available from: https://www.socialwatch.org/node/18673

European Commission (2018) 'The European Commission's Action Plan on Financing Sustainable Growth' (COM(2018) 97), [online], Available from: https://www.greenfinanceplatform.org/policies-and-regulations/european-commissions-action-plan-financing-sustainable-growth

Fine, B. (2020) 'The value of financialization and the financialization of value', in P. Mader, D. Mertens and N. Van der Swan (eds), *The Routledge International Handbook of Financialization,* Abington/New York: Routledge, pp 19–30.

Gabor, D. (2021) 'The Wall Street consensus', *Development and Change* 0(0): 1–31.

Gaillard, N. and Waibel, M. (2018) 'The Icarus syndrome: How credit rating agencies lost their quasi-immunity', *Southern Methodist University Law Review*, 71(4): 1077.

Greer, R.J. (1997) 'What is an asset-class, anyway?', *Journal of Portfolio Management*, 23(2): 86–91.

Honneth, A. (2014) *El derecho de la libertad: esbozo de una eticidad democrática*, Buenos Aires: Katz.

ICMA (2022) 'Social Bond Principles', [online], Available from: https://www.icmagroup.org/sustainable-finance/the-principles-guidelines-and-handbooks/social-bond-principles-sbp/

ICMA, UN Women and IFC (2021) 'Bonds to bridge the gender gap: A practitioner's guide to using sustainable debt for gender equality', ReliefWeb [online] 16 November, Available from: https://reliefweb.int/report/world/bonds-bridge-gender-gap-practitioner-s-guide-using-sustainable-debt-gender-equality

IMF (2019) 'Sustainable finance', in *Global Financial Stability Report: Lower for Longer.*

Inderst, G. and Stewart, F. (2018) *Incorporating Environmental, Social and Governance (ESG) Factors into Fixed Income Investment,* Washington, DC: World Bank, [online], Available from: https://documents1.worldbank.org/curated/en/913961524150628959/pdf/Incorporating-environmental-social-and-governance-factors-into-fixed-income-investment.pdf

International Regulatory Strategy Group (2021) 'Accelerating the S in ESG – A roadmap for global progress on social standards', [online] June, Available from: https://www.irsg.co.uk/assets/Reports/AA_IRSG_S_ROADMAP_008.pdf

Langley, P. (2020) 'Assets and assetization in financialized capitalism', *Review of International Political Economy*, 28(2): 382–93.

Lupo-Pasini, F. (2022) 'Sustainable finance and sovereign debt: The illusion to govern by contract', *Journal of International Economic Law*, 25(4): 680–98.

Moore, P. (2022) 'Greenium set to stay, say sovereign debt issuers", Official Monetary and Financial Institution Forum [online] 7 February, Available from: https://www.omfif.org/2022/02/greenium-set-to-stay-say-sovereign-debt-issuers/

Muniesa F.; Doganova L. and Ortiz H. (2017) *Capitalization: A Cultural Guide*, París: Presses des Mines.

Noel-Vaeza, M. (2021), "Por qué hay que invertir en mujeres, hoy más que nunca", UN Women Latin America and the Caribbean, at https://lac.unwomen.org/es/noticias-y-eventos/articulos/2021/03/op-eds---por-que-hay-que-invertir-en-las-mujeres-8m

Núñez, G.; Velloso, H. and Da Silva, F. (2022) 'Corporate governance in Latin America and the Caribbean. Using ESG debt instruments to finance sustainable investment projects', *Project Documents* (LC/TS.2022/23), ECLAC [online] March, Available from: https://www.cepal.org/en/publications/47778-corporate-governance-latin-america-and-caribbean-using-esg-debt-instruments

Park, S. (2018) 'Investors as regulators: Green bonds and the governance challenges of the sustainable finance revolution', *Stanford Journal of International Law*, 54: 1.

Pistor, K. (2019) *The Code of Capital: How the Law Creates Wealth and Inequality*, Princeton: Princeton University Press.

Semet, R; Roncalli, T. and Stagnol, L. (2021) 'ESG and sovereign risk. What is priced in by the bond market and credit rating agencies?', [online] October, Available from: http://www.thierry-roncalli.com/download/WP_Sovereign_ESG.pdf

Sklair, J. (2022) *Brazilian Elites and their Philanthropy. Wealth at the Service of Developmen* t, New York: Routledge.

Sustainable Stock Exchange Initiative (2022) 'How exchanges can advance gender equality – Updated guidance and best practice', Sustainable Stock Exchanges (SSE) and IFC [online], Available from: https://sseinitiative.org/publication/how-exchanges-can-advance-gender-equality-updated-guidance-and-best-practice/

Sustainable Stock Exchange Initiative (2023) 'ESG Disclosure Guidance Database', periodically updated and available from: https://sseinitiative.org/esg-guidance-database/

UNDP (2022) 'Identifying the greenium', UNDP Blog [online] 25 April, Available from: https://www.undp.org/blog/identifying-greenium

UNEP and Global Compact (2021a) 'Why and how investors should act on human rights', Principles for Responsible Investment [online], Available from: https://www.unpri.org/download?ac=11953

UNEP and Global Compact (2021b) 'ESG engagement for sovereign debt investors', Available from: https://www.unpri.org/sovereign-debt/esg-engagement-for-sovereign-debt-investors/6687.article

Vaeza, M-N. (2021) 'Por qué hay que invertir en mujeres, hoy más que nunca', UN Women Latin America and the Caribbean [online] 8 March, Available from: https://lac.unwomen.org/es/noticias-y-eventos/articulos/2021/03/op-eds---por-que-hay-que-invertir-en-las-mujeres-8m

Williams, J. (2020) 'Recidivists, rough sleepers, and the unemployed as financial assets: Social impact bonds and the creation of new markets in social services', in K. Birch and F. Muniesa (eds), *Assetization: Turning Things into Assets in Technoscientific Capitalism,* Cambridge: The MIT Press, pp 287–318.

20

Institutionalization of the Gender Approach in Public Finances: How to Strengthen – Rather than Dilute – Feminist Demands?

Magalí Brosio and Mariana Rulli

1. Introduction

The institutionality of gender consists of a network of international commitments, laws, mechanisms, institutions, actors and persons that have managed to make visible and institutionalize the demands related to gender inequality in society and the State (Guzmán, 2001; Guzmán and Montaño, 2012). In the last four decades, the institutionalization of gender in the State (in all its levels) has involved the crystallization of a series of political and technical processes that have not been univocal. On the contrary, it has been a dynamic process affected by economic, social and cultural changes at both internal and international levels that, driven by the demands of the feminist and LGTBIQ+ movements, has enabled the design of public policies aimed at ensuring the rights of women and LGTBIQ+ people. All of this journey can be observed in the different advances of public policies that have been implemented throughout this period: from the policies for women and those of affirmative action in the 1980s and 1990s to the development and incorporation of a gender approach, and more recently to the policies aimed at gender mainstreaming.

The main advances have involved the enactment of international and national regulations aimed to fight gender-based violence, guarantee sexual and reproductive health and rights, promote the political participation of women, expand the rights of LGTBIQ+ people and create mechanisms for the advancement of women, among others. In turn, in recent years, policies have increasingly started to address economic inequalities, such as: those aimed at the recognition of the unequal distribution of unpaid domestic and care work, and its measurement through time use surveys, as well as income transfers, the reforms of care leave (such as maternity leave), the creation of national comprehensive care systems and the recognition for women of years of retirement/pensions contributions for each child.

At the same time, and in parallel with the advances in gender institutionality in the States, there have also been changes in a similar direction in both international organizations and international financial institutions (IFIs) that have shown an increasing interest in applying a gender approach to their work and formalizing it. Thus, discussions on gender inequality are no longer restricted to world conferences on women organized by the United Nations (UN), but they are increasingly common topics in the Davos Economic Forum[1] and in the Annual Meetings of the International Monetary Fund (IMF) and the World Bank (WB).[2]

However, when analyzing these phenomena through the theoretical guidelines of feminist economics, it becomes evident that gender equality advances both at national and supranational levels have found significant limits in the economic realm, especially in the policies related to public finances in general and sovereign indebtedness in particular. In this context, this chapter has a twofold objective. On the one hand, to identify the scarce and insufficient advances in the institutionality of gender in the States of Latin America[3] in the field of public finances and sovereign debt. Through this exercise, we offer a critical reflection that contributes to identifying the barriers that have limited these initiatives and understanding why these obstacles have been more difficult to avoid in certain areas, such as the case of debt. On the other hand, to analyze how, why and with which effects the IMF has been including in its agenda and its organizational structure a (self-proclaimed) gender perspective, and to consider what potential effects this may have on the processes at a national level that were previously identified.

The chapter is divided into four parts. In the second section, we analyze the advances in gender-based institutionality in the public finances of Latin American States. In the third section, we focus on the experience of institutionalization with a gender perspective in the IMF. In the fourth section, we reflect on the main findings from the previous analyses with the goal of contributing to understanding the reason for the proliferation of instrumentalist strategies promoted by moderate feminism at a State level and in the IFIs, as well as the existing limits to the development of truly transformative approaches. Lastly, we offer proposals to advance and deepen the gender-based institutionality in the field of public finances and more specifically regarding sovereign debt.

2. Institutionalization of the gender perspective in public finances in Latin America

In this section, we analyze the advances in the gender-based institutionality in the public finances of the Latin American States considering the following pillars: the institutionalization of the Mechanisms for the Advancement of Women and the creation of gender areas and policies in State economic and financial agencies (for example, Ministries of Economy and Finance, Central Banks and the participation of women in the decision making of these agencies); the implementation of gender-responsive public budgets and their degree of formalization; and the institutional design and the core characteristics of both the tax systems and the sovereign debt management in the region.

The institutionalization of the Mechanisms for the Advancement of Women and in State economic and financial agencies

Since the 1980s, institutional mechanisms aiming to guide and coordinate the policies of gender equality in the States with different degrees of hierarchy and institutionality started to emerge in Latin America. These mechanisms, known as the Mechanisms for the Advancement of Women (MAW), were promoted through a number of regulatory frameworks, as well as recommendations and agreements among States. In accordance with the United Nations Economic Commission for Latin America and the Caribbean (ECLAC) Gender Equality Observatory, today, 60 per cent of Latin American countries have high-level MAW (that is, they have the institutional status of ministry or their head holds the position of minister with full participation in the cabinet), while in the Caribbean, 83.3 per cent of countries still have a low level of institutionalization (that is, they depend on a ministry or an authority with a lower rank, such as vice-ministers, institutes, councils and other institutional forms). In the case of the countries under study, most of them (six) have a high level of MAW (Argentina, Brazil, Chile, Costa Rica, Mexico and Dominican Republic), two of them have a medium level (Ecuador and Guatemala), and the Bolivian case has a low-level MAW.[4]

However, the situation of gender-based institutionality in public finances presents a more complex picture. First, regarding the existence of specific gender-based areas within the Ministries of Economy and/or Finance, it is worth noting that six of the countries of the study do not have any kind of institutionality related to gender issues (Bolivia, Brazil, Chile, Costa Rica, Dominican Republic and Mexico[5]). In the other three cases, gender-based areas were created in the framework of the Ministries of Economy and Finance: in Argentina, the National Office of Economy, Equality and Gender under the purview of the Ministry of Economy was created in 2019

313

with the goal of analyzing and planning public policies to reduce gender inequality gaps in the economy. In turn, Ecuador has a National Office of Fiscal Equality within the Undersecretariat of Fiscal Policy of the Vice-Ministry of Finances of the Ministry of Economy. In Guatemala, the area of Gender, Indigenous People and Disabled Persons was created, under the Ministry of Economy.

Second, it is also worth noting that, to date, except for the Undersecretariat of Economy in Mexico and the Ministry of National Planning and Economic Policy of Costa Rica, all high hierarchy agencies in the area of economy and finances of the countries under study are in the charge of men.

Third, national central banks are agencies tasked with the design and implementation of monetary, exchange rate, credit, financial policies and, specifically, price control and inflation measures. As a consequence, despite the fact that this issue has been hardly studied in the literature and the public agenda, the policies carried out by these agencies have a potential impact on the human rights of women. In the case of central banks of the nine countries under study,[6] in eight of them, the main authorities are men and only in the case of Mexico is the main authority of the central bank (governor) a woman, and the government board is gender-balanced. The analysis of the bank organizational charts shows that in none of these cases are there formal gender units in place. Moreover, none of the strategic goals, missions and plans of central banks analyzed contain specific references to a gender perspective.

Finally, it is worth mentioning that, even in the few examples where gender-based agencies and institutions are being created with the aim of working in public finance issues, they have had scarce decision-making power on the guidelines of the macroeconomic policy at a national level, their responsibilities being mainly limited to some specific issues.

The institutionalization of gender-responsive budgets: advances and unfinished issues

From the expenditure perspective, the public budget is the main instrument of fiscal policy. The distribution of resources affects different social groups in an unequal way, including men and women, as well as LGBTIQ+ people, due to preexisting structural socioeconomic inequalities. Therefore, the initiatives of gender-responsive budgets may contribute to the elimination of these gaps, ensuring that public funds are collected and spent in a more effective way, and they can contribute to guarantee the achievement of gender-equality goals, as well as improve the compliance with current international regulations (Elson, 2008).

The implementation of gender-responsive budgets (GRB) is still the most developed and institutionalized strategy of a gender-responsive economic and fiscal policy today. In the mid-1980s, budget analyses from a gender perspective started to be implemented in Australia and, since then, these initiatives have been growing and proliferating in all the regions of the world, today reaching more than 80 countries at different levels of the State. However, there are still only a few countries with such a degree of institutionalization and implementation that covers the whole budget cycle, as well as the identification of the 'transformative gender needs' to be met using fiscal policies. Moreover, the different realities in which these initiatives have been developed have created a wide range of models that cover the methodologies used, the participating agents and the goals pursued through their implementation (Jubeto, 2008).

The institutionalization of GRB, driven by feminist movements, has taken different forms. On the one hand, through different international instruments, and, on the other hand, in some countries, they have been included as mandates in the legal frameworks that regulate the budget process (Almeida, 2021). At the international level, this process began with the Charter of the UN of 1945, and gained momentum through the International Conferences of Women promoted by this organization since 1975, creating guiding instruments for its member states (Jubeto, 2008). Specifically, the Convention on the Elimination of All Forms of Discrimination against Women (CEDAW) sets forth that member states shall take all appropriate measures in the economic area to ensure the full development and advancement of women (United Nations, 1979). Although the CEDAW does not have specific provisions on budgets, the Committee on the Elimination of Discrimination against Women, which monitors its implementation, has issued Concluding Observations and Recommendations in which it suggests that budget policies and processes should be gender responsive and consider the principles and criteria of the Convention (Elson and United Nations Development for Women, 2006). At the regional level, in the context of the last Regional Conferences on Women in Latin America and the Caribbean,[7] agreements among the States have been established to ensure enough resources in order to implement equality policies and commitments related to fiscal issues and gender-responsive countercyclical fiscal policies (Almeida, 2021).

At a national level, in Latin America and the Caribbean, the degree of institutionality and regulatory commitment of the different countries regarding gender-responsive budgeting varies (see Table 20.1 in the Appendix): from the political will of some governments (Argentina) to its formalization in the constitution (as in the case of the Plurinational State of Bolivia, where it is also established in the Framework Law of Autonomy and Decentralization, which includes its enforcement in territorial entities), or at the level of national laws that govern the budget process (Ecuador, Guatemala and Mexico). However, in all these cases, the labelling system[8] is restricted to (some) expenses without establishing a comprehensive analysis or considerations on the impact on fiscal revenues.

Concerning instruments, there are also a wide range: some countries establish the obligation to introduce the gender perspective in the planning exercise (Ecuador and Guatemala); others include it in the development of budget programmes and projects (Bolivia); budget categories or classifiers are also included (Bolivia and Guatemala), as well as the obligation to allocate specific budget percentages (Bolivia), the creation of specific gender appendixes (Ecuador) and the prohibition to modify the allocated budgets at the time of execution (Mexico) (Almeida, 2021). In the case of the countries under study that still do not have legal mandates, there exist different initiatives that, in some cases, are recent (such as in the case of Argentina and the Dominican Republic); in others, its sustainability in time has not been guaranteed, such as in Brazil or Chile, where the gender-responsive budget is only made in some programmes of the government (see Table 20.2 in the Appendix).

In addition to the legal mandates and the GRB initiatives, there are other types of policies linked to public finances in the region that include gender budget institutional programmes, labellers or classifiers, gender-based public purchases and the development of follow-up, assessment and accountability reports. Classifiers enable the quantification of the proportion of public expenditure in terms of gender, which later makes it possible to see advances or setbacks; hence the importance of institutionalization. In Argentina, in 2019, gender expenditure represented 3.8 per cent of the total budget and 0.9 per cent of the Gross Domestic Product (GDP). In Ecuador (2016), it represented 2 per cent of the budget and 0.6 per cent of the GDP; in Guatemala (2020), 6.4 per cent and 0.9 per cent, respectively. Finally, in Mexico (2020) the expenditure percentage in terms of gender involved 1.6 per cent of the total budget and 0.3 per cent of the GDP (Almeida, 2021).

Despite the fact that the institutionalization of a gender perspective in public finances – especially through the formalization of GRB initiatives – represents an extremely valuable step forward, it is important to recognize that this has not necessarily been translated into an automatic increase of the budget resources allocated to policies that contribute to gender equality. In many cases, for example, experts on GRB do not have enough power to modify budgets as they are top-tier political tools that are very difficult to influence for those who are not in the highest positions. This is particularly true in the countries of the Global South, where bilateral donors and the IFIs are often the ones with the greatest decision-making power in terms of budget (Elson, 2021).

At the same time, the implementation of GRB led to feminist critiques that suggest that quantification depoliticizes and domesticates feminism, translating political demands into technocratic management (Budgeon,

2011) and, therefore, neoliberalizes the agendas of the feminist movement, or what Nancy Fraser has called 'corporate feminism', the pinkwashing that has legitimized strategies of progressive neoliberalism. However, it is important to mention that quantification contributed to the visibilization and massification of key demands of the feminist movement, providing political legitimacy and entering into the institutional and governmental agendas: the gender pay-gap analysis and the quantification of (paid and unpaid) work time have been key examples of that.[9]

Elson (2021) states that two core challenges need to be addressed in order to release the transformative potential of GRB. The first one is to guarantee that the gender analysis enters the budget as a whole and it does not focus only on those expenses explicitly aimed at gender equality. Even though many countries have made significant advances in this field, still there is a lot to be done. In particular, it is worth highlighting that most of the gender-responsive analysis has focused essentially on predicted expenses, but, as will be discussed in the following section, estimated revenues and the source of these resources have received significantly less attention. The second challenge is to consider the underlying macroeconomy in the budget. Feminist economists have shown again and again the negative impacts of the measures linked to the globalization of trade, investment and finances, as well as the reduction of the resulting fiscal space, on women, especially when they are combined with austerity measures that, despite their reputation, are still in vogue, as will be discussed later.

The gender-based institutionality in tax systems

The tax system is the main fiscal instrument that States have to guarantee the fulfilment of human rights and to deal with the structural income inequality that has characterized this region for decades, including in particular gender income inequality. In other words, financing, through tax collection, is an enabling condition to mobilize the maximum available resources in order to reach gender equality. However, with their nuances, the institutional characteristics of the tax systems of most countries of the region have a strong regressive component, and, therefore, (implicit and explicit) gender biases that causes a negative impact on the human rights of women. Consequently, these structural institutional characteristics of the tax systems of the region cause those tax systems to be producers and reproducers of inequalities. About 50 per cent of the total tax collection of the countries of the Latin American and Caribbean region is based on indirect taxes so that the burden falls disproportionately on the persons with less contributory capacity, especially affecting women who live in poverty.

Furthermore, abusive tax practices of companies and the limited monitoring capacity of the States have a decisive impact on the collection of fiscal resources and, through this, on the protection of human rights, including the prohibition to discriminate for gender reasons. In accordance with ECLAC (2019), tax evasion and avoidance continue to be one of the main obstacles to mobilize internal resources to finance the 2030 Sustainable Development Agenda in the region. The most recent estimates show that tax evasion reaches an amount equal to 2.2 per cent of the GDP in the case of the value-added tax (VAT) and 4.1 per cent of the GDP in the case of the income tax, an amount equal to US$335,000 million (ECLAC, 2019: 7). Hence, evasion and avoidance are even worse in the case of the income tax that is levied on active taxpayers with a higher contributory capacity, which again shows the need to address this issue considering the principle of progressivity.

Gender-based institutionality in the management of sovereign debt

In accordance with the WB, 60 per cent of low-income countries today (end of 2022) are in a situation of debt distress or close to being in such situation (World Bank, 2022). Despite recognizing this complex context, IFIs have continued to require – even during the pandemic – the implementation of orthodox economic measures (Ortiz and Cummins, 2022) with the well-known negative effects on the rights of women.

In spite of the fact that the negative impact of debt distress and the conditionalities required by IFIs on women's human rights has been widely shown (Experto Independiente, 2019),[10] and that from a human rights perspective it has been argued that both States and IFIs have obligations in this field, the development of gender-based institutionality and the transversality advance in the areas of decision making related to public debt management have been very scarce or non-existent.

Despite the academic and legal developments in the field and the contributions of social activism, virtually no public policies have been implemented aimed at assessing the sustainability of public debt, as well as the conditionalities of the loans from a human rights approach, that includes a feminist perspective as a central component with the goal of foreseeing potential negative impacts on the rights of women in order to avoid, correct, mitigate or compensate them, as necessary. For instance, two core aspects that should be monitored in any indebtedness process are how requested funds will be used (and to what extent those additional funds will contribute to closing gender gaps) and how the resources to repay the debt will be obtained (and again, who specifically will shoulder the impact of this burden).

The lack of advances in this field is to some extent explained by the fact that carrying out a feminist analysis of debt requires acknowledging the need for a radical reform of the way in which the economic policy is conceptualized in States and IFIs, as well as a review of their roles, duties and responsibilities.

In the next section, these structural barriers will be discussed in more detail through the study of the IMF case and its recently adopted gender strategy.

3. The institutionalization of the gender perspective in IFIs

In parallel with the advances in gender-based institutionality in public finances at a national State level, there have also been changes in the same direction in the IFIs. In this section, we propose to report on how this process has taken place, particularly in the IMF, and what its approach has been regarding gender budgeting. Recognizing the substantial importance that this agency has on macroeconomic decisions in the Southern region, and understanding the way in which it conceptualizes the gender-based approach to fiscal policy, is crucial for understanding how it can have an impact on the ability to face the pending challenges at a national level discussed in the previous section.

The interest in addressing gender issues is not new among IFIs. In particular, the WB has paid attention to the unequal impact of development policies on women since at least the 1970s, although this issue has become even much more prominent since 1995. While the WB claims to have made 'important efforts and substantial progress' since the implementation of its first gender-based strategy in 2001 (World Bank Group, 2015: 29), scholars and civil society organizations have qualified these assessments, concluding that the approach has been partial – as it has not contributed to review the economic orientation of the agency and the type of polices it promotes (Berik, 2017) – and instrumental because the value of gender equality is determined by its alleged ability to contribute to economic growth (Chant, 2012).

The institutionalization of the gender perspective in the IMF

For their part, the IMF has only started to venture into these matters in the last decade. The changes began from within the organization. On the one hand, more women were appointed to leadership roles: apart from the fact that the last two persons who chaired the institution (in the role of managing director) have been women, 34 per cent of leading positions and 40 per cent of department leadership positions are currently in the charge of women (IMF, 2022).[11] On the other hand, specific roles have been created within the institutional machinery to address gender issues, with a progressive increase of human resources for this purpose (see Table 20.1). Additionally, these efforts (mainly focused on incorporating personnel to the existing departments) will in time be supplemented with the creation of a specific unit[12] in charge of centralizing this work within the institution.[13]

Table 20.1: Projection of resources allocated (in number of persons full-time employed) to gender issues within the IMF (2021–24)

	Fiscal year			
	2021	**2022**	**2023**	**2024**
Area departments	4.2	6.3	8.1	8.1
Functional departments, except SPR	4.9	9.4	9.9	9.9
SPR	1.7	2.0	4.0	6.0
All the departments	10.8	17.7	19.5	19.5

Note: SPR refers to the Strategy, Policy and Review Department. The formalization of a core gender unit is expected to take place within this department.

Source: Own elaboration based on International Monetary Fund, 2022

In July 2022, the IMF Executive Board approved the first strategy for the mainstreaming of a gender approach in the institution. The adoption of this strategy is a historical milestone as it implies the explicit recognition not only of the link between gender gaps and the economy, but also the consequences it has for the work of the IMF. Particularly, this proposed strategy aims to mainstream the gender approach into the main activities of the institution: surveillance, lending and capacity building. However, this does not involve a formal expansion of the IMF mandate as the matters related to gender inequality will only be considered in so far as they are 'macrocritical'.[14]

It is worth highlighting that the process to create such a strategy took place mainly within the IMF, with scarce opportunities for civil society to substantially contribute to its development. The consultation spaces were limited and notified with short notice, which hindered the participation of Global South organizations, which are in turn those that work more directly with the population groups that are more likely to be impacted by such a strategy. Even though this does not represent a complete departure from the common practice of the IMF, whose coordination with civil society has been infrequent and often superficial (Action Aid International et al, 2022), it becomes more relevant as the institution itself recognizes its limited expertise in this matter.

In this context, and considering the limited changes that the IFIs have made after announcing their intention to move away from their traditional orthodox stances (Berik, 2017; Oxfam, 2017), it is no surprise that the news of the adoption of such a strategy has been received with concern and even refusal by activists and scholars in the field of feminist economics (Latindadd, 2022). Notwithstanding the specific criticisms that one may pose to the proposed strategy,[15] the big elephant in the room is whether a gender perspective is compatible at all with the theory of change of the IMF and the resulting conditionalities.

In particular, from feminist economics it has been shown that austerity measures – which still have a central place in the IMF's lending agreements[16] – as well as the economic model proposed by this institution – based on the extractivism of natural resources and the exploitation of low-cost workforces – disproportionately and negatively impact women, exacerbating preexisting gender gaps.[17]

The IMF approach to gender-responsive budgets: one step forward, two steps backwards

In this context, a very specific concern arising from the implementation of the IMF gender strategy is how it will impact on the several processes of institutionalization of the gender perspective in public finances in the regions where this credit agency has high levels of influence, as in most countries of Latin America.

In this respect, as we have previously explained, in the region there have been some advances, albeit limited ones. Thus, the question that arises is whether the adoption of a gender-based strategy by the IMF will contribute to support them or, on the contrary, will limit even more their transformative potential. Likewise, it is not clear if the IMF is willing to review its own actions under this same lens and discuss the gender impacts of its own lending policy at a national level. Although it is too soon to provide a final answer to this question, the case of GRB may show some valuable insights to reflect upon.

In 2017, the IMF carried out an assessment of GRB initiatives in G7 countries. Later on, and based on the findings of this research, it developed its own approach to the elaboration of GRB, promoting the 'the holistic integration of a gender perspective across each phase of the budget cycle through gender-responsive fiscal policies and gender-specific practices of public financial administration' (Alonso-Albarran et al, 2021).

In turn, and using this framework as the basis, the IMF developed a survey to collect information on how different governments implement practices of gender-responsive budgeting. An interesting aspect of this survey is that it mainly addresses formal aspects as to how GRB is implemented at a national level, for instance, if there is a legal framework in place, or if the government collects and releases disaggregated fiscal statistics (Alonso-Albarran et al, 2021). Absent from the survey are more substantial questions, such as if a minimum percentage of the budget or GDP exists that the government must commit to allocate to measures aimed at gender equality, or if a commitment exists with a progressive increase of the resources allocated to these type of policies. In this way, the IMF contributes to a formalist understanding of the tool that at the same time limits its transformative potential.

In this respect, Elson (2021) suggests that GRB analyses need to show how certain economic policies exacerbate gender inequalities in order to be truly transformative (and in line with the proposals from feminist economics), but she recognizes that this is not the type of analysis that most governments nor the IMF are interested in doing. This conclusion is in line with the findings of the previous section regarding the type of policies that the IMF continues to promote – or even impose – in indebted countries.

Thus, it is clear that the IMF (as many governments) has interpreted and implemented the GRB tool in an instrumentalist way that significantly limits its transformative potential. Improving available tools and data are necessary steps, but they are certainly not enough to transform reality (Elson, 2021). These matters become crucial in a context in which the IMF tries to make its way to the field of gender and the economy, deploying its internal line on the countries where it has high levels of influence.

4. Conclusions and work agenda

The creation and hierarchization of State gender units, together with the advances and the increase of women's participation in public decisions (especially in parliaments, and more slowly in the executive branches) during the last four decades have impacted the design of gender-responsive public policies in several key areas in the field of women's autonomy. Yet, despite these advances, this chapter has evidenced that there are still important limitations in the way institutionalization and gender mainstreaming have been implemented, both at national and international levels, in public finances.

As has been analyzed, the process of institutionalization of the gender perspective has not been univocal nor linear, let alone regarding the demands that have been permeating into the governmental agendas. In this process, fiscal and financial matters, like the ones related to the sovereign debt, have been left out despite the fact that they have in recent years been increasingly pushed forward and made visible by feminist movements and scholars (Cavallero and Gago, 2019). Feminists have correctly suggested that debt is not a technical matter, but a political and systemic one as it consolidates a direction of the economic policy that is harmful for the human rights of women.[18] The demands of the most radical or transformative feminisms not only face the counteroffensive of moderate and corporate feminism – dominant schools of thought linked to private corporations that have legitimized the progressive neoliberalism that promotes an instrumentalist vision of gender equality – focused on the incorporation of women into the labour market with the ultimate goal to contribute to the growth of the GDP, but also to the arising and reactions of even more conservative political positions, such as the one that Jair Bolsonaro personified in the last years in Brazil.

In this respect, the GRB case, one of the tools with the greatest levels of advance and implementation in a large number of countries, is a clear example of the political and institutional limitations that still persist. Particularly, perhaps one of the nodal points is that advances in its institutionalization have been interpreted almost unambiguously as advances in its formalization, without necessarily moving forward in the reconceptualization of gender-responsive budgeting as a political programme aimed at the transformation of public budgets as power technologies (Marx, 2019). In the same line of thought, limitations and ideological biases of the gender-based strategy developed by the IMF are evident even from the early stages of its implementation as its purely instrumental approach prevents a deep review of the institution and the policies it promotes.

The tension to be solved involves a twofold challenge: On the one hand, how to continue promoting and developing strategies to strengthen the quantification of gender gaps, especially in the economy, without losing its transformative potential, and, on the other, how to consolidate the process of gender-based institutionalization from a transversal approach that may permeate and influence the agendas of fiscal and financial decisions.

We present here some proposals to contribute to the debate on how to face those challenges and advance towards a gender-based institutionalization in public finances at national, regional and international levels, which is substantive, transformative and truly enables the closing of gender gaps in the economy through a radical reorganization of the economic system and the role that women play in it:

- Strengthen and promote multilateral institutional and cooperation opportunities among countries in the Global South that ensure, during both indebtedness and debt reduction processes, as well as at the time of designing strategies to fight tax evasion and tax avoidance and illicit financial flows, a feminist and human rights perspective that draws more resources for gender equality policies, in line with the provisions of the Buenos Aires Commitment (ECLAC, 2022b).[19]

  Binding international human rights obligations of both States and creditors (particularly the IFIs) provide the grounds for these multilateral opportunities of cooperation. These standards enable that creditors be required not to propose, condition or require debtor States to implement economic policies that violate human rights, essentially through the excessive erosion of the fiscal space thought the full debt repayment. As an implication of these principles, creditors might be held accountable for complicity in the violation of human rights.[20]

- Promote and guarantee a clear and participative monitoring of indebtedness processes and the resulting conditionalities to assess the potential gender impacts and propose the necessary changes to avoid, correct, mitigate or compensate them, as appropriate.

  Furthermore, following the Guiding Principles related to the assessments of the effects of the economic reforms on human rights, assessments of the effects of the debt and the conditionalities on women's rights by the States and the IFIs must be implemented (Guiding Principle 15.1), whose goal should be to ensure that the ability of the borrower State to respect, protect and comply with its obligations in terms of human rights is not undermined, going beyond the instrumentalist approach. In other words, these assessments must accept the transformative potential of economic policies that do not have an exclusive short-term fiscal and compensatory purpose for gender inequalities.

- At a national level, increase the degree of institutionalization of gender in public finances (through formalization, but also through the increase of related resources), creating specific units in the related ministries and central banks from which a work programme aimed at reducing gender gaps in the economy should be designed and implemented.

  In this respect, it is highly important that these units are not isolated and categorized as only related to those issues a priori considered relevant to women, but they should be given sufficient hierarchy and decision-making power to contribute to the debates of macroeconomic policies, including those related to indebtedness.

- The tools to assess debt sustainability should take into account gender gaps and be able to predict the differential impact on women. This may include the development of relevant indicators that can quantify some of these aspects, as well as qualitative information that provides information on those dimensions that cannot be measured by those indicators.[21]

As a final point, it is worth highlighting that a series of conditions must be fulfilled so that these initiatives can truly have a transformative power and be less vulnerable to be co-opted by 'pinkwashing' strategies. Firstly, their goals should be the promotion and guaranty of the human rights of women. Under this assumption, these initiatives should aim at changing preexisting structures of power relations, as well as redistributing resources to the most vulnerable segments of the population. In turn, in order not to be merely performative, these initiatives should be hierarchized within the political agenda, and they should be given power, autonomy and resources to achieve their goals. Finally, monitoring mechanisms that allow civil society and particularly women to oversee them and demand their compliance to the State are needed.

Appendix

Table 20.2: Legal mandates to incorporate gender-responsive budgets (selection of four countries of Latin America and the Caribbean)

Country	Regulatory framework	Brief description
Bolivia	Framework Law of Autonomy and Decentralization 'Andrés Ibañez' (Plurinational Legislative Assembly, 2010)	Autonomous territorial entities create and execute policies and budgets to reach gender equality. Autonomous government departments might allocate up to 5% of intergovernmental transfers to non-recurring programmes of support for gender equity.
Ecuador	Organic Code of Planning and Public Finances	It sets forth that gender budgeting should take into account the different needs of women and men to enhance equality and fair actions that make governmental commitments with equity and equality real.
Guatemala	Organic Law of Budget (Congress of the Republic of Guatemala, 1997)	Public budgets shall be created in the context of the strategy of economic and social development (Congress of the Republic of Guatemala, 1997), where women's human rights, Mayan women, garífunas, xinkas and mestizas are included (SEPREM, 2019).
Mexico	Federal Law of Budget and Treasury Responsibility (INDESOL, 2006)	It sets forth a series of mandates to include the gender approach in the whole budget process: for instance, it provides for its inclusion in programmatic structures, a gender classifier, a gender transversal appendix in the project of expenditure budget and a performance assessment with gender indicators, among other matters.

Source: Own elaboration based on Almeida, 2021

Table 20.3: Initiatives of gender-responsive budgets (selection of four countries of Latin America)

Countries	GRB initiative
Argentina	There is no regulation in this respect, but since 2018 the Argentine Budget Office promotes the identification of budget programmes related to gender issues (Circular No. 1/2020). In 2021, the first national gender-responsive budget was implemented.
Brazil	Until 2016, the 'Woman Budget' was presented, but the labelling protocol was not systematic.
Chile	Some government programmes adopt a gender-based perspective.
Dominican Republic	Since 2019, a gender-responsive budget is undertaken.

Source: Own elaboration based on national regulations

Notes

[1] See for example the panel 'Women's leadership: Towards parity in power', carried out during Davos Economic Forum in January 2023.

[2] See for instance the panel 'Empowering women to unleash green, resilient, and inclusive development: Should development policy be feminist?', carried out during the Annual Meetings of the IMF and the WB in October 2022.

[3] To that end, a selection of nine representative cases was made by using two indicators: the indebtedness level (as a percentage of the GDP) and the hierarchical level of the Mechanism for the Advancement of Women (MAW). Argentina, Brazil and Costa Rica are among the countries with a high level of indebtedness (more than 60 per cent of the GDP) in 2021 (ECLAC, 2022a), and these three countries also have a high level of MAW; among the ones with a medium level of indebtedness, the cases of Bolivia and Dominican Republic with a low level of MAW were selected, as well as Ecuador with a medium level, and Chile and Mexico with a high level of MAW. Finally, the case of Guatemala with a low level of indebtedness and a medium level of MAW was selected (OIG, ECLAC, 2022a).

[4] Although in the analyzed countries a process of strengthening of the institutional rank can be observed, it is worth highlighting that at a regional level there is a twofold trend: in some cases, the mechanism rank improves, while in others their autonomy and strength have been reduced with time (ECLAC, 2012: 54). In some countries where institutionality was originally created as a ministry, as in the case of Bolivia, it lost its status on two occasions, with five-year intervals, until it recovered it in 2009, when the Ministry of People's Power for Women and Gender Equality was created (ECLAC, 2012: 53). Brazil can be found in this same category, where the solid agency of women's policies incorporated in the movement of women turned into an anti-feminist agency (Rodríguez Gustá, 2021).

[5] In the case of Mexico, the full organizational chart is not available on the official website of the Secretary's Office of Economy.

[6] In order to analyze the gender-based institutionality and gender mainstreaming in the agency, a desktop search was made on the official websites regarding the authorities, organizational charts, mission, goals and plans when they were posted online. This search was carried out during the month of November 2022.

[7] See Brasilia Consensus in ECLAC, 2010, paragraph 2.C; Santo Domingo Consensus in ECLAC, 2013b, paragraphs 65 and 113; Montevideo Strategy in ECLAC, 2016, measures 5.a, 5.c, 5.d, 5.g, 5.h; Santiago Commitment in ECLAC, 2020, paragraphs 24 and 29.

[8] In accordance with ECLAC (2013a), '[b]udget labelling refers to the allocation of funds to a specific programme or purpose. Expenditure labelling for women and gender equality is an important affirmative action and a strategy to include the gender perspective in the public expenditure, and it implies working on the proper labelling and the tracking of the budget to ensure that resources have an impact on inequality and help to reduce gender gaps' (p 4).

[9] See chapter 16 by Marx in this book.

[10] See chapters 10 by Perrons, 11 by Kubrink and 9 by Villard Durán in this book.

[11] However, Pamela Blackmon (2021) suggests that during the term of Christine Lagarde (2011–19), most of the incorporations were at a professional level and not at a managing level, evidencing then that there exists a glass ceiling in the institution, even when the maximum authority is a woman.

[12] See chapter 9 by Camila Villar Durán in this book.

[13] It is quite interesting that this area is not expected to be made up of 'gender experts', but of 'fungible' macroeconomists (that is to say, interchangeable among them).

[14] The IMF uses the concept of 'macrocritical' to refer to the factors that it considers as crucial to ensure macroeconomic and financial stability.

[15] See chapter 6 (letter of mandate holders of United Nations Special Procedures submitted to the IMF in March 2022).

[16] A group of civil society organizations reviewed 267 recent country reports (January 2020–April 2022) made by the IMF and found that currently there is an important range of austerity policies that are being implemented or considered by governments all over the world (Ortiz and Cummings, 2022). In this same line, Shahra Razavi et al (2021) highlight that even though during the COVID-19 pandemic, when the IMF showed support to an increase of resources for health or direct transfers programmes (although often in a temporary manner), the recommendation to implement measures of fiscal consolidation and public expenditure reduction were even more frequent.

[17] See chapters 10 by Diane Perrons and 11 by Alicja Krubnik in this book.

[18] See chapter 2 by Rodríguez Enríquez in this book.

[19] See chapter 8 by Perceval and Rulli in this book.

[20] See chapter 5 by Bohoslavsky and Rossi in this book.

[21] See chapter 17 by Pautassi and Navarro in this book.

References

Action Aid International et al (2022) 'Joint civil society position on IMF Gender Strategy', [online] March, Available from: https://www.brettonw oodsproject.org/wp-content/uploads/2022/03/Joint-Civil-Society-Posit ion-on-IMF-Gender-Strategy-FINAL.pdf

Almeida Sánchez, M.D. (2021) 'La política fiscal con enfoque de género en países de América Latina' (LC/TS.2021/105), Serie Macroeconomía del Desarrollo, No 217, Santiago: Economic Commission for Latin American and the Caribbean (ECLAC).

Alonso-Albarran, V.; Curristine, T.; Preston, G.; Soler, A.; Tchelishvili, N. and Weerathunga, S. (2021) 'Gender budgeting in G20 countries' (IMF Working Paper WP/21/269), International Monetary Fund.

Berik, G. (2017) 'Beyond the rhetoric of gender equality at the World Bank and the IMF', *Canadian Journal of Development Studies / Revue Canadienne d'études Du Développement*, 38(4): 564–9, Available from: https://doi.org/ 10.1080/02255189.2017.1377062

Blackmon, P. (2021) 'The Lagarde effect: Assessing policy change under the first female managing director of the International Monetary Fund (IMF)', *Global Society*, 35(2): 171–90, Available from: https://doi.org/10.1080/ 13600826.2020.1763925

Budgeon, S. (2011) *Third Wave Feminism and the Politics of Gender in Late Modernity*, Basingstoke: Palgrave Macmillan.

Cavallero, L. and Gago, V. (2019) *Una lectura feminista de la deuda*, Buenos Aires: Fundación Rosa Luxemburgo.

Chant, S. (2012) 'The disappearing of "smart economics"? The World Development Report 2012 on Gender Equality: Some concerns about the preparatory process and the prospects for paradigm change', *Global Social Policy*, 12(2): 198–218, Available from: https://doi.org/10.1177/1468018112443674

ECLAC (2010) 'Brasilia Consensus' Eleventh session of the Regional Conference on Women in Latin America and the Caribbean (2010), Brasilia, Available from: https://repositorio.cepal.org/bitstream/handle/11362/47951/S2200521_en.pdf?sequence=4&isAllowed=y

ECLAC (2012) 'Políticas públicas e institucionalidad de género en América Latina (1985–2010)' (LC/L.3531), Santiago de Chile: CEPAL, División de Asuntos de Género [online], Available from: https://www.cepal.org/es/publicaciones/5847-politicas-publicas-institucionalidad-genero-amer ica-latina-1985-2010

ECLAC (2013a) 'El Gasto Etiquetado para las Mujeres y la Igualdad de Género (GEMIG) en México: Un avance para garantizar la autonomía de las mujeres', Observatorio de Igualdad de Género de América Latina y el Caribe [online], Available from: https://oig.cepal.org/sites/default/files/el_gasto_etiquetado_para_las_mujeres_en_mexico_esp.pdf

ECLAC (2013b) 'Santo Domingo Consensus' Twelfth session of the Regional Conference on Women in Latin America and the Caribbean (2013), Santo Domingo, Available from: https://repositorio.cepal.org/bitstream/handle/11362/47951/S2200521_en.pdf?sequence=4&isAllowed=y

ECLAC (2016) 'Montevideo Strategy' Thirteenth session of the Regional Conference on Women in Latin America and the Caribbean (2016), Montevideo, Available from: https://repositorio.cepal.org/bitstream/handle/11362/47951/S2200521_en.pdf?sequence=4&isAllowed=y

ECLAC (2019) 'Panorama fiscal de América Latina y el Caribe 2019: políticas tributarias para la movilización de recursos en el marco de la Agenda 2030 para el Desarrollo Sostenible' (LC/PUB.2019/8-P), Santiago de Chile.

ECLAC (2020) 'Santiago Commitment' Fourteenth session of the Regional Conference on Women in Latin America and the Caribbean (2020), Santiago de Chile, Available from: https://repositorio.cepal.org/bitstream/handle/11362/47951/S2200521_en.pdf?sequence=4&isAllowed=y

ECLAC (2022a) *Balance Preliminar de las Economías de América Latina y el Caribe* (LC/PUB.2022/1-P), Santiago de Chile [online], Available from: https://repositorio.cepal.org/bitstream/handle/11362/47669/5/S2100698_es.pdf

ECLAC (2022b) 'Compromiso de Buenos Aires, documentos de órganos subsidiarios, Conferencia Regional sobre la Mujer de América Latina y el Caribe', [online], Available from: https://www.cepal.org/es/publicacio nes/48737-compromiso-buenos-aires-xv-conferencia-regional-la-mujer- america-latina-caribe

Elson, D. (2008) 'Los retos de la globalización y los intentos locales de crear presupuestos gubernamentales equitativos', Cuadernos de Trabajo 43, Instituto de Estudios sobre Desarrollo y Cooperación Internacional, Universidad del País Vasco [online], Available from: https://www.ucm.es/data/cont/docs/3-2016-03-02-gen_cuadernos_de_trabajo_43_hegoa.pdf

Elson, D. (2021) 'Gender budgeting', in G. Berik and E. Kongar (eds), *The Routledge Handbook of Feminist Economics* (1st edn), London: Routledge, Available from: https://doi.org/10.4324/9780429020612

Elson, D. and United Nations Development Fund for Women (2006) *Budgeting for Women's Rights: Monitoring Government Budgets for Compliance with CEDAW*, New York: United Nations Development Fund for Women.

Experto Independiente en Deuda y Derechos Humanos de Naciones Unidas (2019) 'Impacto de las reformas económicas y medidas de austeridad en los derechos humanos de las mujeres' (A/73/179), Consejo de Derechos Humanos.

Guzmán, V. (2001) 'La institucionalidad de género en el estado: Nuevas perspectivas de análisis', Serie Mujer y Desarrollo 32, Santiago de Chile: CEPAL.

Guzmán, V. and Montaño, S. (2012) 'Políticas públicas e institucionalidad de género en América Latina (1985–2010)', Serie Mujer y Desarrollo 118, Santiago de Chile: ECLAC.

International Monetary Fund (2022) 'Gender: IMF strategy toward mainstreaming gender'. Policy paper.

Jubeto, Y. (2008) 'Los presupuestos con enfoque de género: una apuesta feminista a favor de la equidad en las políticas públicas', Cuadernos de Trabajo 43, Instituto de Estudios sobre Desarrollo y Cooperación Internacional, Universidad del Pais Vasco [online], Available from: https://www.ucm.es/data/cont/docs/3-2016-03-02-gen_cuadernos_de_trabajo_43_hegoa.pdf

Latindadd (2022) 'Feministas rechazan la estrategia del Fondo Monetario Internacional para incorporar la perspectiva de género', [online] 14 October, Available from: https://www.latindadd.org/2022/10/14/feministas-rechazan-la-estrategia-del-fondo-monetario-internacional-para-incorporar-la-perspectiva-de-genero%EF%BF%BC/

Marx, U. (2019) 'Accounting for equality: Gender budgeting and moderate feminism', *Gender Work Organ*, 26: 1176–90.

Ortiz, I. and Cummins, M. (2022) 'End austerity: A global report on budget cuts and harmful social reforms in 2022–25', Initiative for Policy Dialogue [online] 10 October, Available from: https://policydialogue.org/publications/working-papers/end-austerity-a-global-report-on-budget-cuts-and-harmful-social-reforms-in-2022-25/

Oxfam (2017) 'Great Expectations: Is the IMF turning words into action on inequality?' Oxfam Briefing Paper.

Razavi, S. et al. (2021) 'Social policy advice to countries from the International Monetary Fund during the COVID-19 crisis: Continuity and change', ILO Working Paper 42, Available from: https://www.ilo.org/global/publications/working-papers/WCMS_831490/lang--en/index.htm

Rodríguez Gustá, A. (2021) 'Women's policy agencies and government ideology: the divergent trajectories of Argentina and Brazil, 2003–2019', *International Feminist Journal of Politics*, 23(4): 625–47.

United Nations (1979) 'International Convention on the Elimination of All Forms of Discrimination against Women New York, 18 December 1979', Available from: https://www.ohchr.org/en/instruments-mechanisms/instruments/convention-elimination-all-forms-discrimination-against-women

World Bank Group (2015) 'World Bank Group Gender Strategy (FY16–23): Gender equality, poverty reduction and inclusive growth', World Bank [online] 16 December, Available from: https://openknowledge.world bank.org/handle/10986/23425

World Bank Group (2022) *International Debt Report 2022. Updated International Debt Statistics*, World Bank [online], Available from: https://openknowledge.worldbank.org/bitstream/handle/10986/38045/978146 4819025.pdf?sequence=8

Index

References to figures appear in *italic* type; those in **bold** type refer to tables; and the letter 'n' indicates a chapter endnote.